Understanding Latin American Politics

Gregory Weeks

University of North Carolina at Charlotte

PEARSON

Boston Columbus Indianapolis New York San Francisco Upper Saddle River
Amsterdam Cape Town Dubai London Madrid Milan Munich Paris Montréal Toronto
Delhi Mexico City São Paulo Sydney Hong Kong Seoul Singapore Taipei Tokyo

Editor in Chief: Ashley Dodge
Senior Acquisitions Editor: Melissa Mashburn
Editorial Assistant: Courtney Turcotte
Marketing Coordinator: Jessica Warren
Managing Editor: Denise Forlow
Program Manager: Kathy Sleys
Project Manager: PreMediaGlobal/Doug Bell
Senior Operations Supervisor: Mary Fischer
Operations Specialist: Mary Ann Gloriande
Art Director: Maria Lange

Cover Designer: PreMediaGlobal
Cover Image: Tifonimages/Fotolia; Galyna
 Andrushko/Fotolia
Digital Media Project Manager: Tina
 Gagliostro
Full-Service Project Management and
 Composition: PreMediaGlobal/Murugesh
 Namasivayam
Printer/Binder: Courier/Westford
Cover Printer: Courier/Westford

Credits and acknowledgments borrowed from other sources and reproduced, with permission, in this textbook appear on appropriate page within text.

Many of the designations by manufacturers and seller to distinguish their products are claimed as trademarks. Where those designations appear in this book, and the publisher was aware of a trademark claim, the designations have been printed in initial caps or all caps.

Library of Congress Cataloging-in-Publication Data

Weeks, Gregory Bart.
  Understanding Latin American politics / Gregory Weeks.
    pages cm
  Includes bibliographical references and index.
  ISBN 978-0-205-64825-2 (alk. paper)—
  ISBN 0-205-64825-8 (alk. paper)
  1. Latin America—Politics and government.   I. Title.
  JL960.W38 2015
  320.98—dc23

                        2014007091

10 9 8 7 6 5 4 3 2 1

ISBN 10: 0-205-64825-8
ISBN 13: 978-0-205-64825-2

BRIEF CONTENTS

CONTENTS

3 Dictatorship, Democracy, and Revolution in the Modern Era 35

4 The Politics of Capitalism and Socialism Through the Twentieth Century 55

PART II MEXICO, CENTRAL AMERICA, AND THE CARIBBEAN

5 Mexico   79

PART IV   BRAZIL AND THE SOUTHERN CONE

11 Brazil   253

12 Argentina   281

PREFACE

Imagine a president disappears from public view, leaves his country for extended periods to get cancer treatments, and even misses his inauguration. There is clamoring by the opposition to prove he's alive, expressions of concern by other countries, and shows of support on the streets. The interim president says he's still receiving orders from the sitting president, but the evidence for this is disputed. The president then returns to his home country and not long after is pronounced dead. This example describes what happened in Venezuela with its president, Hugo Chávez, in late 2012 and early 2013. How should we unravel Chávez's secretive behavior and why different political actors responded as they did?

As its title suggests, the ultimate goal of this book is to lay the foundation for a better understanding of Latin American politics. The main audience is undergraduate students, who can use some guidance to navigate what they read and hear from friends, family, and the media. There is almost too much to consider at once: Why was Hugo Chávez such a polarizing figure? What developments led Venezuelan politics to this moment? Why did presidents and heads of state of other nations react in different ways to the crisis? Answers to these questions often defy easy explanation.

If we want to understand why certain political events are occurring in Latin America, we need to get a bird's-eye view and then zoom in to get a look at people on the ground. By doing that in a comparative way, we can uncover not only why events are happening, but also whether they are likely to occur in other countries as well. In this book, these different perspectives all come together to form a more complete picture. The Venezuelan case, with all its surprises and uncertainties, can start making more sense.

The essence of this book is to highlight three different levels of analysis: international, national, and local. Decisions are not made in a bubble, political forces are often not isolated, and interaction with other countries creates multiple layers of complexity. The chapters ask students to ponder how each level of analysis is integral to political and economic outcomes.

Text Features

This book begins with an introductory chapter that lays out major theoretical frameworks and initiates the conceptual discussion. Chapters 2 through 4 provide the historical grounding necessary to grasp the major political and economic themes that developed in the nineteenth and twentieth centuries in Latin America. From there we move to country case studies, sixteen countries in nine chapters: Central American and three Andean countries are grouped together. All of the country case study chapters include clear comparative discussions to show how we can make generalizations that further our understanding of political and economic events.

The chapters provide a host of analytical tools that go beyond just a narrative:

- Timelines of key events
- Key economic indicators (gross domestic product growth, inflation, unemployment, poverty rate, and the human development index)
- Boxes discussing key country characteristics
- Boxes discussing important political institutions in each country
- Annotated lists of additional readings and Web sites
- Annotated primary documents
- A glossary of key terms
- Suggested topics for student term paper research

From long experience, I know it is no easy task to present the right combination of country studies and analytical tools in a single class, but I believe students will come away from using this book with a better understanding of Latin American politics.

This book is available in a variety of formats—digital and print. To learn more about Pearson programs, pricing, and customization options, visit www.pearsonhighered.com.

Acknowledgments

This book originated with a lengthy phone conversation I had with then Longman Acquisitions Editor Vik Mukhija back in 2007, just after I had completed another book on U.S.-Latin American relations. I talked about how none of the existing texts really fit the structure and content of my Latin American politics class. Vik is an energetic and enthusiastic editor and encouraged me to consider tackling another book. Almost seven years later, here we finally are. At Pearson thanks must also go to Beverly Fong and Melissa Mashburn, who ushered me through various stages of the process and brainstormed with me. At the tail end, I appreciate the help of Doug Bell, who led me through the tortured but necessary process of obtaining all necessary permissions.

Mulling over Latin American politics was in part a public exercise. As ideas or topics occurred to me, I blogged about them at Two Weeks Notice: A Latin American Politics Blog (http://weeksnotice.blogspot.com/) where I have been writing since early 2006. Thanks to all the readers, anonymous or otherwise, who commented—positively or otherwise—on my meandering posts. Further, I am very grateful to the many undergraduates in my Latin American Politics course at UNC Charlotte who read draft versions and directly or indirectly made me think of ways to improve the manuscript. I was also pleased at the high quality of the external reviews I received, and I expect some of you will recognize the impact of your own suggestions on the final book. I would like to thank the following reviewers: Stephen Morris, Middle Tennessee State University; Gratzia Villaroel, St. Norbert College; Richard Levy, Salem State University; Candice Ortbals, Pepperdine University; Adrian Hull, SUNY Cortland; Velma Garcia, Smith College; David Scott Palmer, Boston University;

Jose M. Vadi, Cal State Polytechnic University at Pomona; Lourdes Gil, Baruch College—CUNY; James G. Stamsad, San Diego State University; Ted Henken, Baruch College; Amy Below, Oregon State University.

Through it all, I appreciate all the love and support from my wife Amy and my children Benjamin, Julia, and Elizabeth. When I felt like tossing the computer out the window, I just went and hung out with them.

CHAPTER 1

Theoretical Perspectives on Latin American Politics

LEARNING OBJECTIVES

- Identify the main theories related to Latin American politics.

- Explain how theories contribute to an understanding of specific political events.

- Differentiate between the three main levels of analysis.

In January 2006, Evo Morales was inaugurated president of Bolivia. Hailing from a poor family, he had become an influential local union leader of the "cocaleros," or coca growers. He then proceeded in 1997 to win election to the national Congress. His rise was due specifically to local concerns about national and international policies. In particular, for years discontent with the government's anticoca policies had led to civil discontent. Considerable anger was aimed at the United States, which used economic leverage to push Bolivian presidents to enact strict laws intended to eliminate the coca plant. Coca had been part of indigenous cultures for hundreds of years and was essential to the livelihood of many rural Bolivians.

Those local concerns combined with discontent over national economic policy. Morales' organization led large national protests that ultimately unseated the recently elected Gonzalo Sánchez de Lozada (more commonly known as *Goni*). When he resigned in 2003, Goni blamed his ouster on criminal behavior and sedition, labeling protests like Morales' as creating "national disintegration" and "fratricidal violence."

Before Morales' official swearing-in ceremony in the capital, La Paz, he attended an indigenous ceremony at Tiwanaku, an important pre-Columbian political center. Of Aymaran descent, Morales emphasized his commitment to indigenous issues and was reelected in 2009 in a very divided country. He also argued that key natural resources, such as natural gas, should be in national rather than international hands. That meant nationalization, where the state took over industries. How to distribute wealth and services in Bolivia, though, did not suddenly become easier. He faced opposition even within his movement.

Morales' overall policy orientation highlighted the deep national divisions within Bolivia, a country historically split between east and west. His national political struggles and the international disputes that ensued serve as reminders that understanding Latin American politics requires a comprehensive view of the region. Political actors do not function on only one level. Instead, they must seek delicate and ever-shifting balances between different levels.

The Complexities of Latin American Politics

Political pressures come from above and below. As we will see, many theories and hypotheses about Latin America tend to focus on the "above" and exclude the "below." International factors and elite-level politics are extremely important, but they are not the whole story. There is also a lot happening on the ground, at the grassroots level, that has an impact on political and economic development. Further, there is a constant interaction—harmonious or conflictive—that major theories don't necessarily capture.

Latin America has always experienced major international influence, first from Spain as a colonial power and then from the United States. Latin American countries also have long-standing national-level projects, such as economic development and democratization, which are affected by international actors. Yet they also have critical local-level developments that must be integrated into political analyses because they shape national politics and international responses. Evo Morales created a local power base, moved into a power vacuum at the national level, and once there had to deal immediately with a wide variety of national and international pressures. This book will consider Latin America from a wide-angle lens to provide a full understanding of its politics.

Bolivia is the second poorest country in the Western Hemisphere (ahead only of Haiti). Why has it remained so poor? Historically, it has arguably been the weakest democracy in the region, with nearly 200 **coups d'état** since independence in 1825. What are the root causes of political and economic instability in Bolivia and around the region? Bolivia offers an example of the recent rise of national political leaders challenging the status quo, professing greater appreciation of and sympathy for the downtrodden at the most local level, which in Bolivia refers in large part to the indigenous population. Once president, Morales faced serious conflict with the national legislature, local governments, and the United States. Why is there so much discontent and what has been the result? Answering these and other critical questions requires the examination of local, national, and international factors that all come together to help us understand political outcomes. That will also facilitate comparisons.

Making Comparisons in the Context of Complexity

This book is a comparative analysis of Latin American countries. Within the discipline of political science, "comparative politics" is the subdiscipline focusing on a comparison of different cases as a means of reaching generalizable conclusions. It rests on the assumption that what happens in one place very well might help explain events elsewhere because the causes and effects may be similar. At the most basic level, comparativists identify an independent variable that explains variations in the outcome of the dependent variable. This allows us to formulate hypotheses (if/then statements that specify causal relationships), which can then be tested by examining other countries. Constructing hypotheses and testing them can lead to the development of theories.

Theory building is a critical element of comparative politics, as it helps us understand causal relationships. Theories link concepts to real-world events and, if the theories are successful, help explain *why* things did happen in the past or will happen in the future. In fact, theories often have the potential to be very controversial, because they may be linked to certain **ideologies** (visions about the way the political world should work), which in turn offer suggestions for what types of policies should be pursued. In short, theory matters at a very practical level. Evo Morales, for example, forged an **ideology** of socialism and nationalism that strongly emphasized local and national indigenous rights. Both specific hypotheses and broader theories are also important because they point to ways in which different levels of analysis come together.

Before discussing some of the major theoretical and conceptual frameworks that have guided scholars' understanding of Latin American politics, it is necessary first to acknowledge a tension that often surfaces in theoretical debates. There is often disagreement about the importance of systemic (generally, internationally driven) influences versus more local factors. This is commonly framed as "structure" versus "agency." For example, political and economic structures constrain individual choices—that is, individual agency—in many ways. On the other hand, it is an exaggeration to argue that what individuals and groups do is unimportant in the larger scheme of things. Local-level actions, such as protests in Bolivia, should not get lost in the shuffle. What individual people do is important.

One goal of this book is to unpack these relationships and demonstrate how existing theories sometimes have problems explaining politics. It will take into consideration three levels of analysis, or political levels: international, national, and local. The idea of explicitly addressing levels of analysis has received considerable attention in political science since the 1950s, especially in the subfield of international relations. In his seminal work *Man, the State and War*, Kenneth Waltz asked why states go to war. To do so, he examined the nature of human beings as individuals making decisions, the internal structures of states, and the nature of the international system, where there is no world government dictating what states can or cannot do. This approach ensures that all possible variables and effects receive at least some attention.

For the purposes of this book, the approach serves as a reminder that different levels of analysis deserve more scrutiny than they often receive. Not only that, but political actors at different levels are working together or at least having an impact on others literally all the time. There are times when one particular level seems to be the most influential, but none of them are fully isolated from each other.

International Level

The international level refers to political actors outside the state, which means governments of other countries and international organizations. The role of the United States will come up again and again because of its considerable—and sometimes controversial—influence. In the Bolivian case, for example, the United States has pressured the government to engage more actively in counternarcotic operations. But at various historical moments, other countries, most notably Spain and the Soviet Union, have had important impacts. Organizations as disparate as the International Monetary Fund (IMF) and the Organization of American States (OAS) or a **nongovernmental organization** such as Amnesty International also should be taken into account. The international level can even include the fluctuation of international prices for exports.

National Level

The national level centers on the central government. This means the executive, legislative, and judicial branches, as well as groups that lobby those branches at high levels to pursue their political goals, such as national business elites or religious organizations. This also includes political parties, which operate on all levels but are fundamentally national. All these political actors connect in many ways to both the local and international levels—Evo Morales' Movement for Socialism party grew out of local alliances—but are focused on the national government. In a federal system, state-level governments fall in the middle between local and national.

Local Level

The local level includes groups that are either not part of the state or peripheral to it, yet still seek to influence politics. Examples can include local unions, protest organizations, human rights activists, neighborhood associations, or regional indigenous groups. It can also include local government, because the mayor is the political official most in touch with the local population. At this grassroots level, one essential challenge is to figure out *how* to change policies further up. As the leader of a coca union, Evo Morales championed small farmers in their quest to defy U.S. coca eradication policies.

How the Levels Intersect

Think about this example of how different levels intersect: A farmer in Bolivia decides to protest a government tax by putting up roadblocks. That is the local level. But that farmer is part of the national association that helps coordinate it. Alone, that individual farmer wouldn't have much effect. But the national level is critical, because the Bolivian government is in debt and needs the cash that the tax provides. Why does it need that cash right now? The international level helps explain that, because the government is in debt to international creditors and faces globally high prices of food. This 360-degree view makes it much easier to understand Latin American politics.

We also have to acknowledge that there are no clean lines between these different levels. For example, the Catholic Church is an international actor, with national leaders chosen by the Vatican. However, at times priests at the local level—in the poverty-stricken urban slums or isolated rural areas—have interpreted Catholic doctrine in ways that diverge widely from either the national or international dictates. Political parties also commonly operate on a number of different levels, down even to the neighborhood. A mayor, for example, deals with all sorts of local problems but usually is also part of a national political party that might even have international connections.

Ultimately, for a complete picture of Latin American politics, we want to neither rob agency nor underestimate systemic forces. Presidents and grassroots organizers alike do have some leeway to make decisions and take action, but the latitude varies widely, and constraining—or liberating—pressures can come from many different sources. Cases like Bolivia also illustrate the fact that a leader like Evo Morales at the local level can at times be catapulted to the national level, where both the constraints and the opportunities are suddenly different.

How Levels of Analysis Inform Theory

Paying closer attention to different levels of analysis and how they interact puts us in a better position to evaluate the many hypotheses and theories that claim to explain different aspects of Latin American politics. For example, two of the most prominent and lasting theories—modernization and dependency—privilege international influences. Despite the fact that their essential arguments are still made all the time by politicians across the hemisphere, they miss important national and local factors.

Modernization Theory

The core of **modernization theory** is simple (as is the case with any influential theory). The way to develop economically and achieve political stability, to become "modern," is to emulate the countries that have already done so. The entire theory is centered on international effects. The diffusion of western values will pull less developed countries in a modern direction as they rid themselves of the backward practices of their failed past. In a highly influential book, W. W. Rostow, who became a top aide to U.S. Presidents John F. Kennedy and Lyndon Johnson, argued that there are five stages of economic growth: the traditional society, the preconditions for take-off, the take-off, the drive to maturity, and the age of high mass consumption.[1] Following the correct policy prescriptions could propel a country in the right direction. For Rostow, modernization was a direct challenge to the Marxist assertion that class conflict must inevitably lead nations toward Communism. Instead, modernization would foster capitalism and peace. It is a theory based on international influence, which is supposed to trickle down first to the national and then to the local levels.

In the specifically Latin American context, sociologist Seymour Martin Lipset argued that value systems were still preindustrial, based on the Iberian (referring to the Iberian Peninsula of Spain and Portugal) tradition that rejected hard work and favored hierarchy and obedience over individual initiative.[2] A revamped educational system could be one means of transforming society, as well as breaking the grip of traditional elites who block the rise of new talent and resist modernization.

Modernization theory was developed in the 1960s, but there is no doubt that it remains relevant. It is illustrated in the widely read book *Guide to the Perfect Latin American Idiot*, which ripped at dependency theory and argued that "[o]nly at the end of the [nineteenth] century did this faith in U.S. progress, this confidence in the pragmatic, this amazement for material achievements begin to fall apart."[3] The solution? Reexamine the U.S. model and take on many of its characteristics. Speeches by U.S. presidents often echo this sentiment, with references to how we all have shared values of progress. There are widespread laments that leftist governments are pursuing failed policies of the past, based on wishful thinking rather than clear-headed realism. Get rid of the old thinking, follow international models, and progress will follow. The original modernization theorists would have agreed heartily.

What Modernization Theory Can't Explain

By looking at other levels gives us more leverage for understanding Latin American politics. Many national and local solutions boost both democracy and stability without copying international models. As matter of fact, homegrown solutions to national challenges often work better than foreign-inspired solutions. And, as the Bolivian case will show, sometimes pushing for those models too hard actually creates serious local backlash.

Dependency Theory

There was a theoretical reply as **dependency theory** emerged as a direct challenge to both modernization and the ideas of neoclassical economics. It was also fundamentally international and structural in its emphasis. The foundation of dependency theory coalesced in the 1950s, and formal works on the topic were published largely in the 1960s in response to the major works of modernization theory.

It started with a basic question. If free-market capitalism was so good, why were the results often so negative in the developing world? Dependency theory originated in Latin America, as academics and members of the United Nations' Economic Commission for Latin America and the Caribbean (usually known through its Spanish acronym, CEPAL) noted an element of "modernization" that had not yet been explored. Whereas modernization theorists believed that greater connection to the developed world would be beneficial, because traditional societies could take on their characteristics, dependency theorists argued that the relationship was negative.

The theory views the world in terms of a "core" and a "periphery" in the international system. The core refers to wealthy, developed countries, whereas the latter is composed of less developed, poorer countries. As part of the periphery, Latin American countries exported raw materials to the core, especially—though not exclusively—to the United States. The prices for these products, such as Argentine beef, Bolivian tin, Colombian coffee, Cuban sugar, or Guatemalan bananas, did not appreciate over time, and often dropped. Meanwhile, the core exported finished manufactured products back. Those items, such as cars, refrigerators, farming equipment, or other durable goods (meaning they last and do not wear out quickly), tend to increase in price. The terms of trade, therefore, were getting worse, and as a result, Latin America was becoming heavily dependent on the core for all the goods it was not producing. The core was responsible for keeping the periphery down and routinely intervened or invaded whenever threats to the arrangement emerged. The developed world would also work to keep leaders in power who would not disrupt the flow of primary products and the consumption of finished goods from abroad. The national and local levels were, therefore, largely victims that could do very little in response.

Fernando Henrique Cardoso (who was elected the president of Brazil in 1994) and Enzo Faletto compared dependency to a banker and client relationship. The client has no money, and even though he or she may do something productive with the loan, there are clear lines of dependence: "In most cases, when such an economy flourishes, its roots have been planted by those who hold the lending notes."[4] Cardoso and Faletto emphasized that dependent industrialization by its nature created inequalities because only a small elite benefits from industrial output, whereas the large majority of the population continues with traditional methods of agricultural production and extraction. Interestingly, though, Cardoso's views changed as he moved from intellectual to politician (Box 1.1).

Some scholars of dependency, such as Andre Gunder Frank, asserted that the only way to open the door for development was not only to sever ties with the international core but also to destroy the national bourgeoisie (meaning the economic elite) that was closely tied to foreign economic interests.[5] You had to destroy national and international influences to become free. Many of the works of the time were inspired by Marxism, so the logical solution was to eliminate

███████████████ **BOX 1.1** ███████████████

Theory and Practice: International Factors and the Ideological Transformation of Fernando Henrique Cardoso

International: With his coauthor Enzo Faletto, Brazilian Sociologist Fernando Henrique Cardoso published one of the most influential and important works on dependency theory, originally published in 1969 (the English version was released in 1979). The entire analysis centered on the negative effects of international economic factors.

National: In 1982, he was elected senator of São Paulo, and his political career took off after the end of military rule in 1985. In 1988, he helped found the Brazilian Social Democratic Party (PSDB). Unlike the leftist Brazilian Worker's Party, the PSDB and Cardoso claimed to ignore ideology and seek common-sense solutions to long-standing national and local problems of poverty, inequality, and injustice. As minister of finance in 1993, he spearheaded "Plan Real," which created a new currency (the "real") and drastically reduced inflation. He was elected president in 1994 and reelected in 1998.

Local: What critics noted was the ways in which his policies as president conflicted with the theoretical precepts he had developed years before. His economic strategies were perfectly in line with prevailing market-based policies of privatization and limited government spending. In short, in looking for solutions for national and local problems, he began to view international influences such as globalization—and thereby the "core" as well—in largely positive terms. Poverty, for example, which is a major local problem in Brazil, could not be addressed effectively with a large state but required *more* integration into the international system.

In his memoirs, published in 2006, Cardoso denies that his theory was leftist at all. Far from rejecting the developed world, he argues, he felt Latin American countries should "harness" multinational corporations for their benefit.[6] He writes that he was unfairly labeled a Marxist because he was involved in study groups that read Marx, but that they did so critically and also read many other points of view.

Discussion Questions
- If an individual who has something to sell is connected to global markets, can you think of what the costs and benefits might be?
- Can you think of specific ways in which international actors can have an effect on poverty at the local level?

███

capitalism and cease trading with capitalist countries while embracing socialism. That meant taking up arms and starting a revolution.

It also continues to stay highly relevant. The rhetoric from the Latin American left echoes its main points. The United States is taking advantage of the region, the argument goes, and we need to break away from its domination and sell new products in new markets—even more just to each other. More than ever, Latin American policy makers are seeking opportunity in places such as China and India, which had largely been absent from the region for most of its history. In fact, dependency theory is no longer associated with only the left. Even center-right presidents, such as Felipe Calderón of Mexico, have talked openly and unambiguously about reducing dependency on the United States and looking globally for new opportunities. It has proven much harder to diversify economies, but at least there has been diversification of trading partners away from a reliance on the United States. Many of the original dependency theorists would have approved.

What Dependency Theory Can't Explain

Dependency theory leaves holes at the national and local levels. Many policy makers have developed successful national economic strategies that defy dependency's predictions. Brazil, for example, sells its Embraer jets around the world, including to airlines in the United States. Local economic initiatives across the region have also demonstrated that dependency theory's international focus too often fails to integrate specific ways in which national and local realities do not correspond to the generally deterministic dependency argument. There is far more autonomous action at those levels that prominent theories like these often overlook.

Defining Democracy and Development

Remaining mindful of levels of analysis also clarifies key definitions that are essential for understanding Latin American politics. The two broad challenges faced by Latin American governments have been how to achieve and maintain democracy and to foster sustainable economic development and prosperity. We will be coming back to these issues again and again, with particular attention to how the different local, national, and international contexts must each be considered.

Democracy

Democracy is a term that has had many different definitions applied to it, ranging from simply having competitive elections to a broad conception that includes quality of life. As we will see, constitutions in Latin America reflect the ways in which democracy is conceived in different countries and in different eras. Political scientist Guillermo O'Donnell, for example, has argued that democracy is intimately tied to human development and human rights, and therefore, they all must be viewed together to determine the quality of a given democracy.[7] In other words, there are central national concerns but also local ones. Democracy must involve competition but also satisfaction of local needs. As he acknowledges, this is no easy matter.

We will pay particular attention to what has been called a *procedural* definition, which reflects the influence of political scientist Robert Dahl. It focuses on the procedures a political system utilizes to elect its leaders. People must have freedom of expression and the right to create and join organizations at either the local or national levels, for example. Then political leaders compete to get their votes. He refers to a **polyarchy**, which refers to a system that is "highly inclusive and extensively open to public contestation."[8] This type of definition is useful for two main reasons. First, from a political perspective, elections (at any level) are the core of any democracy and, therefore, deserve to be front and center. Without elections, democracy cannot exist. This is especially relevant for Latin America, where the fight simply to have free and fair elections has been long and difficult. Coups have plagued Bolivia, and a large swath of the indigenous population was excluded for many years; therefore, the local population felt politically powerless. Second, it is easier to do comparative analysis because the outcomes are visible and obvious. A downside to a procedural definition is that it tells us much less about the quality of democracy and very little about accountability. Once a president is elected, how much can he or she do without political repercussion?

The intent of this book is not to stick a label on each country to determine which is more or less democratic than the others, though that is a constant and seemingly entertaining pastime for both academics and politicians. Instead, it will focus on the mechanics of democracy—the procedural aspect—while also taking into consideration how democracy (or relative lack of it) affects different groups in a country. Looking at it from all three levels will yield insights the major theories may overlook. Chapter 3 will dive into the development of democracy.

Development

Development is not much easier to define. At its core, development means prosperity. Are you better off than you were last year or even ten years ago? On its face, it seems simple. We can look at a wide variety of national economic indicators (which we will discuss in detail in Chapter 4) and answer yes or no. But it quickly gets more complicated. We need to know how many of a country's citizens are becoming better off. A country might have high economic growth rates at the national level, but if the wealth is limited to only a few, then there might still be political upheaval and discontent bubbling up from the local level, especially in rural areas. We also need to know how sustainable it is. If your country is dominated by one or two key exports (e.g., oil or metals), you might do well when prices are high and then face disaster when they drop.

Growth is a necessary but not sufficient factor for development. No matter how good your intentions, you cannot develop economically without growth. And each chapter will also examine the human side of the equation, the local effects. Doing so will also provide insight into why political discontent grew through the 1990s and, eventually, led to the election of political outsiders who challenged—to greater or lesser degrees—the status quo. Even when the economy looks great from a bird's-eye view, there may be serious problems at the local level that need attention.

Conclusion

Only a decade or so before Evo Morales assumed office, Bolivia was seen as a model of economic reform and democratic transition. Yet his inauguration was a clear sign that national-level policies put in place with international influence did not take into account the responses at the local level. Bolivia is just one example of how Latin American politics must be viewed from all angles. Ironically, before becoming president, Morales had organized the very sorts of local protests that later would be aimed directly at his administration.

Keeping our eyes on the three different levels gives us some analytical leverage. Why would a local leader reach national fame if influential international actors believed that a country was doing so well? That outcome doesn't seem to make much sense until we take into account the fact that growth based on commodity exports does not necessarily benefit everyone equally. Down at the local level, many people were becoming unhappy that the highly touted growth didn't seem to be improving their lives as much as they hoped.

Thus, the relationship between economic development and democracy is not always obvious because of how they play out at the international, national, and local levels. What we might believe is "progress" or "success" may not be perceived the same way at different levels. Such disagreement can then spark political debate and at the extremes even political violence. We get a much fuller picture of Latin American politics when we keep all the levels in mind.

Key Terms

- Coup d'état
- Ideology
- Nongovernmental organization
- Modernization theory
- Dependency theory
- Polyarchy

Discussion Questions

- Can you think of ways that international factors might be positive for a country in the process of democratizing?
- What are important aspects of a democracy that the term *polyarchy* does not capture?
- Why are theories useful even though they can't explain everything?
- What are some positive aspects of a presidential system?
- In what ways might locally generated protests start to influence national-level politics?

Further Sources ▮▮▮▮▮▮▮▮▮▮▮▮▮▮▮▮▮▮

Books

Collier, David, ed. *The New Authoritarianism in Latin America* (Princeton: Princeton University Press, 1980). This collection of essays analyzes why modernization theory incorrectly argued that Latin American countries would become more democratic.

Evans, Peter. *Dependent Development: The Alliance of Multinational, State, and Local Capital in Brazil* (Princeton: Princeton University Press, 1979). Like Cardoso, in this classic work Evans argues that economic development is possible within a dependent economic context.

Klarén, Peter F., and Thomas J. Bossert. *Promise of Development: Theories of Change in Latin America* (Boulder: Westview Press, 1986). This is a very useful collection of excerpts from major works on theory, with key examples from both modernization and dependency.

Munck, Gerardo L., ed. *Regimes and Democracy in Latin America: Theories and Methods* (New York: Oxford University Press, 2007). Different authors examine theory building in the study of Latin American democratization and economic development.

Packenham, Robert. *The Dependency Movement: Scholarship and Politics in Development Theory* (Cambridge: Harvard University Press, 1992). A highly critical look at dependency theory, the book argues that the theory is politicized and not scientific.

Endnotes ▮▮▮▮▮▮▮▮▮▮▮▮▮▮▮▮▮▮▮▮▮

1. W. W. Rostow, *The Stages of Economic Growth: A Non-Communist Manifesto* (New York: Cambridge University Press, 1961).
2. Seymour Martin Lipset, "Values, Education, and Entrepreneurship," in *Elites in Latin America, eds.* Seymour Martin Lipset and Aldo Solari (New York: Oxford University Press, 1967), 3–60.
3. Plinio Apuleyo Mendoza, Carlos Alberto Montaner, and Alvaro Vargas Llosa, *Guide to the Perfect Latin American Idiot* (Lanham: Madison Books, 2000), 11.
4. Fernando Henriquez Cardoso and Enzo Faletto, *Dependency and Development in Latin America* (Berkeley: University of California Press, 1979), xxi–xxii.
5. Andre Gunder Frank, *Capitalism and Underdevelopment in Latin America: Historical Studies of Chile and Brazil* (New York: Monthly Review Press, 1967).
6. Fernando Henrique Cardoso, *The Accidental President of Brazil* (New York: Public Affairs, 2006), 98.
7. Guillermo O'Donnell, "Human Development, Human Rights, and Democracy," in *The Quality of Democracy: Theory and Applications, eds.* Guillermo O'Donnell, Jorge Vargas Cullell, and Osvaldo M. Iazzetta (Notre Dame: University of Notre Dame Press, 2004).
8. Robert A. Dahl, *Polyarchy: Participation and Opposition* (New Haven, CT: Yale University Press, 1971), 8.

CHAPTER 2

State Formation and Economic Development in the Nineteenth Century

LEARNING OBJECTIVES

- Explain the main challenges of state building after the independence era.

- Differentiate between the strategies used to achieve political stability.

- Evaluate the importance of international influences on early political and economic development.

In 1812, the legendary revolutionary Simón Bolívar was doing his best to keep up the morale of his troops and beleaguered local populations in the fight for independence. This was not easy, but he had a high level of confidence and had taken command of the revolutionary forces. He wrote his first major declaration, called *The Cartagena Manifesto*. Bolívar emphasized how unity was critical and how democracy would not work well, at least in the short term as national identities were forged in a context of international war. "The American provinces," he wrote, "are involved in a struggle for emancipation, which will eventually succeed."[1] He was right on all counts.

The Challenges of Independence

The wars for Latin American independence, which took place from about 1808 until 1825, were sparked in large part by international factors, most prominently Napoleon Bonaparte's invasion of the Iberian Peninsula in 1807 (Portugal) and 1808 (Spain). The toppling of the Portuguese and Spanish monarchs served to unmoor the ties between the colonies and the homeland, and consequently political splits within the colonies quickly boiled over. These wars were bitter, violent, and terribly destructive, leaving devastation in their wake. In Mexico, which was the Viceroyalty of New Spain, somewhere between 250,000 and 500,000 were killed out of a total population of about 6 million.[2] The new nations that slowly emerged faced serious obstacles as a result. For much of the nineteenth century, state building would be primarily a national-level activity—fighting against local interests; only in the latter half would international factors—particularly, but not exclusively, the rising influence of the United States—become a part of that project as well in Mexico, Central America, and the Caribbean.

This early period is critical for understanding future political developments in Latin American countries. Events sparked by international factors had huge national consequences. For example, the strong militaries we still see across the region are a direct result of nation- and state-building efforts in the nineteenth century. This chapter will examine the early evolution of Latin American politics and economics. The constitutions written and political patterns established during that time created legacies that are still being felt in the twenty-first century. For economic development, there were of course many individual policy decisions being made (i.e., "agency"), but the newly independent countries must be placed within a very specific political and economic context that constrained those decisions (i.e., "structure").

The International Level: Peninsular Wars and Latin American Declarations of Independence

After the United States broke free of Great Britain, the next taste of independence in the region came in Haiti, where a slave revolt against the French in 1791 sparked years of fighting that culminated in victory in 1804. Military leader Toussaint L'Ouverture had first worked with the French to abolish slavery and then led the independence forces against them after French authorities resisted his efforts to take political control over Haiti, which included writing a new constitution. L'Ouverture was captured and died in prison before independence, but his example of resistance to white rule continued to resonate. The racial aspect of Haitian independence would not go unnoticed in the Spanish- and Portuguese-speaking world. **Creoles** were native born and lighter-skinned elites in the colonies and feared the possible ramifications of wars that might arm blacks and/or the indigenous.

Race and Nation in Latin America

However, those same creoles resented the **pensinsulares**, referring to the Spanish- and Portuguese-born elites. By virtue of being born in the Iberian Peninsula, they were favored and more trusted by their respective monarchies and, therefore, monopolized the highest political offices. In turn, dominance by the peninsulares was contested by **mestizos**, people whose ancestry was that of a mix between the Iberian conquerors and natives. They soon came to be a majority in most of Latin America and demanded more political power. In social (and economic) terms, the lower strata were composed of the indigenous and blacks who were slaves or descendants of slaves brought from Africa.

In Carlos Fuentes' novel about the wars for independence, *The Campaign*, the protagonist sums up the racial aspect of the struggles: "The whites ran the war—the wars, the guerilla wars—and killed one another off. The mestizos died in battle, and the Indians provided food, labor, and women."[3] Racial discrimination was central to Spanish and Portuguese control. Independence would change the dynamic, because mestizos took more positions of political authority, but by no means would the foundations of racial domination disappear.

By 1806, Napoleon wished to weaken Great Britain by forcing the rest of Europe to accept the blocking of all British imports into the continent. Portugal attempted to remain neutral, which only brought Napoleon's attention to bear on that country. He made a pact with Spain to allow French troops to march on Portugal, at which point the Portuguese royal family fled to Brazil. This created a very different dynamic for Brazil compared to its Spanish American counterparts, because no Spanish king or queen ever set foot in their Latin American colonies. The Portuguese king eventually returned in 1821, but his son (who became King Pedro I) remained and became emperor of an independent Brazil.

National Response to International Factors in Spanish America

The political transition was much more traumatic in Spanish America. King Ferdinand VII was imprisoned after the French invasion, and the inability of the Spanish monarchy to exert effective authority emboldened creoles in the colonies. Without these international factors, independence movements would still have existed but would not have occurred precisely in this time frame. Venezuela was the first colony to declare independence, in 1811 (and Spain did not acknowledge the independence of any of its colonies until 1836, when it recognized Mexico).

Independence was a protracted and confusing process, because national loyalties remained quite weak. Local leaders fought to liberate themselves from Spanish control but often with only minimal connection to a cause much greater than themselves. It was during this time that the word **guerrilla** came into usage. The literal Spanish translation is "little war," and it refers to small groups of fighters using hit-and-run tactics to defeat a larger, stronger enemy. It was coined in Spain during the war against French occupation and used to great effect. Spanish rebels successfully engaged French soldiers, who were in unfamiliar territory and facing a hostile local population. Guerrilla warfare helped drain French resources. In Spanish America, the strategy was then turned on the Spanish, who found strong pockets of local resistance all across the region.

There was, however, a very strong dose of conventional war as well. Soldiers such as Simón Bolívar, Bernardo O'Higgins (Chile), José de San Martín

(Argentina), Antonio José de Sucre (Bolivia), José Gervasio Artigas (Uruguay), and many more found glory on the battlefield and would become part of the mythology of the new nations. They would also establish the view that the armed forces of Latin America preceded independence and, therefore, should be the ultimate defenders of the state.

Nonetheless, the mere existence of these iconic figures was obviously insufficient to immediately generate a widespread sense of "nation." When, in colony after colony, independence from Spain was ultimately gained, there was little in the way of national unity. Ties formed during the colonial era and wartime did not necessarily translate into nationality. In all ways, Latin American countries were starting from scratch.

The National Level: Nations and States

International events were instrumental in launching the wars for independence and explaining why they occurred at this particular time. However, once Latin American countries won independence, their immediate goals were national. New borders had to be drawn and defended, and new political institutions were constructed. Therefore, it is important first to emphasize the conceptual differences between **nations** and **states**.

The Challenge of Nation Building

These terms are often tossed around loosely and sometimes seem to mean the same thing, but they should be viewed as complementary rather than synonymous. The essential difference is that the former is about the deeply shared common characteristics that people feel, whereas the latter refers to the concrete institutions that allow a government to function both domestically and as part of an international system. A nation represents a close sense of belonging and, in the international arena, fosters a sense of difference between different countries. Nations share a common history, with shared heroes. Everyone is reminded of this history through symbols such as flags, money (which shows people and places deemed important), monuments, oaths, songs, poems, and important commemorated days. All this shared history is then taught to children in schools and becomes part of the fabric of everyday life.

Creating a sense of nationality to bridge local differences is no easy task, especially in countries with people who may not speak the same language (very common in Latin America), who are of different races and ethnicities, or even who live in very large countries with regional variations. This was a major task for nineteenth-century Latin America, and one that is still not yet completely resolved. Well into the twentieth century, indigenous peoples became victims of political violence because they were not considered insufficiently part of the nation. In the context of the Cold War, for example, many people were killed simply because their "otherness" made them seem like a threat to the government's idea of national unity.

The Challenge of State Building

Building states was also critical. This simply refers to the basic characteristics of a country that distinguishes it from other countries, rather than to the more symbolic nation. A state must have a defined territory and be sovereign, meaning that it exerts sole control over its population through laws and the use of force. This entails creation of a central government to impose order and facilitate economic growth. Building a military force to protect your borders is essential, as is creating a system of taxation to raise revenue. The terms *state* and *government* are also often used as if they mean the same thing, but a state is more permanent, whereas governments come and go. No Latin American state has disappeared despite changes in government, though some have changed in size due to wars. Obviously, building a strong state is indispensable for prosperity. Weak states, especially referring to states whose governments do not effectively control much of the territory, create a "survival of the fittest" scenario in which the majority of people tend to lose out and where foreign incursion is therefore more likely.

In Latin America, state building proved difficult. As historian Robert Holden writes about Central America, "[t]he state could not hope ... to nonviolently induce compliance with its law because it was not perceived as a legitimate or ultimate source of any latent power to enforce compliance."[4] Citizens did not consider the state to be a real authority no matter what government happened to be in charge, which then led to the habit of the state of using violence as a way to get people to obey the law. That pattern persisted, and it was difficult to break.

This was precisely the lament of Domingo Faustino Sarmiento, an Argentine intellectual who eventually became the president. In 1845, he published *Life in the Argentine Republic in the Days of the Tyrants; or, Civilization and Barbarism*, which he wrote while in political exile and which made him famous. In the book, his main target is the dictator Juan Manuel de Rosas, a caudillo who ruled in Buenos Aires from 1829 until 1852. Sarmiento championed the pursuit of national greatness over local interests and wrote of the extreme and arbitrary violence of the Argentine caudillos. As we will discuss in subsequent chapters, some countries were more successful than others in breaking that mold.

ANALYZING DOCUMENTS

Domingo Sarmiento wrote an eloquent analysis of how local caudillos could rise to national prominence and lay waste to the political system. The local population was thereby terrorized, and as he notes, the money spent reduced the country's ability to take advantage of international trade opportunities.

Life in the Argentine Republic in the Days of the Tyrants; or, Civilization and Barbarism (1845)

Have Facundo or Rosas ever done the least thing for the public good, or been interested in any useful object? No. From them come nothing but blood and crimes. I have given these details at length, because in the midst of horrors such as I am

(Continued)

obliged to describe, it is comforting to pause on the few progressive impulses which revive again and again after being apparently crushed by savage barbarians. Civilization will, however feeble its present resistance, one day resume its place. There is a new world about to unfold itself, and it only awaits some fortunate general to put aside the iron heel which has so long crushed it. Besides, history should not be considered merely a tissue of crimes, and for this reason it is desirable to bring before the mind of a subjugated people a remembrance of past epochs. If they desire for their posterity a better record than they themselves have, let them not hope for it because the cannibal of Buenos Ayres is just now tired of shedding blood, and permits exiles to return to their homes. This fact is of no import in the progress of a people. The great evil to be dreaded is a government which fears the influence of thoughtful and enlightened men, and must either exile or kill them. This evil results from a system which gives one man such absolute power that there can be no liberty of thought or action, no public spirit—the desire of self-preservation outweighing all interest for others. Every one for himself, and the executioner for all without discrimination, this is the *résumé* of the life and government of an enslaved people.

...

But no evils are eternal, and a day must come when the eyes of this people will be opened, who are now denied all liberty of progress, and are deprived of all capable and intelligent men, who could carry on the great work, and bring about in a few years the prosperity for which Nature has destined this now stationary, impoverished, devastated country. Why are such men persecuted? Brave, enterprising men, who employed their lives in various social improvements, encouraging public education, introducing the water-courses, with only the national interest at heart, and desiring no other reward than the satisfaction of serving their fellow-citizens! Why do we not see again arising the spirit of European civilization which, however feeble, did once exist in the Argentine Republic? . . . Why has not even a twentieth part of the millions employed in a fratricidal war been used to educate the people or to facilitate trade? What has been given to this people in exchange for its sacrifices and sufferings? A red rag! This is the extent of the government's care of them for fifteen years; this is the only measure of the national administration; the only relation between master and slave, the mark upon the cattle!

Discussion Questions
- Why might a dictator want to crush all local caudillos?
- Why was Sarmiento so critical of the way the national government was being run?

Source: D. F. Sarmiento, *Life in the Argentine Public in the Days of the Tyrants; or, Civilization and Barbarism* (New York: Collier Books, 1961), 144, 158.

Local Challenges of State Building

A persistent obstacle to state building was the existence of regional **caudillos.** A caudillo is a military figure who, through personal favors, charisma, and of course the use of force, develops a large following and establishes some variant of authoritarian rule. Caudillos resisted centralized control and ruled their fiefdoms. This represented a serious political challenge from the local level.

Many were also heirs of a colonial system that encouraged large **haciendas**—plantations—that became towns in themselves, and they fought to protect their private property and their exclusive control over those who worked for them. Although some caudillos would break out of their regions and come to lead entire countries, their local power base was always an important source of support and authority. So, for example, although Mexico's Antonio López de Santa Anna was president at various times (eleven in all between 1833 and 1855), he remained firmly embedded in the state of Veracruz, to which he would periodically retreat. The Mexican state would not solidify until the dictatorship of Porfirio Díaz (1876–1911), who himself was always strongly tied to the state of Oaxaca.

As regional leaders, they were not easy to dislodge. For people living far from the few major cities, caudillos represented a source of order. It is one thing to ratify a constitution guaranteeing specified rights but quite another for those rights ever to be respected. The caudillos provided protection and predictability for the local population, even though in many cases they might abuse their power. Fear was an important factor and, combined with military power, made the caudillos a potent adversaries to politicians with ambitions of extending national authority.

The Role of the Military in State Building

So what could governments do to strengthen the state? The role of Latin American militaries was central to state-building projects across the region. From the ashes of revolution, the armed forces represented the most organized institution, and their leaders the most highly visible. They were better positioned than any other institution to expand state authority throughout national territories, which were often vast and/or hard to navigate (through mountains, jungles, or deserts). In addition, they were not fighting international wars. In the first half of the nineteenth century, there were only two wars within Latin America. Argentina and Brazil fought over territory between 1825 and 1828, which ultimately yielded Uruguay as a buffer state between them. Chile also fought successfully against Bolivia and Peru (1836–1839), after Bolivia under Andrés Santa Cruz invaded Peru and created the Peruvian-Bolivian Confederation.

But was the military's role positive or negative? This is a matter of some debate, generating various hypotheses. Fernando López-Alves argues that it was often positive.[5] At times, wars facilitated the definition of towns and regions, imbued citizens with national symbols, and fostered incorporation. Those who entered the military enjoyed a **fuero** (privileges and immunity) that continued from the colonial period, which also made it an attractive career option. When the military allied itself with urban elites, such as in Argentina, democracy was less likely to develop because elites were able to repress opposition and limit political competition. But when militaries were tied to parties in rural areas, the state never became domineering and democracy could take root.

On the other hand, Miguel Angel Centeno notes that the military's role did little to foster the construction of strong states.[6] In fact, the weakness of the postindependence states prompted the military to focus largely on internal enemies. The only "benefit" was that interstate wars did not occur very often compared to other regions of the world, because governments were preoccupied with conquering their own land rather than others. The ultimate result, though, was a military institution well aware of its relative strength and determined to attack what it believed were the government's domestic enemies threatening the status quo. From the beginning, the armed forces viewed their role as protecting "la Patria" (the motherland) by any means necessary. As the main conflicts were internal, that is where their energy was focused. Officers felt that the military's historical roots predated independence, and therefore, it should enjoy an exalted status. As political scientist Brian Loveman writes, "According to this view, the armed forces preceded, and then created, *la patria* in glorious struggles for independence, defended it against internal and foreign enemies, and became the reservoir of nationalism and patriotism."[7]

We therefore have a conundrum, or at least the question of whether the glass was half full or empty. Weak states certainly may have facilitated the growth of parties, political competition, and sparked fewer wars, but they also tended to create internally oriented militaries, which were all too often a threat to civilian rule. They also opened the door for foreign intervention, because no government was in a position to defend itself effectively.

Although this dilemma was evident in most countries, there were exceptions. Cuba, for example, remained part of the Spanish empire until 1898. Brazil, meanwhile, experienced a peaceful shift from colony to monarchy in 1822, independent from Portugal but still ruled by Dom Pedro, the son of King João VI. Furthermore, Chile established a strong central government that became much more civilian than military. For the most part, however, states in Latin America faced more or less constant challenges, and the armed forces played a central role in politics.

The Problem of Weak States

In addition, we need to be careful about the very notion of a "weak" state. Those in power may find it difficult to control their territory and face foreign incursions, but that does not necessarily mean that they cannot exert tremendous control over their citizens, such as the peasantry. A **peasant** is an individual who lives in a rural area and makes a living by engaging in agriculture. In nineteenth-century rural Latin America, as in many other parts of the world, most peasants subsisted on land owned by others and would be allowed to spend some of their time growing food for themselves. In some cases, they might be held there by debt peonage, referring to the practice of forcing someone with no money to go into debt in return for use of the land. They would remain in a cycle of debt from which they could not escape, and the landowner would benefit from their indentured servitude.

By the late nineteenth century, even seemingly very weak states, such as those in Central America, were able to impose a wide range of controls over peasants. In El Salvador, for example, governments worked in tandem with large landowners ("hacendados," after the term *hacienda*) to construct systems—both formal and informal—of surveillance and violence intended to keep the peasantry compliant. The relationship between the rulers and the ruled was repressive. Indeed, for the indigenous and black populations, in addition to mestizo peasantry across the region, independence brought little substantive local change.

The same was true for women. As in the United States at the same time, women enjoyed very few political rights and would not be granted suffrage until the twentieth century. In the first years of the new Latin American republics, women were not even considered citizens and were legally relegated to private, rather than public, life. In some cases, women did have legal rights (e.g., widows becoming official head of household, such as in Mexico), and some countries (e.g., Colombia) passed civil matrimony and divorce laws, though they received staunch opposition from the Catholic Church and were therefore later rescinded. These came from local efforts of women activists struggling to convince male legislators to make changes. None of these efforts, though, extended to voting or holding political office.

Constitutions and the National Seeds of Democracy and Authoritarianism

Part of state building, of course, involves writing the national political rules of the game, which are enshrined in constitutions. Venezuelans wrote the first Latin American constitution even before winning independence (though it lasted only eight years), and almost 200 years later, the country continued to debate and reform, with a new constitution put into effect in 1999 and more reforms passed in 2009. Either amending or completely rewriting constitutions has often coincided with political upheaval in Latin America. Political leaders view them as elements of an overall political project, to be shaped and reshaped over time.

The writers of the first nineteenth-century constitutions had the imposition of order as an immediate challenge. Both in rural areas and in cities, economic and military elites recognized the poor and displaced as threats, because economic dislocation brought desperation. They felt a pressing need to control local politics as much as possible and stifle local dissent. Yet there was also a strong liberal streak, inspired by the American and French revolutions. Politically, **liberal** refers to principles that honor representative republican government, with pluralism and protection of individual liberties. In fact, a key impetus for the new constitutions was the fact that Ferdinand VII, besieged by French troops, accepted the liberalism of the 1812 Spanish constitution (in 1814, he rejected it and then later reaccepted it as political conditions in Spain changed). That acknowledgment spread to the colonies. Unfortunately, such ideals collided with reality, so that although the constitutions enshrined many of the same rights as in the United States, they also included military prerogatives and states of emergency, which grant the executive broad authority and suspend normal constitutional rights. Both of these veered much more toward authoritarianism.

The French constitution of 1791 asserted that the armed forces were "essentially obedient" and could not "deliberate," meaning they would not become embroiled in political disputes. Latin American constitutions took this exact wording.[8] In practice, this was unworkable in most countries, because the military became an arbiter of political conflict and could hardly remain out of politics. Therefore, also tucked into constitutions were articles outlining the military's role in protecting "la Patria." That sidestepped the prohibition against deliberation by giving the military what it considered an obligation to save the country if political conflict threatened order.

Further, constitutions across the region codified "regimes of exception," meaning the suspension of civil liberties in times of emergency, as declared by the executive with varying degrees of consultation with the legislature. Once invoked, the average citizen's rights in a specific area (sometimes national, at other times more localized) were strictly limited, martial law might well hold, and security forces wielded tremendous power. Indeed, the removal of such constitutional provisions has proved a lasting and difficult task for reformers over the years, and many constitutions still retain language that is strikingly similar to the nineteenth-century examples. This centralist tendency was a hallmark of Simón Bolívar, the most visible and well-known figure of the wars for independence. Limitations on freedom were viewed as necessary, if perhaps unfortunate, vehicle for protecting the state from the many threats it faced, both internal and external.

At least on paper, the legislature constituted a brake on executive authority. Its members would be elected separately from the president, and there would be a divide between the two branches. So, as in the United States, the president would have to obtain legislative approval for the country's budget. The formal role, however, was very different from the way that politics really played out. Throughout the nineteenth and well into the twentieth century, Latin American legislatures rarely exerted much authority. There are some exceptions, as in the Chilean case, but most commonly legislators followed the president and were rewarded for doing so. This bestowing of favors worked to mutual benefit.

Constructing Accountable Political Institutions

Thus, the pattern that became established in the nineteenth century was an absence of **horizontal accountability** because of the presidential power. The *horizontal* refers to other state institutions that exist alongside the president, particularly the legislature and the judiciary. In a democracy, all these institutions should hold the others accountable so that no single one garners too much political power. In the United States, this is usually called *checks and balances*. In countries where governments have difficulty keeping order and perhaps where resources are scarce, it is tempting for the president to ignore, shut down, or otherwise reduce the authority of any institution that might stand in his or her way. That is still a problem in Latin America today.

The debate over horizontal accountability was not confined only to the power of the presidency. Also in the mix was whether these new governments should be **centralist, federal,** or **confederal,** all of which denote the relationship between the central government and different regions of the country. As its name suggests, a centralist system invests virtually all political power in the central government. This was the example left by colonial rulers, where the monarchy named viceroys who carried out their orders. Power came directly from the top without representative institutions. In the postindependence period, centralism clashed immediately with federalist tendencies.

In a federal system (e.g., in the United States, Mexico, or Brazil), power is formally shared between the central government and state governments. Governors (sometimes called *prefects*) have their power bases but ultimately must answer to the central government. The idea is to combine autonomy and central authority. By the nature of the arrangement, there will always be tension between the two, because both the federal and state governments have a strong incentive to acquire as much power as possible. The resulting competition, however, can have a positive effect on democracy because there will be a balance between national and more local interests. In the nineteenth century, however, especially in the absence of competitive elections Latin American federalism remained largely dictatorial.

Finally, a confederation places most power (e.g., raising money or creating a military force) to the states, which may or may not voluntarily accept central government requests. The Articles of Confederation did not work out so well in the United States, and in Latin America, confederations (e.g., the Central American Confederation or the Peru-Bolivia Confederation of 1836) were short-lived in the face of governments deciding not to participate when it was not in their interest.

Vertical accountability was also rare in Latin America and would only become more commonplace in the twentieth century, and even then with periodic setbacks. The "vertical" relationship is between the elected rulers and the voters. For example, if a president enacts policies that are terribly unpopular in a democracy, he or she will have to be accountable to voters in the next election. Obviously, the core of vertical accountability is the existence of regular free and fair elections. These were few and far between in this period of time, and those that took place were limited to elites (not unlike, though more extreme than, the United States at the time). The average person at the local level had almost no opportunities for participation.

The Liberal–Conservative Divide

We can better understand the question of constitutional accountability when we consider it in light of the conflicts between liberals and **conservatives** in Latin America. There were many different factions in the region, defined by geography, wealth, race, gender, and many other factors, but the liberal–conservative divide grew out of the independence wars and remained overarching, in some cases for well over a hundred years.

Liberals looked to political philosophy in the United States and parts of Europe, which preached the gospel of individual rights (though certainly, as in the United States these rights were applied unevenly). This meant an emphasis on the separation of church and state, international trade, and in general a challenge to the traditional order. Conservatives, as the name implies, were committed to maintaining many of the political and social characteristics of the Spanish (or Portuguese) regimes. This included the preservation of the Catholic Church's prerogatives, opposition to popular sovereignty, and a commitment to social order. They often had a rural power base (in some cases because the Church owned land) and therefore advocated for protection of agriculture versus industry and the small fiefdoms that rural life entailed. Each had very different ideas about what the role of the state should be and who it should favor. Both viewed the local level in elite terms, as something that needed to be controlled.

We cannot understate the importance of the Church throughout the nineteenth century. It determined who could get married, dominated education, owned extensive tracts of land, and enjoyed a broad range of fueros similar to the military that protected it. It acted as a connector between national and local (even international, given the power of the Vatican in Rome) forces. This could mean legal protection or even exemption from paying taxes. The stakes of political conflict were therefore very high, because any alteration in the church's position would affect not only the political system but society at large. Struggles between liberal and conservative forces were therefore the source of civil wars, chronicled in the chapters that follow.

By the end of the century, however, liberals held sway in much of the region. Although the Catholic Church remained influential, most countries had separated church and state. Borders were still under dispute (the War of the Pacific is by far the most famous example, especially because it continues to rankle both Bolivia and Peru), but the contours of modern-day states were largely formed. As Box 2.1 demonstrates, nationhood was also firming up as time went on, which had the effect of accentuating the differences between citizens of different countries. Bolivar's goal of unification was more distant than ever.

This coincided with the rapid growth of the U.S. economy after the civil war (1861–1865), and so foreign investment poured in. Liberal presidents, very often unelected, worked to consolidate centralized power over regional conservative strongholds and embarked on infrastructure projects, which served to facilitate both trade and central control. The occurrence of coups decreased in the late nineteenth century, which did not necessarily entail democracy, but it did encourage an infusion of capital that sparked economic growth. As we will discuss in Chapter 12, nowhere was this more evident than in Argentina, which moved from a country ripped apart by violence to an economy rivaling Europe (and then back again).

Thus far, our discussion of state building has focused on the national and regional levels. However, with regard to economic development, we need to examine the international level to a much greater degree.

BOX 2.1

The Legacies of Andean Conflict: The War of the Pacific
The Interplay Between National and International
Causes of Conflict

International: The most lucrative area for guano deposits was in Bolivia, which in 1878 imposed an export tax on nitrate and even made it retroactive, which infuriated Chilean exporters. The war was fueled by long-standing distrust the Bolivians and Peruvians felt for Chile, which had been far more stable, more prosperous, and widely viewed as a potential expansionist threat.

The Bolivian government proceeded to seize the properties of Chilean companies for nonpayment, and so in 1879 the Chilean government sent naval ships to take the Bolivian port city of Antofagasta. Five years earlier, Bolivia and Peru had signed a secret treaty ensuring that if either country were attacked, the other would come to its defense. Thus began a three country war (though Bolivia and Peru unsuccessfully tried to entice Argentina to join as well).

The war still resonates. In 2008, the Peruvian army chief remarked that "The Chilean that enters (Peru) doesn't leave or he leaves in a coffin; if there aren't enough coffins, they'll leave in plastic bags."[9] He was forced to resign, but not before noting that his comments "only express the feelings of every soldier who loves his homeland."

National: Bolivia has a navy but no sea in which to sail. In 2006, Vice Admiral José Alba Arnez gave an interview, saying rather sadly, "We don't want it all back.... All we want is a ten-kilometer strip to call our own."[10] After his 2005 election, President Evo Morales worked with both the Chilean government and the Organization of American States to regain some type of ocean access. Bolivia's coast was lost in war well over a century ago, but the national wound is still gaping.

Local: The superior Chilean navy quickly gained control of the Pacific, and then a bloody land war ensued.[11] Local populations were displaced and ultimately territories changed nationality. The Battles of Tacna and Arica (which at the time were the south of Peru) broke the back of the defending armies, and Chilean troops took Lima in 1881, which they would occupy for two more years. The ultimate result was that Peru gave up part of its southern territory (Tarapacá and Arica), whereas Bolivia entirely lost its access to the ocean (its former province of Litoral).

Discussion Questions
- In what kinds of ways does war have a deep and long-lasting impact on feelings of nationalism?
- What impact can invasion have on local populations?

International Influences and the Challenge of National Economic Development

One of the most basic problems facing Latin American states was a lack of capital. With fields burned and towns in tatters, where would governments obtain the money necessary to rebuild and launch projects of national economic development? The answer was to be found with European, and later also U.S., creditors. Thus would begin the relationship so closely analyzed by dependency theorists. Latin American countries would borrow and produce primary products, which would be sold to the more developed world—often the same countries as the banks—in return for finished goods that Latin America was unable to produce for itself.

It is worth noting that the buzzword *globalization*, which entails an increasing interconnectedness between countries and comes up almost constantly these days, is not really new. Leaders of all Latin American countries were immediately aware that they could not possibly survive in isolation, and consequently they actively sought to connect more to other countries that could supply capital and/or become a market for their exports. There was also talk of unification, as a way to gain strength against international forces, especially the growing power of the United States. Simón Bolívar was the most vocal in this regard, as he repeated the theme in countless letters. He commonly used grand phrases to show his passion for the idea, so that not only would unity make the region stronger, but it would create a body politic "greater than any that history has recorded."

ANALYZING DOCUMENTS

Simón Bolívar was dedicated to merging the national and the international, viewing newly independent Latin American countries as fraternal enough that they could join together in formal ways. The local and national struggles for freedom could forge a united region that could become a formidable global power.

Simón Bolívar, Letter to Juan Martín Pueyrredón, Supreme Director of the United Provinces of the Río de la Plata (1818)

I have the honor to reply to the communication which Your Excellency had the honor to send me under date of November 19, 1816. Its long-delayed arrival, although easily understood, has not diminished the inexpressible joy in my heart on witnessing the inauguration of the relations we have so long desired. Your Excellency, overcoming the barriers presented by distance, isolation, and lack of direct routes, has taken a forward step that gives both governments new life by making them better known to each other.

Your Excellency honors my country by regarding her as a solitary monument which will remind America of the price of liberty and which will recall the memory of a magnanimous and incorruptible people. There is no doubt but that Venezuela, in devoting everything to the sacred cause of freedom, regards her sacrifices as triumphs. Upon the altars of patriotism she has offered her blood in torrents, her towns in flames, to the absolute ruin of all her works of man and even of Nature.

…

Your Excellency may assure your noble countrymen that they will be received and honored here, not merely as members of a friendly republic, but as members of our Venezuelan commonwealth. There should be but one country for all Americans, since we have been perfectly united in every other way.

Most Excellent Sir, when the triumph of Venezuela's arms has completed the work of independence, or when more favorable circumstances permit us more frequent communication and closer relations, we, for our part, will hasten, with lively interest, to establish the American pact; which, in forming a body politic comprising all our republics, shall present America to the world in an aspect of majesty and grandeur, greater than any that history has recorded. An America thus united—should Heaven grant us that devout wish—could truly style herself the Queen of Nations and the Mother of Republics.

I hope that the Rio de la Plata, with her powerful influence, will cooperate actively in perfecting the political edifice which we initiated on the first day of our struggle for freedom.

Discussion Questions
- Can you think of possible reasons why it was impossible to unify all the different revolutionary movements in Latin America?
- Why would Simón Bolívar want international unity so badly?

Source: Vicente Lecuna (comp.) and Harold A. Bierck, Jr., ed., *Selected Writings of Bolívar, Volume One, 1810–1822* (New York: The Colonial Press, Inc., 1951), 160–161.

Spain and Portugal had enforced mercantilist policies, which meant tightly controlling colonial exports. To ensure a favorable balance of trade, the colonial powers forced the colonies to trade only through the motherland. Not surprisingly, this monopolistic policy grated on colonial subjects, whose taxes went straight to the crown. After independence, Latin American governments were free to trade anywhere, and new economic relationships soon sprouted up. This also meant that many foreigners began arriving in Latin American cities, looking for opportunity. However, the late 1820s would also see the first round of debt defaults in the region, and so it took several decades before Latin America was widely considered a profitable place to invest.

The failure to construct strong central governments in the nineteenth century meant that internal taxation was either spotty or nonexistent. It was often simply impossible for the government to extract taxes, and because economic elites had close ties to rulers (or were the rulers themselves), there was little incentive to do so. As a result, government revenue came primarily from import and export duties. Customs houses, situated at borders and especially at ports, became central to the accumulation of state wealth.

Becoming Dependent Internationally

This had three intertwined effects. First, it contributed to the precedent of being heavily dependent on the trade of primary products. Because prices for commodities routinely rise and fall, this was no stable foundation for economic growth. This would become particularly evident in the latter half of the century. Dependence would turn the liberal goal of trade on its head, because for the most part trade did not foster the kind of sound financial foundation that liberals sought. It should be noted, however, that the price of some primary products—cattle is one example—were often very favorable. Indeed, Argentine leaders saw no reason to push for an industrial policy when meat and hides generated considerable profit, enough to prop up the entire economy (with the Argentine gaucho—loosely translated as *cowboy*—an international symbol). In no country, however, would those continuously favorable conditions last into the twentieth century.

Second, given shortfalls governments often turned to foreign countries for loans, which made them subject to pressure from those doing the lending. Foreign companies also established a close relationship with corrupt leaders who were willing to provide highly favorable terms (e.g., buying land, receiving tax breaks, receiving guarantees of a docile labor force) in return for money in their pockets. These arrangements rarely constituted the source of long-term economic development and left the vast majority of citizens in most countries in a state of poverty.

Third, it made customs houses the periodic target of foreign countries (particularly Europe and the United States) when debt was owed and not being repaid. Dominican dictator Ulises Heureaux shuffled national debt from European to U.S. creditors, which fostered such a threat of invasion that the U.S. government (under President Theodore Roosevelt) took over the country's finances in 1905. The general importance—both domestic and international—of customs houses is vividly portrayed in Joseph Conrad's 1904 novel *Nostromo*, which takes place in the port city of a fictional Latin American country ("Costaguana"). Silver deposited in the customs house became the primary target for opposing forces and therefore is the site of a bloody battle for control over it.[12] The practice became so prevalent that in 1902 the Argentine minister to the United States Luis Drago penned what became known as the "Drago Doctrine," arguing that states had no legal right to collect debt by force.

Dependency and Lack of Development

Scholars have argued for years about why the United States, which became independent only a few decades before Latin America, became an economic powerhouse while Latin American countries did not. Our discussion has shown that the failure of political institutions is a key explanatory variable for understanding why Latin America so quickly lagged behind the United States in terms of economic development. The wars for independence were brutal and far more destructive than the revolution in the United States. Into the power vacuum came despots, further fuelled by the longtime Spanish example of harsh and un-yielding central authority. Dependency theory offers important insights about the unfavorable position of Latin American countries, which we will return to in subsequent chapters, but it does not take the problems with political institutions into account.

It might be tempting to view the tumult of the nineteenth century in cultural terms. Certainly many in the United States viewed it as such. The main thrust of the argument is that certain qualities inherited from Spain and Portugal are incompatible with good governance and economic development, or at least pose obstacles that Europe and the former British colonies do not face. This became conventional wisdom. In his history of Latin America, Columbia professor William R. Shepherd wrote in 1914 that by copying colonial political structures, the new nations created leaders "who either thought and acted for them, or else prevented them from thinking and acting for themselves."[13] In economic terms, "the Latin Americans, whatever their nationality, appear to lack the business instinct of the British, the German, and the American."[14] He added that they followed the Spanish and Portuguese model of business too closely. This general perspective has been echoed more recently in the scholarly literature as well, though it is widely disputed. The essence of the argument is that Latin Americans inherited certain negative characteristics from their colonizers and by the Catholicism brought by the conquerors. According to this argument, these characteristics crippled these new nations. This is the essence of modernization theory.

For many years, U.S. officials were openly critical of Latin American culture. As a foreign aid official noted in 1812 after landing in Venezuela, the people he found were "timid, indolent, ignorant, superstitious, and incapable of enterprise or exertion. From the present moral and intellectual habits of all classes, I fear they have not arrived at that point of human dignity which fits man for the enjoyment of free and rational government."[15]

This view has even been expressed by Latin Americans. As early as 1830, Mexican historian and journalist Lorenzo de Zavala wrote that people in the United States were hard working and independent, whereas Mexicans were "easy going, lazy, intolerant, generous almost to prodigality, vain, belligerent, superstitious, ignorant, and an enemy of all restraint."[16] This is a sentiment that has been repeated over the years. Lawrence Harrison has argued that Latin America requires "progressive" cultural change that would replace the "traditional" culture that pervaded the region for centuries.[17] According to this argument, hallmarks of traditional culture include excessive deference to authority, too much religious influence, little orientation toward the future, and a lack of emphasis on work and education. Howard Wiarda sums it up in the following way:

> Latin America was a product of the Counter-Reformation, of medieval scholasticism and Catholicism, of the Inquisition, and of frankly nonegalitarian, non-pluralist, and nondemocratic principles. Many of these early characteristics, now obviously modified, updated, or "modernized," are still present today, embedded in cultural, social and political behavior and in the area's main institutions.[18]

The essential drawback to the cultural argument, however, is that it cannot account well for change. For example, when many Latin American countries made the transition from dictatorship to democracy in the 1980s, was the change primarily cultural rather than political? When Brazil, Mexico, or Chile underwent periods of rapid economic growth, were they somehow changing their cultures as well? Were they somehow less "Latin American" than before? No doubt culture is part of the equation, but as the driving force of underdevelopment, it is less than convincing. When we examine specific countries in the chapters that follow, the importance of political institutions will become even clearer.

Social Structure and Local Politics

Social structure is also a factor contributing to the persistent underdevelopment in Latin America, both then and now. **Commodities**—meaning goods that are mined and farmed—were the traditional engines of economic growth and wealth, and they required a constant supply of labor in conditions that were often inhumane. Eighteenth-century dictatorships had every incentive to keep the poor and uneducated, which were the vast majority of Latin Americans, right where they were. Economic elites, whose wealth was primarily in land, needed that acquiescent labor. Inequality therefore became entrenched in every country, with variations according to differences in racial, ethnic, and other characteristics of the population.

Indeed, local-level politics in Latin America during much of the eighteenth century was characterized by repression. A tiny percentage of the population owned the vast majority of land and political offices. Individuals could find no support from law enforcement, judges, or politicians when they felt their rights were being violated. Local elites essentially decided what rights people would have. This state of affairs deepened both political and economic inequalities.

From a strictly economic perspective, long-term inequality poses a problem for development. If the majority of the population is very poor, then the country's purchasing power is quite low, which stunts the creation of prosperous domestic businesses aimed at an internal market. People who are struggling to make ends meet on a daily basis are less likely to become entrepreneurs (except perhaps on a very small scale) or own a business that will hire others at good wages. In addition, it decreases the tax base for government revenues. Not only does income taxation require an efficient bureaucracy, but it needs a relatively well-off citizenry to pay them. So while inequality will contribute to the wealth of a small percentage of the population, the country as a whole cannot move forward.

Inequality also serves to point out the difference between growth and development. Growth is about production. How much more is being produced now compared to the past? How much money is moving around in the country? How much investment is being made? These days, growth is most commonly measured as **gross domestic product** (GDP). GDP is the value of all goods and services produced within a country in one year (the citizenship of the producer is not relevant). It is the most widely used figure, and the one that this book will employ. It tells you a lot about the amount of wealth being produced, but nothing about how it is distributed. National-level figures don't tell us much about whether the majority of people on the ground are benefiting as well. Another measure that was developed in 1990 is the **Human Development Index (HDI)**. It combines three different parts: life expectancy at birth, average years of schooling, and average income. That provides a more detailed view of how growth affects individuals.

Development, on the other hand, is all about sustainability and durability. It can mean physical infrastructure (roads, bridges, dams, sewers), human capital (education, healthcare), or investment in industries that generate jobs over the long term (targeted subsidies, tax breaks). If tremendous wealth flows into a country, but goes primarily into the pockets of political elites, there might be high growth but not development. In Latin America, from independence to the present, the enduring challenge has been to translate economic growth into development. That means transforming national-level prosperity into local growth as well.

Subaltern Groups: National and Local Levels

The end of colonial rule also meant the end of tribute laws that forced indigenous populations in Latin America to pay a tax to the crown or to give their labor if they could not pay. Forced labor, however, remained widespread. In some countries, such as Guatemala, a tribute tax was reinstated in 1831, which prompted local support for the caudillo Rafael Carrera, who had darker skin and appealed to indigenous interests. Further, the loss of colonial authority meant it was even easier for large landowners to take peasant land because of weak central control.

The newly formed states worked to forcibly assimilate Indians. From the liberal perspective, the cultural backwardness of the indigenous posed an obstacle to westernization and modernization. Conservatives, meanwhile, viewed native practices with even more distaste, as something blasphemous. Despite their political differences, liberals and conservatives alike considered Indians as a potential threat that must be controlled in one way or another.

Slavery even continued in Brazil and Cuba, though it was abolished elsewhere. From the perspective of race, independence represented a major step forward, but many limitations remained. Mestizos would soon take positions of greater authority than during the colonial period, but for the most part blacks and indigenous peoples would not see significant socioeconomic improvement after independence and would remain subordinate to local elites. But as historian John Chasteen writes, "The old social hierarchies, no matter how stubborn, had lost much of their explicit, public justification."[19]

Conclusion

Simón Bolívar argued that the wars for independence would be won but that democracy would not immediately result. In fact, democracy would not develop for many years. Civil wars pitted national and local leaders against each other.

At the end of the nineteenth century, there were several patterns that proved durable. First, at the national level the aftermath of the independence wars had encouraged strong presidential systems, with very powerful executives and weak legislatures. Second, international influence was important. The heyday of selling primary products abroad for high prices was ending and Latin American leaders were not in a good position to industrialize. Third, foreign capital was extremely important to Latin American economies, and the United States in particular increasingly loomed over the region.

Despite these persistent patterns, the twentieth century marked major changes in Latin American politics. Traditional local caudillo politics transformed by the growth of national mass political parties, social movements, international wars, the introduction of new ideologies, and the expansion of foreign capital, especially from the United States. The traditional divide between liberals and conservatives splintered into many different factions and organizations with cross-cutting interests. Twentieth-century political development had its own dynamics but was strongly conditioned by nineteenth-century institutions.

Key Terms

- Creoles
- Peninsulares
- Mestizos
- Guerrilla
- Nation
- State
- Caudillo
- Hacienda
- Fuero
- Peasant

- Liberal
- Horizontal accountability
- Centralist
- Federal
- Confederal
- Vertical accountability
- Conservative
- Commodity
- Gross domestic product (GDP)
- Human Development Index (HDI)

Discussion Questions

- What kinds of local problems might GDP not measure very well?
- In what ways might guerrillas gain the support of local populations?
- Can you think of reasons why nation building is so difficult?
- How can caudillos pose a challenge to national political authority?
- In what ways did international factors make it more difficult for newly independent Latin American countries to develop economically?

Further Sources

Books

Chasteen, John Charles. *Americanos: Latin America's Struggle for Independence* (New York: Oxford University Press, 2008). A highly readable and balanced political history of Latin American independence movements. In addition to the narrative, it includes timelines, short biographies of key figures, and suggestions for additional readings.

Franko, Patrice. *The Puzzle of Latin American Economic Development*, 3rd edition (Lanham: Rowman and Littlefield Publishers, Inc., 2007). This is an indispensable and thorough textbook for understanding virtually every aspect of Latin American economic development. It includes useful definitions, charts, tables, narrative examples, and other features that allow for a broad analysis of development.

Fukuyama, Francis, ed. *Falling Behind: Explaining the Development Gap Between Latin America and the United States* (Oxford: Oxford University Press, 2008). This is a collection of essays about why Latin American economic development so quickly fell behind the United States. The authors come both from different disciplines (particularly political science and history) and from different countries.

Loveman, Brian. *The Constitution of Tyranny: Regimes of Exception in Spanish America* (Pittsburgh: University of Pittsburgh Press, 2003). A detailed analysis regarding the formation of constitutions in the nineteenth century and how they enshrined the suspension of civil liberties in times of emergency. Of particular importance is the way in which constitutional language has endured to the present day.

Lynch, John. *Caudillos in Spanish America, 1800–1850* (Oxford: Clarendon Press, 1992). This book provides an exhaustive view of the role of caudillos in the decades immediately following independence. It analyzes the different roles that caudillos played, and how the national contexts led to different political outcomes. It also includes specific country examples and examination of several different individual caudillos.

Websites

Digital Library of the Caribbean (http://dloc.com/). This site includes a large collection of historical documents, maps, and newspapers for the Caribbean.

History of Cuba (http://www.historyofcuba.com/cuba.htm). This website has an extensive collection of essays, documents, reviews, photos, and links related to the history of Cuba.

H-LatAm (http://www.h-net.org/~latam/). This is a website portal for scholars studying Latin American history. It includes essays, book reviews, and message boards.

Latin American Information Network Center (http://lanic.utexas.edu/). The University of Texas at Austin hosts a site that has links to many different useful online sources for Latin American history. It includes sources both in the United States and in Latin American countries.

Latin American Pamphlets (http://vc.lib.harvard.edu/vc/deliver/home?_collection=LAP). Harvard University has a digital collection of over 5,000 Latin American pamphlets from the nineteenth and twentieth centuries, illustrating the political development of the region.

Endnotes

1. Quoted in Simón Bolívar, *El Libertador, Writings of Simón Bolívar* (New York: Oxford University Press, 2003), 27.
2. Robert L. Scheina, *Latin America's Wars: The Age of the Caudillo, 1791–1899* (Washington, DC: Brassey's, Inc., 2003), 84.
3. Carlos Fuentes, *The Campaign* (New York: Harper Perennial, 1990), 68.
4. Robert H. Holden, *Armies Without Nations: Public Violence and State Formation in Central America, 1821–1960* (New York: Oxford University Press, 2004), 26.
5. Fernando López-Alves, *State Formation and Democracy in Latin America, 1810–1900* (Durham: Duke University Press, 2000).

6. Miguel Angel Centeno, *Blood and Debt: War and the Nation-State in Latin America* (University Park: The Pennsylvania State University Press, 2002).

7. Brian Loveman, *For La Patria: Politica and the Armed Forces in Latin America* (Wilmington, DE: Scholarly Resources, 1999), xxi.

8. Brian Loveman, *The Constitution of Tyranny: Regimes of Exception in Spanish America* (Pittsburgh: University of Pittsburgh Press, 1993), 61.

9. *International Herald Tribune*, "Peru Removes Army Chief, Says Spat with Chile Over," December 6, 2008.

10. Simon Romero, "Bolivia Reaches for a Slice of the Coast That Got Away," *The New York Times*, September 24, 2006.

11. See Scheina 2003, Chapter 34, for a detailed narrative of the war.

12. Joseph Conrad, *Lord Jim & Nostromo* (New York: The Modern Library, 1999 [1904]).

13. William R. Shepherd, *Latin America* (New York: Henry Holt and Company, 1914), 82.

14. Shepherd 1914, 170.

15. Quoted in Lars Schoultz, *Beneath the United States: A History of U.S. Policy Toward Latin American* (Cambridge: Harvard University Press, 1998), 7.

16. Enrique Krauze, "Looking at Them: A Mexican Perspective on the Gap with the United States," in *Falling Behind: Explaining the Development Gap Between Latin America and the United States,* ed. Francis Fukuyama (Oxford: Oxford University Press, 2008), 50.

17. Lawrence Harrison, "Promoting Progressive Cultural Change," *Culture Matters: How Values Shape Human Progress,* eds. Lawrence E. Harrison and Samuel P. Huntington (New York: Basic Books, 2000).

18. Howard J. Wiarda, *The Soul of Latin America* (New Haven: Yale University Press, 2003), vii.

19. John Charles Chasteen, *Born in Blood and Fire: A Concise History of Latin America* (New York: W.W. Norton and Company, 2001), 113.

CHAPTER 3

Dictatorship, Democracy, and Revolution in the Modern Era

LEARNING OBJECTIVES

- Explain the challenges to democracy that emerged after independence.

- Evaluate how the United States affected the development of democracy in the region.

- Identify the relationships between economic development and democracy.

Porfirio Díaz, who ruled Mexico from 1876 to 1911, was from the southern state of Oaxaca. As president, of course he ruled the entire country but always focused attention on his home state. His minister in Washington actively promoted it for international audiences. In return, local leaders mostly accepted demands Díaz made about who would be the main political leaders in the state. He developed personal relationships with Oaxacan politicians even at the local level to maintain their support. When in 1911 he was overthrown and forced to leave the country, the Oaxaca state congress was the only one to send him a telegram of congratulations for his accomplishments.[1] As in so many Latin American countries, in both democracies and dictatorships, national and more local power bases were bound together in many ways and further spiced with international pressures.

The nineteenth century was not an auspicious one for Latin American democracy. Caudillos had often dominated the political landscape, and weak political institutions had contributed to the rise of militaries that either ruled directly or were hovering over civilian governments. Thus, in the first decade of the twentieth century, there were still dictators such as Porfirio Díaz, Juan Vicente Gómez of Venezuela, and José Santos Zelaya of Nicaragua. They viewed themselves as modernizers, bringing a needed iron fist to nations that could not advance otherwise. But an era was passing. The age-old liberal–conservative divide was mutating and becoming more complicated. New forces and ideologies emerged that challenged the old order and sparked new divisions, with dissent bubbling up from the local level. This chapter will introduce background and concepts about the struggle for democracy that we will keep coming back to in the case studies.

As we discussed in Chapter 1, Robert Dahl's concept of *polyarchy* is a useful place to start for analyzing democracy. The procedures behind free and fair voting, political competition, and representations are the essential building blocks of democracy. They do not guarantee broader rights and liberties, but **liberal democracy** cannot exist without that foundation. As political scientist Gerardo Munck notes, however, it is easy for a focus on **procedural democracy** to exclude participation.[2] For example, people must have the right to vote (which can be easily measured by examining the constitution and relevant laws, as well as the ways in which they are enforced) but they must also be free from informal means (e.g., intimidation or elite-based decision making) of keeping them out of the political system.

Political scientist Peter Smith emphasizes the need to include accountability in any analysis of democracy.[3] Thus, rulers must not simply be elected. There must also be a way to judge their actions while in power, and they must consistently justify their policies in a formal manner. Voters put politicians into office, but there may or may not be ways to judge that ruler once he or she is in office. Examples include regular elections, freedom of speech and media scrutiny, and the ability for citizens to organize and protest, which reverberates all the way to the local level. Horizontal accountability refers to what in the United States is commonly known as *checks and balances*. Do state institutions have the authority to hold each other accountable? In the context of Latin American presidentialism, to what extent can presidents make decisions that cannot be checked by the legislature, the courts, or other institutions?

In Parts II to IV, we will see why this is so important, particularly with regard to contemporary politics. Countries with long records of democratic elections convulsed with discontent because the elections masked underlying problems of minimal participation. In addition, presidents might be elected but then rule in a manner that circumvented accountability, either vertical or horizontal. The first step, however, remains the free and fair election. In the early twentieth century, they were few and far between.

The wide variation that we see, both now and a century ago, creates analytical challenges. Very often, a particular regime does not conform perfectly to the characteristics of polyarchy, or even if it holds competitive elections, it lacks in terms of participation or accountability. This variation has given rise to what has been called *democracy with adjectives*, whereby "democracy" is qualified.[4] Thus, governments may be "protected democracy," "oligarchic democracy," "illiberal democracy," "restrictive democracy," "electoral authoritarianism," and so on. Scholars have used hundreds of such subtypes to describe how particular governments deviate from polyarchy. Although it may increase precision, it makes comparison more difficult. Is a "tutelary democracy" more or less democratic than a "guarded democracy"? There isn't much agreement.

National and International Influence in the First Half of the Twentieth Century

We have already examined the development of presidential systems in the nineteenth century, characterized by a very strong president and weak national legislatures. But in the twentieth century, the gradual growth of an independent **civil society**, referring to groups organizing at the local level to push for change of some sort, also prompted the development of a wide variety of political parties, in some cases very radical. These parties emerged from below, as voluntary associations (e.g., unions) came together to make specific political demands. The ability of these emerging movements to create functional governing organizations also helped translate into parties that were unified enough to engage existing political structures and even challenge the executive. We need to remember that these movements were sometimes threatening to the status quo and therefore sometimes found themselves under attack. In particular, local demands could translate into national action. Despite some resistance, the parties these movements helped create would alter the presidential–legislative relationship in ways that had different effects in different countries. As a result, the presidential domination of the nineteenth century gradually gave way to a more complicated interaction.

Early Weakness of Democracy: National Challenges

As Scott Mainwaring and Matthew Soberg Shugart point out, presidential power in Latin America is mediated by a country's constitution and by its party structure.[5] In some countries, such as Mexico, a single party would extend its reach throughout the country, down to the lowest possible level, even a neighborhood. With its power, for most of the twentieth century the Mexican president wielded tremendous influence that was almost totally uncontested by Congress. But elsewhere, political parties began defining new issues and contesting the status quo.

The gelling together of national parties is important for the process of democratization, both then and now. Parties are vehicles for stable political negotiation and provide guidance for voters with specific issue interests. But there is a delicate balance to keep. Where there were relatively few parties that had clear platforms, that had coherent leadership, and avoided being dominated by single personalities, democracy was more likely to take root. Party disintegration would become a challenge later in the century, when a variety of populist leaders (which we will discuss shortly) ran without an established party. Too many parties can also be problematic because debate becomes more like a cacophony, which makes negotiation and compromise much trickier.

It took a very long time for parties and presidents to work together in a democratic way. In 1900, there were no democracies at all in Latin America. In most countries, there were elections of some sort, but they can be characterized as "oligarchic domination through electoral means."[6] In other words, the elections were rigged or at least elites tightly controlled the choices of candidates. Even the more democratic countries, such as Chile, greatly restricted participation and vertical accountability was minimal. Other Southern

Cone countries, especially Argentina and Uruguay, also started moving in the direction of procedural democracy. Elite competition came before broader political participation.

We can also see the lack of democracy by how many times the rules of the political game changed. There has also been a multitude of constitutions, which demonstrates the high degree of instability. From 1800 to 2006, there were a total of 251 constitutions in Latin America, for an average of 12.6 per country.[7] Most of those, however, were ratified in the nineteenth century (the Dominican Republic had an astounding twenty-four constitutions between 1827 and 1929). After 1977, only two countries (Guatemala and Nicaragua) had as many as two. Nonetheless, periodic rewriting of all those rules of the game undermined predictability and the formation of strong democratic institutions, especially in the nineteenth and early twentieth centuries. And in some cases, the absence of democracy helped prompt revolution.

National Threats to Democracy

Presidential power would also be leavened with **revolution**, or armed overthrows of the entire political system, which became more common in the twentieth century as new groups pushed their way into the political system and demanded rights. These are the most radical political transformations. The first major revolution of the century occurred in Mexico, where the dictator Porfirio Díaz was forced out in 1910. Emiliano Zapata emerged as the revolutionary leader most attuned to the Mexican peasantry. He excoriated the country's political leadership, especially Francisco Madero.

The main tenets of Zapata's 1911 "Plan de Ayala" would be echoed throughout the century in different countries and contexts. The main argument was that a single dictator should not run a country, and that a combination of corruption and repression had made revolution necessary (and perhaps even inevitable). In its place, the country needed to have more representative institutions that would allow the voice of "the people" (whoever they might be) to be heard at the local level. Similar sentiments were later heard in Cuba, Nicaragua, and elsewhere.

In general, however, revolutions were sporadic during the first part of the century, because local discontent had not yet come together at the national level. There were a few, however. Fueled by discontent in the countryside, the 1925 July Revolution in Ecuador ended three decades of liberal rule and increased the state's role over the economy. In Paraguay, after winning the Chaco War against Bolivia in 1935, soldiers expressed their disgust with the liberal government in February 1936. That "Febrerista Revolution" created a short-lived, fascist-leaning government that redistributed land but was overthrown. After years of instability, in 1952 Bolivia experienced upheaval with the Bolivian National Revolution, which nationalized tin mines and incorporated the rural population into the political system with universal suffrage and land reform.

The Cuban revolution, which we will discuss in Chapter 7, was the model for many Marxist revolutionary movements after 1959. **Che Guevara**, the Argentine who fought alongside Fidel and Raúl Castro in the Sierra Maestra mountains of Cuba, penned a famous work on guerrilla warfare that was intended to be a manual for future revolutionaries. He argued that a small "foco," or group of guerrillas, could establish themselves in the countryside, the very heart of the local level, where they are harder to find than in the cities. He summarized the strategy as "Hit and run, wait, lie in ambush, again hit and run, and thus repeatedly, without giving any rest to the enemy."[8] Guerrilla fighters could win the support of the peasants and destabilize the government regardless of conditions in urban areas. As in Cuba, revolution would radiate out from the rural area, destroy capitalism, and bring a Marxist government to power. Although that strategy failed in most cases (and Guevara was executed in Bolivia in 1967, unable to attract the support of a skeptical and fearful peasantry), it had a massive impact on the Latin American left and on the United States, which considered the Cuban revolution to be a hemispheric threat. In general, revolutions have had a very shaky relationship with democracy. Radical change does not mesh well with the normal push and pull of polyarchies.

International Influence: The United States and Democracy

Until fairly recently, the U.S. government has only sporadically supported democracy in Latin America. By the end of the nineteenth century, U.S. troops were being deployed as a way to keep European influence out of the region and protect U.S. businesses. That, in turn, led to support for nondemocratic governments that were more likely to maintain order and by extension protect U.S. interests. As the Nicaraguan foreign minister put it delicately in 1912, "my Government desires that the Government of the United States guarantee with its forces security for the property of American citizens in Nicaragua and that it extend its protection to all the inhabitants of the Republic."[9]

In practice, this would mean the beginning of an extended period of U.S. intervention in Latin American politics, focused on Central America and the Caribbean, which of course were the closest. These interventions were antidemocratic in nature and sparked considerable local resistance. In 1898, the United States sent troops to Cuba to finally push the already teetering Spanish Empire out forever. General Leonard Wood was sent to govern the island, and he noted, "It is next to impossible to make them believe we have only their own interests at heart."[10] That would remain a very common lament, as many Latin Americans resented the dictatorships supported by the United States.

Woodrow Wilson (president from 1913 until 1921) was committed to spreading what he believed to be the benefits of U.S. democracy. As the diplomatic historian Samuel Flagg Bemis put it admiringly back in 1943, there was "a sincere Wilsonian zeal for saving the people from bad government, tyranny, and economic exploitation in order that they might be made fit and stable for self-government, liberty, and the pursuit of happiness under protection of the United States."[11] Therefore, in the name of all things good, Wilson had Marines almost constantly on the move around the Caribbean.

Of course, not everyone viewed occupation as synonymous with "protection." The presence of these troops was unpopular to most of the population (though political elites often enjoyed the enforced stability), and resistance found a strong voice in Nicaragua, where a rebel named Augusto Sandino took to the hills to fight against not only the United States but the political elites—"shameless hired assassins"—who accepted and even encouraged their presence. Sandino's message was that Nicaragua should belong to Nicaraguans, including the long-awaited (and never completed) canal. Foreigners—he gave specific and scathing attention to the United States—and elites subverted Nicaraguan development: "The world would be an unbalanced place if it allowed the United States of America to rule alone over our canal."

ANALYZING DOCUMENTS

Augusto Sandino was an ardent nationalist, which in turn stemmed in large part from the international presence of the United States. He celebrated the local population, "the lap of the oppressed," from the national oligarchies and the U.S. government.

Augusto Sandino, Manifesto, July 1, 1927

To the Nicaraguans, to the Central Americans, to the Indo-Hispanic Race:

The man who doesn't ask his country for even a handful of earth for his grave deserves to be heard, and not only to be heard, but also to be believed.

I am a Nicaraguan and I am proud because in my veins flows above all the blood of the Indian race, which by some atavism encompasses the mystery of being patriotic, loyal, and sincere.

The bond of nationality give me the right to assume responsibility for my acts, without being concerned that pessimists and cowards may brand me with a name that, in their own condition as eunuchs, would be more appropriately applied to them.

I am a mechanic, but my idealism is based upon a broad horizon of internationalism, which represents the right to be free and to establish justice, even though to achieve this it may be necessary to establish it upon a foundation of blood. The oligarchs, or rather, the swamp geese, will say that I am a plebeian, but it doesn't matter. My greatest honor is that I come from the lap of the oppressed, the soul and spirit of our race, those who have lived ignored and forgotten, at the mercy of the shameless hired assassins who have committed the crime of high treason, forgetful of the pain and misery of the Liberal cause that they pitilessly persecuted, as if we did not belong to the same nation.

...

The world would be an unbalanced place if it allowed the United States of America to rule alone over our canal, because this would mean placing us at the mercy of the Colossus of the North, forcing us into a dependent and tributary role to persons of bad faith who would be our masters without justifying such pretensions in any way.

Civilization requires that a Nicaraguan canal be built, but that it be done with capital from the whole world, and not exclusively from the United States. At least half of the cost of the construction should be financed with capital from Latin America, and the other half from other countries of the world that may want to hold stock in this enterprise, but the share of the United States should be limited to the three million dollars that they paid to the traitors Chamorro, Díaz, and Cuadra Pasos. And Nicaragua, my Fatherland, will then receive the taxes that by right and be law belong to it, and we will then have income enough to crisscross our whole territory with railroads and to educate our people in a true environment of effective democracy. Thus we will be respected and not looked upon with the bloody scorn we suffer today.

Fellow citizens:

Having expressed my ardent desire to defend my country, I welcome you to my ranks without regard to your political tendencies, with the one condition that you come with good intentions to defend our nation's honor. Because keep in mind that you can fool all of the people some of the time, but not all of the people all of the time.

Discussion Questions
- What does Sandino think about the international influence on Nicaragua and how it affects nationalism?
- Why is Sandino so angry about the "Colossus of the North"?

Source: http://www.latinamericanstudies.org/sandino/sandino7-1-27.htm

The United States helped seal decades of dictatorship by maneuvering to make Anastasio Somoza García head of the National Guard in 1933 just as the U.S. Marines were leaving the country. Somoza lured Sandino to a meeting, where he had him murdered the following year. Somoza, and then his sons after his death, ruled Nicaragua until the Sandinistas—a guerrilla group named after their hero—overthrew the dictatorship in 1979. Support for dictatorships was the norm in Central America and the Caribbean. By that time the United States had established a hegemonic position in Latin America, meaning that it had far more economic and military power than any other country in the hemisphere. Hegemony does not mean the ability to determine events, but it does entail considerable political leverage, especially over the governments of smaller, weaker countries. Over the years, the United States would commonly use force or economic sanctions, or at least the threat of one or the other, to ensure that a friendly government came to power. Whether or not that government ruled (or even came to power) democratically was not necessarily a primary consideration. Before the Cold War, hegemony was less relevant for South America, which by virtue of distance was less of a concern for policy makers in the United States.

The National Effects of Economic Policy

Particularly, once the Great Depression of the 1930s settled in, old oligarchies were challenged politically in newly insistent ways, mostly undemocratic. The military was deeply involved in resolving socioeconomic conflict by taking over the political system. Between 1900 and 1935, coups hit fifteen Latin American countries.[12] In Ecuador, there were nineteen governments between 1931 and 1948, with none of them finishing their term.

As the region recovered from the economic ravages of the Depression, however, democracy did emerge in many countries. The growth of the middle class was an important factor, but only when the middle class allied itself with the similarly growing working class.[13] This is where politics at the local level became increasingly relevant, as the working class organized. Combined, the middle and working classes pushed for greater political inclusion and participation. When the middle class chose to ally itself with the military, broad political participation was restricted. In those cases, the middle class felt more threatened by what they considered radical working-class demands and looked to the military to maintain order. Or, as political scientists Ruth Berins Collier and David Collier argue, when the working class was incorporated into the political system by political parties, this was deemed to be a threat and a backlash—such as a military coup—ensued.[14] Most governments were pursuing some version of import substitution, but only later in the century would government spending be viewed as more leftist.

Presidentialism became even more pronounced in this context, as the executive guided state-led development strategies at the national level. Constitutions already concentrated power in the executive branch, and it became even more common to rule by decree through the use of emergency powers. As Colombian President Alberto Lleras Camargo (1958–1962) put it, the president had to be "a magician, prophet, redeemer, savior, and pacifier who can transform a ruined republic into a prosperous one, can make the prices of the things we export rise and the value of the things we consume drop."[15] Political elites considered a strong president as the most effective tool to overcome economic difficulties and push through reforms.

As Table 3.1 demonstrates, polyarchies were not uncommon in Latin America in the middle of the twentieth century. In some cases, such as Chile, Colombia, Costa Rica, and Venezuela, they were long lasting if at times imperfect. But as time would show, many of them were quite fragile.

TABLE 3.1 Latin American Polyarchies in Mid-Century

Argentina 1946–1951; 1958–1962; 1963–1966

Bolivia 1952–1964

Brazil 1945–1964

Chile 1932–1970

Colombia 1936–1949; 1958 to present

Costa Rica 1919–present

Ecuador 1948–1961

Guatemala 1944–1954

Peru 1939–1948; 1956–1962; 1963–1968

Uruguay 1942–1973

Venezuela 1958 to present

Source: Dietrich Rueschemeyer, Evelyne Huber Stephens, and John D. Stephens, *Capitalist Development and Democracy* (Chicago: University of Chicago Press, 1992), 162.

The Cold War (1947–1991)

Structural change, particularly with regard to international politics, meant that period of democratic rule was short-lived. Militaries across Latin America were already deeply involved in politics since independence and most commonly retained close ties to ruling elites. That combination already posed a major obstacle to democratization. The advent of the Cold War, however, made the process even more difficult and, in many cases, more violent. In most countries, military leaders viewed Marxism—and any leftist group by extension—as a threat to the existence of the nation. In military journals, Communism was routinely portrayed as a "cancer" that needed to be removed from the political body. Continuing the medical metaphor, the armed forces were the doctors, and because cancer is insidious and ever spreading, it needed to be cut out by whatever means necessary. Eventually that would mean simply taking over the entire country, cancelling elections, and ruling by force.

This phenomenon has aptly been called the "politics of antipolitics."[16] Military leaders professed disgust at the ways in which civilians would create unstable conditions, and thus how "politics" had become too important at the expense of the national interest. Antipolitics therefore entails restoration of order, both political and economic, and a subordination of individual rights to the needs of the fatherland. The level of repression might vary, but the rhetoric across different countries was strikingly similar. As the manifesto of the more leftist Peruvian military government put it in 1968, "Overwhelming personal ambition in the exercise of the responsibilities of the executive and legislative branches in the discharging of public and administrative duties, as well as in other fields of the nation's activities, has produced immoral acts which the public has repudiated."[17] If politics is producing immorality, then the armed forces are not only justified to act but indeed required to do so decisively. As subsequent chapters will demonstrate, that militarized aspect of Latin American politics has now diminished greatly, particularly since 1990, though still has not entirely disappeared in some countries.

The Military and International Influence

Latin America was not developing in a vacuum. The United States and the Soviet Union were allied in the effort to defeat the Axis (the most important components of which were Nazi Germany and Japan), but the alliance was one only because of necessity. The ideological divide between the two immediately became apparent once the war was over and the two sides began the process of consolidating new borders and spheres of influence in Europe and Asia. What became known as the Cold War is commonly considered to have begun in 1947, as the Soviet Union consolidated control over parts of Eastern Europe and President Harry S. Truman announced the Truman Doctrine, asserting that the great power rivalry pitted freedom against tyranny. It emphasized containment, referring to a strategy of preventing the spread of Communist, or Communist-inspired, governments. This would have a tremendous, and mostly negative, impact on Latin American democracy.

Latin America soon became part of the battleground. Enhanced freedoms of the press and of opposition in many countries motivated locally inspired reform efforts, which ran up against deeply entrenched and suspicious oligarchies. Their views coincided with, but were not created by, the United States. In 1948, the **Organization of American States (OAS)** came into being, the culmination of over fifty years of periodic hemispheric meetings intended to cultivate some sort of common vision. For the United States, the essential purpose of the OAS was to add another layer of protection against what policy makers considered Communist infiltration in the region. Many Latin American leaders agreed, but they also believed the OAS could act as a block against U.S. hegemony by providing a space for defending against intervention.

Nowhere was the new era more evident than in Guatemala, where the dictator Jorge Ubico was forced out in the midst of a general strike in 1944. Elections held soon thereafter brought Juan José Arévalo to the presidency. He proclaimed his project was "spiritual socialism," which in practice meant a focus on labor reform, empowerment of unions, and expansion of civil liberties. Although he was careful to couch his ideology in anti-Communist terms, and not to antagonize United Fruit in the countryside, U.S. officials became convinced that Guatemala was traveling on the road toward Communism. He was succeeded in 1951 by his defense minister, Jacobo Arbenz, who took the reformist project into the countryside, brought members of the Communist party into his cabinet, and prompted the United States to launch Operation PBSuccess, which successfully overthrew Arbenz in 1954 (see Box 3.1).

From that point on, support for authoritarian governments became common if they were anti-Communist. Truman's idea of "containment" was also not always enough. Rather than simply contain leftist governments, the United States worked to oust them and install a more friendly replacement. Obviously, this new war was not "cold" in Latin America. The influential former State Department official George Kennan neatly summed up the Cold War view of Latin America: "It seems to me unlikely that there could be any region on earth in which nature and human behavior could have combined to produce a more unhappy and hopeless background for the conduct of human life than in Latin America."[18] Latin America was not only vulnerable, but it was really incapable of democracy. Therefore, Kennan concluded that only "harsh governmental measures of repression" would protect them from Communist advances. In this view, dictatorship might be the only answer for many governments. That assessment would be echoed by countless policy makers over the next several decades.

The struggle for democracy in Latin America in the early Cold War developed a certain circular quality. Nascent efforts at reform were turned back, which led to resistance, violence, military coups, and dictatorships. In turn, those dictatorships spurred on even greater resistance and guerrilla warfare, which alarmed the United States and led to increased repression. Very few countries escaped some aspect of this vicious cycle, which accelerated after the Cuban revolution of 1959. But even the most stable democracies, such as Chile

████ **BOX 3.1** ████

International Pressures: The Overthrow of Jacobo Arbenz

International: The United States watched the election of Jacobo Arbenz with considerable alarm. President Dwight D. Eisenhower cut off all economic and military aid. Covert action began in 1952, and the newly formed Central Intelligence Agency (CIA) used every means at its disposal to create a sense of crisis and obtain support from the Guatemalan military. An analyst in the Department of State wrote an influential memo titled, "Our Guatemala Policy," positing that Guatemala could be used "as a base from which to operate against the political and social structures of other Latin American states, and from which to organize sabotage of physical installations that contribute to the defense of the Hemisphere."[19]

The plan was enacted in 1954 after a shipment of weapons Guatemala purchased from Czechoslovakia was intercepted. The operation was quick and effective, as Arbenz's internal support crumbled under the CIA's radio broadcast of a massive invasion (which in reality was only 250 soldiers). Arbenz fled the country and a military junta took control. Guatemala's fledgling democracy ended, and the resulting civil war would not officially end until peace accords were signed in 1996.

National: Under Arbenz, both political exiles and foreigners came into the country, bringing with them ideas that had been banned during the previous dictatorship. They introduced Marxism into the country, especially to the country's largest union, the Central Labor Federation. Arbenz allied himself with the Community Party and enacted land reform that included nationalization and expropriation of land owned by the large U.S. company United Fruit. That set into motion a series of events that culminated in the CIA-orchestrated overthrow of Arbenz and the installation of a military government.

Local: Elected president of Guatemala in 1944, Juan José Arévalo advocated for what he called *spiritual socialism*, the core of which was emphasis on the dignity of the individual. Long oppressed, the large local indigenous populations had little connection to the national government and received almost no benefits from it. Arbenz sought to deepen the connection between the national government and the local level even more. That challenged local elites, who then supported his overthrow.

Discussion Questions
- How legitimate is it for international actors such as the United States to intervene in the national (or even local) affairs of other countries?
- Why was the United States so concerned about national policy making in a very small country?

and Uruguay, eventually succumbed to military coups in the face of intense ideological polarization. Research has also shown that increased spending on military institutions has a negative effect on economic development. As a result, dictatorships have been detrimental not only to democracy but also to basic socioeconomic indicators.

National Factors in Democratic Breakdown

Latin American military ideology and international influences are not the only explanations for democracy's fragility. One prominent hypothesis about political outcomes relates to political institutions, particularly presidential versus parliamentary forms of government. A very common argument is that presidentialism—the norm in Latin America—has been detrimental to democracy. This can help explain democracy's periodic breakdown in the region, but it can also provide insight into how democracies struggle on a constant basis without necessarily succumbing to dictatorship. The hypothesis is focused largely on the national level, though it does acknowledge the destabilizing effects of local discontent.

In presidential systems, the executive and legislative branches are elected separately, sometimes by voters with very different priorities. If the president and a majority of legislators are at odds, then a "zero-sum game" ensues, meaning that a win for one side necessarily entails a loss for the other. Presidential systems do not offer any means for resolving disputes, because each side is elected separately from the other, and only in extreme circumstances (e.g., criminal behavior) can a legislature impeach and convict a president. The president, meanwhile, has no power to dissolve the legislature as in a parliamentary system or otherwise force it to compromise. As the well-known political scientist Juan Linz has argued, "The zero-sum game raises the stakes in a presidential election for winners and losers, and inevitably increases the tension and polarization."[20]

In countries with weak political institutions that are experiencing a high degree of conflict, this tension may lead to democratic breakdown. Traditionally, this has taken the form of military intervention but, in recent years, has also manifested itself in what is known as a **self-coup** (from the Spanish "autogolpe") where the president illegally forces the dissolution of the legislature, thus overthrowing part of the government. The essential hypothesis is that presidentialism makes political conflicts worse and thereby represents a threat to democracy. By contrast, a parliamentary system in which the executive is chosen by a majority in the legislature, and then must maintain the confidence of a majority of legislators or be forced out of office, is viewed as a preferable alternative that would alleviate—if not necessarily eliminate—the sometimes disastrous effects of polarization.

This line of argument, while influential, has been challenged. The rules governing presidential systems may not be to blame; instead, other external (or "exogenous") factors may be more responsible. Presidential systems in Latin America "tend to exist in countries that are also more likely to suffer from dictatorships led by the military."[21] Therefore, presidentialism may not be the most important variable, as other aspects of Latin American countries have led to military intervention, such as historically powerful and politicized militaries. Furthermore, there are many different variations of presidentialism that also account for breakdown. Scott Mainwaring and Matthew Soberg Shugart note the importance of the number of political parties, how disciplined they are, and also of electoral law (i.e., the rules governing how presidents and legislators are elected).[22] Some combinations might therefore keep presidential governments more stable.

Even if there is no consensus about the most relevant variables, there is widespread agreement that presidentialism plays an important role in determining how politics plays out in Latin American countries. Since independence, presidential power has been substantial, which in turn has led to political conflict of varying intensity. Between 1964, when the Brazilian military overthrew the elected government (subsequently ruling for twenty-one years), and 1990, when the Chilean dictatorship finally left power, Latin American democracy was at a low point. The ideology of the Cold War had literally overwhelmed the region. A few polyarchies remained, most notably Colombia, Costa Rica, and Venezuela, but political violence had replaced democratic governance in many countries (see Table 3.2). In 1979, Ecuador was the first dictatorship to launch a transition to democracy, and gradually others followed suit. It is no coincidence that many of these transitions occurred just as the Cold War was winding down, as the Soviet Union ceased to exist in 1991. Once the ideological battle was no longer so relevant, even the brutal Central American civil wars slowly concluded. The United States gradually ended its support for these wars and showed less patience with dictatorships than in the past.

The transitions from authoritarian rule took a number of different forms. In a widely cited work, political scientist Terry Lynn Karl identified four broad "modes" of transition.[23] In a pacted transition, the dictatorship and the opposition negotiate an end to authoritarian rule. Transition by imposition means the governing regime is forced out. Transitions by reform entail using existing laws to democratize the political system and end authoritarian practices. Finally, as its name suggests, revolution involves overturning the entire political system and installing something radically different in its place. Each of these different

TABLE 3.2 Women's Suffrage in Latin America

Argentina 1947	Guatemala 1945
Bolivia 1952	Honduras 1955
Brazil 1932	Mexico 1953
Chile 1949	Nicaragua 1955
Colombia 1957	Panama 1945
Costa Rica 1949	Paraguay 1961
Cuba 1934	Peru 1955
Dominican Republic 1942	Uruguay 1932
Ecuador 1929	Venezuela 1947
El Salvador 1939	

Source: Peter H. Smith, *Political Change in Comparative Perspective* (New York: Oxford University Press, 2005), 186.

modes of transition suggests different political outcomes and, therefore, represents a "path-dependent" argument. This generated considerable scholarly debate, as analysts struggled to explain what happened once authoritarian governments fell. As we go through the country case studies, we will examine some of these transitions in more detail.

We should keep in mind, however, that despite authoritarian setbacks, even short-term experiences with electoral democracy had some long-lasting and positive consequences. Structural transformations brought new political actors to the fore. Women in Latin America were pushed to the periphery of the political system until the nineteenth century, when (as in the United States) they won the right to vote. Middle- and upper-class women spearheaded the suffrage movements from the grassroots, spurred on by the example of the United States, which amended the constitution to allow women to vote, effective in 1920. From the perspective of modernization theory, this would be a cultural step on the path toward copying the model of the developed world, because many activists explicitly pointed to the advances that women were making in the United States. As Table 3.3 shows, South American countries took the lead in the 1920 and 1930s, though in some countries (e.g., Colombia and Paraguay) that change did not take place until at least well into the 1950s.

Women's societies around Latin America linked together in a 1922 meeting in Baltimore and formed the Pan American Association for the Advancement of Women. By virtue of their social status, participating women had the opportunity to make their views known to relevant policy makers. In 1922, for example, Brazilian activists were able to attend a luncheon with the U.S. ambassador to Brazil, the Brazilian vice president, the minister of foreign relations, the director of public education, and congressmen.[24] Change came slowly, but within a decade Brazilian women could vote.

A second surge of women participating in politics came as a result of authoritarian governments. Especially in the 1970s and 1980s, women took on

TABLE 3.3 Latin American Military Dictatorships After 1959

Argentina 1966–1973; 1976–1983	Guatemala
Bolivia	Honduras
Brazil 1964–1985	Nicaragua
Chile 1973–1990	Panama
Cuba 1959 to present	Paraguay
Dominican Republic	Peru 1968–1980
Ecuador	Uruguay 1973–1985
El Salvador	

active political roles to protest the mistreatment of their relatives and joined together to overcome the repression and economic deprivation they suffered. They were partially protected because of their cultural status as wives and mothers and carved out political space that did not exist before (the Argentine mothers of the Plaza de Mayo is probably the most famous example, along with Rigoberta Menchú in Guatemala, which will be discussed in more detail in later chapters). Once the dictatorship, and hence the common enemy, was gone, women found it challenging to maintain the same level of unity and commonality of purpose. This is a dilemma that continues today.

Political participation of indigenous groups proved even thornier. There have been periodic moments when the virtues of indigenous cultures have been promoted (e.g., the Mexican revolution), but the benefits tended to be either mostly symbolic or short-lived. The 1991 Colombian constitution, for example, lays out indigenous rights in detail but periodic protests demonstrate the depth of concern about how political violence there has negatively impacted those rights. Even in the latter part of the twentieth century, there was a severe imbalance between the percentages of indigenous people in the legislature versus the population as a whole. Indigenous populations in some countries constitute a majority or at least close to a majority of the entire population, yet have barely any political representation. It has proven very difficult to get their demands heard at the national level.

By 2012, for example, the American Declaration on the Rights of Indigenous Peoples remained only in draft form. As with many other issues, there remains considerable distance between the rhetoric of rights and the implementation of specific policies intended to ensure their protection. In Chapter 8, we will examine the dynamics of indigenous rights in Andean countries, but the outcomes of these struggles remain very much in doubt, particularly because they are hotly contested.

Contemporary Democracy in the Post–Cold War Era (1991 to Present)

By the time the Cold War officially came to a close, Cuba was the only remaining dictatorship in Latin America. Despite periodic reversals, such as a self-coup in Peru (2000), along with coups in Ecuador (2000), Venezuela (2002), and Honduras (2009), polyarchies persist in the region. Plus, even the coups that have occurred have not led to military dictatorships as in the past. Parts II to IV that follow will analyze the political effects of the widespread of election of self-proclaimed leftists to the presidency. Their platforms and policies are far more diverse than conventional wisdom suggests, but they do raise important questions about the dynamics of accountability and participation in polyarchies. In general, left-leaning governments have arisen because of simmering discontent with market-driven reforms that began in the 1980s and gained momentum in the 1990s. Processes of privatization, spending and subsidy cuts, and deregulation were unpopular in many countries. New political leaders emerged who harnessed that resentment and ran successful campaigns focusing on bringing the state back in.

Much ink has been spilt trying to categorize the rise of leftist governments. Some argue about "good" versus "bad" lefts, with the former more social democratic and the latter more authoritarian.[25] *Social democratic* refers to the idea that the state should play an important role in the economy to alleviate the problems generated by market forces, but at the same time the rules of democratic governance are strictly followed. The authoritarian argument is that more radical leftist governments seek to force state-led development and increase the power of the executive, thus endangering both vertical and horizontal accountability. Our case studies will show that it is difficult to make such sweeping generalizations. Indeed, research has shown that despite the election of so many governments of the left, the median voter is still slightly to the right of world opinion.[26] In other words, in general Latin Americans lean a bit to the conservative side.

The National Impact of Populism

This debate also centers on **populism**, which has a complex relationship with democracy. Populism involves the rejection of established political parties, an emphasis on the individual leader's direct and personal connection to the populace, and the establishment of direct ties to different segments of the population. Kurt Weyland sums it up as "a political strategy through which a personalistic leader seeks or exercises government power based on direct, unmediated, uninstitutionalized support from large numbers of mostly unorganized followers."[27] It also involves a discourse that focuses on duality, of good and evil, with of course the charismatic leader embodying the good.[28] Latin America has experienced populism of both the left and the right, and its essential danger is that the president bypasses formal political channels and makes policy according to his or her whim. Hugo Chávez is the current figure most associated with the concept, but past leaders as ideologically varied as Alberto Fujimori (Peru) and Juan Perón (Argentina) also fit the populist label.

Populism past and present involves leaders making personal connections to people at the local level. They see parties as national elites that are uninterested in the common person. In practice, this often generates a lot of excitement and intense loyalty. Individuals feel that, for the first time, a president is really paying attention to them and even promising to solve local problems that have been totally ignored in the past.

Newfound Strength of Democracy

The strength of party systems must also be considered in the context of populism. Well-functioning parties provide connections between the local and national levels, place obstacles in the way of individuals who want to concentrate power in their personal hands, and allow for clear avenues of policy discussion and debate. In Venezuela, the strong traditional parties literally disintegrated, leaving a gaping power vacuum. Yet in Uruguay, where the left has won two consecutive presidential elections (including former guerrilla José Mujica, elected in 2009), the parties are very strong and the shift from the right to the left has been smooth and peaceful. Other countries fall in between. Brazil, with leftist president Dilma Rousseff, has a chaotic party system but the Worker's Party is disciplined and well organized, which has also ensured a tranquil transition and no move toward populist rule.

The mere fact that so many leftist presidents have been elected and remained in office (with Honduras a glaring exception) represents a step forward for a region that has experienced so many conservative military coups in its history. Also positive is the alternation of power from left to right, as occurred in Chile after a runoff presidential election in 2010. Whether or not populist governments continue to rule in a democratic fashion, and accept elections that force them to step down, remains an open question that we will explore. The wide variety of these new analytical terms that have come into vogue refer to a government that is freely elected but attacks other institutions—the legislative and judicial branches, the media, even organizations within civil society—once it is in power. There are worrisome signs in this regard in Venezuela, for example, but once again, generalizing too much is problematic.

Conclusion

The process of democratization in Latin America has been very gradual and, many times, has suffered setbacks in the form of coups and other types of authoritarian intrusions. Porfirio Díaz's rule in Mexico exemplifies how difficult it was even for authoritarian leaders to reconcile local, national, and international demands. The middle of the century saw an increase in polyarchies, although they did not necessarily offer expansive political participation and either vertical or horizontal accountability. In practice, this means that many local-level concerns have gone largely unnoticed from national politicians, and that has created discontent. In addition, for decades international influence was very high. The Cold War was characterized by a literal explosion of coups and military governments, demonstrating the importance of international factors. Between 1979 and 1990, Latin American dictatorships began transitions to democracy (with the exception of Cuba).

Currently, Latin America is more moderate and democratic than at any other time in its history. That may be hard to believe given the sometimes alarmist headlines, but—with some exceptions—elections take place in a much more fair and much less contentious atmosphere, the armed forces are more likely to stay in the barracks, and the state persecutes fewer of its citizens. There are glaring exceptions to be sure, but the chapters that follow will show the gains made by many countries that have suffered tremendous instability in recent decades. We can't make predictions about the future, but we can take a close look at the political development of specific countries and get a sense of where they seem to be headed.

Key Terms

- Liberal democracy
- Procedural democracy
- Civil society
- Revolution

- Che Guevara
- Organization of American States (OAS)
- Self-coup
- Populism

Discussion Questions

- What consequences did U.S. intervention tend to have on democracy in Latin America? Why?
- What historical and doctrinal characteristics of the armed forces have made them an obstacle to democracy in the region?
- Which political parties in the region have been the most stable? Can you think of ways parties connect to people at the local level?
- Are there discernable time periods where democratic rule has been more common in Latin America?
- In what ways might populism connect national-level politics to the local level?

Further Sources

Books

Bowman, Kirk S. *Militarization, Democracy, and Development: The Perils of Praetorianism in Latin America* (University Park: The Pennsylvania State University Press, 2002). This book uses both quantitative and qualitative methods to argue that militarization has a negative impact on democracy, economic growth, and equity. It includes detailed case studies of Costa Rica and Honduras.

Diamond, Larry, Jonathan Hartlyn, Juan Linz, and Seymour Martin Lipset, eds. *Democracy in Development Countries, Latin America*, 2nd edition (Boulder: Lynne Rienner Publishers, 1999). Although now dated for contemporary politics, this is an excellent single-volume analysis of the historical development of democracy in specific Latin American countries.

O'Donnell, Guillermo, Jorge Vargas Cullell, and Osvaldo M. Iazzetta, eds. *The Quality of Democracy: Theory and Applications* (Notre Dame, IN: University of Notre Dame Press, 2004). This book seeks to look beyond formal democratic regimes in Latin America and instead to examine the quality of democracy, using the concept of "citizenship" as a starting point. This makes possible an audit of democracy across the entire region.

Drake, Paul W. *Between Tyranny and Anarchy: A History of Democracy in Latin America: 1800–2006* (Stanford: Stanford University Press, 2009). As the title suggests, this is a broad historical comparative historical analysis of democracy. It focuses on major institutional trends in Latin America.

Smith, Peter H. *Democracy in Latin America: Political Change in Comparative Perspective* (New York: Oxford University Press, 2005). This is a long-term analysis of Latin American democracy, focusing on the different cycles of democracy and authoritarian rule. Chapters center on different aspects of democracy, such as the role of the military, presidentialism, international influences, social equity, and civil liberties.

Web Sites

Fitzgibbon Survey of Scholarly Images of Democracy in Latin America (**http://www2. kenyon.edu/Depts/PSci/Fac/klesner/fitzgibbon/default.htm**). Named after Professor Russell Fitzgibbon, who began the project in 1945, this is the Web site of a survey taken every five years. It asks scholars of Latin America their perceptions of various aspects of Latin American democracy, using a specific set of criteria.

Latinobarómetro (**http://www.latinobarometro.org/**). This is data generated by a private company in Santiago, Chile. Every year, it conducts public opinion polling across Latin America and releases a lengthy summary. The Web site does not allow access to the data, but it does include past reports back to 1995. The site is in both English and Spanish.

The National Security Archive (**http://www.gwu.edu/~nsarchiv/**). This independent, nongovernmental organization has unearthed countless U.S. government documents through Freedom of Information Act requests. Its archival projects includes details on Chile, Colombia, Cuba, Guatemala, Honduras, and Mexico (in addition to many other countries outside Latin America).

Center for Latin American Studies (Research) (**http://pdba.georgetown.edu/**). The Center for Latin American Studies at Georgetown University offers a database focusing on political institutions. This includes constitutions, information on branches of government, political parties, indigenous peoples, and civil society.

Vanderbilt University Latin American Public Opinion Project (**http://www.vanderbilt. edu/lapop/**). Latin American Public Opinion Project (LAPOP) conducts extensive public opinion polling, culminating in the Americas Barometer. The Web site includes an extensive list of publications on the topic, access to the data, and the option to sign up for email releases of new polling analyses.

Endnotes

1. Paul Garner, *Porfirio Díaz* (New York: Longman, 2001), 204.
2. Gerardo L. Munck, *Measuring Democracy: A Bridge Between Scholarship and Politics* (Baltimore: The Johns Hopkins University Press, 2009), 17.
3. Peter H. Smith, *Latin America: Political Change in Comparative Perspective* (New York: Oxford University Press, 2005), 7.
4. David Collier and Steven Levitsky, "Democracy with Adjectives: Conceptual Innovation in Comparative Research," *World Politics* 49, 3 (1997): 430–451.
5. Matthew Soberg Shugart and Scott Mainwaring, "Presidentialism and Democracy in Latin America: Rethinking the Terms of the Debate," in *Presidentialism and Democracy in Latin America*, eds. Scott Mainwaring and Matthew Soberg Shugart (New York: Cambridge University Press, 1997).
6. Peter H. Smith, *Latin America: Political Change in Comparative Perspective* (New York: Oxford University Press, 2005), 27.
7. Paul W. Drake, *Between Tyranny and Anarchy: A History of Democracy in Latin America: 1800-2006* (Stanford: Stanford University Press, 2009), 29.
8. Che Guevara, *Guerrilla Warfare, with an Introduction and Case Studies by Brian Loveman and Thomas M. Davies, Jr.* (Lincoln: University of Nebraska Press, 1985), 53.
9. Quoted in Karl Bermann, *Under the Big Stick: Nicaragua and the United States since 1848* (Boston: South End Press, 1986), 162.

10. Quoted in Lars Schoultz, *That Infernal Little Cuban Republic: The United States and the Cuban Revolution* (Chapel Hill: The University of North Carolina Press, 2009), 24.
11. Samuel Flagg Bemis, *The Latin American Policy of the United States: An Historical Interpretation* (New York: Harcourt, Brace and Company, 1943), 85.
12. Brian Loveman, *For La Patria: Politics and the Armed Forces in Latin America* (Wilmington, DE: Scholarly Resources, 1999), 101.
13. Dietrich Rueschemeyer, Evelyne Huber Stephens, and John D. Stephens, *Capitalist Development and Democracy* (Chicago: University of Chicago Press, 1992).
14. Ruth Berins Collier and David Collier, *Shaping the Political Arena* (Princeton: Princeton University Press, 1991).
15. Quoted in Drake 2009, 175.
16. Brian Loveman and Thomas M. Davies, Jr., eds., *The Politics of Antipolitics: The Military in Latin America* (Wilmington, DE: SR Books, 1997).
17. Quoted in Loveman and Davies 1997, 186.
18. Quoted in Weeks 2008, 106.
19. Quoted in Gregory Weeks, *U.S. And Latin American Relations* (New York: Pearson Longman, 2008), 107.
20. Juan J. Linz, "Presidential or Parliamentary Democracy: Does It Make a Difference?" in *The Failure of Presidential Democracy: The Case of Latin America*, Volume 2, eds. Juan J. Linz and Arturo Valenzuela (Baltimore: The Johns Hopkins University Press, 1994), 19.
21. José Antonio Cheibub, *Presidentialism, Parliamentarism, and Democracy* (New York: Cambridge University Press, 2007), 3.
22. Scott Mainwaring and Matthew Soberg Shugart, "Conclusion: Presidentialism and the Party System," in *Presidentialism and Democracy in Latin America*, eds. Scott Mainwaring and Matthew Soberg Shugart (New York: Cambridge University Press, 1997).
23. Terry Lynn Karl, "Dilemmas of Democratization in Latin America," *Comparative Politics* 23, 1 (1990): 1–21.
24. Francesca Miller, "The Suffrage Movement in Latin America," in *Confronting Change, Challenging Tradition: Women in Latin American History*, ed. Gertrude M. Yeager (Wilmington, DE: SR Books, 1997), 159.
25. For example, see Jorge G. Castañeda, "Latin America's Left Turn," *Foreign Affairs* 85, 3 (2006): 28–43.
26. Mitchell A. Seligson, "The Rise of Populism and the Left," in *Latin America's Struggle for Democracy*, eds. Larry Diamond, Marc F. Plattner, and Diego Abente Brun (Baltimore: The Johns Hopkins University Press, 2008).
27. Kurt Weyland, "Clarifying a Contested Concept: Populism in the Study of Latin American Politics," *Comparative Politics* 34, 1 (2001): 1–22.
28. Kirk Hawkins, "Is Chávez Populist? Measuring Populist Discourse in Comparative Perspective" *Comparative Political Studies* 42, 8 (2009): 1040–1067.

CHAPTER 4

The Politics of Capitalism and Socialism Through the Twentieth Century

LEARNING OBJECTIVES

- Explain the key differences between capitalism and socialism.

- Evaluate the effects of economic dependence on the United States.

- Identify the variety of responses in Latin America to economic underdevelopment.

In 1890, Carlos Pellegrini became president at a difficult time in Argentine history. Economic policy had long emphasized foreign investment and loans, and so both national and local governments were spending far more than they brought in. In fact, the previous president had just been forced out because of the economic crisis. Working with economic elites, he diversified the Argentine economy and boosted exports. Within a few short years, the economy had revived because of, as he put it, "peace and work."[1] Yet that prosperity didn't last long, as those same elites began to fight amongst themselves and as a result were responsible for economic decline and national political violence. Argentina's rising star was plummeting.

At the threshold of the twentieth century, most of Latin America depended largely on primary products and foreign capital. In the case of Argentina, the focus on cattle (and the wonders of refrigeration to transport beef around the world) spurred growth that left the impression the country would soon move into the ranks of the developed world. On the other side of the spectrum, countries such as Guatemala relied on foreign companies to manage the fruit industry. That created wealth, but it remained in the hands of foreign companies and a small domestic elite.

Overall, manufacturing output in Latin America was low, such that even in a relatively highly developed economy such as Argentina's, it represented only 16.6 percent of gross domestic product (GDP) by 1913. The majority of exports across the region were processed foods and textiles. Export partners were diverse. In 1913, only 29.7 percent of exports went to the United States, followed by the United Kingdom (20.7 percent), Germany (12.4 percent), and France (8.0 percent).[2]

This picture, however, would soon become much more complicated with the introduction of new political and social actors, who brought with them new ideas about how economies should be organized. Eventually, it also brought pressures to industrialize. Of course, these developments would have important political implications. This chapter will analyze the changes that were taking place, while also explaining the economic concepts that will help us make more sense of the types of policies that were pursued in the twentieth century.

Throughout the century, much political, economic, and social conflict revolved around the divergence of international and national influences. Ideologies such as Marxism, which originated elsewhere, were adapted to local conditions but faced stiff resistance that in many cases descended into violence. The United States in particular watched the region with great interest, pushing for more open economies, foreign investment.

International Influences: Capitalism and Socialism

In previous chapters, we've discussed "economic development" but not its ideological underpinnings. Throughout the nineteenth century, that development was capitalist. **Capitalism** entails a small role for the state in the economy. Instead, the economy relies on signals from the market, which refers to the sum total of all the buying and selling that occurs. If there is high demand for a given product, then its price may rise, and more producers will try to gain a share of that market. As production increases, prices will likely decrease. In a truly capitalist economy, the state's role is just to ensure a basic level of stability, but otherwise it should not become involved, because interference will distort supply and demand.

The Foundations of Capitalism

The key to capitalism is incentive. Any individual (or firm) should be able to fulfill his or her goals by finding the right market. Those who are entrepreneurial will always be looking for innovations that will make a profit. From this perspective, innovation benefits society as a whole. Advances in technology, infrastructure, health, and other areas occur because individuals and companies saw the possibility of profit.

Nineteenth-century Latin America was indeed very capitalist, but the state still played a role, albeit an often corrupt one. Government officials are always involved in the nuts and bolts of business, such as granting licenses, approving construction or land purchases, and resolving disputes. Corruption, in the form of payoffs, was an all too common accompaniment to doing business. It opened the door for monopolies to form, where competition is squeezed out by large companies, such as in the Central American fruit industry. In an oligarchic environment, inequality was extremely high, and that would change very little. Currently, Latin America has higher rates of inequality than any other region of the world.

The politics of capitalism in the early twentieth century revolved around stability, and this generally precluded democracy. Foreign capital required a conducive business atmosphere. That meshed perfectly with local political and economic elites (including the military), whose livelihoods were tied directly to maintaining the status quo. With regional variation, the traditional oligarchy was careful to quash labor organizers and peasant leaders. Political activism at the local level was therefore difficult to generate and maintain. In her novel *The House of the Spirits*, Isabel Allende provides a vivid depiction of hacienda life in early-twentieth-century Chile, where the "patrón" controlled virtually every aspect of a worker's life, even paying them with his credit rather than cash. He taught them the basics of reading and writing to increase their productivity, but "he was not in favor of their acquiring any additional learning, for fear they would fill their minds with ideas unsuited to their station and condition."[3] Although the stock market crash of 1929 and the resulting global depression tends to get most of the attention, the first decades of the twentieth century were difficult economically in most Latin American countries.

World War I upset trade in the Western Hemisphere. This was especially true for countries, such as Argentina, Chile, and Uruguay, which had strong European ties. European investors abruptly pulled out, European capital evaporated, and export markets disappeared. Indeed, it is for this reason that the United States became such a major economic player in this time frame. But trade in general was threatened by German submarines in the Atlantic (which torpedoed Argentine, Bolivian, Brazilian, Peruvian, and Uruguayan ships). The war's aftermath saw a brief boom (1919–1920) followed by a crushing depression (1921–1922).

The Foundations of Socialism and Communism

Economic disruption helped fuel nascent Socialist and Communist parties. The dawn of the twentieth century saw the rise of competing ideologies in Latin America. Of these, **socialism** and **communism** are the most relevant. Karl Marx first published *The Communist Manifesto* in 1848, so these ideologies were hardly new, but they only gained real significance in Latin America when urbanization and industrialization created a new and politically active working class.

There is tremendous confusion about what socialism and communism mean. In part, this is due to the fact that even advocates define them in different ways. Marx would not have labeled most "communist" countries of the twentieth century (e.g., Cuba) as such at all. It is also because opponents emphasize their most negative features in an effort to demonize them. Finally, there are many different possible variants that elude easy labels.

The essence of socialism is that the state plays a central role in the economy. The ideological foundation is the assertion that capitalism fosters certain problems—most notably poverty—and cannot solve them. But capitalism also does not guarantee education, health care, or retirement benefits. Under a purely capitalist system, those benefits would only emerge if they were profitable and a private company sought to provide them. In addition, capitalism distributes wealth unequally, so that a relatively small proportion of society gains the lion's share. In socialism, the state takes total or partial ownership over a wide variety of enterprises, paying for it with a higher rate of taxation than in a capitalist economy (or owning it completely). The overall goal is cooperative control over the means of production, and then equitable distribution of resources. Down to the local level, individuals are shielded from market disruptions typical of capitalism.

Socialism can easily coexist with democracy, and often does. **Democratic socialism** is standard in much of the European Union. Citizens have the opportunity to vote and there is considerable debate in legislatures about what types of socialist policies to pursue. The degree of socialism therefore waxes and wanes with time according to different variables, such as which party is in power and how the economy is doing. Of course, there are also countries that are both socialist and dictatorial. In Latin America, Cuba has been the most prominent example by far. Marxist government force policies on the population from the top down, arguing that state control is necessary to block counterrevolutionary forces and ensure that everyone receives equal benefits. The economy is centrally planned (though, as we will see, in Cuba that has changed in recent years).

Inequality is a central issue for these ideologies, and we can measure it. The most common measure is the **Gini coefficient**, which is a value between zero and one. Perfect equality (where everyone has the same amount of wealth) would mean a coefficient of zero. Total inequality—which in theory means that one individual has all the wealth and the rest of the population has nothing—would result in a coefficient of one. Latin America currently has the highest regional Gini coefficient of any region in the world, usually around 0.50 (for comparison, the United States is commonly about 0.45).[4]

Because of their emphasis on redistribution of wealth, countries with socialist economies tend to have lower Gini coefficients. The relationship between socialism and economic equality is the reason why governments seeking to alleviate inequality increase the state's role in the economy. As Latin America is the most unequal region in the world, the political battles over socialism are all the more intense. Historically, a large proportion of the population feels left out, and so at various times political leaders have successfully mobilized them to roll back capitalism. Not surprisingly, such efforts are not always peaceful. Opponents argue that socialism takes resources away from productive parts of the economy, such as business, and then just gives them away, thus increasing poverty in the long term.

Perhaps the most difficult concept is communism. Marx considered communism the natural and inevitable evolution of industrialized countries. Industrialization would foster class conflicts, and over time these would bring down the global capitalist system and transform it into a socialist one. What we usually refer to as communism, however, is really Marxism-Leninism. The Russian revolutionary Vladimir Lenin argued that Marx's slow march toward communism could be sped up through revolution. Furthermore, Lenin contested Marx's assertion that countries must undergo industrialization to achieve communism. Instead, Lenin argued, peasants could be mobilized and the country could become industrial after the revolution succeeded. They would overthrow the old capitalist system by force and a communist party would be required to install a new system that would remove all class distinctions and create a society based on equality. Marx coined the famous phrase "from each according to his ability, to each according to his need." Communism would make that possible, and the Communist party would act as the director.

In Latin America, the attraction of Marxism-Leninism was its promise to liberate the poor and destroy the traditional elite bases of power. It gained momentum as European immigrants helped to diffuse ideas such as socialism, anarchism (a rejection of government), and syndicalism (which offers a collectivist view of working, where traditional politics is rejected and everyone works together in a democratic setting). Communist parties would not be organized until the 1920s (the first was in Mexico) after the Russian revolution of 1917 put the principles of Marxism-Leninism into practice.

The Dynamics of Dependence

Latin American governments therefore walked a delicate line but still faced the essential problem of dependence. Dependence on primary products is problematic for several reasons. In Chapter 1, we outlined dependency theory, which emphasizes how developed countries are in a position of considerable advantage. In many ways, Europe and the United States grew economically at the expense of the less developed world, exploiting their natural resources and then reaping the profits.

But there are other problems. Prices tend to be much more volatile than for industrial goods. For example, the metal, rubber, leather, and other components of a car go up and down all the time, whereas the price of, say, a new car stays very stable and usually rises over time. Food products may shoot up when there is a drop in supply (say, because of natural disasters that destroy crops) but then plummet when harvests are plentiful in other countries and supply exceeds demand. Latin American countries have consistently suffered from weak terms of trade. This means the revenue from exports has not been enough to pay for what the country needs to import. Such a situation leaves a country very vulnerable to economic shocks and leads to debt. Economic alternatives in the mid-twentieth century centered largely on creating buffers from global supply and demand, with an active state role.

The question of dependence relates directly to the debate over "structure" and "agency." Economic arguments that place Latin America within the context of its place in the international system are called *structural*. This refers to the fact that economic outcomes (income inequality, for instance) can best be understood by examining the structural conditions of a country. Does it generally export raw materials? Does it generate any manufactured products of its own? Does it rely on foreign sources of capital? As economic structures are deeply rooted and difficult to change, most structural arguments maintain that change requires drastic action to overcome well-entrenched obstacles.

Structural arguments stand in contrast to those that emphasize "agency," which refers to the ability to make decisions and influence one's destiny. Free-market theories going back to eighteenth-century philosopher Adam Smith hold that individuals (or firms or even governments) can improve their situations through good planning, hard work, and an entrepreneurial spirit. Their individual decisions will lead to better collective outcomes as well, because everyone will be working as hard they can, thus creating more wealth overall.

For much of the twentieth century, the "structure" versus "agency" debate boiled down to the basic question of how large a role the state should play in the economy. Structuralists see an expanded role as necessary because only the state has the power and resources to resist broad global forces. This argument has reemerged in recent years. In 2009, Venezuelan President Hugo Chávez gave U.S. President Barack Obama a copy of famed Uruguayan intellectual Eduardo Galeano's *Open Veins of Latin America*, which offers a scathing analysis of the structural inequalities that have contributed to underdevelopment. The gesture was a signal of agency, as Chávez was clearly indicating that individual leaders can counteract structural constraints.

Anti-mperialist and revolutionary ideology was also evident in a sprinkling of different political parties, but for the most part Marxism took years to germinate in Latin America and did not flower until the Cold War. The United States and other anti-Communist governments eyed the Soviet Union—dominated at that time by Josef Stalin—warily, but the Soviets were focused on internal developments such as industrialization and so did not yet pose an immediate threat to the United States. World War II changed that. The Soviet Union suffered terribly (upward of 23 million dead) but emerged victorious with a large, strong military and a commitment to self-protection. Most prominently, that meant developing a nuclear weapons program and controlling border countries. But it also involved listening to Latin American communists, directing their activities through the Communist International (Comintern) and helping them when possible. Contrary to popular opinion, the Soviets did not sponsor revolution in Latin America. Yet when conditions were favorable, they stepped in with aid, advisors, and weapons (in the case of Cuba, that even meant nuclear missiles).

Nonetheless, the very possibility that Marxism could take hold in Latin America horrified many, especially after World War II when the Soviet Union expanded its hold over Eastern Europe and developed a nuclear weapons program. The United States worked quickly to counter the threat, encouraging the ratification of the Inter-American Treaty of Reciprocal Assistance (more commonly known as the Rio Treaty) in 1947. It stated that an attack from out-side the hemisphere on one country would be considered an attack on all. As communism originated outside the Western Hemisphere, by definition it would trigger the Rio Treaty even if no outside powers were involved.

Opposition to unrestrained capitalism was therefore growing but only slowly and in no unified form. By the 1920s, however, skepticism grew about the power of primary products to bring prosperity. As countries become wealth-ier, their demand for primary products does not increase significantly. Around the world, people with more money may well buy more cars, but they will not eat more bananas. Thus, a country such as El Salvador, where by 1938 coffee still constituted 92 percent of total exports, could go no further. That fostered restlessness from below.

The 1929 stock market crash accelerated popular support for alternatives to capitalism, for three reasons. First, it obviously entailed severe economic de-privation, and the struggle to stay afloat opened the door to new and perhaps even radical ideas. On the ground, people did not have enough money to buy basic goods. Second, the Russian revolution of 1917 provided a concrete exam-ple of how a dictatorship could be overthrown and replaced by a government that claimed goals of equality. No matter how different the circumstances, or how weak the actual commitment to equality Soviet rulers demonstrated, the revolution was real. Activists therefore found it easier to attract support. Third, the 1930s and 1940s was a period of political flux in Latin America. As noted in Chapter 3, Latin American governments during that period were fragile at best, and elite preferences still tended to dominate. The friction between efforts to try new economic models from below and resistance from above was the precursor to the much more violent ideological wars that appeared in the 1950s and 1960s.

Economic Alternatives: International and National Influences

There has always been confusion about the relationship between national and international influences, engendered by Cold War assumptions. From the per-spective of most Latin American economic and political elites, as well as the U.S. government, leftist ideology was fundamentally foreign. Thus, what many advo-cates considered to be nationalist policies based on placing more land or natural resources in domestic rather than foreign hands was immediately viewed as an orchestrated effort by communists (ultimately controlled by the Soviet Union) to take over the region. While reformer Jacobo Arbenz was in power in Guatemala, the United States pushed for a resolution proclaiming communism to be an ex-ternal threat to the hemisphere, which would then trigger action through the Rio Treaty. Secretary of State John Foster Dulles was unable to garner enough votes, but the assessment would become embedded in U.S. foreign policy. There would be only a few exceptions, where (like in Peru from 1968 to 1975) land reform was accepted as long as the government clearly opposed communism.

The Impact of Nationalization

The emphasis on national origins of economic reform was particularly complex with regard to nationalization. For many years, natural resources in Latin America were controlled and operated by foreign firms. This arrangement brought in the necessary capital and resources but began to grate on nationalist sensibilities. Profits, of course, flowed outward, whereas those who worked in the mines or the fields were routinely treated poorly. The local population was repressed and mistreated.

One of the most famous cases of nationalization was Mexican President Lázaro Cárdenas's seizure of the oil industry—dominated by U.S. companies—in 1938 after the companies refused a government order to accept worker demands. Avoiding foreign intervention required skilled maneuvers, which included strong criticism of foreign companies while also giving clear signals that the Mexican government had no plans for widespread nationalization and expected U.S. private capital to play an important role in the economy. He phrased the nationalization decree carefully, even referring to how it would benefit foreign investment generally: "It is the social interest of the working class in all the country's industries that demands it. It is the public interest of Mexicans and even of foreigners living in the Republic who require peace and the dynamics of petroleum for work." Cárdenas sought to convince the administration of Franklin Delano Roosevelt that oil was a unique national asset and that nationalization was not part of an ideological program aimed at foreign capital. There was some retaliation, as the United States refused to buy Mexican silver and some countries boycotted Mexican oil, but those petered out as the Cold War got underway, and PEMEX became a large company.

███████████   **ANALYZING DOCUMENTS**   ███████████

The decision by President Lázaro Cárdenas to nationalize the oil industry had a major impact on both the Mexican economy and nationalism. He focused on how oil was too vital to the economy to be controlled by foreign investors, and to this day any proposal to privatize the national oil company, PEMEX, is extremely controversial.

Speech by President Lázaro Cárdenas Regarding Oil Expropriation

[T]he oil companies, despite the calm attitude of the Government and the considerations they have been given, have persisted in following, both in and out of the country, a dirty and skillful campaign that the Federal Authorities told one of the directors of the companies about two months ago, who denied it. The result has been that the companies are attempting to seriously damage the economic interests of the nation, seeking by these means to nullify the legal dictates of the Mexican authorities.

...

And in this delicate situation, the Public Power finds itself besieged by the social interests of the nation that would be the most affected, since insufficient petroleum production for the diverse activities of the country, which includes those as important as transportation, or even production that is zero or made too expensive by difficulties, would create in a short time a situation of chaos that is incompatible not only with our progress, but peace itself in the nation. It would paralyze banking, commercial life in many of its aspects, public works of general interest would be made almost impossible and the existence of the Government itself would be placed in grave danger, since losing the State's economic power would also mean losing political power, thus producing chaos.

It is evident that the problem the oil companies have presented the Executive Power with their refusal to obey the ruling from the High Court is not a simple case of carrying out a judgment, but rather a definitive situation that needs to be resolved with urgency.

It is the social interest of the working class in all the country's industries that demands it. It is the public interest of Mexicans and even of foreigners living in the Republic who require peace and the dynamics of petroleum for work.

It is the very sovereignty of the nation, that would be left exposed to the maneuvering of foreign capital which, forgetting that previously they had been part of Mexican enterprises, under Mexican law, attempts to avoid orders and the obligations placed on them by the country's authorities.

This consists of a clear and evident case that obliges the Government to apply the Expropriation Law with vigor, not only to subject the oil companies to obedience and submission, but because having broken the work contracts between companies and workers and leaving them thus, for the Government not to occupy the companies' institution would bring on immediate paralysis of the oil industry, creating incalculable evils for the rest of industry and the general economic of the country.

For these reasons the corresponding decree has been expedited and it has been ordered that its rules be followed, and this manifesto informs the people of my country the reason why everything has proceeded in this way and asks of the entire nation the moral and material support necessary to confront the consequences of a decision that we neither desired not sought of our own accord.

Discussion Questions
- Why are so many governments sensitive to international control over national natural resources?
- What seems to be Cárdenas's concern about how national law is respected by international investors?

Source: Colosio Foundation Web site, http://web.archive.org/web/20090523073516/ http://comunidad. fundacioncolosio.org/_Discurso-del-Presidente-Lzaro-Crdenas-con-motivo-de-la-Expropiacin-Petrolera-/ blog/44696/24409.html?b=

A similar dynamic held in Bolivia, where mines were nationalized in the 1950s as part of a broad program of reform by the Revolutionary Nationalist Movement (MNR). The government of Víctor Paz Estenssoro was careful to emphasize his anticommunist credential and stay within the U.S. "camp" by resisting internal pressures not to compensate the former owners. We will come back to the consequences for Bolivia in Chapter 8.

But these were the exceptions. Most often, elites as well as U.S. policy makers considered nationalization—even with full compensation—to be associated with communist infiltration. Later, after the Cold War erased the threat of communism, state seizure of private industry would still be viewed as potentially threatening but not nearly to the same degree.

Economic Reform Within Latin America

World War II had several important economic impacts on Latin America. It sparked a boom in raw materials, which the Allies needed for the war effort, and increased reserves in many countries. It also fostered nascent industrialization (though the capital goods were largely imported from the developed world), and especially in South America, industrial trade between countries began. After the war concluded, Latin American political leaders looked to the United States to provide aid and some measure of price stability for primary products, something along the lines of a Marshall Plan that contributed to rebuilding Europe after the war. The administration of Harry S. Truman was not interested "because the problems of the countries in this hemisphere are different in nature and cannot be relieved by the same means and the same approaches."[5]

Faced with uncertainties, Latin America looked for alternatives. Created in 1948, the Economic Commission for Latin America and the Caribbean (known as both ECLAC and CEPAL [its Spanish acronym]) became the center of debate over economic reform. Its most influential director, the Argentine Raúl Prebisch, held the position from 1950 until 1963 and spearheaded a regional push for import substitution industrialization. The policy was not new, as it dated back to the 1930s, and the struggle to overcome the global depression by enacting protectionist tariffs aimed at limiting imports (see Box 4.1). Under Prebisch's leadership, however, it gained intellectual weight and broader support.

▬▬▬▬▬▬▬▬ **BOX 4.1** ▬▬▬▬▬▬▬▬

Raúl Prebisch and the Import Substitution Model: Using National Resources to Overcome International Structural Constraints

International: Created in 1948, the United Nations' Economic Commission for Latin America and the Caribbean developed a structural economic view of Latin America. The driving idea was that the global capitalist system left Latin America at a disadvantage. There was, the argument went, no way to create and then nurture industry because it would be immediately overwhelmed by competition from the more developed world, particularly the United

States. Countries at the "core" of the international system to a significant extent controlled prices and prevented the "periphery" from moving forward. This idea of unequal exchange dated back to European theorists from the nineteenth century.

National: Therefore, the only way to develop was through targeted protection of specific industries. Unlike the more blanket protectionism so often used in the 1930s, the new policy would bring the state together in cooperation with industry only in certain sectors. This would spur on development but also would satisfy the growing (and restive) urban population, which was clamoring for work.

It was called *import substitution industrialization*. Domestic industry would gradually substitute for imports. It would do so by imposing tariffs, which were intended to be temporary. Once the industry was mature, it would be ready to compete in the global market, at which time further protection would no longer be necessary. The state's role was critical, because only it had the resources and power necessary to foster industrialization in the face of international competition.

ISI would indeed bring growth, but by the late 1970s it was widely viewed as "exhausted." From an economic perspective, there was a problem of both incentive and efficiency. The state became deeply involved in creating industrial employment, which in turn became a source of political support. Workers and unions were politically active and tied to ruling political parties, which in turn were unwilling to make economic decisions that might jeopardize that support. Industries therefore continued even if they were not becoming competitive.

Given the continued flow of capital from the state, companies had little incentive to change course or respond to market demand, which entailed restructuring and risk. Meanwhile, given the reasons just mentioned, policy makers had no incentive to force such changes given the strong potential for political backlash. Governments were therefore saddled with inefficient industries, and they borrowed abroad as a result. That borrowing became a cause of the catastrophic economic crash of the 1980s.

Local: The model's main successes were also limited to countries with large and wealthy enough domestic markets to purchase the domestically produced goods. Brazil, for example, produced cars (actually in collaboration with foreign companies), which would have been impossible in most other countries. Plus, in Brazil (and other prominent examples include Argentina, Chile, and Mexico), economic growth under ISI provided an industrial foundation for future economic development.

Discussion Questions
- Why do Latin American governments want to sell industrial rather than primary goods to international markets?
- Why might local and national markets be so important for at least partial success for the model?

CEPAL was but one of several important international financial institutions that emerged in the postwar years. After World War II, the United States was instrumental in the creation of the **World Bank**, the **International Monetary Fund (IMF)**, and the Inter-American Development Bank (IDB). Originally, the World Bank's purpose was to fund and coordinate development projects, and it began lending in 1947. The IMF was intended to create monetary stability through a system of financing.

These institutions became more central after the Cuban revolution in 1959. They acquired foreign policy relevance to the United States, which considered them a bastion of capitalist assistance to the developing world that could stem the tide of communism. Under President John Kennedy, the United States also launched the Alliance for Progress in 1961, which had the same goal. Throughout the 1960s, the United States sent over a billion dollars a year in economic assistance to Latin America, focusing intently on those countries (e.g., Chile) that had strong leftist parties. The intended goal of alleviating poverty did not come to pass, and the political left continued to make important advances. In general, the Alliance for Progress did not entail any structural changes to Latin American economies, so inequality and poverty remained persistent and widespread.

Our discussion thus far might lead one to believe that the search for economic alternatives was led only by the left, but this is not the case. In fact, in South America right-wing dictatorships were also seeking new models that often included a central role for the state. This is particularly striking because modernization theory would assert that countries such as Argentina, Brazil, and Chile should be moving briskly toward democracy. Modernization theory was challenged by scholars such as Guillermo O'Donnell, who noted the serious problems that arose when the ISI model began to stagnate.

Why Do Democracies Break Down? Economic Factors at the National Level

As mentioned, the most developed South American countries suffered military coups in the 1960s and early 1970s. A prominent and widely discussed middle-range theoretical response came from Guillermo O'Donnell, who coined the term *bureaucratic-authoritarian* to label these new modern dictatorships. According to O'Donnell, in the South American cases modernization was also accompanied by exclusion. If the popular sectors (e.g., labor) started making demands at a time when they could not be met economically (i.e., the policies of industrialization were coming to a halt), and those demands were then ignored or suppressed, modernization might actually compel elites to support a dictatorship. He asserted that the "easy" stage of import substitution industrialization was ending. It had been characterized by "horizontal" industrial growth, meaning they were aimed at satisfying domestic demand for finished goods. However, this demand was being met by foreign, not national, producers.

Rising political and economic demands prompted the upper class, those with money and land, to ally themselves with the armed forces to reestablish what they viewed as order, usually meaning stamping out unrest at the local and national levels. Such a dictatorship would be not only authoritarian—nondemocratic—but also bureaucratic, because it would have all the trappings of a modern state, including a functioning bureaucracy, trained experts (**technocrats**), and a professional military.

O'Donnell's work contradicted assumptions about modernization. Still, it received its criticisms. Different countries—such as Argentina, Brazil, Chile, and Uruguay—that at first glance seemed to support his hypothesis were pursuing different economic policies and had widely varying political characteristics. In addition, why did some more developed countries such as Mexico manage not to succumb to dictatorship? In other words, O'Donnell's primarily national argument had some holes. Nonetheless, his hypotheses forced a rethinking of the relationship between modernity and democracy as well as between economic policy and political outcomes. These are puzzles that we need to explore.

There are other reasons for ISI's decline. One serious problem was that governments kept their exchange rates overvalued as a way to encourage the cheap import of industrial goods required to equip factories. Therefore, the finished product was handicapped because it was expensive for buyers in other countries, while the internal market was too small to fill the gap. Plus, governments were not willing to allow inefficient industries to go under. Rather than face the potentially explosive results of greater unemployment, they continued to subsidize regardless of performance. Economic elites benefited greatly from state assistance, but ISI did not spark much improvement for the lot of the majority. High growth rates only led to more inequality, which in turn produced unrest. It is worth mentioning, however, that ISI did create an industrial base that contributed to economic growth in the long term.

The short-term economic challenges were becoming evident in the 1960s, in the wake of the Cuban revolution and amidst massive protests worldwide against the status quo. The Brazilian coup was the first of a decade-long wave of military overthrows of civilian governments across Latin America. By no means, however, did military government automatically mean the state reduced its presence in the economy. In the Brazilian case, by 1973 (almost a decade after the coup) the state still owned 100 percent of railways and port services, 99 percent of water, gas, and sewers, 97 percent of telegraph and telephone, and over 50 percent of a wide range of other economic sectors.[6]

Thus, in some of the largest and most dynamic economies of Latin America, such as Argentina, Brazil, and Chile, modernization in the 1960s and 1970s contributed to authoritarian rule. Yet despite the shift away from democracy, with the exception of Chile, the economic models did not change drastically. A prominent role for the state was posed in nationalist terms, sidestepping the fact that these anti-Communist governments were in fact retaining important socialist policies. Even in Chile, which moved more toward pure capitalism than any other government, the copper industry remained largely in the state's hands for nationalist reasons (and much of it remains there now).

International Factors in the Late Twentieth Century

Clearly, the import substitution model was started to show cracks, but it received a boost in the early 1970s. The countries of the Organization of the Petroleum Exporting Countries (OPEC) unified and established various measures to increase the price of oil. Those governments, primarily in the Middle East but also including Ecuador and Venezuela, soon were awash in dollars. Their response was to invest that money in foreign banks, which in turn needed to loan it out. Governments across the region embarked on large projects and kept many state-run businesses afloat that otherwise would have gone bankrupt. The good times rolled, at least for a short while. Concerns about risk were disregarded, and Latin American governments were able to pile new debt onto old.

The Debt Crisis

Meanwhile, throughout the 1970s interest rates in the United States and Europe began to climb as a way to combat inflation—the way to get people to stop spending money is to entice them to save with high interest rates. For Latin America, it resulted in loan terms that required an ever greater share of their payments to be interest rather than principal. In 1979, debt payments constituted 11.1 percent of the exports of goods and services, and by 1982 that had grown to a whopping 24.2 percent.[7] But it also meant an increase of imports, which in turn led to trade deficits. As competitiveness dropped, investors started getting nervous, and capital flight ensued.

When the global economy contracted in 1981, the ride was officially over. Lenders began questioning the wisdom of approving new loans to much of the developing world, yet without new loans it was not possible to pay off past existing loans. The inevitable conclusion was nonpayment. Beginning in 1982 with Mexico, Latin American governments announced they were defaulting.

At that point, the United States and the IMF took center stage, as the latter became a clearinghouse for any loans. Treasury Secretary James Baker pushed for structural adjustment in 1985 for the larger debtor countries. The assumption of the Baker Plan was that increased exports could spark the economic growth necessary to reduce debt. As the plan called for banks to increase lending to spur industry, it actually also increased debt. Continued failure to repay ended the plan after less than two years. In 1989, Treasury Secretary Nicholas Brady developed what became known as the Brady Plan, which replaced old Latin American bonds with new, dollar-denominated bonds. The idea was that investors would feel more confident with choices of new bonds (the values of which were negotiated) that had more protections and that could be traded if companies felt they were too risky. Unfortunately, no solution reduced Latin American debt. For the most part, it was restructured but still increased.

Along with U.S. policy makers, the IMF had the leverage to compel Latin American governments to enact its desired economic reforms. Refusal would mean no new loans, because banks would not come calling without an IMF stamp of approval. Lenders dealt with each country on a case-by-case basis, determining exactly what types of market reforms would be necessary to resume a flow of credit. In practice, this meant reversing many aspects of the state's role to achieve greater economic efficiency and tackle debt.

State-owned enterprises were privatized, meaning they were sold to private companies, which brought in revenue. Governments were very hesitant to do so, but by the late 1980s privatization became commonplace. Trade barriers, such as tariffs, were dismantled so that domestic business would either sink or swim according to whether it was competitive globally, not whether the state was protecting it. Latin American countries joined the General Agreement on Trade and Tariffs (GATT, created in 1947), which became the World Trade Organization (WTO) in 1995. Their purpose was to set rules for free trade, which included reduction of tariffs. Public spending was cut, and so were the subsidies that kept prices for specific goods (including food) artificially low.

All these measures taken together became widely known as the *Washington Consensus*, which emphasizes the international influence. Their ultimate sources were headquartered in Washington, DC, and they were pushed hard by the U.S. government, which, not coincidentally, is also centered in Washington, DC. To be sure, there were plenty of Latin American leaders who supported these policies, but many others were not pleased at how the Washington Consensus was forced onto them.

The market-driven approach had varying results. From a macroeconomic perspective, the reforms successfully addressed some of the most pressing challenges. As so much money was being taken out of the economy, inflation dropped, which stabilized prices. Inflation had been a serious problem, especially for the poor, because wages did not keep up. In some cases, governments had resorted to printing more money, which ultimately had the effect of making inflation worse.

But debt did not go away. In fact, it often increased. Plus, as governments still had to pay off interest, government spending as a percentage of GDP actually increased despite all the cuts in services. For example, by 1987 more than 50 percent of Mexico's central government expenditures went to interest payments.[8] Debt repayment is a constant problem.

Chile as an Alternative Model

Unlike the rest of Latin America, Chile already had market-oriented policies in place before the debt crisis. Several years after the 1973 coup that ended the country's experiment with socialism, the dictatorship put the economy into the hands of a young group of economists, many of whom had studied in the United States (they became known as the *Chicago Boys* because of their ties to the University of Chicago). They had been meeting informally to discuss Chile's economic future and soon after the coup made sure that a copy of their diagnosis and prescriptions got into the hands of the new military government. The report became known as *El Ladrillo,* or *The Brick,* because of its size. It argued that state intervention was at the heart of Chile's economic stagnation and that only dramatic shifts toward free-market capitalism would open up its potential. The report harshly criticized the "asphyxiating statism" followed by the government of Salvador Allende and became the intellectual model for economic reform in Chile and later for other countries as well.

▬▬▬▬▬▬ ANALYZING DOCUMENTS ▬▬▬▬▬▬

The Chilean economic model that emerged in the mid-1970s had a strong international influence. The Chicago Boys found inspiration in the United States and used ideas found there to address what they considered a disastrous national economic model. They also believed that negative international factors—such as the popularity of Marxism—had brought the country to the brink of economic ruin.

El Ladrillo
Introduction

This report is the result of long study by a group of distinguished economists from high academic levels, whose object was to define a collection of coherent and interrelated policies that would resolve the deep economic crisis the country is experiencing, and at the same time to propose the basic elements of a global political economy that would make accelerated economic development possible.

The group began its activities in a totally informal manner, with the object of exchanging opinions among professionals of the same academic level about the grave results that could be foreseen regarding the harmful political economy initiated by the Popular Unity government. It became evident that we shared the basic diagnostic elements, and that it fell to us, as professionals and as citizens, the unavoidable responsibility of adding our intellectual contribution to the effort to reconstruct the country and to liberate it from the chaos in which it finds itself.

...

Chapter I—Diagnosis

This anxiety to obtain a more rapid economic development and the failure of successive programs intended to generate it have opened the door for the triumph of Marxist demagoguery that presented itself with the halo of an untested scheme and which promised substantial improvements in the quality of life for the vast majority of Chileans, where no one but the very rich would have to make sacrifices. According to this scheme, it was enough to expropriate the large monopolies and *latifundia,* and transfer their surplus to social investment and the redistribution of wealth, in order to achieve accelerated economic development in an atmosphere of price stability (the end of inflation) and justice in the distribution of income. Less than three years have been enough to demonstrate the complete failure, constantly more evident, of the Marxist recipe....

Another characteristics, in large part associated with the first, has been the growing and asphyxiating statism that myopically has created a vicious cycle of stagnation-statism. In effect, since the end of the 1930s, Chile has been following a line of state intervention with which it has hoped to resolve the crisis of growth.

...

One of the most pernicious aspects of the statist tendency has been the growth formula that has been tried: "excessive industrial protectionism to induce the substitution of imports" that has had the contrary effect to that desired, and has resulted in a concentration of our productive resources in the service of restricted internal markets, which because of their small size are condemned to a slow rate of development.

Discussion Questions
- For the authors of *El Ladrillo*, what role should the state have in national development?
- What does their view seem to be about the benefits of international markets?

Source: Ladrillo, 15–16, Centro de Estudio Públicos, http://www.cepchile.cl/dms/lang_1/cat_794_inicio. html

---

This model was not followed anywhere else in Latin America at the time, but it can be seen as a precursor to the Washington Consensus. Nowhere else was there the same combination of a dictatorship (which ensured that labor remained fully controlled), ideological unity, and a generalized feeling that the previous statist economic policies had failed. As inflation was tamed and foreign investment flowed in, Chile was often held up as an example of what other Latin American countries could achieve. The "Ladrillo" tenets would spread.

As the Cold War came to a close, a new debate over political economy emerged. Had the world, to use a rather tired but common phrase, reached the "end of history" in which Marxism and command economies been permanently discredited? Was there no other model than that of capitalism? In Latin America, the initial answer seemed clear. The state-led development strategies of past decades had contributed to the debt crisis of the 1980s, and market reforms were slaying hyperinflation and increasing rates of economic growth. Once the state began to retreat from the economy, private industry moved in.

Another Alternative: Mixed Economies

One problem was that many countries experienced serious and sometimes very violent protests against policies of privatization. As a result, a number of scholars and policy makers, many associated with CEPAL, began proposing a balance between markets and state intervention in the economy. It became known as the *third way* (between capitalism and socialism) or sometimes as *neostructuralism*. One scholar has labeled it the "political economy of the possible."[9]

No matter what it is called, the idea is that an export-driven model of development is the best engine for growth. However, it also recognizes that capitalism is attuned to supply and demand rather than to people. Therefore, advocates seek to include an ethical dimension to economic policies, using carefully targeted government spending to provide a safety net for the disadvantaged.

Advocates argue that economic growth alone is not the answer to a country's problems and that poverty must also be reduced to take full advantage of its human resources.

In fact, "pure" neoliberalism is no longer common in Latin America. Policy makers of all ideological stripes agree that at times the state must take an important economic role, especially in times of crisis. The basic ideas of the famous economist John Maynard Keynes are widely held. Keynesian economic policy asserts that free markets can be inefficient, which leads to negative economic outcomes. As a result, the state should intervene (e.g., through spending) to encourage growth and unemployment. In the wake of the global economic crisis of 2008, many Latin American governments implemented stimulus packages to boost employment and growth.

In subsequent chapters, we will see how such policies have functioned in practice. The most widely cited contemporary examples are Brazil and Chile, where governments have followed market-driven policies while also working to alleviate the negative effects of capitalism through targeted social programs and spending, which show Keynesian tendencies. We will get a grip on their political ramifications and examine the ways in which they are perceived at different levels.

The Local Level: Formal and Informal Economies

These macro-level factors have real micro—that is, local—impacts as well. Understanding the state's involvement in the economy also requires examining the local level, where there is a lot of economic activity that doesn't get noted in the official, national-level statistics. In addition to the formal, there is an **informal economy**. This refers to people who perform work and earn money that is not sanctioned or recorded by the government. There are countless examples, from very small (selling items on the street) to very large (including narcotics) transactions. Yet most are local, composed of individuals seeking small-time work. It may consist of anywhere between one-third and one-half of the economically active population.[10] Many people participate in both, using the informal to augment formally earned income.

The informal economy is a direct result of state failure at the national level. The most common argument is that the government could not generate enough decently paying jobs, thus forcing many people to search for alternate sources of income. This is particularly true in time of deep economic crisis, such as the aftermath of the debt crisis. However, others have argued that overly complex and burdensome state regulations make life too difficult for would-be entrepreneurs, who opt for the freedom of less formal work. Regardless of economic policy, it is also a consequence of rapid urbanization. In the past several decades, millions of people migrated from rural to urban areas, as the former could no longer sustain a growing population.

The informal economy is both there and not there, though of course government officials are well aware of its existence. Vendors may be selling things and quickly disappear when strolling police approach. The police know they are all around. Sadly, there are many instances of corruption, where people must pay not to be officially noticed by the state. The sales—and certainly the kickbacks—are not reflected in official tallies. But the state cannot afford to crack down too heavily, because it would face an enraged population no longer able to make a living.

Informality falls heavily on the shoulders of women. A lack of income pushes women into the informal workforce as a way to make enough money to provide for a family. Women still have to do all their traditional tasks but then are expected to add that additional labor. For example, they may sell food, or provide childcare, or otherwise perform services for others that are not official and are not taxed. Needless to say, it is a tremendous hardship.

This dual economy poses a serious obstacle to economic development. The state does not officially capture any of the benefits (e.g., taxation), the jobs tend not to create stable enterprises, it decreases faith in the rule of law, and it increases inequality because the informal economy is composed overwhelmingly of the poor and does not offer much upward mobility. Therefore, it can be both crucial to survival and problematic for a life that goes beyond simply surviving.

Dollarization: The Ultimate International Influence

Faced with extremely high—roughly 50 percent or more a month—inflation (called **hyperinflation**) in the 1980s, some Latin American policy makers looked to a solution that would ensure a stable currency indefinitely. **Dollarization** means making the dollar the official currency. It is a radical solution because it takes much of a country's fiscal policy out of its hands. For example, printing money (called *seignorage*) is no longer possible. Indeed, part of dollarization's rationale was to prevent that very action because it contributes to inflation. This has major impacts on the local level, because people who don't have money suffer badly when inflation hits. A loaf of bread and other basic goods could go up drastically from day to day and that generates a lot of resentment and often leads to protests.

There are historical precedents for dollarization. By virtue of a very large U.S. presence and the widespread use of dollars, Panama became dollarized in 1904. A Cuban law passed in 1914 allowed the dollar to circulate along with the peso; even by 1931, over 80 percent of Cuban economic exchanges were in dollars.[11] At various times, governments have pegged their currency to the dollar (e.g., Honduras, the Dominican Republic, and Haiti during the 1930s) to avoid exchange rate shocks. As we will discuss more in later chapters, Ecuador made the full switch in 2000 and El Salvador in 2001. For Ecuador, economic crisis in the late 1990s combined with heavy debt to raise the specter of default, inflation, and capital flight, so President Jamil Mahuad eliminated the "sucre" currency and adopted the dollar. In El Salvador, the decision was made preemptively as there was no immediate economic crisis to overcome.

Dollarization does lead to macroeconomic stability (with low inflation and interest rates) and consequently encourages a continuous flow of investment. Exchange rate volatility is no longer a problem because the dollar is much steadier.

But it does not necessarily have a major impact on debt or budgetary discipline. It also makes the economy even more heavily dependent upon policy decisions made in the United States as well as the performance of the U.S. economy. If major trading partners devalue against the dollar, they automatically also do so against dollarized economies. In Chapter 12, we will examine the problems that Argentina faced when its peso was pegged to the dollar.

At the same time, it is notable that Rafael Correa, elected president of Ecuador in 2006 (and who also holds a Ph.D. in Economics), has not called for an end to the policy, despite his strong criticisms of capitalism and the United States. Similarly, when Mauricio Funes of the leftist FMLN party was elected president of El Salvador in 2009, his platform did not include any challenge to dollarization. The combination of its stabilizing properties and the difficulty of reversing it tend to leave it off the table. No matter what ideology a president has, he or she values macroeconomic stability.

An International Constant: The Exchange Rate

An important final point to make is that with all the booms and busts and ideological evolution, an economic constant is the **exchange rate**. No matter what the ideological orientation, policy makers must make decisions about the value of their currencies. At a very basic level, at times they must decide whether the current value compared to other countries is benefiting or hurting them economically.

The exchange rate refers to the value of one country's currency in relation to another. Policy makers are always greatly concerned about how their currency relates to the dollar, because business around the world is often conducted in dollars. However, it is also critical for any countries that trade a lot of goods with each other. Anyone who has traveled internationally has firsthand experience with the exchange rate, because when you arrive in a country, typically one of your first actions is to take your money (let's say, Mexican pesos) and exchange it for the money of the country you are visiting (e.g., the Brazilian real). If day after day, your pesos get you more and more reais (the plural for real), that means the Mexican peso is strong, and the real is weak.

The nominal exchange rate is the amount that each currency can be exchanged for the other when governments do not intervene. The market, meaning the combination of supply and demand, determines the nominal rate. Very often, though, governments want to influence what goods will be worth to fulfill their economic goals. Governments sometimes have to deal with overvalued currencies. This is a situation in which the "real" value of the money has decreased, but the government has not yet changed the official exchange rate. The real value is the price of a domestic good compared to the price of a foreign good. How do we figure this out? The answer is by looking at purchasing power parity (PPP). The idea behind PPP is that the value of a good that is traded internationally—meaning it is exported and imported—can tell us the nominal exchange rate. You just look at the cost of a particular good—a toaster—in the United States, which might be $10. Then, using the official exchange rate, you

FIGURE 4.1 An Overvalued Exchange Rate: Mexico and the United States

calculate what $10 would exchange for Mexican pesos. That price in Mexican pesos is the nominal exchange rate.

So although the official exchange rate may be one peso to one dollar, the real exchange is something like 1.5 pesos : 1 dollar. Further, assume a company in the United States exports radios to Mexico, and they sell for $10 each. Using Figure 4.1, let's say a Mexican company makes the exact same radio. With an overvalued exchange rate, the imported radio costs $10, and the Mexican radio costs the equivalent of $15. What would a person in Mexico likely do? They would go to the bank, exchange their pesos for dollars, and then buy the radio from the United States. With an overvalued exchange rate, imported goods become cheaper, and that country's exports become more expensive to sell abroad. Many domestic businesses complain when this occurs, because, of course, they cannot compete well with the foreign goods coming into the country.

The problem with this scenario is that many people will be exchanging their pesos to get dollars. Speculators, in fact, will likely do so in large quantities. But even more importantly, the government sometimes must sell its dollars to maintain the overvalued exchange rate. Its dollar reserves then dwindle. If that process continues, a panic may ensue, which further reduces the currency's value and sparks a run on reserves. That sort of downward spiral is very difficult to reverse.

Now, why would a country keep its currency overvalued? One reason is to give local producers privileged access to important foreign raw materials, which become cheaper than they otherwise would be. That also helps if domestic industries need those imports for parts, machinery, and so on. However, sometimes it is an unintended consequence of having a currency pegged to another currency, discussed next.

Therefore, before long we would expect Mexico (or any other country in the same position) to **devalue**, which reduces the value of your currency relative to others. People will then stop running to exchange their money for foreign money. Furthermore, that country's exports will become more competitive, which will then bring more foreign currency back into the country, thus restoring reserves.

But how does a government actually accomplish the changes in currency values? In the case of Latin America, it is essential for governments to maintain dollars in reserve. Dollars are the international currency of business (though in recent years some Latin Americans have called for an emphasis on the euro instead to decrease dependency on the dollar and, by extension, the United States) and so it is critical to keep them on hand to reassure investors. It is a sign of macroeconomic stability.

Conclusion

Although Carlos Pellegrini was in power well over a century ago, the types of challenges he faced have changed remarkably little over the years. International influence is particularly important for understanding the dynamics of political economy in Latin America, and governments have moved back and forth from market-led to state-led development. As the twentieth century progressed, the proposed alternatives to free-market capitalism multiplied. Given the stakes involved, challenges to capitalism created conflict, sometimes very serious. Some variation of socialism or communism enjoyed support from the working class in particular but was staunchly opposed by business and political leaders. However, government did periodically nationalize core natural resources for nationalist, rather than primarily ideological, reasons. Of course, such policies have important and often immediate impacts at the local level.

Development requires capital, and like other parts of the developing world, Latin America has experimented with virtually countless strategies to raise capital and maintain a stable economic environment for investment to flourish but also for the alleviation of poverty and inequality. These strategies have gone to different extremes, from free-market capitalism in Chile to a command economy in Cuba. In places such as Ecuador and El Salvador, it has entailed formal adoption of the dollar as national currency. The ideological divide that currently exists in Latin America revolves around the questions of capital accumulation and macroeconomic stability. The more things change, the more they stay the same. The chapters that follow will analyze how this played out in different countries.

Key Terms

- Capitalism
- Socialism
- Communism
- Democratic socialism
- Gini coefficient
- World Bank
- International Monetary Fund (IMF)

- Technocrats
- Informal economy
- Hyperinflation
- Dollarization
- Exchange rate
- Devalue

Discussion Questions

- In what ways is inequality an obstacle to national economic growth?
- Why does dollarization help with hyperinflation?
- Can you think of ways that capitalism in Latin America can lead to a larger informal economy?
- Why would the United States consider Latin American Marxism to be such a threat?
- In what ways can decentralization put more power in the hands of local politicians?

Further Sources

Books

Bulmer-Thomas, Victor. *The Economic History of Latin America Since Independence,* 2nd edition (New York: Cambridge University Press, 2003). This is a very useful resource, with well-written analyses of different eras of economic development, from the macro to the micro levels. It also includes dozens of tables and clear explanation of key terms.

Cárdenas, Enrique, José Antonio Ocampo, and Rosemary Thorpe, eds., *An Economic History of Latin America* (New York: Palgrave, 2000). This is an ambitious and useful three-volume series. The first focuses on the late nineteenth and early twentieth centuries, the second solely on the 1930s, and the third on industrialization in the postwar years. It has both general chapters and specific country case studies.

Graham, Carol, and Eduardo Lora, eds. *Paradox and Perception: Measuring Quality of Life in Latin America* (Washington, DC: Inter-American Development Bank, 2009). This collection takes a unique look at economic development in Latin America by focusing more specifically on perceptions of well-being.

Kingstone, Peter. *The Political Economy of Latin America: Reflections on Neoliberalism and Development* (New York: Routledge, 2011). This is a thoughtful analysis about how weak institutions have prevented either neoliberalism or its leftist alternatives from achieving their stated goals.

Ignacio Leiva, Fernando. *Latin American Neostructuralism: The Contradictions of Post-Neoliberal Development* (Minneapolis: University of Minnesota Press, 2008). This book argues that current economic strategies across Latin America have failed to address power relations (i.e., the political struggle to determine where profits should go).

Wilkie, James, ed. *Statistical Abstract of Latin America* (Los Angeles: UCLA Latin American Institute). The abstract is an invaluable resource on Latin American economic statistics of all kinds and is updated annually. It is both extensive and comparative.

Web Sites

The Economic Commission for Latin America and the Caribbean (www.cepal.org). This is a major source of economic data on Latin America, including annual reports covering all countries and public access to economic publications.

Inter-American Development Bank (http://www.iadb.org). Unlike other Web sites, the IDB Web site is focused not solely on economic indicators but rather on development projects that it sponsors across Latin America.

Latin American Economic Outlook (http://www.latameconomy.org/en/). This Web site is sponsored by the Organization of Economic Cooperation and Development. It includes a lengthy annual report on the economies of each Latin American country.

Latin Focus (http://www.latin-focus.com/index.htm). It is a Web site dedicated to maintaining updated links to news stories about the economies of Latin American countries, along with charts and tables on economic indicators.

The World Bank: Latin America (http://web.worldbank.org). The official Web site of the World Bank has a section on Latin America, which has a variety of data and publications. It includes detailed summaries of ongoing developments projects, which are organized according to economic sector.

Endnotes

1. Douglas W. Richmond, *Carlos Pellegrini and the Crisis of the Argentine Elites, 1880–1916* (New York: Praeger, 1989), 66.
2. Victor Bulmer-Thomas, *The Economic History of Latin America Since Independence* (New York: Cambridge University Press, 2003), 74.
3. Isabel Allende, *The House of the Spirits* (New York: Bantam, 1993), 89.
4. Patrice Franko, *The Puzzle of Latin American Economic Development*, 3rd edition (Lanham: Rowman and Littlefield Publishers, Inc., 2007), 396–399.
5. Quoted in Lars Schoultz, *Beneath the United States: A History of U.S. Policy Toward Latin America* (Cambridge: Harvard University Press, 1998), 332.
6. Franko 2007, 62.
7. Rudiger Dornbusch, "The Latin American Debt Problem: Anatomy and Solutions," in *Debt and Democracy in Latin America*, eds. Barbara Stallings and Robert Kaufman (Boulder: Westview Press, 1989), 9.
8. Bulmer-Thomas 2003, 377.
9. Javier Santiso, *Latin America's Political Economy of the Possible* (Cambridge: The MIT Press, 2006).
10. Miguel Angel Centeno and Alejandro Portes, "The Informal Economy in the Shadow of the State," in *Out of the Shadows: Political Action and the Informal Economy in Latin America,* eds. Patricia Fernández-Kelly and Jon Shefner (University Park: The Pennsylvania State University Press, 2006).
11. Kenneth P. Jameson, "Dollarization in Latin America: Wave of the Future or Flight to the Past?" *Journal of Economic Issues* 37, 3 (2003): 643–663.

CHAPTER 5

Mexico

LEARNING OBJECTIVES

- Identify how the three levels of analysis interact in Mexico.

- Use theoretical propositions to understand political and economic development in Mexico.

- Explain how and why political and economic development in Mexico differs from other Latin American countries.

TIMELINE

1821	Independence
1848	Treaty of Guadalupe Hidalgo
1876–1910	Porfiriato
1910–1920	Mexican revolution
1917	Constitution ratified
1929	National Revolutionary Party (PNR) created
1938	PNR becomes the Party of the Mexican Revolution (PRM)
1946	PRM becomes the Institutional Revolutionary Party (PRI)
1968	Massacre in Tlatelolco square
1982	Government announces debt default
1994	NAFTA goes into effect; Zapatista rebellion begins
2000	PRI loses presidency
2006	Felipe Calderón wins disputed presidential election
2012	PRI regains presidency with Enrique Peña Nieto

MEXICO'S POLITICAL INSTITUTIONS

Last constitution: 1917

Federal system with thirty-one states

Executive: President with six year terms; no reelection

Legislative: Bicameral with 128 Senators and 500 deputies (300 through plurality vote in single-member districts and 200 through proportional representation based on party's share of total votes)

Judicial: Supreme Court with judicial review

In 2010, a twenty-year-old criminology student named Marisol Valles agreed to become police chief of Praxedis G. Guerrero, a small town near the border with the United States. She took the position because no one else was willing, as rival drug trafficking gangs were ripping the town apart. As a result, she received worldwide press attention. A mere five months later, she sought asylum in the United States, meaning that she believed persecution made it too dangerous to stay. At least in northern Mexico, local politics was coming apart at the seams. The international influence of drug demand in the United States has had serious impacts in many

1. Aguascalientes
2. Distrito Federal
3. Guanajuato
4. Hidalgo
5. Mexico
6. Morelos
7. Queretaro de Arteaga
8. Tlaxcala

MEXICO
Population: 113.7 million
Size: 762,000 square miles
Capital: Mexico City
Currency: Peso

Map of Mexico Showing Regions

Latin American countries. In Mexico, both democracy and economic development suffer, as corruption, fear, and intimidation all collide in a volatile mix.

One of the most interesting developments in Latin American politics in recent years was the peaceful end to one-party rule in Mexico, a gradual process that came to an official conclusion after the presidential election of 2000. Democracy bubbled from the bottom up, as opposition parties organized locally and were elected to towns and cities across Mexico, and then moved up the political ladder. Domestic influences were paramount.

Nonetheless, given Mexico's geography, international factors are also prominent in politics and often not in a positive way. Probably, the most famous quote about Mexico is "So far from God, so close to the United States," which is attributed to the dictator Porfirio Díaz. It symbolizes the very strong international influence that has always been part of Mexican politics, and not always in a particularly positive manner. A border with the United States has often meant that policy making must take the northern neighbor into consideration.

Historical Roots of Political and Economic Development

When Mexico won its independence in 1821, it had a vast, unwieldy territory that included much of the west and all of the southwest of the current United States. In the colonial era, it had been part of the Viceroyalty of New Spain, an important part of the Spanish empire. The Catholic Church exerted tremendous political power and became entrenched in all parts of the region. More than elsewhere in Latin America, its position would be challenged after Mexico became independent.

Postindependence Challenges

The first half of the nineteenth century was disastrous for Mexico because of international factors. Like much of the region, Mexico emerged bankrupt from independence. In time-honored fashion, foreign governments eyed customs houses in port cities as a way to force repayment. Spain invaded and took Veracruz in 1829 and the French blockaded in 1838 (the so-called *Pastry War* as France pursued a claim of damage for a pastry shop, among other demands). Even worse, in 1846 the United States invaded and under the 1848 Treaty of Guadalupe Hidalgo took roughly half the country (the United States paid out $15 million, which the Mexican government used to pay off debt). During this time, Mexico was ruled by leaders such as Antonio López de Santa Anna, who was president seven different times between 1833 and 1855, switching political allegiances in whatever way best served him.

International influences combined with the liberal–conservative divide in Mexico to spark the War of the Reform (1857–1861), a civil war won by liberal forces under the leadership of Benito Juárez. As president, he suspended all debt repayments for two years, which prompted Spain, Great Britain, and France to attack Veracruz in 1862. All the while, Mexican conservatives had been searching Europe for someone who might head a new monarchy that would reestablish both political and economic order and crush the liberal project. That person was the Austrian Ferdinand Maximilian Joseph, who became Maximilian I, the emperor of Mexico, in 1864. President Juárez and military officers such as Porfirio Díaz fought back, and his reign lasted only three years (Maximilian was then executed).

Roots of the Mexican Revolution

From then on, liberals dominated Mexican politics, but that did not mean stability. Within a few years of Maximilian's defeat, Díaz began a series of revolts against the government, which culminated in his self-appointment as president in 1876 and election in 1877. Thus began what became known as the *porfiriato*, or era of Porfirio. Ironically, one of his public criticisms of the government had been about presidential reelection, which he claimed to oppose. But he would then amend the 1857 constitution to allow indefinite reelection. The term *reelection* should be taken with a grain of salt, as the elections became shams that papered over a dictatorship.

Under Porfirio Díaz, the Mexican state solidified. He helped put the country back on its economic feet by expanding foreign trade and inviting investment. He embarked on an ambitious plan of infrastructure, most importantly railroads, which connected the country while also facilitating trade. Further, he established a lengthy period of internal peace that allowed economic development to take root. Politically, Mexico was clientelist, as Díaz offered benefits to all major social and political groups, including the Catholic Church. Liberalism usually entailed strong antagonism toward the church, but Díaz brought them into the clientelist fold. Overall, this system of favors, combined with internal repression and no accountability (either horizontal or vertical), became a source of friction over time.

The eventual result of that political conflict was the Mexican revolution, prompted by Díaz reneging on a promise to allow free elections. His opponent in the 1910 election was Francisco Madero, who headed the "no reelection" faction. But then Díaz had Madero imprisoned and held a fraudulent election that kept him in the presidency. That sparked the revolution, led by heroes such as Pancho Villa in the north and Emiliano Zapata in the south, both of whom called in particular for land reform. This national uprising forced Díaz to resign and flee the country in 1911, but the turmoil continued until 1917. Madero became president, who was then ousted and killed by Victoriano Huerta. Huerta was eventually forced to resign, and finally Venustiano Carranza's army took over the country. Carranza would initiate the negotiations that culminated in the 1917 constitution (plus his election as president) and the end of the revolution.

The Legacies of the Revolution

The revolution is notable for so many reasons, but race and class are two issues that merit attention. Revolutionary leaders and their followers came from all walks of life. Carranza was a wealthy landowner, for example, whereas Zapata was poor and of indigenous origin. (This helps explain why the former ended up having the latter killed and why almost ninety years later an uprising in the southern state of Chiapas would use Zapata's name.) To forge a lasting agreement, the demands of the lower strata of Mexican society had to be acknowledged. As a result, the constitution guarantees extensive rights, granting numerous protections to workers and land to many peasants. A new brand of nonelite politician emerged—72 percent of public figures who were combat veterans were from the working class.[1]

Further, the constitution explicitly recognized the indigenous population and the multicultural nature of Mexico, laying out a considerable list of rights, including preservation of land and self-determination. Peasants were recognized through the **ejido** system, a traditional system of communal land dating before Spain's arrival. Porfirio Díaz in particular had contributed to its erosion, as land was taken over by private interests. The new constitution restored it, though widespread distribution would not occur until Cárdenas became president, when he distributed land to 800,000 families.

From the perspective of workers, Article 123 guarantees a host of different rights, including an eight-hour day, the ability to strike, and the ability to file a grievance for wrongful termination. The allowance of such rights marked a radical turn for Mexico, because as in the rest of Latin America workers had often been abused. It is also important to note that Article 130 stipulated a separation of church and state and regulated the actions of the church and its representatives. This was a considerable shift for a very Catholic country. Nonetheless, most often constitutional rights remained primarily on paper, and Mexican governments generally ignored the indigenous population and repeated that racism was not a problem (at times emphasized as a contrast to racial conflict in the United States).

There was also an important gender element to the revolution. Women were actively engaged in revolutionary activities, in a wide variety of combat roles. So in 1914 they were given the right to divorce and remarry. Then, the 1917 Law of Family Relations gave women legal rights to own property, sue in a court of law, and have custody of their children.[2] Yet they did not receive the right to vote in national elections until 1953. Instead, women worked at the state level for suffrage rights, and in the 1920s several states allowed women to vote in state and local elections. They also entered the workforce in greater numbers, but decades would go by before the PRI acknowledged their demands at the national level.

Contemporary Politics in Mexico

Another revolutionary hero, Plutarco Calles, created the National Revolutionary Party (PNR) in 1929 as a way to bring the various political strands (political leaders, peasants, military, labor, etc.) of the revolution together. It would go through another name change before becoming the **Institutional Revolutionary Party (PRI)** in 1946. The name is evocative because of its contradictory nature. By definition, institutions are solid and lasting, whereas revolutions represent rapid and radical change. The PRI managed to hold this contradiction together for about seventy years. It has been called a *perfect dictatorship* because the party maintained a firm grip on power from the national to the local level, but the authoritarian nature of the regime did not include the brutal repression of military dictatorships elsewhere in Latin America. Instead, it kept a democratic façade that was not seriously punctured until the 1980s.

The Influence of Clientelism and Corporatism

Understanding Mexico requires an examination of clientelism, the essence of which is a *quid pro quo*. The government scratches the back of all major organizations in the country by providing them with resources and access to political power. In turn, they scratch the back of government by giving their political support and strengthening the government's legitimacy. Similar to the Venezuelan case, the concept of clientelism helps explain why Mexico was exceptional with regard to military coups. After the revolution, military heroes became presidents, and they depoliticized the armed forces by granting them relatively generous budgets and then staying out of internal military decisions. At the same time, government-controlled labor unions did not become radical as they did in many other Latin American countries. Neither economic elites nor the military considered labor to be a threat to their interests, and consequently the political system remained stable.

The formalized nature of Mexican clientelism represents **corporatism**, which involves forming institutions that channel the back scratching. For example, at the national level the Confederation of Mexican Workers was formed in 1936 as the primary labor union. It was entwined with the PRI, which allowed for constant dialogue between the two. The arrangement made it easier for the PRI to respond to social demands. It went all the way down to the level of small cities or towns, where PRI mayors would have discussions with major groups, from landowners to shopkeepers to the Catholic Church. At the national level were "camarillas," or groups of like-minded politicians who help each other move upward, often with a mentorship quality. These informal relationships facilitated being placed in formal positions of power. Down at the local and regional levels were the "caciques," political bosses who controlled smaller fiefdoms, channeling demands up and handling the resources being sent down. It was truly a well-oiled machine.

But it was also entirely fraudulent and made a mockery of democratic principles. Everyone was free to vote for whomever they wished, but votes were routinely and openly bought, while the counting was famously corrupt. For example, there might be a convenient power outage just as the votes were to be tabulated, at which time new ballot boxes suddenly appeared, stuffed with votes for the PRI candidate. Further, presidents were chosen with what became known as the *dedazo*, or pointing of the finger. The sitting president signaled who would become the next PRI candidate, in consultation with other PRI leaders. That individual would be pointed to in figurative terms and then would be guaranteed to win the election. The trappings of democracy were all there, including an opposition candidate, but the outcome was preordained.

Mexican Presidentialism

The president in Mexico is not granted broad powers under the constitution, or at least no more extensive than in most presidential systems. That was in line with the revolution's foundational ideal of limiting presidential power. However, the PRI's position gave the president "meta-constitutional" powers, meaning authority that is not spelled out anywhere but is nonetheless real and binding. So, for example, PRI presidents named candidates for the legislature or for governor.

But after the 1988 election, the PRI acceded to a number of measures that formally reduced presidential authority. The head of government of Mexico City became an elected position rather than appointed by the president (and Cuahtémoc Cárdenas won the position in 1997) and the Bank of Mexico became an independent institution, thus more protected from presidential manipulation. Perhaps even more important was the agreement to allow the Federal Electoral Institute to become independent (which it did by 1996), thus ending the PRI's stranglehold on voting. That opened the door for free and fair elections to become reality. In 1997, the PRI lost its majority in the lower house of Congress, which for the first time forced it to work with the political opposition to get legislation passed. That set the stage for the historic 2000 presidential election.

National Economic Restructuring

The strong presidency also fostered important economic changes. Like many other Latin American countries, Mexico embarked on an economic project of import substitution industrialization. Lázaro Cárdenas, president from 1934 to 1940, spearheaded that effort. His most prominent legacy is the nationalization of the oil industry in 1938 (the text of which we examined in Chapter 4), which also involved the creation of the government-owned petroleum company Petróleos Mexicanos (known as PEMEX). By 2009, oil revenue from PEMEX would constitute 40 percent of the federal budget. Despite calls for privatization from some quarters, its nationalist origins still resonate, so there is considerable resistance to handing it back over to private interests.

The constitution explicitly states that the Mexican state controls all land and water and could nationalize for "public utility," though compensation is required. Cárdenas nationalized electricity, railroads, and the telephone industry. Revenue from state-owned industry became an important source of the capital required to subsidize and protect domestic industries, though it would have to be supplemented—sometimes massively—with foreign loans. He also redistributed land to peasants, who became part of the corporatist model of governing. Subsequent governments similarly focused on state-led industrialization, which would continue until the debt crisis.

Cárdenas thus established the foundations for successful one-party rule, giving something to almost everyone. By creating different organizations, he ensured that peasants, workers, business, and the middle class were all loyal to the party, but distinct so that they did not come together in opposition. For example, the National Peasant Federation remained separate from the Mexican Workers Confederation. They served different parts of the economic model (agriculture versus industry) and, therefore, were treated differently. Workers benefited more than peasants from the corporatist model because there was less political pressure to improve the lot of the rural population.

Drawbacks to the Economic Model

At least on the surface, that model was very successful, and especially in terms of economic growth Mexico seemed to be modernizing rapidly. From the 1940s until the early 1970s, average gross domestic product (GDP) growth annually was 6.5 percent. That fell slightly through the 1970s as Mexico went further into debt. Inflation was also low during this period, under 5 percent, which sustained purchasing power. The real minimum wage rose steadily through the 1960s until the mid-1970s. Mexico's National Bank developed a measure, the "Well-Being Index," with variables related to standard of living. It shows a growth rate of 3.7 percent in the 1960s and 2.3 percent in the 1970s.[3] The PRI hoped that the so-called *Mexican Miracle* would propel the country toward developed status.

Yet there were still serious problems, particularly with regard to inequality, which remained high, like in other countries in the region. Internal migration—spurred on by high fertility rates and inattention to the plight of smaller farmers struggling to make a living—was also creating crises in cities. The percentage of the economically active population in agriculture had dropped from 58 percent in 1950 to 39 percent in 1970. Urbanization is an expected outcome of industrialization, but there were insufficient resources to address its effects. By 1970, rural-to-urban migration resulted in 452 slums (called *lost cities*) with around 1.5 million people around Mexico City. By 1977, 41 percent of households had total earnings below the minimum wage. Education and healthcare were lacking. According to the 1980 census, half of Mexican households did not even have running water. In his novel *An Easy Thing*, published in 1977, Mexican author Paco Ignacio Taibo II wrote, "It was part of what it meant to him to be Mexican, sharing in the general bitching over the rise in prices, the cost of *tortillas*, increases in bus fares, pulling his hair out over the TV news, cursing the police and government corruption."[4]

There were also signs of discontent with the nondemocratic nature of the political system. As in much of the world, including of course the United States, during the 1960s Mexican students organized politically. Demographic change that increased the younger populations vis-à-vis the older, along with global events such as decolonization and the Vietnam War, prompted many young people to make their voices heard. They protested the repression of the Gustavo Díaz Ordaz administration (1964–1970), and waves of student strikes were met with a hard-line response by the government. Just days before the beginning of the 1968 Olympic Games in Mexico City, the army fired on a gathering of approximately 10,000 students in the Tlatelolco part of the city, killing and wounding hundreds (the exact number is hotly disputed). The "perfect dictatorship" was indeed sometimes dictatorial.

Theory and Politics of Mexican Development: Local, National, and International Influences

The 1970s saw important changes in both economic and political terms. Public expenditures jumped, and the state expanded its economic presence in key industries such as electricity and steel. Revenues, however, were not keeping pace, and so deficits and debt ballooned. A hint of future crisis arrived in 1976 when the Mexican government was compelled to devalue and obtain a loan from the International Monetary Fund (IMF). Politically, it was undergoing a transition by reform, whereby a process of democratization occurs within the existing rules of the game instead of a sharp break from authoritarian to democratic. The PRI had always wanted some opposition to exist because that granted the regime greater legitimacy. Electoral reforms in 1977 gave opposition parties even more influence, in particular because it added 100 seats to Congress to be allocated according to proportional representation. Parties were also given more access to media. The result was that parties other than the PRI gradually gained a greater political foothold. At first these victories were almost entirely at the provincial level but by the 1980s spread to governorships as well. As the conservative National Action Party's influence grew, so did its support from the business community.

Political Impact of Economic Reforms

The 1980s was therefore a critical decade for both Mexican politics and economics. After years of borrowing and splurging under the ISI model, in 1982 its government became the first to announce its inability to continue paying creditors, and the "lost decade" began. Mexico embarked on a series of reforms, as discussed back in Chapter 4. The IMF worked with the government of Miguel de la Madrid (1982–1988) to enact structural adjustment policies that would reduce government spending, tame inflation, and reestablish economic stability. State industries (though, importantly, not oil) were privatized, spending on infrastructure and social services was cut, subsidies were slashed, and Mexico joined the General Agreement on Trade and Tariffs (which later became the World Trade Organization), thus signaling a new orientation to free trade instead of protecting domestic industry. As in other Latin American countries that underwent structural adjustment policies, the overall result was economic contraction and increased unemployment, but macroeconomic indicators (e.g., inflation) showed clear success.

Many within the PRI believed the de la Madrid administration did not respond adequately to the increasingly insistent demands for political liberalization, a further democratic opening of the political system. The economic crisis and political inflexibility was giving rise to internal discontent. The most visible was led by Cuauhtémoc Cárdenas (son of former president Lázaro Cárdenas), a former PRI governor, who broke away and formed his own party, the Democratic Revolutionary Party (PRD). It represented a new center-left opposition. Cárdenas ran for president in 1988 but lost to PRI candidate Carlos Salinas de

Gortari. Despite the loss, the election was a critical moment because Salinas's vote totals were widely viewed as inflated by fraud (some even claim Cárdenas should have won, though there is no way to be certain), which weakened the PRI's legitimacy. In addition, Cárdenas's strong showing demonstrated that the PRI's grip on power was no longer as strong as in the past.

President Salinas became a polarizing figure in Mexican politics, as he was committed to pushing the country even more rapidly away from the traditional state capitalist economic model. He privatized banks, airline industry, telecommunications, and steel, along with smaller industries such as hotels and funeral parlors. This move brought in badly needed capital and greatly reduced the role of the government in the Mexican economy. He also renegotiated the country's foreign debt, working with the United States to reduce the payment amounts (but thereby increasing the total amount of debt). He reformed the ejido system (through a constitutional amendment), which he argued was not productive, by allowing and even encouraging the sale of land, while simultaneously allowing the land to be used as collateral for loans. This was a major break from a key part of the revolution. Soon, corporations could buy land that was originally intended for poor individuals.

The Importance of NAFTA

Finally, President Salinas reduced the regulations for foreign investment, which was an entrée to his proposal for the **North American Free Trade Agreement (NAFTA)** with the United States and Canada, which went into effect at the beginning of 1994. NAFTA reduced tariffs between the participating countries (which eventually would also include Chile) over a fifteen-year period and created mechanisms for resolving trade-related disputes.

Salinas believed that individual agreements were not sufficient to lock in his reforms. The PRI was openly split between free-market reformers such as Salinas and the "dinosaurs," who believed that the party's traditional corporatist model required a strong state role in the economy. Although Salinas was careful to give the dinosaurs some political space (e.g., cabinet positions) to avoid a rupture, he also sought to protect the policy changes he was making. Passage of NAFTA—a treaty that would be very difficult to roll back—ensured that market reforms would endure and foreign investors would feel confident. In particular, it protected property rights, ensuring that a future government would not nationalize and it allowed for 100 percent foreign ownership of some Mexican companies, rather than forcing joint ventures with Mexican investors.

Deciphering the effects of NAFTA is complicated. It increased the flow of foreign direct investment in the short term, but by 2005 the amount was almost the same as in 1994 (just over $10 billion).[5] It provided access to U.S. markets that were not available before, particularly for agriculture. Trade between the United States and Mexico did grow, but approximately 91 percent of the growth of Mexican exports would have occurred even without NAFTA.[6] Thus, overall trade has increased, which has created jobs and brought in more foreign capital, but it has not necessarily transformed the economy in the way its advocates claimed it would.

NAFTA's impact also depended on geography. In southern Mexico, which is far less developed, farmers found that they could not compete with large agricultural companies that produced crops such as corn and beans with much lower costs. That in turn sparked migration (discussed later in this chapter). In the more industrial north, it brought assembly jobs, as companies wanted a location close to the United States as a way to reduce transportation costs for the finished products. These factories are called *maquiladoras* (see Box 5.1). Wages in maquiladoras remain relatively low, and tax breaks used to lure companies mean that local communities face the challenge of providing services to the mass of people migrating from other parts of Mexico in search of employment.

BOX 5.1

The Maquiladora Program: Local Impacts from International Agreements

International: The maquiladora industry dates back to 1965, as the Mexican government worked to industrialize the northern part of the country (part of the Border Industrialization Program). Its purpose was to bring companies from the United States into Mexico, where they could enjoy lower production and labor costs, and then export the finished goods back into the United States. In practice, it meant creating special economic zones (SEZs) that were exempt from normal Mexican trade laws. In particular, companies can import raw materials, parts, or other necessary components without paying import duties on them. They are also granted tax breaks in return for their investment. Border cities such as Tijuana and Ciudad Juárez burst at the seams with Mexicans from across the country coming to work.

National: Over time, it has become apparent that a gender imbalance exists within the maquiladora industry, though in recent years it has been narrowing (even as that occurs, however, the absolute number of women working in *maquilas* has increased steadily). The majority are women. This trend began as factory owners determined that women were more likely to accept orders than men and less likely to complain or organize. They were also deemed to be more dexterous and so better able to do precision work quickly. These stereotypes persisted to the point that there was a shortage of female labor. Against that backdrop, many Mexican women discovered they could successfully come together to demand better wages and working conditions.

But there is a dark side as well, with evidence of *maquila* managers forcing women to take pregnancy tests. Pregnant women were fired because their condition reduced their ability to work and increased the potential for demands to be made of the factory. Further, although Mexico had developed large (albeit clientelist) labor unions, *maquila* workers were overwhelmingly nonunionized, leaving more open to abusive management.

(Continued)

Labor flexibility was part of the appeal for foreign investors.

Local: There are also complex social consequences of the predominantly female workforce. Young women are becoming more independent, even in financial terms, which forces their families to navigate new relationships, especially in terms of men taking more responsibility for household and childcare duties. For many women, then, assertiveness at work has translated into more independence at home as well. Yet discrimination, both at home and at work, continues to persist.

Discussion Questions
- Can you think of local costs and benefits to inviting foreign investment to a developing country?
- Given the gender implications, what local consequences might we see from an increase in the numbers of women working in maquiladoras?

One challenge for Mexico's economic miracle is that it required a continued and constant flow of foreign investment. The Salinas government worked to maintain a stable exchange rate and, therefore, issued dollar-denominated "tesobonos," bonds that investors felt comfortable with because being in dollars ensured that they were devaluation-proof. Salinas also followed a long tradition of stimulating the economy at the end of his term to boost the chances of his chosen successor.

Changes in the Mexican Economic and Political Models

By the time Ernesto Zedillo took office in 1994, the exchange rate was no longer viable, because the current account deficit was widening. Rebellion in the south, the assassination of a PRI presidential candidate (Luis Donaldo Colosio, whose campaign manager was Zedillo), and concerns about a corrupt banking system prompted investors to cash in their tesobonos. With the fixed exchange rate, Mexican reserves were rapidly being depleted as dollars flowed out.

Zedillo therefore decided to devalue the peso against the dollar, expecting a relatively minor adjustment. Unfortunately, the effect was to create even more of a run on pesos, meaning that investors tried to dump their pesos and get dollars in exchange, which drained Mexico's reserves even more when combined with widespread selling of the tesobonos. Facing economic collapse, Zedillo turned to the United States, which issued an emergency loan of $50 billion to bolster Mexican reserves and reassure skittish investors.

Mexico's recovery was quicker than many expected, particularly because the devaluation made Mexican products cheaper in the United States, thus boosting exports, but the crisis became yet another rallying cry for the growing political opposition. Those cries were bolstered when the newly privatized banking industry collapsed in 1995, requiring a multibillion dollar bailout and thereby calling even more into question the PRI's fitness to lead.

The Zapatistas: Local Response to National and International Influences

Timed deliberately on the same day that NAFTA went into effect, on January 1, 1994, several thousand Zapatistas seized control of a number of towns in Chiapas, the southernmost and poorest state in the Mexican federal system. They issued a declaration, arguing they were following the 1917 constitution and their revolution was intended to free the country. They would march to Mexico City, overcome the army, and free the Mexican people. They were particularly critical of Carlos Salinas, whom they blamed for putting the country into the hands of an elite few: "the supreme and illegitimate federal executive who today holds power." To transmit their message, the Zapatistas used a wide range of technologies, from laptops to cell phones, in a highly effective manner that gave them global publicity and prevented the government from suppressing them.

███████ **ANALYZING DOCUMENTS** ███████

The Zapatista National Liberation Army (EZLN) rocked Mexico at a delicate time, just as it was struggling to recover from economic crisis and enter into a major trade agreement with the United States. Its official declaration was a stark reminder that many Mexicans were not benefiting from economic reform and felt excluded from the national political system.

EZLN Declaration of War December 31, 1993
TODAY WE SAY ENOUGH IS ENOUGH!
TO THE PEOPLE OF MEXICO:
MEXICAN BROTHERS AND SISTERS:

We are the product of 500 years of struggle: first against slavery, then during the War of Independence against Spain led by insurgents, then to avoid being absorbed by North American imperialism, then to promulgate our constitution and expel the French Empire from our soil, and later the dictatorship of Porfirio Díaz denied us the just application of the Reform Laws, and the people rebelled and leaders like Villa and Zapata emerged, poor people just like us. We have been denied the most elemental preparation so that they can use us as cannon fodder and pillage the wealth of our country. They don't care that we have nothing, absolutely nothing, not even a roof over our heads: no land, no work, no health care, no food, no education. Nor are we able to freely and democratically elect our political representatives, nor is there independence from foreigners, nor is there peace nor justice for ourselves and our children.

But today, we say ENOUGH IS ENOUGH. We are the inheritors of the true builders of our nation. The dispossessed, we are millions, and we thereby call upon our brothers and sisters to join this struggle as the only path, so that we will not die of hunger due to the insatiable ambition of a 70-year dictatorship led by a clique of traitors who represent the most conservative and sell-out groups. They are the same ones who opposed Hidalgo and Morelos, the same ones who betrayed Vincente Guerrero, the same ones who sold

(Continued)

half our country to the foreign invader, the same ones who imported a European prince to rule our country, the same ones who formed the "scientific" Porfirista dictatorship, the same ones who opposed the Petroleum Expropriation, the same ones who massacred the railroad workers in 1958 and the students in 1968, the same ones who today take everything from us, absolutely everything.

To prevent the continuation of the above, and as our last hope, after having tried to utilize all legal means based on our Constitution, we go to our Constitution, to apply Article 39, which says:

"National Sovereignty essentially and originally resides in the people. All political power emanates from the people and its purpose is to help the people. The people have, at all times, the inalienable right to alter or modify their form of government."

Therefore, according to our Constitution, we declare the following to the Mexican Federal Army, the pillar of the Mexican dictatorship that we suffer from, monopolized by a one-party system and led by Carlos Salinas de Gortari, the supreme and illegitimate federal executive who today holds power.

According to this Declaration of War, we ask that other powers of the nation advocate to restore the legitimacy and the stability of the nation by overthrowing the dictator.

We also ask that international organizations and the International Red Cross watch over and regulate our battles, so that our efforts are carried out while still protecting our civilian population. We declare now and always that we are subject to the Geneva Accord, forming the EZLN as the fighting arm of our liberation struggle. We have the Mexican people on our side, we have the beloved tri-colored flag, highly respected by our insurgent fighters. We use black and red in our uniform as a symbol of our working people on strike. Our flag carries the following letters, "EZLN," Zapatista National Liberation Army, and we always carry our flag into combat.

Beforehand, we reject any effort to disgrace our just cause by accusing us of being drug traffickers, drug guerrillas, thieves or other names that might be used by our enemies. Our struggle follows the Constitution, which is held high by its call for justice and equality.

Therefore, according to this declaration of war, we give our military forces, the EZLN, the following orders:

First: Advance to the capital of the country, overcoming the Mexican Federal Army, protecting in our advance the civilian population and permitting the people in the liberated area the right to freely and democratically elect their own administrative authorities.

Second: Respect the lives of our prisoners and turn over all wounded to the International Red Cross.

Third: Initiate summary judgments against all soldiers of the Mexican Federal Army and the political police who have received training or have been paid by foreigners, accused of being traitors to our country, and against all those who have repressed and treated badly the civilian population, and robbed, or stolen from, or attempted crimes against the good of the people.

Fourth: Form new troops with all those Mexicans who show their interest in joining our struggle, including those who, being enemy soldiers, turn themselves in without having fought against us, and promise to take orders from the General Command of the EZLN.

Fifth: We ask for the unconditional surrender of the enemy's headquarters before we begin any combat to avoid any loss of lives.

Sixth: Suspend the robbery of our natural resources in the areas controlled by the EZLN.

To the People of Mexico: We, the men and women, full and free, are conscious that the war that we have declared is our last resort, but also a just one. The dictators have been waging an undeclared genocidal war against our people for many years. Therefore we ask for your participation, your decision to support this plan that struggles for work, land, housing, food, health care, education, independence, freedom, democracy, justice and peace. We declare that we will not stop fighting until the basic demands of our people have been met by forming a government of our country that is free and democratic.

JOIN THE INSURGENT FORCES OF THE ZAPATISTA NATIONAL LIBERATION ARMY!

Discussion Questions
- Why do the Zapatistas consider international influences to be very negative?
- For the Zapatistas, who are the "true builders of the nation"?

Source: http://lanic.utexas.edu/project/Zapatistas/chapter01.html

Their direct influence never spread much beyond Chiapas, but the political impact of the Zapatistas was significant. It accelerated the pace of electoral reform and brought international attention to the government's failure to address long-standing rural poverty and allow adequate local representation. The government granted the Zapatistas the right to create their local governments and legitimize the use of indigenous languages. The Zapatista's beginnings were highly public and media saturated. That is no longer the case because the media has turned its attention elsewhere, but there is no doubt that their control of many towns in southern Mexico remains in place. In some places, there are essentially dual governments, or at least split governments.

It is not entirely clear, however, how much indigenous identity is a cement that holds indigenous peoples in Chiapas (or elsewhere) together. As political scientist Todd Eisenstadt argues, "state residents harnessed the movement to redress the state's historically inequitable land distribution through state and federal government agencies."[7] The Zapatistas provided a certain amount of political leverage where before it did not exist, but did not create a unified indigenous movement that could successfully pressure the state to enact desired reforms.

Political Resistance at Other Levels

In addition to the Zapatistas, women mobilized at the grassroots in the 1980s and 1990s, largely as a result of the economic crisis, but also due to the feeling that the PRI was paying too little attention to women's working conditions, gender violence, and health. Prior, there was more of a gulf between women at the local level and those in academia who were studying women's issues. The rise of non-governmental organizations (NGOs) since then has been important for sustaining political momentum. By 1991, all three major parties included women's issues in their platforms, though they did not run many female candidates for office.

The local organization therefore had a national effect. By a law passed in 2002, 30 percent of candidates for the Senate had to be women, excluding 300 districts that have primaries, and by 2008, 40 percent in the Chamber of Deputies. The result was that in the 2003 midterm elections, women won 23 percent of the seats, a 7 percent increase from 2000 (and, indeed, the number would likely have been higher had the primary exemption not been in place). In the newly competitive electoral environment, all parties saw an advantage to including women as a way to garner more votes and thereby win more congressional seats.

Other local-level strategies were also in play. Although the candidacy of Cuauhtémoc Cárdenas was a high-profile national example, the PRD and the older National Action Party (PAN) worked to organize at the local level, running well-organized campaigns that gradually brought victory at, for example, the mayoral level. The PAN was most successful in the north and west of Mexico, with the PRD more in the center and south of the country. From the local level, they moved upward to the state, where the first opposition governor won for the first time in 1989. It is no coincidence that PAN presidential candidate Vicente Fox was a former governor of Guanajuato. Electoral success was built from the ground up. By 1999, 45.4 percent of the Mexican population was governed by either the PAN or the PRD at the municipal level.[8]

In 2000, Cárdenas ran once again for the PRD, against Fox and Francisco Labastida of the PRI. Reformers within the PRI had changed the party's internal rules to allow registered voters to participate in a primary, thus ending the dedazo. Fox won with 42.5 percent (in Mexico no second round is required if a majority is not reached), with Labastida at 36.1 percent and Cárdenas a distant third with 16.6 percent (which effectively ended his political career).

The Process of Democratization in Mexico

Not only did Fox's victory mean the end of the PRI's seventy years of political dominance in Mexico, but it transformed Mexican presidentialism. For years, the legislature had largely been a rubber stamp, convening to follow the general path determined by the president. However, once the PRI lost the presidency in 2000, it suddenly discovered the relevance of the legislature in a presidential democracy. Out of 500 seats in the lower house, the PAN and the Mexican Green Party (PVEM, its coalition partner) won 221, far short of a majority. The PRI won 211. In the Senate, the PAN won only 51 seats out of 128, whereas the PRI garnered 60. Thus, in both houses the PRI had the power to block virtually anything President Fox proposed. Indeed it did so, which meant Fox was unable to fulfill many of his campaign promises. Some, such as creating 1.4 million jobs a year, may well have been impossible regardless. In 2003, the PAN was hit again when it won only 149 seats in the Chamber of Deputies, following the common pattern in democracies of the incumbent party losing seats in midterm elections.

It should be noted, however, that the legislature has built-in weaknesses. It prohibits consecutive reelection, so legislators tend not to have much expertise. During the 2000–2003 legislative session, only 15 percent had previous experience with state or national legislatures.[9] Yet at the same time, the staff in the legislature is quite small compared to the executive, so there is also relatively little permanent support for legislators who require assistance regarding highly specialized and technical topics.

After the more technocratic styles of Salinas and Zedillo, Fox represented a return to a more personal mode of governing. He was charismatic and highly attentive to his public image, successfully appealing to younger Mexican voters who wanted change. The attacks on the United States on September 11, 2001, represented a serious blow to his economic policy because as the U.S. economy slowed down, inevitably so did the Mexican. Mexico slid into a recession that lasted several years, as GDP growth dropped. The Fox administration remained committed to basic market policies inherited from Zedillo but did implement a number of programs aimed at assisting small and medium-sized businesses focused on exports. The goal was to reach at least 10 percent of the firms that required assistance.[10]

The second major political shock for Mexico's presidential system came in the 2006 presidential election. After initial counting, the PAN's Felipe Calderón had a very narrow (0.58 percent) lead over the PRD's Andrés Manuel López Obrador (who ran as part of a leftist coalition), who demanded a recount. Mexico's Federal Electoral Tribunal (IFE) agreed only to recount the votes in specific precincts where alleged irregularities occurred and eventually named Calderón the victor. In response, López Obrador called for a campaign of civil disobedience (which included blocking major thoroughfares in Mexico City and even preventing President Fox from going to give his annual address to Congress). In a dramatic statement, López Obrador proclaimed himself the "legitimate president" of Mexico and laid out his views of Mexican politics. His government would strive to "observe, to listen, and to collect the feelings of all the sectors and all the regions of the country."

▮▮▮▮▮▮▮ ANALYZING DOCUMENTS ▮▮▮▮▮▮▮

Few Mexican politicians in recent years have been as dramatic as Manuel Andrés López Obrador. After the contested 2006 presidential election, he refused to accept Felipe Calderón's victory and gave a speech accepting his supporters' claim that he was the true president of Mexico. Polyarchy in Mexico was stronger, but national unity remained elusive.

Manuel Andrés López Obrador Speech, September 16, 2006

Today is an historic day. This National Democratic Convention has proclaimed the abolition of the current regime of corruption and privilege and has established the foundation for the construction and establishment of a new Republic.

...

This political crisis has as its immediate antecedent the Salinista project, which converted the government into a committee at the service of a minority of bankers, businessmen tied to power, speculators, influence traffickers, and corrupt politicians.

Since the creation of this network of interests and complicities, national politics have been subordinated to the goal of maintaining and increasing the privileges of a small group, without care for the destiny of the country or the fate of the majority of Mexicans.

...

Let's remember that Zedillo, with the support of the PRI and the PAN (the PRIAN) decided to convert private debts of some into public debt.

(Continued)

With the arrival of Vicente Fox this network of complicities was reinforced and made even more vulgar, to the point that an employee of the banker Roberto Hernández was put in charge of the government's finances.

But even more grave is that Fox became a traitor to democracy and dedicated himself tenaciously and blindly, with all the resources at his disposal, to try and destroy us politically.

…

This Convention has decided … to create a new government, founded to exert and defend the rights of the people.

The government that emerges will be obligated to be national. It will have headquarters in the capital of the Republic and, at the same time, it will move in order to observe, to listen, and to collect the feelings of all the sectors and all the regions of the country.

…

I accept the position of President of Mexico because we reject the imposition and rupture of constitutional order. To accept electoral fraud, as some are proposing, and to recognize the usurper government, would imply postponing indefinitely democratic change in the country.

Long live Mexico!

Discussion Questions

- For Andrés Manuel López Obrador, what seems to be the proper connection between the national and local levels?
- What is his view of the other national political parties?

Source: AMLO Web site, http://web.archive.org/web/20080629155759/http://www.amlo.org.mx/noticias/discursos.html?id=55435 (translation by the author)

López Obrador's actions had the unforeseen result of pushing the PRI closer to the PAN. The PRI's presidential candidate, Roberto Madrazo, finished a distant third with only 22 percent of the vote. Further, it won only 106 seats in the Chamber of Deputies and 35 seats in the Senate. All these results represented a significant drop from 2000 and demonstrated to the PRI leadership that some type of political accommodation was necessary to maintain the party's profile. Alarm about the radical rhetoric of many members of the PRD made it even more attractive for the PRI to establish a better working relationship with the PAN. This helps explain why President Calderón faced less gridlock with Congress than his predecessor.

The López Obrador phenomenon also highlights some of the unintended consequences of democratization. As they struggled against the PRI, leaders of the PAN and the PRD were committed to allowing the rank and file of the parties a strong voice and thus maintaining internal democracy. Once the political system broke open, however, winning elections sometimes trumped broad internal dialogue. This has created a dynamic where the push to win at the national level can sacrifice some of the ideals that had been earlier hallmarks of the parties.[11] President Fox was often criticized for not listening to the rank and file at the local level.

Indeed, during Mexico's extended transition (from the hotly contested 1988 presidential election until Vicente Fox's victory in 2000), the parties engaged with each other in "concertacesiones," or gentlemen's agreements that came after extensive negotiations. They are defined more precisely as an "act by which, in cases where official electoral results do not correspond to a reality sensed and witnessed by the electorate, the official winner steps down and cedes to the candidate of the party which was really thought to have won."[12] This reflected the weakness of formal electoral institutions, which had not functioned in the past because the PRI ultimately decided who won and who lost. Eventually, the PAN stopped participating in concertacesiones because the party worked hard to empower the formal institutions. But the results of 2006 presidential elections demonstrated that many Mexicans were still suspicious of electoral machinations.

Nonetheless, twelve years of PAN rule—with considerable drug-related violence during the Calderón administration—led to decreased support for the party, and the PRD was unable to increase its support, which opened the door to the PRI's return to the presidency. Enrique Peña Nieto, a young former governor of the State of Mexico, defeated López Obrador 39–32 percent, with PAN candidate Josefina Vázquez trailing with 28 percent. The PRI was back, but Mexico was a much more democratic country than the last time the party had controlled the executive branch.

Democratization with Decentralization

At the same time, it is interesting to note how the process of democratization has accelerated an already existing move toward decentralization. There was some decentralization after the 1968 massacre in Tlatelolco as a way to re-inspire confidence in the government and create a greater sense of autonomy within the PRI-dominated state. The National System of Democratic Planning was created in 1982 to coordinate economic development planning between local, state, and federal authorities. However, power over the economy was still gripped by the hands of the federal government.

Once opposition parties coalesced, the PRI allowed more decentralization to occur, in part to appease this newly empowered opposition (thereby avoiding open conflict) and also to shift blame away from the national government for problems that arose. Especially after Salinas took office, this went hand in hand with an overall policy of reducing the federal government's role in the economy. Thus, for years state and local elections were more competitive than at the national level. Gradually, the opposition leaders at the local level pushed for more political and fiscal autonomy from the federal government. As these new elected officials were no longer simply political lackeys, suddenly they had an incentive to seek more autonomy and gain control over more policy areas.[13] That is, after all, how you win support and votes.

A major challenge for decentralization in Mexico is the continued inequality between different states. Northern states are much richer than those in the south, and the process of decentralization has not addressed that inequality. By the 1990s, inequality was 10–20 percent worse than it had been in the 1960s and 1970s. Some Mexican states have per capita incomes similar to less developed African countries. Decentralization was occurring precisely when national economic development strategies focused on the industrial north.

As decentralization accelerated along with Mexican democratization, so did judicial reform, which has increased horizontal accountability. Until 1994, for example, the Supreme Court had no powers of judicial review and, like the legislature, followed the president's lead. Reforms pushed by President Zedillo in 1994 required the president to obtain a two-third vote in the legislature for approval of a justice (thus making it more difficult to push through a favored candidate). Further, it gave the court the power to adjudicate disputes between branches of the government (or between different levels in the federal system) and decide on the constitutionality of laws at the federal or state levels. Judicial independence has increased, so that the Supreme Court is increasingly asserting itself against the executive branch and hearing more cases than in the past.

Reforms in 2008 also significantly modified the judicial system. Prior, defendants were considered guilty until proven innocent. Under this Napoleonic system, judges made decisions without juries and the proceedings were not public. The reforms switched the system to one that assumes innocence, utilizes juries, and is public. The lower courts are still beset by corruption, which has been a long-standing problem with the Mexican judicial system. Thus, accountability at the local level remains problematic, as average citizens face serious obstacles in seeking justice. With the changes that are occurring at the Supreme Court level, however, it is possible that a new example of probity will filter downward.

Migration: The Confluence of International, National, and Local

An emphasis on political institutions still leaves out an important part of the Mexican political and economic story, namely immigration. Of course, given the long shared border and highly unequal economies, Mexicans had always moved across the border in search of work. That movement was often circulatory, as people went back and forth with regularity. For example, someone might follow seasonal agricultural harvests and then come back to Mexico for a time with the added income. The Mexican government's (meaning the PRI's) official stance was against immigration, in particular because it represented a stark failure of the Mexican revolution to provide economically for the population. If the revolution was so beneficial to the common person, then why were so many of them leaving? However, the Mexican state did not have the capacity to do much about it.

In response to the large numbers of **undocumented immigrants** (especially, but not by no means exclusively, Mexicans), referring to people residing illegally in the United States (i.e., without legal documentation), in 1986 the U.S. Congress passed the Immigration Reform and Control Act (IRCA). The purpose of IRCA was to legalize immigrants already in the country (ultimately about 3 million immigrants were able to become permanent legal residents and roughly 2.3 million were of Mexican origin) and then to "close the door" by requiring more documentation for hiring, cracking down on businesses, and increasing border security (measures along those lines have continued to expand ever since). However, the legislation had unintended consequences. Given the availability of jobs in the United States, migrants kept coming. But as the trip was more difficult than before, there was a strong incentive to remain in the United States rather than moving back and forth. Lastly, it spawned a thriving business of fraudulent documents, particularly social security cards. Businesses needed only to make a good faith effort to check documents, and so fakes were sufficient to obtain employment.

Another unintended consequence came as a result of NAFTA, which policy makers had claimed would reduce undocumented immigration by spurring on job creation in Mexico. However, Mexican farmers with small land holdings could not compete with large agricultural businesses in the United States (and to a lesser degree in Canada). Farmers (and eventually their families) therefore moved to the cities, and given few employment opportunities there (or very low-paying jobs), they made their way to border cities and then into the United States. This has an important local impact, because many small towns in Mexico have lost a large proportion of their working-age population. Grandparents take care of children whose parents are working in the United States and sending **remittances** back home.

Although remittances bring much-needed money into these communities ($22 billion in 2012), there is increasing concern about the social impact of absent parents, as well as the economic impact. Remittances do not necessarily spark economic growth in Mexico and can represent another aspect of dependency on foreign economies. When the U.S. economy crashed in late 2008, the ripple effect hit Mexico quite quickly as remittances dropped. To ensure greater capture of remitted funds, the Calderón administration has implemented programs such as Tres por Uno (Three for One), whereby the government will provide matching funds for remittances used for development projects. In addition, since the 1990s Mexico has enacted a number of policies intended to engage Mexican migrants and keep them connected. This included allowing Mexicans outside the country to vote in presidential elections as well as dual citizenship.

Post-PRI presidents have made migration a priority and have been far more vocal than any past administration. President George W. Bush had signaled that he would tackle the issue, but the September 11 attacks shifted his attention, and when in 2003 President Fox voted against the U.S.-sponsored resolution in the United Nations to authorize the use of force against Saddam Hussein in Iraq (at the time Mexico was one of the rotating members of the Security Council), he received the cold diplomatic shoulder for several years. Felipe Calderón was highly critical after President Bush began pursuing immigration reform again in 2006. He also made the first efforts to address the human rights plight of undocumented immigrants from Central America in southern Mexico.

Drugs: The Local and National Effects of International Trade

Drug trafficking has always been an issue for Mexico, because its long border with the target market, combined with weak and corrupt law enforcement, made it a prime area for transshipment of cocaine from the Andean region. As profits grew, Mexican drug traffickers also began producing marijuana. Drug trafficking organizations such as Los Zetas became entrenched in a number of different cities. But not until the twenty-first century did drug trafficking create the high levels of violence that have become a serious concern, particularly for border cities such as Tijuana and Ciudad Juárez. Between 2006 and 2012, there were about 60,000 deaths due to drug-related violence in Mexico. These murders are often grisly, intended to serve as warnings to anyone—politician, judge, journalist, and so on—that if they dig too deeply, they may suffer the same fate.

The violent atmosphere in Ciudad Juárez has had a serious impact on women. Hundreds of women have been killed in the two decades, and most of the cases are not solved. In response, local NGOs have helped to bring cases to the attention of both the Mexican government and the international community. The lower house of the legislature even created a Special Committee on Femicide to find ways for the national government to take a more active role. The process of finding murderers, however, has been agonizingly slow.

Especially under President Calderón, the Mexican government's response to violence and drug trafficking was to expand the police and employ the military. This approach was bolstered in 2008 when the U.S. Congress approved the Merida Initiative, a security agreement for $1.4 billion over three years that focused on the military and police. President Calderón also successfully advocated for legalization of small amounts of drugs (including marijuana, cocaine, and heroin), a measure that Fox had previously vetoed, as a way to direct resources more at the drug lords. Fox shifted 180 degrees, advocating in 2010 for drug legalization.

Mexico's proximity to the United States remains a core part of the problem. Demand for illegal drugs remains high, and so the rise of the cartels can be viewed in economic terms simply as the market working to generate enough supply. The fight between the cartels and their attacks can be viewed in similar terms. In addition, approximately 90 percent of the guns in Mexico have come from the United States, despite efforts to slow the weapons trade.

Many commentators have therefore labeled Mexico a *failed state*, and a 2009 Defense Department document indicated it was at risk of becoming one, along with Pakistan. The dilemma was whether the Mexican state was strong enough to withstand the barrage of drug-fuelled violence and corruption, or whether parts of the country would be run by the cartels. Such a conclusion is premature. Nonetheless, there is no doubt that lawlessness and murder remain serious obstacles to stability in some parts of Mexico, especially near the border with the United States.

The challenges of both immigration and drugs underline the very complicated relationship Mexico has with the United States. A history of intervention has left Mexican policy makers sensitive to U.S. foreign policy pressure. Thus, Mexico has maintained a relationship with the governments of Fidel and Raúl Castro, voted against the use of force in Iraq, and later openly criticized the failure of the U.S. Congress to pass immigration reform while emphasizing the demand side of the "drug war."

Polls show that Mexicans are greatly concerned with security, along with the effects of the global economic crisis. Confidence in the government to address those problems is not high. Voters punished the PAN in the 2012 legislative elections, as the party won only 114 of 500 total seats. The PRI won 212 and the PRI took 104 (four other parties won the remaining 20 seats). As in any presidential democracy, divided government presents a challenge to the executive, who must coordinate and negotiate more and more with a sometimes hostile opposition that itself is eyeing the next presidential election.

TABLE 5.1 Mexican Economic Indicators, 1991–2011

Year	GDP Growth	Inflation	Unemployment	Poverty Rate	Human Development Index
1991	4.4	18.8	2.7	—	0.842
1992	3.7	11.9	2.8	—	0.804
1993	1.7	8.0	3.4	—	0.845
1994	4.6	7.1	3.7	35.8	0.853
1995	−6.2	52.1	6.2	—	0.771
1996	5.5	27.7	5.5	43.4	—
1997	7.0	17.6	3.7	—	0.786
1998	4.5	18.6	4.7	38.0	0.784
1999	3.8	12.3	3.7	—	—
2000	6.6	9.0	3.4	—	—
2001	0.0	4.4	3.6	—	0.800
2002	0.8	5.7	3.9	39.4	0.802
2003	1.4	4.0	4.6	—	—
2004	4.2	5.4	5.3	—	—
2005	2.8	3.3	4.7	—	0.829
2006	4.8	4.1	4.6	31.7	—
2007	3.4	3.8	4.8	—	—
2008	1.5	6.5	4.9	34.8	—
2009	−6.1	3.6	6.7	—	—
2010	5.3	4.3	6.5	—	0.770
2011	3.9	3.4	6.0	—	0.773

Sources: Unemployment: *GDP and Inflation: Preliminary Overview of the Economies of Latin America and the Caribbean*, 1994–2012.
Poverty rate: *Social Panorama of Latin America*, Economic Commission for Latin America, 1990–2012.
Human Development Index: United Nations, *Human Development Report*, 1990–2013.

Conclusion and Comparative Perspective

Marisol Valles's experience is an excellent example of how democratization is never painless or easy, especially when combined with potent international influences. Drug trafficking and the violence that comes along with it complicate local politics, national policy making, and international relations. A difficult question for Mexican politics is whether democracy can endure when individuals are actively afraid to run even for local office. Colombia in its darkest moments bears some similarity in that regard, and the road toward reducing fear was long and arduous.

In many ways, democratization makes policy making less efficient at the national level. In a presidential system, it can foster legislative inaction as the president of one party struggles to overcome congressional resistance from the opposition. Mexico's presidency is not as strong as many others in Latin America, so once the meta-constitutional powers evaporated, the president had more political rivals to contend with.

Mexico also shows how modernization is a delicate process. As in other countries like Bolivia, economic strategies employed during the "miracle" boom years in Mexico led directly to depression in the 1980s, and even greater dislocation and urbanization. It remains notable, however, that the negative effects of "modernization" did not bring the military into the center of politics. Ironically, the path to democratization was the opposite of modernization theory, because democracy took root largely as a result of modernization's failures. As the PRI could not live up to its promises and maintain ISI, its image shattered and opened political space for the opposition.

International factors continue to be critical both to Mexico's economy and to politics. The long border and looming presence of the United States are impossible to ignore, particularly because the market for immigrant labor and drugs in the United States is close to insatiable. Mexico is dependent in many ways on the economy of its northern neighbor, but political change within the country has had significant effects on the economy as well.

Mexico is unique because it is the only Latin American country to share a border—a very long one at that—with the United States. Nonetheless, its example of political and economic development shares a number of characteristics with its Latin American counterparts. Like Argentina, for example, its experiment with import substitution industrialization led to the piling up of debt and ultimately high inflation and inability to pay. In addition, like Central America and much of the Caribbean its economy is increasingly becoming dependent on the primary product of its human labor, with remittances bringing in billions of dollars annually.

Mexico does not allow presidential reelection, which is unusual for the region, but its concentration of power in the executive branch is a hallmark of many other Latin American countries. However, the constant political fight between the national and state governments is also notable, and similar to those in other federal systems such as Argentina and Brazil. Unfortunately, one of the biggest political challenges for Mexico is how to address drug trafficking, which is becoming sadly similar to the drug cartel wars that took place (and still simmer) in Colombia.

Key Terms

- Ejido
- Institutional Revolutionary Party (PRI)
- Corporatism
- North American Free Trade Agreement (NAFTA)
- Undocumented immigrants
- Remittances

Discussion Questions

- How has Mexican presidentialism changed after the PRI lost the presidency in 2000?
- How has the Mexican government's political response to immigration changed over time?
- What are the key benefits and costs of Mexico's switch from ISI to market capitalism?
- Has the U.S.–Mexican relationship changed significantly after the PRI lost its hold on the presidency?
- To what degree does decentralization in Mexico seem to contribute to democratization?

Further Sources

Books

Camp, Roderic Ai. *Politics in Mexico*, 5th edition (New York: Oxford University Press, 2007). This is an excellent overview of Mexican politics. It covers a wide variety of topics, from the formal structures of Mexican political institutions to the beliefs of Mexicans and foreign policy.

Crandall, Russell, Guadalupe Paz, and Riordan Roett, eds. *Mexico's Democracy at Work: Political and Economic Dynamics* (Boulder: Lynne Rienner Publishers, 2005). A well-written concise analysis, broken into categories of politics, economics, and foreign policy. It has the added benefit of including authors from both the United States and Mexico.

Fitzgerald, David. *A Nation of Emigrants: How Mexico Manages its Migration* (Berkeley: University of California Press, 2009). Fitzgerald examines the changes in Mexican policies toward emigrants, which moved from hostile to ambivalent to supportive over time. It focuses in particular on the relationship between emigrant and nationhood and how the Mexican state has addressed the two.

Haber, Stephen, Herbert S. Klein, Noel Maurer, and Kevin J. Middlebrook. *Mexico Since 1980* (New York: Cambridge University Press, 2008). Written by well-known experts on Mexico, the book provides a very readable and insightful analysis of contemporary Mexican politics, economics, and social change. It is very useful for understanding the interplay between those three variables.

Wuhs, Steven T. *Savage Democracy: Institutional Change and Party Development in Mexico* (University Park, PA: The Pennsylvania State University Press, 2008). The book takes a unique perspective from within political parties in Mexico, which reveals the conflicts that arise in democracies. "Savage democracy" ensues when parties have to compromise internal democracy to win elections.

Web Sites

Bank of Mexico (http://www.banxico.org.mx/indexEn.html). Mexico's central bank maintains a highly detailed Web site in English. It contains up-to-date statistics on a variety of economic indicators, bank publications, speeches, and presentations. It also offers an RSS feed to receive new information as it is made public.

Guadalajara Reporter (http://www.theguadalajarareporter.com/). It is an English-language newspaper. Despite its base in Guadalajara, it publishes national as well as regional political news items. It also offers weekly podcasts.

Mexico Institute (http://www.wilsoncenter.org/index.cfm?fuseaction=topics. home&topic_id=5949). This is the Web site of the Woodrow Wilson International Center for Scholars. It includes a large number of reports and documents on Mexican politics, economics, and immigration. The site also has the Mexico Portal, a free news feed available through RSS feeds.

The National Security Archive: The Mexico Project (http://www.gwu.edu/~nsarchiv/ mexico/). Mexico is one of the National Security Archive's projects, so there is a wide range of primary documents available, including material on the Tlatelolco massacre, the EZLN, the Mexican military, and Mexican elections.

Presidency of Mexico (http://www.presidencia.gob.mx/en/). The government maintains a useful Web site in English, providing information about the presidency and Congress, press releases, news stories, videos, and links to the government's presence on the Internet (YouTube, Twitter, etc.).

Endnotes

1. Roderic Ai Camp, *Politics in Mexico, Fifth Edition* (New York: Oxford University Press, 2007), 46.
2. Carmen Ramos Escandón, "Women's Movements, Feminism, and Mexican Politics," in *The Women's Movement in Latin America: Participation and Democracy,* ed. Jane S. Jaquette (Boulder: Westview Press, 1994).
3. Camp 2007, 284.
4. Paco Ignacio Taibo II, *An Easy Thing* (New York: Penguin Books, 1990), 18.
5. Stephen Haber, Herbert S. Klein, Noel Maurer, and Kevin J. Middlebrook, *Mexico Since 1980* (New York: Cambridge University Press, 2008), 75.
6. J. F. Hornbeck, *NAFTA at Ten: Lessons from Recent Studies.* CRS Report for Congress RS21737, February 21, 2004, 2.
7. Todd A. Eisenstadt, "Agrarian Tenure Institution Conflict Frames, and Communitarian Identities: The Case of Indigenous Southern Mexico," *Comparative Political Studies* 42, 1 (2009), 84.
8. Haber, Klein, Maurer, and Middlebrook 2008, 150.
9. Camp 2007, 187.
10. Manuel Pastor and Carol Wise, "The Fox Administration and the Politics of Economic Transition," in *Mexico's Democracy at Work: Political and Economic Dynamics,* eds. Russell Crandall, Guadalupe Paz, and Riordan Roett (Boulder: Lynne Rienner Publishers, 2005), 103.
11. Steven T. Wuhs, *Savage Democracy: Institutional Change and Party Development in Mexico* (University Park: The Pennsylvania State University Press, 2008).
12. Todd A. Eisenstadt, "Mexico's Postelectoral Concertacesiones: The Rise and Demise of a Substitutive Informal Institution," in *Informal Institution and Democracy: Lessons from Latin America,* eds. Gretchen Helmke and Steven Levitsky (Baltimore: The Johns Hopkins University Press, 2006), 228.
13. Carolina C. Beer, "Electoral Competition and Fiscal Decentralization in Mexico," in *Decentralization and Democracy in Latin America,* eds. Alfred P. Montero and David J. Samuels (Notre Dame, IN: University of Notre Dame Press, 2004).

CHAPTER 6

Central America

TIMELINE

1821	Independence declared
1914	Panama Canal first used
1933	Anastasio Somoza named head of National Guard in Nicaragua
1949	Costa Rica abolishes military
1954	United States overthrows Jacobo Arbenz in Guatemala
1961	FSLN created
1979	Sandinistas overthrow Anastasio Somoza
1980	Civil war in El Salvador begins
1989	United States invades Panama
1990	Violeta Chamorro wins Nicaraguan presidential election
1992	Civil war in El Salvador ends
1996	Civil war in Guatemala ends
2005	CAFTA passed
2009	First leftist president in El Salvador (Mauricio Funes) elected
2009	Coup in Honduras

International influence has been a crucial part of Central American political and economic development. At times this has even led to a sort of chameleon politics, where political elites shift their political preferences according to changes in international political winds. **Daniel Ortega** led a successful revolution in Nicaragua, overthrowing a dictator who remained in power primarily because of support from the United States. Decrying that influence, he embarked on a Marxist-inspired transformation of the country. Yet years later, as a democratically elected president in the postrevolutionary era, he praised free trade with the United States and forged agreements with the International Monetary Fund. As two scholars of Nicaragua put it, despite the fact that Ortega periodically criticized the United States, he was "curiously submissive to the demands of its old enemy." [1] Such is the power of international actors.

Central American countries have faced immense challenges since independence. Persistent poverty and inequality, elite politics, economic dependence, foreign intervention, and military coups are just a few of the obstacles the subregion continues to deal with. International influence in Central America has been very high. A mixture of foreign investors, mercenaries, and external

COSTA RICA	EL SALVADOR
Population: 4.3 million	**Population:** 6.1 million
Size: 20,000 square miles	**Size:** 8,100 square miles
Capital: San José	**Capital:** San Salvador
Currency: Colón	**Currency:** U.S. Dollar

GUATEMALA	HONDURAS	NICARAGUA	PANAMA
Population: 13.8 million	**Population:** 8.1 million	**Population:** 5.7 million	**Population:** 3.5 million
Size: 42,000 square miles	**Size:** 43,300 square miles	**Size:** 50,200 square miles	**Size:** 29,200 square miles
Capital: Guatemala City	**Capital:** Tegucigalpa	**Capital:** Managua	**Capital:** Panama City
Currency: Quetzal	**Currency:** Lempira	**Currency:** Córdoba	**Currency:** Balboa & U.S. Dollar

Regional Map of Central America

intervention of varying kinds has always strongly affected Central American political and economic development. Honduras, for example, was the country for which the term *banana republic* was first used, denoting the very opposite of modern. Instead, Central American countries were considered backward, corrupt, and tied to primary products like bananas.

Yet despite important similarities, the countries of Central America have evolved in different ways. This chapter analyzes the conceptual and empirical similarities between the countries but will then also pay attention to the specific ways in which they have diverged. Costa Rica in particular will offer a very different picture than its neighbors. Central American countries differ considerably in terms of political parties. Guatemala has a fairly chaotic party system, where none remains in existence for long, while the parties in El Salvador have roots going back to the civil wars. Nicaragua is somewhere in between because it has a party (the Sandinistas) dating back to the 1980s, but it has been badly fragmented by defections. All have strong presidential systems.

All Central American countries have unitary governments, and power has traditionally rested within the executive branch. There are still elections for local offices (such as mayors), but local government depends to a significant degree on the central government in the capital. Central government officials can also manipulate rules to harass local candidates and even to disqualify them. In the case of El Salvador, for example, this has been labeled *electoral authoritarianism*.[2]

Historical Roots of Political and Economic Development

Central American countries declared their independence in 1821, at the same time as Mexico. Mexico controlled the region for two years, at which point Central America declared itself independent. Until 1838 it remained a loose confederation. The dream of some sort of Central American union has never completely died, but nationalist rivalries remain a permanent impediment. In the nineteenth century, those antagonisms were even more complex because they included internal divisions within Liberal and Conservative ranks, who were already at each other's throats.

Costa Rica had similar characteristics but was different in important ways. The Spanish considered it a backwater because it had only a small indigenous population (and therefore no source of forced labor) and no precious metals for quick profit. As a result, it developed with less repression and more autonomy. The relative lack of labor meant there were more small landowners and a broader distribution of land. This combination of factors tempered Liberal–Conservative conflicts and reduced the violence associated with them.

Dependency theory is particularly relevant for Central America, which from the beginning was reliant on foreign capital for economic growth and primary products for exports. By the late nineteenth century, fruit and coffee in particular were the main exports, and low-wage laborers remained tied to land owned by a small wealthy elite, much of which was foreign. That in turn led to greater international attention from governments, investors, and mercenaries from other countries. Foreign intervention was a serious problem in the nineteenth century, as in Nicaragua where a U.S. citizen named William Walker briefly took control in the midst of a civil war and proclaimed himself president in 1856. In addition to adventurers, there were many investors seeking their fortunes, both from the United States and from Europe (particularly Great Britain). They built infrastructure, such as railroads, and soon became interested in constructing an isthmus canal. That even led to the Clayton-Bulwer Treaty in 1850, where the United States and Great Britain agreed not to build a canal without the consent of the other. Central American consent was not considered relevant.

Throughout most of the nineteenth and well into the twentieth century, Central Americans lived under dictatorships of varying stripes. As in other parts of Latin America, the struggles between liberal and conservative regimes fostered instability, and all governments were dominated by small minorities that controlled the vast majority of resources. Liberal governments gained supremacy by the latter part of the century, which meant they oriented their economies to exports and invited foreign investment as part of an overall economic development strategy. Liberal governance was aided by an influential international presence, most notably Great Britain (especially in the nineteenth century) and the United States, but also Germany, which had interests in the coffee industry, shipping, and manufacturing. The export of primary products constituted the backbone of the economies, and local needs are all too often ignored.

The late nineteenth and early twentieth centuries are important for understanding the trajectories that each country took. Sociologist James Mahoney argues that decisions made by liberal governments at that time pushed each country in different directions that had long-term local consequences.[3] Liberal elites either attacked communal landholding patterns, which entailed harsh dictatorships (in El Salvador and Guatemala), preserved small farms, which led to more democratic structures (e.g., Costa Rica), or maintained existing traditional structures, which led to less harsh dictatorships (in Nicaragua and Honduras).

Costa Rica

Costa Rica suffered similar national liberal–conservative disputes as its neighbors, including military governments, but they tended to be less violent and both sides were more willing to enact local reforms for small farmers, for example, that served to avoid total domination by a small elite. In the early twentieth century, this contributed to the expansion of suffrage and the introduction of direct elections that provided for greater political competition and vertical accountability. The result was that in 1919 the last military dictatorship left power.

The Great Depression was an important turning point for Costa Rican democracy, as the working class and middle class alike looked for solutions to the economic crisis, but were wary of authoritarian rule. Fraudulent elections in the 1940s, however, intensified political polarization in the country, as did Communist participation in the government. The dominant figure of the times was José Figueres, a coffee grower who had been vocal about the problems of

◾ COSTA RICA'S POLITICAL INSTITUTIONS ◾

Last constitution: 1953 (1949)

Unitary government with seven provinces

Executive: President with four-year term, one nonconsecutive reelection

Legislative: Unicameral Legislative Assembly with fifty-seven members elected by proportional representation

Judicial: Supreme Court of Justice with judicial review

---

corruption in the country (and who planned a so-called Caribbean Pact, intended to overthrow dictatorships across Central America, such as Anastasio Somoza in Nicaragua). Fighting broke out after the 1948 presidential election, and Figueres organized his own troops to defeat the Costa Rican army (which he then disbanded). He set up a junta that ruled until 1949, and a commission wrote a new constitution that abolished the army entirely.

Abolishing the military was an essential element of Costa Rica's future stability and prosperity. Research has shown that the buildup of large militaries had severe consequences for democracy, equity, and long-term economic growth in Central America.[4] In the Costa Rican case, successive governments were able to spend more on economic development projects and social welfare than on defense. In addition, even when political conflict arose (such as in the 1950s), there were only civilian institutions involved and no military to act as political arbiter, as militaries across Latin America often did. The Costa Rican model was not copied elsewhere, and the confluence of domestic and international contexts did not last long. In particular, the Cold War made militaries the most important actors in fighting Communism.

As Costa Rican democracy developed, it was marked by a weak executive, which is exceptional in the region. For example, if the president calls for emergency powers, they must be approved by Congress immediately; the president cannot veto the national budget; presidents must wait eight years before running for reelection; the legislature must approve all treaties; and cabinet members may be censured.[5] The effect has been to enhance the importance of political parties. The National Liberation Party (PLN) has been the dominant party in Costa Rican politics, although it has faced criticism for the effects of market reforms it pushed through in the 1990s. That has led to a split within the party as well as the rise of others, such as the Social Christian Party (PUSC). The PUSC, however, has had its own internal squabbles and smaller third parties have grown significantly in the 2000s.

Costa Rica firmly entered the international stage under President Oscar Arias, who was first president from 1986 until 1990. He won the Nobel Peace Prize for his efforts to forge the Esquipulas II Accords in 1987 (named for the town in Guatemala where it was signed), which sought to end civil war in Central America and assembled a plan for political reconciliation, the end of hostilities, and a path toward democratization. Arias won the presidency again in 2006 and took an active international role by taking the diplomatic lead after the Honduran coup in 2009. Although he was unsuccessful in restoring President **José Manuel ("Mel") Zelaya** to the Honduran presidency (discussed later in the chapter), his efforts were a symbol of the continued relevance of Costa Rica for regional politics.

Like other Central American countries, Costa Rica faces the ever-growing internationally driven problem of drug trafficking, as drugs make their way from South America through Mexico to the United States. That brings violence with it, which is a relatively new phenomenon for the country. For example, it was the last country in Central America to have an MS-13 gang presence. It was also one of the last to sign agreements with the United States to share intelligence and coordinate antigang activities, such as the Central American Law Enforcement Exchange (which brings law enforcement officials from the United States and Central America together), but eventually policy makers felt it was necessary. Although the problem is far less severe than in El Salvador or Guatemala, it is greater than it was a decade ago.

Given the growth of drug trafficking organizations across Central America, it is unfortunately likely that Costa Rica will begin to suffer economic and social costs. Unlike its neighbors, however, it has a more solid economic base to cushion the potential blows. Costa Rica serves as an example that even countries traditionally dependent on primary products can democratize and diversify. Its stability has led to a thriving tourist industry and solid economic growth since the mid-2000s after an economic downturn from 2000 to 2003. Like the rest of the region, Costa Rica experienced contraction after 2008, but both poverty and inequality are still much lower than its counterparts.

El Salvador

In the wake of the global depression, the early 1930s were marked by political upheaval. A 1931 coup brought General Maximiliano Hernández Martínez to power, and the following year he crushed a peasant uprising so violently that it became known just as *la Matanza* (*the killing*). Among the 30,000 dead was Farabundo Martí, an activist in the Communist Party and the leader of a guerrilla organization dedicated to overthrowing the government. Like Augusto Sandino in Nicaragua, he became a martyr and the namesake of a future guerrilla group and later political party, the **Farabundo Martí National Liberation Front (FMLN)**.

The military never left its position of political importance, and from 1931 until 1979 the president was a military officer (sometimes elected, other times not). The Cuban revolution started a process of greater paranoia and increased repression. Political parties did form, most notably the Christian Democratic Party (PDC) and the National Conciliation Party (PCN). The PDC in particular (under the leadership of José Napoleón Duarte) sought to weaken the grip of the small oligarchy on politics, and ideological splinters also appeared in the army. A 1979 coup briefly brought reformist elements within the army to power in alliance with the PDC, but it was badly divided and could not control the more conservative military elements that favored a very hardline response

EL SALVADOR'S POLITICAL INSTITUTIONS

Last constitution: 1983

Unitary government with fourteen departments

Executive: President with five-year term, no reelection

Legislative: Unicameral Legislative Assembly with eighty-four members elected by proportional representation

Judicial: Supreme Court with judicial review

to reform. The FMLN was created in 1980 as a coalition to begin leftist armed insurrection, and the Salvadoran civil war began. That same year, Salvadoran Archbishop Oscar Romero was murdered by a death squad as he gave mass in the cathedral, in retaliation for his strong criticisms of the government. That continues to resound: President Barack Obama even visited his crypt in 2011.

The tipping point of international influence was the election of U.S. President Ronald Reagan, who in 1981 began sending more economic and military aid to the government. Throughout the 1980s, the United States sent upward of $6 billion to El Salvador. The essence of President Reagan's policy toward Central America was that the conflicts were international rather than national and local. From that perspective, unrest should be blamed on Cuba and the Soviet Union rather than on Salvadoran politics. In other words, because of the Marxist flavor of revolutionary movements, especially in El Salvador and Nicaragua, the world was watching and would look for any sign of weakness on the part of the United States. Intervention was therefore not simply desirable but required. Otherwise, U.S. allies would lose faith in the country's resolve, and enemies would be emboldened by the superpower's inaction.

The war lasted until 1992, when the Chapultepec Accords were signed. The FMLN successfully fought the government to a standstill, including high-profile attacks in the capital San Salvador itself. The Cold War was winding down, so international pressures faded. As a result, negotiations began in the late 1980s to end the fighting. The Truth Commission for El Salvador, completed in 1993, lays out the grim facts. Each side targeted anyone deemed even remotely connected to the other down to the smallest village so that thousands of innocent people, even "pleasure-seekers," were killed. The commission report sums it up succinctly: "The warped psychology engendered by the conflict led to a convulsion of violence."

ANALYZING DOCUMENTS

The Commission on the Truth in El Salvador was commissioned in 1992 by the United Nations to investigate human rights abuses committed during the civil war (1980–1992). It details the horrific crimes committed against more than 7,000 Salvadorans. As in other Central American wars, international factors—especially the Cold War and the role of the United States—were central.

(Continued)

El Salvador Truth Commission Report (2003)

Between 1980 and 1991, the Republic of El Salvador in Central America was engulfed in a war which plunged Salvadorian society into violence, left it with thousands and thousands of people dead and exposed it to appalling crimes, until the day—16 January 1992—when the parties, reconciled, signed the Peace Agreement in the Castle of Chapultepec, Mexico, and brought back the light and the chance to re-emerge from madness to hope.

. . .

The warped psychology engendered by the conflict led to a convulsion of violence. The civilian population in disputed or guerrilla-controlled areas was automatically assumed to be the enemy, as at El Mozote and the Sumpul river. The opposing side behaved likewise, as when mayors were executed, the killings justified as acts of war because the victims had obstructed the delivery of supplies to combatants, or when defenceless pleasure-seekers became military targets, as in the case of the United States marines in the Zona Rosa of San Salvador. Meanwhile, the doctrine of national salvation and the principle of "he who is not for me is against me" were cited to ignore the neutrality, passivity and defencelessness of journalists and church workers, who served the community in various ways.

Such behaviour also led to the clandestine refinement of the death squads:

The bullet which struck Monsignor Romero in the chest while he was celebrating mass on 24 March 1980 in a San Salvador church is a brutal symbol of the nightmare the country experienced during the war. And the murder of the six Jesuit priests 10 years later was the final outburst of the delirium that had infected the armed forces and the innermost recesses of certain government circles. The bullet in the portrait of Monsignor Romero, mute witness to this latest crime, repeats the nightmare image of those days.

. . .

The mass of reports, testimony, newspaper and magazine articles and books published in Spanish and other languages that was accumulated prompted the establishment within the Commission on the Truth itself of a centre for documentation on the different forms of violence in El Salvador. The public information relating to the war (books, pamphlets, research carried out by Salvadorian and international bodies); testimony from 2,000 primary sources referring to more than 7,000 victims; information from secondary sources relating to more than 20,000 victims; information from official bodies in the United States and other countries; information provided by government bodies and FMLN; an abundant photographic and videotape record of the conflict and even of the Commission's own activities; all of this material constitutes an invaluable resource—a part of El Salvador's heritage because (despite the painful reality it records) a part of the country's contemporary history—for historians and analysts of this most distressing period and for those who wish to study this painful reality in order to reinforce the effort to spread the message "never again."

Discussion Questions

- What were some of the local effects of the political violence in El Salvador?
- According to the report, what was the overall attitude of the national government during that period?

Source: http://www.derechos.org/nizkor/salvador/informes/truth.html

That intensity of violence prompted large-scale migration to the United States, which connected the two countries well into the future. Not only did the Salvadoran immigrant population grow in the United States, but Salvadoran youth formed the extremely violent Mara Salvatrucha gang in Los Angeles to protect themselves from Mexican-American gangs. The *maras* then exported themselves (or in some cases were forcibly deported) back to El Salvador, where they became heavily involved in drug trafficking. It became a vicious cycle with no clear end in sight.

In the aftermath of the war, the FMLN became incorporated as a political party, but the conservative Republican Alliance (ARENA) party took the presidency and held it until 2009. Since 1992, El Salvador has had a polyarchy without illegal interruptions of government. The FMLN did well in congressional elections, and the balance between the two parties slowly strengthened horizontal accountability. Nonetheless, the country faced daunting problems, especially gang and drug-related violence. ARENA's promarket policies did not reduce poverty or inequality significantly, and the minimal local impact left many Salvadorans more and more dependent on remittances (to the tune of about $4 billion a year). The net result has been a surge in violent crime, with transnational ties. Insecurity is a major complaint of Salvadorans, and has yet to be addressed effectively.

Yet there is potential. Salvador has one of the most industrialized economies of Central America. Widespread privatization in the 1990s spurred foreign industrial investment, especially in the maquiladora industries. Textiles, metals, and chemical fertilizers are examples of these exports. The country also continues to focus on coffee production. Foreign investment has also been encouraged by dollarization, which occurred in 2001. Unlike Ecuador, where dollarization was implemented in 2000, in El Salvador it took place within a context of macroeconomic stability, with solid gross domestic product (GDP) growth and low inflation. The old *colón* can legally circulate with the dollar, but business transactions are denominated in dollars. Its purpose was to create an economic environment conducive to investment. Dollarization followed a policy of a fixed exchange rate with the U.S. dollar, which was put in place in 1993. These measures, accompanied by the Central American Free Trade Agreement (known as **CAFTA-DR** because the Dominican Republic is also a member), have kept the Salvadoran economy very closely tied to the United States, with about two-thirds of exports going there. CAFTA went into effect with El Salvador in 2006 and had been viewed as a way to maintain guaranteed access of Salvadoran goods in the U.S. market. The economy depends heavily on services and light industry exports. Dollarization has served to keep inflation down and to bring in foreign investment, such as maquiladoras, but poverty is high and violence has become economically disruptive.

In El Salvador political conflicts did remain relatively peaceful (though drug-related conflict worsened) in the postwar era, though it offered some drama. In 2009 an FMLN candidate, the journalist Mauricio Funes, won the presidential election with a majority over the ARENA candidate, thus marking the first presidential victory for the FMLN. That opened fissures in ARENA, as later in the year twelve members of Congress split from the party and created their own group, the Grand Alliance for National Unity, or GANA (which is Spanish for *win*). Subsequently the party expelled Antonio Saca, a former president, for supporting that group. Legislative-executive relations immediately shifted, as the GANA members voted in favor of Funes' annual budget, whereas the ARENA members abstained.

Polyarchy in El Salvador has endured since the end of the Cold War, which is a major accomplishment, but the difficulty of changing socioeconomic conditions remains entrenched. The growing and disruptive presence of drug-trafficking organizations seriously complicates any push for reform.

Nicaragua

Nicaragua's political development has been influenced significantly by international actors, especially the United States. In 1856, an adventurer named William Walker took advantage of a Liberal–Conservative civil war to bring troops and proclaim himself president. Because of the opposition of neighboring countries, as well as Cornelius Vanderbilt's, whose effort to expand his railroad empire was being stymied by Walker, he was soon forced out. But U.S. investors remained, as did an interest in possibly building a canal. Eventually, however, the administration of Theodore Roosevelt chose Panama instead. The Liberal–Conservative divide ravaged the country, and relative stability was not achieved until the liberal dictatorship of José Santos Zelaya, who ruled from 1893 until the U.S. government overthrew him for his resistance to U.S. plans to build and operate a canal. Interim governments briefly ruled, but between 1911 and 1933 the United States occupied and controlled Nicaragua. That led to rebellion and to the growing influence of Augusto Sandino, a guerrilla leader who fought against the occupation.

Ultimately, Franklin Roosevelt's Good Neighbor Policy ended direct U.S. intervention, but the strong international influence did not end. Juan Bautista Sacasa became president in 1933, and U.S. officials pushed to have Anastasio Somoza García named as head of the National Guard. The following year, Somoza lured Sandino to a meeting and had him murdered. In 1936, he forced Sacasa to resign and soon took over the presidency himself. The last shreds of polyarchy and either vertical or horizontal accountability disappeared

▆▆▆ NICARAGUA'S POLITICAL INSTITUTIONS ▆▆▆

Last constitution: 1987 (extensive reforms in 1995)

Unitary government with fifteen departments and two autonomous regions

Executive: President with five-year term, no reelection

Legislative: Unicameral National Assembly with ninety-two members, ninety elected by party-list proportional representation

Judicial: Supreme Court

completely. The Somoza family took virtually complete control over Nicaragua, amassing a vast fortune and passing along a personalistic dictatorship. After the first Somoza's assassination in 1956, his son Luís took over, and after his death by heart attack in 1967, his younger son **Anastasio Somoza Debayle** assumed power. The political system was highly clientelist, emanating from the Somoza family itself, and repressive.

In 1961, a group of dissidents formed a local group that would become known as the **Sandinista National Liberation Front.** Inspired by the Cuban revolution and named for the rebel Sandino, the Sandinistas embraced Marxism and sought to overthrow the Somoza dynasty through guerrilla warfare based on local support. One of the movement's leaders was Daniel Ortega, whose family had been targeted by the dictatorship and who would later become president. The Sandinistas gained momentum in the aftermath of a massive earthquake in 1972, when Somoza and his close supporters stole relief aid and profited while the capital Managua went unrepaired and large numbers of Nicaraguans suffered without assistance. At the same time, more moderate groups, even within business, began calling for political liberalization, a call that became even more intense after a prominent newspaper editor, Pedro Joaquín Chamorro, was murdered in 1978. This prompted greater national and international isolation of the Somoza regime.

Even those who disagreed with the Sandinistas' ideology believed that Somoza represented an obstacle to both modernization and democracy. That sentiment spread to the administration of Jimmy Carter, which exerted pressure on him to step down. In 1979, Somoza fled into exile (he was killed the following year in Paraguay) and the Sandinistas took over the country. Somoza left unrepentant: "In my conduct of the presidency, I have no remorsefulness. The people of Nicaragua know that I tried to do my job properly. They also understand that our small nation did not have the power or the means to taken on the International Conspiracy which destroyed our country."[6]

The initial government was broadly inclusive because anti-Somoza sentiment spanned the political spectrum, but soon a small Sandinista directorate led by Daniel Ortega established control over policy making. That soon put many former allies (albeit uneasy ones given ideological differences) into the opposition.

Women played an important role in Somoza's overthrow (in which they constituted about 20 percent of the combatants) and then the Sandinista government, both at the national and local levels. The Louisa Amanda Espinosa Women's Association (AMNLAE) was a broad-based local organization that affiliated with the Sandinista party, and attracted many housewives and mothers of those killed, who had previously not been involved in politics.[7] As in so many conflict-ridden countries, women bore a tremendous burden as they balanced work at home with war-created shortages of food, fuel, and other necessities. The *Frente Sandinista de Liberación Nacional* (FSLN) created a draft that included women, so they were also called to bear arms. The AMN-LAE was tied closely to the Sandinistas, so at times came under criticism for following orders from the leadership even if that meant putting gender issues on the backburner.

Even under the Carter administration, which recognized the new government, relations with the Sandinistas were strained because of the Cold War. Republicans in the United States lashed out at the idea of "another Cuba." Indeed, Fidel Castro immediately sent advisors and brought the new Nicaraguan leaders to Havana to discuss strategy and begin the process of strengthening the Sandinista army.

The CIA (along with the Argentine military regime) helped organize former National Guardsmen in Honduras to begin sabotage operations. When Ronald Reagan took office, he immediately increased funding for these programs, and the "Contra" (Spanish for *against*) force became stronger and bolder. The 1980s in Nicaragua were therefore marked by almost constant war, which killed tens of thousands and displaced even more. In 1985 that effort would include an illegal operation (dubbed "Iran-Contra") whereby U.S. National Security Council official Oliver North ignored Congress and sold weapons to Iran in exchange for cash that would go to the Contras. Peace negotiations were finally launched in 1988 as the Cold War wound down and similar to El Salvador it became clear that neither side could achieve victory. Mutual recognition of stalemate eventually led to elections in 1990. The end of the Cold War greatly facilitated the process because the war lost its international ideological importance. For years, Nicaragua disappeared from the U.S. foreign policy radar.

Economically, the Sandinista government did not copy policies of other socialist governments such as Cuba. It did implement programs designed to improve health and education for the poor. The government empowered local groups, down to the neighborhood level, to find solutions, in a way that did resemble Cuba under Fidel Castro, though with much more autonomy and less repression. Nonetheless, there was periodic harassment of the political opposition and media censorship, which grew worse as the war intensified. Despite its professed Marxist orientation, the Sandinista government felt compelled to impose austerity policies in the late 1980s to curb runaway inflation (which had exceeded 30,000 percent). Elections were scheduled for 1990, and weariness from the extended war plus concern about the economy put Daniel Ortega on the defensive. He ran against Violeta Chamorro, the widow of the slain newspaper publisher. Chamorro won with 55 percent versus Ortega's 41 percent. The revolutionary era thus ended. Before leaving power, the Sandinistas gave supporters money and properties in what became known as the "piñata," a final seizing of resources before handing over the government.

After the conclusion of the civil war, vertical accountability in Nicaragua—which had improved during the Sandinista era versus the Somozas—increased even more. The country's experience with social mobilization required presidents to take heed of local popular sentiment.[8] That has been essential for pushing the legislature to resist the executive. Such resistance was bolstered by the continued strong presence of the FSLN (which became a formal political party) in the legislature. The Chamorro administration was marked by economic stagnation and strikes, though inflation was finally reined in.

Since then, politics in Nicaragua have been characterized by unusual and shifting coalitions. Despite his revolutionary pedigree, Daniel Ortega (who ran and lost in every presidential election until he finally won in 2006) forged an alliance with the conservative Constitutional Liberal Party (PLC), especially with Arnoldo Alemán, who was president from 1997 to 2002 (and then later convicted of corruption). That agreement involved giving the Sandinistas important bureaucratic positions in exchange for political support, which had the effect of blocking other political parties.

When Daniel Ortega won the 2006 election, he was much different politically from the 1980s. He had rejected Marxism, embraced Catholicism, and owed his ability to govern by a political alliance with conservatives who previously had been his enemies. In fact, in 2009 the Supreme Court overturned Alemán's conviction and set him free, which was widely viewed as Ortega's doing. Ortega's term in office has received much criticism for its exertion of presidential power, including a successful lobbying of the Supreme Court to remove the restriction on his running (and then winning) for another term in 2011, a move of dubious legality. Journalists have also complained of harassment and/or criminal charges against them when they write critically of the government.

Like so many other countries, the Nicaraguan economy depends heavily on remittances, which grew to over $1 billion a year. Given its high level of dependence on the United States, after the global crash in 2008, the country's GDP went into negative figures. There has been very little diversification, as the main exports are agricultural goods (like coffee) and textiles. Becoming part of the CAFTA has also facilitated the development of maquiladoras. Given Ortega's ideological affinity with Hugo Chávez and Nicolás Maduro, Nicaragua has also benefited from aid through the Bolivarian Alliance for the Americas, or ALBA, as Venezuelan initiative that channels development funds to poor member countries. Both poverty and unemployment remain high, so Nicaragua faces serious challenges.

Guatemala

The overthrow of Jacobo Arbenz in 1954 set in motion decades of civil war deeply tied to international influences, during which 200,000 Guatemalans were killed. As one army general put it, "Before, the strategy was to kill 100 percent . . . But you don't need to kill everybody to complete the job . . . There are more sophisticated means . . . We instituted civil affairs [in 1982], which provides development for 70 percent of the population while we kill 30 percent."[9]

Military governments and military-backed civilian governments engaged in a violent counterinsurgency effort, and the civil war would not officially end until 1996. The country experienced both military governments and oligarchic civilian regimes, but the armed forces were always a dominant force.

▮ GUATEMALA'S POLITICAL INSTITUTIONS ▮

Last constitution: 1985

Unitary government with twenty-two departments (though mayors are elected)

Executive: President with four-year term, no reelection

Legislative: Unicameral Congress with 158 members elected by party-list proportional representation

Judicial: Supreme Court and Constitutional Court with broad judicial review

---

That in turn led to widespread repression and consequent launching of rebel movements to fight back, such as the Rebel Armed Forces (FAR). One major army offensive in 1968 killed 10,000 people. Using counterinsurgency techniques taught by the United States, the government maintained ongoing war in the countryside.

In 1987 representatives of the government and the rebels met for the first time as a result of the Esquipulas Agreement, led by Costa Rican president Oscar Arias. They did not come to an agreement, but it set a precedent for future negotiations. There was some resistance from the army because its campaign against the guerrilla organization Guatemalan National Revolutionary Unity (URNG) had been successful. By 1990, these negotiation efforts received a boost when the United States became more vocal about human rights violations. Not only was the Cold War ending, but also the administration of George H. W. Bush was much more pragmatic and less ideological than Ronald Reagan. As part of the peace process, a truth commission was established, known as the Commission for Historical Clarification. It noted the abuses of the Guatemalan security forces, especially for Mayans. The plight of the Maya is best exemplified by Rigoberta Menchú (see Box 6.1), who received international fame for her efforts to make her suffering public. The Truth Commission labeled the violence against the indigenous as genocidal, and her story highlighted how pervasive the repression became.

▮ BOX 6.1 ▮

The Local Becomes International Rigoberta Menchú

International: International influence was always central to Guatemala's civil war, as the country was a Cold War ideological battleground. But it took an indigenous (Quiche Mayan) Guatemalan woman named Rigoberta Menchú to make the local suffering of the conflict better publicized internationally. She lived in a village that was attacked both by guerrillas and by the Guatemalan army. She lost members of her family (including her parents and two brothers), killed by the army or paramilitary groups tied to the government. As time went on she became more active politically in the Committee of the Peasant Union (CUC). Fearing persecution for her own activism, she eventually escaped to Mexico, where she met the anthropologist Elizabeth Burgos, who assisted her in publishing a first-person testimonial book *I, Rigoberta Menchú*.

National: The book attracted attention from across the world and highlighted the atrocities being committed, particularly in the Guatemalan countryside. Yet it was also important in Guatemala itself, where many nonindigenous people did not believe atrocities were occurring or that they were overstated. Menchú had come out of obscurity and raised issues no one had been able to raise beyond the local level. She traveled extensively to promote human rights—particularly for indigenous peoples—not only in Guatemala but across Latin America. For this work, she was awarded the Nobel Peace Prize in 1996.

Local: It is a no holds barred view of life in the countryside during civil war and how villages came together to protect themselves. "The moment I learned to identify our enemies was very important for me. For me now the landowner was a big enemy, an evil one. The soldier too was a criminal enemy."[10]

Yet even the local depictions connected to the international level. Anthropologist David Stoll investigated her claims, and in 1999 Stoll published a book refuting some of them, including the status of her father's land, her own education, and the way some of her family members were killed. He argued further that Rigoberta Menchú's book painted the guerrillas in too positive a light. His book was controversial and generated considerable public and academic debate. Regardless, the essential elements of the story, such as the violence, repression, and indiscriminate murder of indigenous rural Guatemalans, are true.

Discussion Questions
- How can local political actors raise international awareness about their plight?
- How did international factors help create Rigoberta Menchú's plight in the first place?

The civil war generated a culture of impunity that has lasted. Horacio Castellanos Moya's novel *Senselessness*, first published in Spanish in 2004, wonderfully (and sadly) captures the fear, suspicion, and paranoia that persisted after the end of the conflicts as civilians attempted to investigate past abuses. The military was very strong, with close political allies as well as the means to intimidate those who threatened its members, including the novel's protagonist. Although he is sometimes delusional, the legitimate root of his paranoia is made clear at the end, as Bishop Juan Gerardi was assassinated in 1998 for his role in assembling a document detailing human rights abuses, echoing the murder of Archbishop Romero in El Salvador. Before and since, countless judges, prosecutors, and witnesses have been murdered or "persuaded" not to continue their work under threat of death.

Problems with Guatemalan democracy were also evident when in 1993 President Jorge Serrano suspended the constitution and announced the dissolution of the legislature. He hoped to emulate the so-called self-coup (or *autogolpe* in Spanish) of Peruvian President Alberto Fujimori in 1990, but failed when both national and international protests forced his resignation. Another example is the continued political presence of former dictator Efraín Ríos Montt, who was in power during 1982–1983 at the height of the vicious campaign against accused "subversives" in the countryside. He founded the Guatemalan Republican Front (FRG), which became a platform for a postauthoritarian political career. He attempted to run for president in 1990, but was forbidden because the 1985 constitution ruled out anyone who had previously taken part in a coup. However, he did get elected to Congress, where he served from 1990 until 2004 (which also provided him with immunity from prosecution for human rights abuses). Then in 2003 the Constitutional Court ruled that he could run, though he received only 11 percent of the vote. His presence all those years, however, symbolized the continued presence of the civil war years after it concluded.

Of even greater concern is the spillover of international drug trafficking and its associated violence in Guatemala. All of Central America had become a transshipment area for drugs going from Colombia to the United States, but as the drug trade grew in Mexico, organized gang activity also increased in neighboring Guatemala. The Mexican drug-trafficking organization Zetas are active in Guatemala, not only in shipping drugs but also in stockpiling weapons. Drug smugglers also take advantage of ties to active duty and retired members of the Guatemalan military. Not coincidentally, the homicide rate rose 40 percent between 2002 and 2008, from 4,507 to 6,292. The police are inefficient and often corrupt, while the court system is unable or unwilling to pursue prosecution. Overall, this leads to a condition of impunity, where perpetrators of crimes feel emboldened. This is devastating down to the local level, because Guatemalans feel almost as insecure as they did during the civil war, which prompts emigration.

A brighter point for Guatemala is that in 2007 it elected its first leftist president, Alvaro Colom of the National Union of Hope Party (UNE), since Jacobo Arbenz. Although no radical, Colom's election demonstrated that, as in El Salvador (2009), the right could cede power without armed conflict. He vowed to reduce poverty, but the struggle against drug trafficking is often overwhelming. Plus, UNE won only 30 of 158 seats in the unicameral Congress, which makes reforms of any kind problematic. Yet even Colom's presidency ran into controversy. Because the constitution prohibits relatives of the president from running for the office, in 2011 his wife divorced him in the hopes that she could become a candidate for that year's presidential election, though eventually the Constitutional Court turned down her petition. Instead, given their fears about violence, Guatemalans leaned toward a more conservative, "iron fist" candidate, retired General Otto Pérez Molina, in the first round.

The Guatemalan economy has never emerged from its dependent agricultural roots. It does have a solid tourist industry, but this is threatened by the expansion of drug-trafficking organizations whose violence at times is indiscriminate. Poverty rates are high, and even higher for the indigenous population, while Guatemala has the greatest income inequality of any Central American country. The economy depends greatly on remittances, which are roughly 10 percent of GDP, and is the fourth highest in Latin America. That growth has been dramatic, as in 2001 remittances constituted only about 3 percent of GDP.

Overall, then, international factors well out of Guatemala's control condition both politics and economics. Both economic growth and political stability were already weak as a result of Cold War–fuelled war and tentacles of international drug trafficking threaten to choke them further, regardless of whether the presidency is controlled by the left or the right.

Honduras

Honduras was the novelist O. Henry's inspiration for the phrase *banana republic* in his book *Cabbages and Kings*. The name stuck, and evoked an image of underdevelopment, foreign intervention, and a fruit-based economy. All of these were true of Honduras, where the United Fruit Company had large banana plantations and the political elites of the National and Liberal parties shared power, with periodic authoritarian governments. During the Cold War, the country was not as repressive as its neighbors, in particular since its elites did not have a long history of unity. However, the country did enter into the conflict, remaining firmly anti-Communist and serving as the staging point for the Contra war in Nicaragua. However, the armed forces allowed parties to function as a way to avoid the polarization of its neighbors, particularly after 1979. Thus a pacted transition occurred in 1982 rather than more violent political change. The military left power, but was still very influential. The 1982 constitution was intended to instill a pattern of one-term presidential rule, and the single-term limit was one of the constitution's unreformable articles (i.e., the constitution prohibits the reform of some specific articles). That stability, however, would not arrive until the 1990s, when presidents began alternating power without military interruptions.

The Honduran political system is highly centralized, with power concentrated in the presidency. Regardless of which party has been in power, corruption is rampant and poverty rates high. Polls routinely show that Hondurans have one of the lowest rates of confidence in government institutions and in democracy more generally. There are elections for local government, but patronage and clientelism are hallmarks of elections at all levels.

In 1990, President Rafael Callejas implemented structural adjustment reforms that liberalized the Honduran economy and brought more foreign investment. The number of *maquiladoras* increased to promote exports, and privatization of state-owned industries also accelerated. The serious downside to these reforms has been increased poverty and unemployment, exacerbated by serious natural disasters like Hurricane Mitch in 1998, which killed over 10,000 Hondurans. Further, crime and drug trafficking grew along with popular dissatisfaction. The homicide rate is now among the highest in the world, a prevalent problem across Central America.

HONDURAS' POLITICAL INSTITUTIONS

Last constitution: 1982

Unitary government with eighteen departments

Executive: President with four-year term, no reelection

Legislative: National Congress with 128 members elected by proportional representation

Judicial: Supreme Court

The continued power of the armed forces in Central America came into sharp relief in June 2009, when President José Manuel Zelaya was detained by the military and then forced out of the country. In the case of Brazil, we discuss the idea of the armed forces being a "moderating power" in Chapter 11, which certainly was the case in Honduras. Zelaya attempted to hold a national referendum asking whether Hondurans wished to allow for a constitutional convention. The Supreme Court ruled that the vote should not go forward, but Zelaya pressed on anyway. The court then ordered his arrest, but the military proceeded to forcibly exile him to Costa Rica in clear violation of the constitution.

Once again in Latin America, the military had stepped in mediate disputes between other state institutions. Afterward, international actors were central to resolving the conflict. Months of internationally sponsored mediation failed to bring a solution, as the de facto government insisted that Zelaya could not be reinstated and that only the upcoming presidential election would resolve the crisis. He even snuck back into the Honduras and took refuge at the Brazilian embassy. Ultimately the "Tegucigalpa–San José Accord" was signed by all parties, and it had stipulations about the way to proceed. Among the points was that no one would seek to reform the constitution, in either direct or indirect form.

ANALYZING DOCUMENTS

The overthrow of José Manuel Zelaya rocked all of Central America and sent presidents and international organizations scrambling to respond. The crisis demonstrated the continued weakness of national political institutions in Central America. A fragile agreement was reached in 2009, though it still left many questions—such as Zelaya's own fate—unanswered.

San José–Tegucigalpa Accord (2009)

We, Honduran citizens, men and women convinced of the necessity to strengthen the state of law, to protect our constitution and the laws of our Republic, deepen democracy and assure a climate of peace and tranquility for our people, have carried out an intense and frank process of political dialogue to seek a peaceful and negotiated exit to the crisis in which our country has been submerged in recent months.

As fruit of this dialogue, in which the wisdom, tolerance, and patriotic spirit of all the participants has predominated, we have drafted a political accord that will permit the reestablishment of civic harmony and assure an appropriate climate for democratic governability in our country. This accord, we are sure, will mark the road to peace, reconciliation, and democracy, which are urgent demands of Honduran society.

The agreement on this accord demonstrates once again that Honduran men and women are capable of successfully carrying out dialogue and thanks to that and by means of it, reach the high goals that society demands and the country requires.

In virtue of the forgoing, we have agreed on the following accords:

The Government of National Reconciliation and Unity
To achieve reconciliation and strengthen democracy, we will form a Government of Unity and National Reconciliation made up of representatives of the various political parties and social organizations, recognized for their capabilities, honesty, aptness, and willingness to dialogue, who will occupy the distinct secretariats and subsecretariats, as well as other dependencies of the State, in conformity with article 246 and following of the constitution of the Republic of Honduras.

In light of the fact that before the 28th of June, the Executive Power had not submitted a General Budget of Income and Expenses for consideration to the National Congress, in conformity with that established in article 205, number 32 of the Constitution of the Republic of Honduras, this government of unity and national reconciliation will respect and function on the basis of the general budget, recently approved by the National Congress for fiscal year 2009.

Renouncing the Convocation of a National Constituent Assembly or Reforming the Unreformable Articles of the Constitution
To achieve reconciliation and strengthen democracy, we reiterate our respect for the Constitution and the laws of our country, abstaining from making calls for the convening of a National Constituent Assembly, in direct or indirect manner and renouncing also promoting or aiding any popular poll with the goal of reforming the Constitution in order to permit presidential reelection, modify the form of government or contravene any of the unreformable articles of our Magna Carta.

In particular, we will not make public declarations nor exercise any type of influence inconsistent with articles 5, 239, 373, and 374 of the Constitution of the Republic of Honduras, and we reject energetically every manifestation contrary to the spirit of said articles and of the special law that regulates the referendum and the plebiscite.

The General Elections and the Transfer of Government
To achieve reconciliation and fortify democracy, we reiterate that, in conformity with the articles 44 and 51 of the Constitution of the Republic of Honduras, the vote is universal, obligatory, egalitarian, direct, free and secret, and it corresponds to the

(Continued)

Supreme Electoral Tribunal, with full autonomy and independence, to supervise and execute everything related to the electoral acts and processes.

At the same time, we make a call to the Honduran people to peacefully participate in the next general elections and to avoid all kinds of demonstrations that would oppose the elections or their results, or promote insurrection, antijuridical conduct, civil disobedience or other acts that could produce violent confrontations or transgressions of the law.

With the goal of demonstrating the transparency and legitimacy of the electoral process, we ask urgently that the Supreme Electoral Tribunal that it authorize and accredit the presence of international missions from now until the declaration of the results of the general elections, as well as the transfer of powers that will take place, in conformity with Article 237 of the Constitution of the Republic, the 27 of January of 2010.

The Armed Forces and National Police

To reach reconciliation and strengthen democracy, we affirm our will to comply in all its measures with article 272 of the Constitution of the Republic of Honduras, according to which the Armed Forces remain at the disposition of the Supreme Electoral Tribunal from one month before the general elections, for the purpose of guaranteeing the free exercise of suffrage, the custody, transparency, and guarding of the electoral materials and all the other aspects of security of the process. We reaffirm the professional, apolitical, obedient and nondeliberative character of the Honduran Armed Forces. In the same way, we agree that the national police should be strictly subject to that prescribed in its special legislation.

Executive Power

To achieve reconciliation and strengthen democracy, in the spirit of the themes of the proposed San José Accord, both negotiating commissions have decided, respectfully, that the National Congress, as an institutional expression of popular sovereignty, in the use of its powers, in consultation with the points that the Supreme Court of Justice should consider pertinent and in conformity with the law, should resolve in that proceeding in respect to return the incumbency of Executive Power to its state previous to the 28 of June until the conclusion of the present governmental period, the 27 of January of 2010. The decision that the National Congress adopts should lay the foundations to achieve social peace, political tranquility and governability that society demands and the country needs.

The Normalization of Relations of the Republic of Honduras with the International Community

On committing ourselves to faithfully comply with the promises assumed in the present Accord, we respectfully ask the immediate revocation of those measures and sanctions adopted at a bilateral or multilateral level, that in any manner would affect the reinsertion and full participation of the Republic of Honduras in the international community and its access to all forms of cooperation.

We make a call to the international community that it should reactivate as soon as possible the projects of cooperation in effect with the Republic of Honduras and continue with the negotiation of future ones. In particular, we ask urgently that, on the request of competent authorities the international cooperation be made effective that might be necessary and opportune for the Verification Commission and the future Truth Commission to assure the faithful completion and follow-through of the commitments acquired in this Accord.

Discussion Questions

- What was the report's main strategy for promoting national unity?
- What importance does the report attach to international actors?

Source: http://web.archive.org/web/20101022072136/http://www.latribuna.hn/web2.0/?p=57987&cpage=1 (translation by author)

The 2009 elections went forward and Porfirio "Pepe" Lobo, a member of the National Party, became the new president. Zelaya left the country—flew into exile to the Dominican Republic—and did not return until 2011. There have been widespread demonstrations against the government, organized by an umbrella group, the National Front of Popular Resistance (FNRP), which has brought people together at the local level. It has endeavored to remain united even after Roberto Micheletti, who served as the interim de facto president from June 28, 2009, to January 27, 2010, left office.

Honduran economic growth has been weak and damaged further by hurricanes, organized crime, the global recession, and the aftermath of the 2009 coup because aid and trade were both reduced. One particularly pernicious international influence has been the drug trade, as Mexican cartels have become more active in the absence of a strong national government. In 2011, for the first time a cocaine lab was found in rural Honduras, yet more evidence of growing drug-related activities and violence. Thus, even the rural local level is deeply affected. This combination of factors led to negative GDP growth, while over 40 percent of the population lives on about $2 a day. Coffee and bananas are still key exports (mostly going to the United States) while as elsewhere CAFTA has fostered foreign investment in maquiladoras, particularly textiles. Honduras has been, and still is, one of the least developed and most poverty-stricken countries in the Western Hemisphere.

Panama

The timing of Panama's independence from Colombia is tied directly to international influences, namely, the administration of Theodore Roosevelt in the United States. As noted in the Nicaraguan case, the United States had long sought a canal to span the Central American isthmus as a way to facilitate trade from the Pacific to Atlantic oceans. Costa Rica had even been considered. But the Panama route became more attractive when a French company began a project and then went bankrupt, meaning that a U.S. company could step in and continue (and the French company lobbied heavily for that outcome so that it could repay its debts). In addition, Nicaraguan

■ PANAMA'S POLITICAL INSTITUTIONS ■

Last constitution: 1972

Unitary government with nine provinces

Executive: President with five-year term, no reelection

Legislative: Unicameral National Assembly with seventy-one members (mixed plurality and proportional representation)

Judicial: Supreme Court of Justice

President José Santos Zelaya was making demands that the United States refused to accept.

Although Panama was part of Colombia at the time of independence, there had been numerous secessionist movements in the eighteenth century clamoring for local autonomy. At various times the U.S. government had even sent troops with the consent of Panamanian authorities to protect its railroad interests when unrest broke out. Panama was a remote part of Colombia, which only sporadically enforced centralized control. Once the Roosevelt administration decided Panama was a propitious location for the canal, in 1902 it sent troops that blocked the already weak Colombian military from responding and the following year Panama declared its independence. In 1914, the canal opened for business, a process entirely driven by international intervention.

From then on, Panama was unique because of the official central role of the U.S. government, which had sovereignty over the ten-mile wide Panama Canal Zone. From a dependency perspective, this arrangement simply formalized the economic domination of the United States. Because of the U.S. presence, the economy has focused predominantly on the service sector and the U.S. dollar circulated. From a modernization viewpoint, however, the United States provided Panama with opportunities it otherwise would not have enjoyed. It promoted relative political stability and a flow of foreign investment.

The United States also created a National Guard in place of the army, which had already unsuccessfully tried to overthrow the government in 1904. Although there was no formal army to intervene in politics, the National Guard became both highly politicized and militarized. That eventually led to a coup in 1968, and in 1969 Colonel Martín Torrijos took the presidency. His rule was both authoritarian and nationalist, with a strong emphasis on asserting control over the Panama Canal. After long negotiations, in 1977 he signed the Torrijos–Carter Treaties, which stipulated handing the operation of the canal to Panama and removing U.S. forces by 1999. The treaties were very popular in Panama across the ideological spectrum. Torrijos died in a 1981 plane crash and was replaced by his intelligence chief (and eventual commander of the National Guard) **Manuel Noriega**.

Noriega's years as executive were marked by authoritarianism, corruption, drug trafficking, and assistance in the U.S. fight against Marxism in Central

America. He nullified presidential elections in both 1984 and 1989 because opposition candidates were clearly going to win, and also reorganized the National Guard, turning it into the Panamanian Defense Forces under his control. The end of his rule was related entirely to international influence.

Given the Cold War context and Noriega's support for the Nicaraguan Contras, the Reagan administration was willing to overlook the drug ties and repression. As the peace process got going in the rest of Central America, however, Noriega's services were no longer needed and the U.S. government ended its support. Most importantly, in 1989 a U.S. federal court indicted him on drug charges. After Noriega annulled the 1989 presidential election, the administration of George H. W. Bush invaded the country, and within a few days captured Noriega after a chase that led him to the Vatican diplomatic mission in Panama City. He was taken to Miami, convicted, and imprisoned. By 2010, his sentence was up, and he was extradited to France, where he started a seven-year term for money laundering.

Panama stabilized considerably in the years after the invasion, which is not always typical of violent political transitions initiated by a foreign power. Although the postinvasion presidency of Guillermo Endara was marked by continued drug trafficking and corruption (which called into question the original rationale for the invasion), the 1994 elections were largely free and fair. Ernesto Pérez Balladares of Torrijos' Democratic Revolution Party won, and Panamanian politics became less violent and more competitive, to the point that the transfer of the Panama Canal in 1999 occurred without a hitch. From then, presidential elections have been both stable and democratic, including a term by Torrijos' son Martín. Polyarchy, if not democracy, was the norm. Panama's socioeconomic indicators, such as poverty rates and the Human Development Index, have been better than its neighbors as well.

Given the long-time presence of the United States, the Panamanian economy is dollarized. As in El Salvador, that has been a source of financial stability. Of course, unique to the country is the canal itself, which is a source of considerable revenue, and which has transformed the service industry into a central economic motor. In 2006 the government announced a plan to widen the canal and double its capacity by 2014, at a cost of about $20 billion. The canal and its associated businesses also cushioned Panama more than its neighbors after 2008, as it continued to have positive, albeit sluggish, GDP growth. Poverty is also slightly lower than in the rest of Central America, but is still over 25 percent.

Regional Issues

International factors continue to affect all of Central America on a constant basis. National and local political dynamics are conditioned in some way by forces originating outside the region. Unfortunately, for the most part this complicates economic development and democratization and leaves Central America more vulnerable.

Migration and Economics

Since the end of the Cold War, remittances have become a rapidly growing source of income as well. In El Salvador, Honduras, and Nicaragua remittances totaled an astonishing 18 to 20 percent of GDP.[11] In Guatemala they reach 13 percent. As discussed in the case of Mexico, this raises important questions about economic dependence. When the U.S. economy crashed in September 2008, Central America was also hit hard not only because trade fell, but because emigrants could no longer send the same amount of money as they had before. Remittances also prompt Central American presidents to spend a considerable amount of time lobbying the U.S. government on behalf of their citizens and for more open immigration policies. This puts a new spin on dependence, as the economic impact of mass migration becomes almost as important as the movement of goods.

Political leaders feel compelled to lobby for temporary protected status (TPS) for many of their citizens. The United States extends TPS to foreign nationals in times of specific crises. For Central America, this referred to civil war in the 1980s, but in more recent years has been granted in the context of natural disasters such as hurricanes, which often hammer the area. The U.S. Congress must renew TPS every 18 months, and in some cases, it has been extended many times. The core problem is that the countries hit by these disasters do not soon recover to the extent that they can absorb a large-scale return of their citizens from abroad.

The Judiciary in Central America

Judicial systems in the region had historically been enmeshed in the families and political elites that governed, so there has been little horizontal accountability. Foreign intervention further weakened it. They were neither insulated from political pressure nor immune to corruption. As a result, in the post–Cold War era judicial reform has been a key goal. In El Salvador, for example, reforms in the 1990s required a two-third majority in the legislature to choose a Supreme Court justice, to ensure that party loyalty alone did not dictate the selection. Reforms also instituted a more rigorous procedure for determining the qualifications of the candidates. Budgets for the judiciary are also a perennial problem, so in Guatemala the Peace Accords included a phased budget increase of 50 percent.[12] Budgets pose two dilemmas. First, inadequate funds mean that courts at all levels develop major backlogs and cannot process cases. Second, if budgets rely too much on the goodwill of the executive or legislative branches, then they can apply pressure on judges with the threat of withholding critical funds.

A broader problem for the judicial branch in Central America is politicization with regard to the investigation of human rights abuses. Outside Costa Rica, the armed forces have exerted considerable influence, including open threats. Of course, this poses a major obstacle to democratization and horizontal accountability. In general, the judiciary enjoys relatively little trust from the public, both in macro terms of major human rights cases or micro terms of simply getting individual civil or criminal cases addressed in a timely and fair manner.

Women and Politics in Central America

Not all international influence has had a negative effect. Women were granted the right to vote relatively late in Central America—the earliest was Guatemala in 1945. Prior to 1945, they were denied many basic rights of citizenship and in fact some constitutions referred specifically to men rather than women.

TABLE 6.1 Costa Rican Economic Indicators, 1991–2011

Year	GDP Growth	Inflation	Unemployment	Poverty Rate	Human Development Index
1991	2.2	25.3	6.0	—	0.883
1992	7.1	17.0	4.3	—	0.848
1993	5.8	9.0	4.0	—	0.884
1994	4.3	19.9	4.3	23.1	0.889
1995	2.2	22.6	5.7	—	0.889
1996	−0.5	13.9	6.6	—	—
1997	3.7	11.5	5.9	22.5	0.801
1998	5.5	12.4	5.4	—	—
1999	8.2	10.1	6.2	20.3	—
2000	1.8	10.2	5.3	—	—
2001	1.1	11.0	5.8	—	0.832
2002	2.9	9.7	6.8	20.3	—
2003	6.4	9.9	6.7	—	—
2004	4.3	13.3	6.7	20.5	—
2005	5.9	14.1	6.6	21.1	0.846
2006	7.9	9.4	6.0	19.0	—
2007	7.9	10.8	4.6	18.6	0.854
2008	2.8	13.9	4.8	16.4	—
2009	−1.1	4.0	8.4	18.9	—
2010	4.0	6.1	7.1	—	0.768
2011	4.2	4.9	7.7	—	0.770

Sources: Unemployment: GDP and Inflation: *Preliminary Overview of the Economies of Latin America and the Caribbean*, 1994–2012.
Poverty rate: *Social Panorama of Latin America*. Economic Commission for Latin America, 1990–2012.
Human development index: United Nations, *Human Development Report*, 1990–2013.

TABLE 6.2 Salvadoran Economic Indicators, 1991–2011

Year	GDP Growth	Inflation	Unemployment	Poverty Rate	Human Development Index
1991	2.8	9.8	7.9	—	0.579
1992	7.3	19.9	8.2	—	0.543
1993	6.4	12.1	8.1	—	0.576
1994	6.0	8.9	7.0	—	0.592
1995	6.2	11.4	7.0	47.6	0.604
1996	2.0	7.4	7.5	—	—
1997	4.0	2.2	7.5	48.0	0.674
1998	3.5	4.2	7.6	—	0.696
1999	3.4	−1.0	6.9	43.5	—
2000	2.2	4.3	6.5	—	—
2001	1.7	1.4	7.0	48.9	0.719
2002	2.3	2.8	6.2	—	0.720
2003	2.3	2.6	6.2	—	—
2004	1.8	5.3	6.5	47.5	—
2005	2.8	4.3	7.3	—	0.735
2006	4.2	4.9	5.7	—	—
2007	4.7	4.9	5.8	—	—
2008	3.0	5.5	5.5	42.7	0.747
2009	−3.5	−0.2	7.1	47.9	—
2010	1.0	3.2	6.8	—	0.678
2011	1.5	5.1	6.6	—	0.679

Sources: Unemployment: *GDP and Inflation: Preliminary Overview of the Economies of Latin America and the Caribbean,* 1994–2012.
Poverty rate: Social Panorama of Latin America. Economic Commission for Latin America, 1990–2012.
Human development index: United Nations, *Human Development Report,* 1990–2013.

International influences were important in this regard, as international nongovernmental organizations worked with local groups to lobby for suffrage. Over the long term that has yielded some important advances. Since 1985 the subregion has matched or exceeded the world average of the percentage of female legislators at the national level.[13]

TABLE 6.3 Nicaraguan Economic Indicators, 1991–2011

Year	GDP Growth	Inflation	Unemployment	Poverty Rate	Human Development Index
1991	−0.3	865.6	14.2	—	0.611
1992	0.8	3.5	17.8	—	0.583
1993	−0.4	19.5	21.8	68.1	0.568
1994	4.0	14.4	20.7	—	0.530
1995	4.5	11.1	18.2	—	0.547
1996	4.8	12.1	16.1	—	—
1997	5.0	8.6	14.3	—	0.616
1998	3.5	18.5	13.2	65.1	0.631
1999	7.0	7.2	10.7	—	—
2000	4.1	9.9	7.8	—	—
2001	3.0	4.7	11.3	69.3	0.643
2002	0.8	4.0	11.6	—	0.667
2003	2.5	6.6	10.2	—	—
2004	5.3	10.1	9.3	—	—
2005	4.3	9.7	7.0	61.9	0.710
2006	3.7	10.2	7.0	—	—
2007	3.1	16.2	6.9	—	0.699
2008	2.8	12.7	8.0	—	—
2009	−1.5	1.8	10.5	—	—
2010	3.0	7.7	9.7	—	0.593
2011	5.1	8.5	—	—	0.597

Sources: Unemployment: *GDP and Inflation: Preliminary Overview of the Economies of Latin America and the Caribbean*, 1994–2012.
Poverty rate: *Social Panorama of Latin America*. Economic Commission for Latin America, 1990–2012.
Human development index: United Nations, *Human Development Report*, 1990–2013.

Why is that? The upheaval of the 1970s and 1980s politicized many women and prompted them to seek political office. This has led to more legislative proposals on issues related to women, more focus on social issues that impact everyone (such as human rights) and more efforts by female legislators to bring women's issues to the nation's attention—especially the impact of economic

TABLE 6.4 Guatemalan Economic Indicators, 1991–2011

Year	GDP Growth	Inflation	Unemployment	Poverty Rate	Human Development Index
1991	3.7	10.2	4.0	—	0.591
1992	4.9	14.2	1.5	—	0.564
1993	4.0	11.6	2.5	—	0.580
1994	4.1	11.6	3.3	—	0.572
1995	5.0	8.6	3.7	—	0.615
1996	3.0	10.9	3.7	—	
1997	4.1	7.1	5.0	—	0.624
1998	5.0	7.5	5.9	53.5	0.619
1999	3.8	4.9	—	—	
2000	3.6	5.1	—	—	
2001	2.3	8.9	—	—	0.652
2002	3.9	6.3	5.4	—	0.649
2003	2.5	5.9	5.2	60.2	
2004	3.2	9.2	4.4	—	
2005	3.3	8.6	—	—	0.689
2006	5.4	5.8	—	—	
2007	6.3	8.7	—	54.8	0.704
2008	3.3	9.4	—	—	—
2009	0.5	−0.3	—	—	—
2010	2.5	5.3	4.8	—	0.579
2011	3.9	6.2	3.1	—	0.580

Sources: Unemployment: *GDP and Inflation: Preliminary Overview of the Economies of Latin America and the Caribbean,* 1994–2012.
Poverty rate: *Social Panorama of Latin America.* Economic Commission for Latin America, 1990–2012.
Human development index: United Nations, *Human Development Report,* 1990–2013.

crisis on women and continued discrimination—and then keep them there as best they can.

National political institutions have an impact on women's elections as well. Women have tended to obtain more representation in countries (such as Costa Rica, El Salvador, and Nicaragua) that utilize proportional representation

TABLE 6.5 Honduran Economic Indicators, 1991–2011

Year	GDP Growth	Inflation	Unemployment	Poverty Rate	Human Development Index
1991	1.8	21.4	7.4	—	0.578
1992	6.3	6.5	6.0	—	0.524
1993	7.2	13.0	7.0	—	0.576
1994	−2.6	28.9	4.0	73.1	0.575
1995	5.1	26.8	5.6	—	0.573
1996	3.3	25.4	6.5	—	—
1997	4.3	15.0	5.8	73.8	0.641
1998	3.0	15.7	5.2	—	0.653
1999	−1.9	11.0	5.3	74.4	—
2000	5.7	10.1	—	—	—
2001	2.6	8.8	5.9	—	0.667
2002	2.7	8.1	6.1	77.3	0.672
2003	3.5	6.8	7.6	—	—
2004	5.0	9.1	8.0	—	—
2005	4.1	7.7	6.5	—	0.700
2006	6.6	5.3	4.9	71.5	—
2007	6.3	8.9	4.0	68.9	0.732
2008	4.0	10.8	4.1	—	—
2009	−1.9	3.0	4.9	—	—
2010	2.5	4.4	6.4	—	0.629
2011	3.6	6.8	6.8	—	0.630

Sources: Unemployment: *GDP and Inflation: Preliminary Overview of the Economies of Latin America and the Caribbean,* 1994–2012.
Poverty rate: Social Panorama of Latin America. Economic Commission for Latin America, 1990–2012.
Human development index: United Nations, *Human Development Report,* 1990–2013.

because that entails expanded options for voters. All countries use party lists, meaning that the political parties determine the rank order list of candidates. The combination of party lists and proportional representation has created an incentive to include more women as a way to increase the party's share of seats.

TABLE 6.6 Panamanian Economic Indicators, 1991–2011

Year	GDP Growth	Inflation	Unemployment	Poverty Rate	Human Development Index
1991	9.0	1.6	19.3	36.3	0.856
1992	8.2	1.6	17.5	—	0.816
1993	5.3	1.0	15.6	—	0.859
1994	3.1	1.3	16.0	29.7	—
1995	1.9	0.8	16.6	—	0.868
1996	2.7	2.3	16.4	—	—
1997	4.4	1.8	15.5	27.3	0.791
1998	3.5	1.4	15.5	—	0.776
1999	4.0	1.5	13.6	24.2	—
2000	2.7	0.7	15.2	—	—
2001	0.6	0.0	17.0	—	0.788
2002	2.2	1.9	16.5	36.9	0.791
2003	4.2	1.5	15.9	—	—
2004	7.5	2.5	14.1	32.9	—
2005	6.9	3.4	12.1	31.0	0.812
2006	8.1	2.2	10.4	29.9	—
2007	12.1	6.4	7.7	29.0	0.840
2008	10.7	6.8	6.5	27.7	—
2009	3.2	1.9	7.9	26.4	—
2010	6.3	4.1	7.7	—	0.770
2011	10.8	5.9	5.4	—	0.776

Sources: Unemployment: *GDP and Inflation: Preliminary Overview of the Economies of Latin America and the Caribbean*, 1994–2012.
Poverty rate: *Social Panorama of Latin America*. Economic Commission for Latin America, 1990–2012.
Human development index: United Nations, *Human Development Report*, 1990–2013.

Conclusion and Comparative Perspective

Daniel Ortega's return to the presidency in Nicaragua highlights the connections between the national and international levels. He had fought against a U.S.-backed dictator, then found his Sandinista government attacked by U.S.-backed forces. Later, through national machinations with his opposition, he was able to win election under very different circumstances. Despite serious challenges, in many ways political development in Central America has strengthened considerably in recent years. As the authors of a prominent book on Central American politics point out about elected officials: "They campaigned, tried to persuade others how to vote, attended party meetings, contacted officials, and protested." [14] There is, therefore, growing engagement with democratic institutions and an interest within civil society to participate politically. In El Salvador, for example, a former guerrilla movement became a political party and successfully gained the presidency with a newly moderate message of reform.

Nonetheless, the 2009 Honduran coup is a stark reminder that Central American politics remains oligarchic, and the armed forces are still powerful political actors, which damages vertical accountability. Central American economies are also heavily dependent on foreign imports, particularly from the United States, for most finished goods while they export many of the same primary products they have exported for many years. The *maquila* industries have brought modest growth and employment, but much of the profit leaves the country.

The history of liberal-conservative conflict is similar to countries like Colombia, where its intensity resulted in widespread killings in the nineteenth and twentieth centuries. The disruption of Cold War–fuelled guerrilla wars resembles Colombia as well, though in fact they were resolved much more effectively in Central America. The effects, however, in countries like El Salvador and Guatemala are still being felt. Insecurity, inequality, and poverty are all high. The combination of indigenous marginalization, poverty, inequality, and instability are quite similar to Bolivia, Ecuador, and Peru, with similar unscheduled changes of government and military intervention.

International influences continue to be central. Drug trafficking and gang activity have been sources of instability and violence, with drugs moving from South America to the United States. That creates a ripple effect into national and local institutions because corruption and intimidation go along with it. Dealing with those problems will be both essential and difficult. Colombia and more recently Mexico have dealt with similar issues, but Central America has much weaker political institutions and its history is more replete with repression.

The importance of remittances is echoed elsewhere in the Caribbean, particularly with Cuba. These economies are tightly intertwined with the United States and heavily dependent on it. El Salvador is fully dollarized, but the dollar is a valuable commodity in countries outside the region as well, including Cuba. Small economies dependent on exporting commodities to the United States are much less able to chart their own economic futures.

Key Terms

- Daniel Ortega
- José Manuel Zelaya
- Farabundo Martí National Liberation Front (FMLN)
- CAFTA-DR
- Anastasio Somoza Debayle
- Sandinista National Liberation Front
- Manuel Noriega

Discussion Questions

- In what ways have international influences hindered or encouraged democracy in Central America?
- In what ways does the local population suffer when there is civil war?
- Does it seem likely that other Central American countries could copy the more stable Costa Rican political model?
- What are the pros and cons of so much Central American emigration to the United States?
- How does drug trafficking affect the local, national, and international levels simultaneously?

Further Sources

Books

Booth, John A., Christine J. Wade, and Thomas W. Walker, *Understanding Central America*, 5th Edition (Boulder: Westview Press, 2009). An informative and well-written analysis of Central American politics. It includes both regional chapters and specific chapters on each country, along with a discussion of the role of the United States.

Dunkerley, James. *The Pacification of Central America* (New York: Verso, 1994). This book provides a good overview of how the conflicts in El Salvador, Guatemala, and Nicaragua ended in the late 1980s and early 1990s. It also includes a lengthy and detailed timeline for each country between 1987 and 1993.

García, María Cristina. *Seeking Refuge: Central American Migration to Mexico, the United States, and Canada* (Berkeley: University of California Press, 2006). García analyzes the political dynamics surrounding the mass emigration of Central Americans and the way they were received. It focuses on the transnational advocacy networks that formed and how that contributed to improved treatment of refugees.

LeoGrande, William. *Our Own Backyard: The United States in Central America* (Chapel Hill: University of North Carolina Press, 1998). A comprehensive look at the policy of the United States during the most intense era of civil war in Central America. It focuses in particular on how U.S. policy makers considered Central America a global threat in the context of the Cold War.

Saint-Germain, Michelle A. and Cynthia Chavez Metoyer, *Women Legislators in Central America* (Austin: University of Texas Press, 2008). This analysis seeks to explain why there has been such an increase of women elected to national legislatures in Central America. It combines primary data and personal interviews to provide a very nuanced view of women in politics.

Web Sites

Office of the United States Trade Representative Page on CAFTA-DR (http://www.ustr. gov/trade-agreements/free-trade-agreements/cafta-dr-dominican-republic-central-america-fta/cafta-dr-tcb). The USTR provides a host of links to primary documents (including the text of the agreement itself) and a good view of how the U.S. government views the benefits of CAFTA.

Guatemala: Memory of Silence (http://www.aaas.org/sites/default/files/migrate/uploads/mos_en.pdf). This is the Web site in English of the Guatemala Truth Commission, with details about the effects of the civil war, particularly on the indigenous populations.

Panama Canal Authority (http://www.pancanal.com/eng/index.html). The PCA's Web site provides information (including webcams) of the Panama Canal, but also extensive information about its functions, its expansion, and its finances.

Tico Times (http://www.ticotimes.net/). The *Tico Times* is an English-language online newspaper based in Costa Rica that covers Central American news.

CISPES (http://www.cispes.org/index.php). The Committee in Solidarity with the People of El Salvador is a pro-FMLN NGO that updates information on political events, focusing in particular on workers, the poor, and free trade.

Endnotes

1. Walker, Thomas W. and Christine J. Wade. *Nicaragua: Living in the Shadow of the Eagle,* 5th edition (Boulder: Westview Press, 2011), 213.
2. Wolf, Sonja. "Subverting Democracy: Elite Rule and the Limits to Political Participation in Post-War El Salvador." *Journal of Latin American Studies* 41 (2009): 429–465.
3. Mahoney, James. *The Legacies of Liberalism: Path Dependence and Political Regimes in Central America* (Baltimore: The Johns Hopkins University Press, 2001).
4. Bowman, Kirk F. *Militarization, Democracy, and Development: The Perils of Praetorianism in Latin America* (University Park, PA: The Pennsylvania State University Press, 2002).
5. Carey, John. "Strong Candidates for a Limited Office: Presidentialism and Political Parties in Costa Rica." In Scott Mainwaring and Matthew Soberg Shugart (eds.), *Presidentialism and Democracy in Latin America* (New York: Cambridge University Press, 1997), 201.
6. Somoza, Anastasio. *Nicaragua Betrayed: As Told to Jack Cox by Former President Somoza* (Boston: Western Islands Publishers, 1980), 261.
7. Chinchilla, Norma Stoltz. "Feminism, Revolution, and Democratic Transitions in Nicaragua." In Jane S. Jaquette (ed.), *The Women's Movement in Latin America: Participation and Democracy* (Boulder: Westview Press, 1994), 177–197.
8. Anderson, Leslie E. "The Authoritarian Executive? Horizontal and Vertical Accountability in Nicaragua." *Latin American Politics & Society* 48, 2 (2006): 141–169.
9. Quoted in Dunkerley, James. *The Pacification of Central America* (New York: Verso, 1994), 79.
10. Quoted in Menchú, Rigoberta. *I, Rigoberta Menchú: An Indian Woman in Guatemala* (New York: Verso, 1984), 120.
11. Booth, John A., Christina J. Wade, and Thomas W. Walker. *Understanding Central America* (Boulder: Westview Press, 2010), 236.
12. Dodson, Michael and Donald W. Jackson. "Horizontal Accountability and the Rule of Law in Central America." In Scott Mainwaring and Christopher Welna (eds.), *Democratic Accountability in Latin America* (New York: Oxford University Press, 2003), 228–265.
13. Saint-Germain, Michelle A. and Cynthia Chavez Metoyer. *Women Legislators in Central America: Politics, Democracy, and Policy* (Austin: The University of Texas Press, 2008), 2–3.
14. Booth et al. 2010, 189.

CHAPTER 7

Cuba

TIMELINE

1898	"Spanish-American War" led to independence
1903	Platt Amendment
1933	Sergeant's Revolt
1934	Platt Amendment repealed
1952	Fulgencio Batista takes dictatorial power
1953	Attack on Moncada Barracks
1959	Fulgencio Batista flees and Fidel Castro takes over
1960	First U.S. embargo measures imposed
1961	Bay of Pigs invasion
1962	Cuban Missile Crisis
1998	Creation of the Varela Project
2006	Fidel Castro steps down as president
2008	Raúl Castro officially becomes president
2010	Government announces major labor cuts and reforms

After hiking for hours, all the while hearing bombs dropped by the Cuban air force in their vicinity, *New York Times* reporter Herbert Matthews met the revolutionary **Fidel Castro** in 1957. While puffing on a cigar, Castro told him, "We are sure of ourselves."[1] Matthews went on to write flattering articles that received international attention and brought considerable favorable press to the young revolutionary who would very quickly become a global force. The Cuban government had been saying that Castro was only a minor irritant, attached to small local populations but not a real threat. That interview proved otherwise. For decades, the government has experienced constant pressure from the United States and has often been labeled as on the brink of implosion. Yet it has persevered, and there is local and national glue that holds it together in the face of international threat. For a number of reasons, the revolutionary leadership has remained remarkably sure of itself.

For a small country—only 42,803 square miles, roughly the size of Pennsylvania—Cuba has exerted tremendous political influence around the world for the past half century. International factors are therefore even more prominent than in other countries. The Marxist revolutionaries Fidel Castro and his brother Raúl became heroes for some and villains for others. Cuba's political and economic trajectories have been different than elsewhere, with very late independence, an even greater presence of powerful foreign countries, and a long-standing revolutionary regime. By the 1990s, Cuba was the only country in the hemisphere without a democratically elected leader and was also the only country with a command economy.

For decades, Cuba has been a symbol. For opponents of the revolutionary regime, it represents everything wrong with state-planned economies and authoritarian government. For supporters, it is a model of independence from U.S. domination and freedom from capitalist pressures, where the local demands of the average person are taken seriously and addressed. Yet over time the regime has shifted in different directions, so easy generalizations are difficult to make.

CUBA
Population: 11.2 million
Size: 42,000 square miles
Capital: Havana
Currency: Peso

Map of Cuba

Historical Roots of Political and Economic Development

Perhaps nowhere else in Latin America do we find a country where political and economic development is more attuned to international influence. Throughout the nineteenth century, Cuba remained part of the Spanish Empire. After Haiti became independent, many slave owners fled to Cuba, bringing their slaves with them. Indeed, royalists from across the region sought refuge in Cuba. This white elite feared the impact that an independence movement might have on slaves, and therefore preferred to retain both slavery and Spanish rule.

International influence eventually clashed with the local level, because over time Cubans felt Spain was treating them unfairly. In 1868, thirty-eight Cuban landowners declared themselves in rebellion against Spain, and initiated thirty years of intermittent warfare that spread throughout the nation. Spain's scorched-earth tactics, which included rounding up inhabitants in rebel areas and putting them in concentration camps, was at times an effective battle strategy, but it also increased the level of resentment toward the colonial government.

Spain's political power, already greatly weakened by the independence movements of the early nineteenth century, continued to dwindle. By the end of the century, it was barely even a shadow of its former self, while the United States was a fast-rising hemispheric power, which intensified the international presence in Cuba. The Cuban war had become a bone of contention for Spanish-American relations because Spain constantly complained about U.S. complacency in the face of U.S. sympathy for the rebels. But the fight was also a threat to U.S. economic interests, so by the time William McKinley won the presidential election of 1896, support for some sort of armed action was widespread.

In 1898, the battleship *USS Maine* exploded in Havana harbor, killing 260 sailors. The blast was blamed on a mine, attributed to the Spanish (later, a naval investigation would argue that it was likely caused by a fire, which then caused an explosion). McKinley announced that enough was enough: "in the name of humanity, in the name of civilization, in behalf of endangered American interests which give us the right and the duty to speak and to act, the war in Cuba must stop."[2] It is notable that in the United States the conflict became known as the "Spanish-American War," thus avoiding the word *Cuba* at all. In many ways, that was a reflection of perceptions at the time, which centered on making sure that Cubans stayed out of the way during combat and then excluding from the peace negotiations (which did not even take place in Cuba).

Dominance of the United States

Within a short time, Spain was defeated and the United States occupied the island. The United States ensured that a Cuban constituent assembly wrote a constitution that guaranteed the right of the United States to intervene (the so-called **Platt Amendment,** named for its author, Senator Orville Platt, who helped craft the language in Congress) and also the long-term lease of four military bases. By 1912, further negotiations reduced that to one—Guantánamo—which of course remains in operation to this day. Thus, with the 1903 Platt Amendment, Cuba had officially won independence, but the dominant presence of the United States precluded any independent action. In the face of instability, U.S. presidents periodically called on the marines to restore order. In 1917 the island hosted a training base for U.S. marines on their way to the European front of World War I, and in the 1920s a drop in the price of sugar led to more intervention, as U.S. officials encouraged private banks and businesses to lend money and buy land as a way to keep the country stable. International factors were central. Policy makers in the United States never believed Cuba would become "modern" because it was considered too backward, but at least they could teach Cubans some basics of governance. Over time that type of attitude grated on Cubans who did not appreciate the paternalistic attitude.

The onset of the Great Depression in 1929 prompted the United States to reduce the size and scope of its military presence across Latin America. In Cuba, the administration of Franklin D. Roosevelt found an ally in **Fulgencio Batista,** an army sergeant who had broad power by virtue of being the military's union leader. In 1933, he conspired with the United States to overthrow the government of Gerardo Machado and install a dictatorship. From then until 1959, when he was overthrown, Batista dominated Cuban politics, either as president or in the shadows.

Fulgencio Batista's Dominance of Cuban Politics

The prevailing view in the United States was that Batista represented a modernizing and stabilizing force in Cuba, which made the island a tourist haven. As one popular book on Latin America noted in 1941, Batista "has sought to reduce the disequilibrium between rich and poor" and "has ended military control of the island and is giving it what promises to be reasonable political stability."[3] A little over a decade later, Vice President Richard Nixon would give him a birthday toast and compare him to Abraham Lincoln. Relative political stability meant turning a blind eye to repression and resentment.

Throughout this period, Batista was in the background. Nonetheless, during the 1940s there was a short era of relatively fraud-free elections and socioeconomic reform. Ramón Grau San Martín, for example, had been president briefly during 1933–1934, then served again from 1944 to 1948 (after losing to Batista in 1940). He enacted reforms aimed at reducing inequality, but his refusal to tackle corruption at times led to violence as different groups sought to obtain their part of the economic spoils. It was within this political context that Fidel Castro came of age politically as he entered law school at the University of Havana. His successor, Carlos Prío, faced the same problems, which amounted to a collection of urban gangs competing for resources. His years in office were notable for the amount of free expression that took place, but the country became increasingly polarized and violent. There was some democratic competition at the presidential level, but it was ravaged by the endless fight for power and money. It was a deeply unequal country, with serious discrimination against its large black population, and with land in the hands of foreigners.

Importantly, though, no president pressed for reforms that would reduce the power of foreign capital, the influence of which was extensive. Sugar and tobacco flowed out, and industrial goods came from abroad. From the dependency perspective, this is an important point. Foreign investment boomed throughout the island, but broader swaths of society considered it more of a negative than a positive force. Nationalist sentiment mixed with populism and gangsterism to generate an unstable stew of discontent.

The Rise of a National Revolutionary Movement

Facing a probable defeat in the 1952 presidential election, Batista deposed President Prío and took power through a coup. His style of ruling soon turned brutal, and he seemed uninterested in the calls for economic and social reforms necessary to reduce poverty and inequality. His ties to organized crime further damaged his image among Cubans. All of this prompted the young lawyer and political activist Fidel Castro to organize a rebellion against the dictatorship. In 1953, Castro led an attack on the Moncada army barracks in Santiago de Cuba. Although the attack failed and Castro (along with his brother **Raúl Castro** and others) was captured and jailed, it marked the opening shots of the Cuban revolution. In recognition of the date, the revolutionary movement became known as the 26th of July. In his own defense, Castro made a four-hour speech in the courtroom, denouncing the dictatorship and extolling the virtues of his own movement, including five specific revolutionary principles. He ended with words that became famous: "Condemn me. It does not matter. History will absolve me." Today that conclusion still sparks debate.

ANALYZING DOCUMENTS

There are few speeches in Latin American history as iconic as this one. With his fiery rhetoric in court, Fidel Castro became famous for his denunciation of the national government and passionate advocacy of the oppressed and call for hemispheric unity. He was savvy enough to write the words down later and circulate them.

"History Will Absolve Me" Speech (1953)

He who speaks to you hates vanity with all his being, nor are his temperament or frame of mind inclined towards courtroom poses or sensationalism of any kind. If I have had to assume my own defense before this Court it is for two reasons. First: because I have been denied legal aid almost entirely, and second: only one who has been so deeply wounded, who has seen his country so forsaken and its justice

(Continued)

trampled so, can speak at a moment like this with words that spring from the blood of his heart and the truth of his very gut.

. . .

The regime has emphatically repeated that our Movement did not have popular support. I have never heard an assertion so naive, and at the same time so full of bad faith. The regime seeks to show submission and cowardice on the part of the people. They all but claim that the people support the dictatorship; they do not know how offensive this is to the brave Orientales. Santiago thought our attack was only a local disturbance between two factions of soldiers; not until many hours later did they realize what had really happened. Who can doubt the valor, civic pride and limitless courage of the rebel and patriotic people of Santiago de Cuba? If Moncada had fallen into our hands, even the women of Santiago de Cuba would have risen in arms. Many were the rifles loaded for our fighters by the nurses at the Civilian Hospital. They fought alongside us. That is something we will never forget.

It was never our intention to engage the soldiers of the regiment in combat. We wanted to seize control of them and their weapons in a surprise attack, arouse the people and call the soldiers to abandon the odious flag of the tyranny and to embrace the banner of freedom; to defend the supreme interests of the nation and not the petty interests of a small clique; to turn their guns around and fire on the people's enemies and not on the people, among whom are their own sons and fathers; to unite with the people as the brothers that they are instead of opposing the people as the enemies the government tries to make of them; to march behind the only beautiful ideal worthy of sacrificing one's life—the greatness and happiness of one's country. To those who doubt that many soldiers would have followed us, I ask: What Cuban does not cherish glory? What heart is not set aflame by the promise of freedom?

. . .

The five revolutionary laws that would have been proclaimed immediately after the capture of the Moncada Barracks and would have been broadcast to the nation by radio must be included in the indictment. It is possible that Colonel Chaviano may deliberately have destroyed these documents, but even if he has I remember them.

The first revolutionary law would have returned power to the people and proclaimed the 1940 Constitution the Supreme Law of the State until such time as the people should decide to modify or change it. And in order to effect its implementation and punish those who violated it—there being no electoral organization to carry this out—the revolutionary movement, as the circumstantial incarnation of this sovereignty, the only source of legitimate power, would have assumed all the faculties inherent therein, except that of modifying the Constitution itself: in other words, it would have assumed the legislative, executive and judicial powers.

This attitude could not be clearer nor more free of vacillation and sterile charlatanry. A government acclaimed by the mass of rebel people would be vested with every power, everything necessary in order to proceed with the effective implementation of popular will and real justice. From that moment, the Judicial Power—which since March 10th had placed itself against and outside the Constitution—would cease to exist and we would proceed to its immediate and total reform before it would once again assume the power granted it by the Supreme Law of the Republic. Without these previous measures, a return to legality by putting its custody back into the hands that have crippled the system so dishonorably would constitute a fraud, a deceit, one more betrayal.

The second revolutionary law would give non-mortgageable and non-transferable ownership of the land to all tenant and subtenant farmers, lessees, share croppers and squatters who hold parcels of five caballerías of land or less, and the State would indemnify the former owners on the basis of the rental which they would have received for these parcels over a period of ten years.

The third revolutionary law would have granted workers and employees the right to share 30% of the profits of all the large industrial, mercantile and mining enterprises, including the sugar mills. The strictly agricultural enterprises would be exempt in consideration of other agrarian laws which would be put into effect.

The fourth revolutionary law would have granted all sugar planters the right to share 55% of sugar production and a minimum quota of forty thousand arrobas for all small tenant farmers who have been established for three years or more.

The fifth revolutionary law would have ordered the confiscation of all holdings and ill-gotten gains of those who had committed frauds during previous regimes, as well as the holdings and ill-gotten gains of all their legates and heirs. To implement this, special courts with full powers would gain access to all records of all corporations registered or operating in this country, in order to investigate concealed funds of illegal origin, and to request that foreign governments extradite persons and attach holdings rightfully belonging to the Cuban people. Half of the property recovered would be used to subsidize retirement funds for workers and the other half would be used for hospitals, asylums and charitable organizations.

Furthermore, it was declared that the Cuban policy in the Americas would be one of close solidarity with the democratic peoples of this continent, and that all those politically persecuted by bloody tyrannies oppressing our sister nations would find generous asylum, brotherhood and bread in the land of Martí; not the persecution, hunger and treason they find today. Cuba should be the bulwark of liberty and not a shameful link in the chain of despotism.

. . .

I know that imprisonment will be harder for me than it has ever been for anyone, filled with cowardly threats and hideous cruelty. But I do not fear prison, as I do not fear the fury of the miserable tyrant who took the lives of 70 of my comrades. Condemn me. It does not matter. History will absolve me.

Discussion Questions
- What does Fidel Castro claim the local response is to the Batista dictatorship?
- How does he view Cuba's place in the international system?

Source: http://www.marxists.org/history/cuba/archive/castro/1953/10/16.htm

In a gesture intended to be taken as magnanimous, but later proving problematic, to put it mildly, Batista pardoned Castro, who in 1955 traveled to Mexico to plot the revolution. There he met the Argentine Ernesto "Che" Guevara, who joined the 26th of July movement and accompanied the Castros in their invasion of Cuba in 1956. The invasion force numbered fewer than 100, but successfully landed and melted into the mountains. From there Castro launched a guerrilla war against the dictatorship. He gained the support of peasants in the mountains, who suffered terribly at the hands of the dictatorship. In that sense, the local level was essential for the revolution, because it provided the lifeblood of the guerrilla movement.

In response to the insurgency, Batista became even more repressive, which only strengthened support in the countryside for the rebels. The local, national, and international levels thus collided as the administration of Dwight D. Eisenhower slowly began to reassess its position. Especially after Vice President Nixon was attacked during a Latin America trip in 1958 (with his car violently rocked in Venezuela), the administration shifted toward a strategy of acknowledging the legitimate desires of Latin Americans struggling against poverty and oppression. This line of thinking, which culminated in the Alliance for Progress several years later, asserted that support for dictatorships could result in swelling the ranks of Communists in the region. President Eisenhower's brother Milton traveled to the region to make policy recommendations, and his book on the topic was published shortly after the revolution. He concluded that "If the intelligent leaders of the other American republics do not move swiftly to correct historic injustices and inequities and to bring about a social revolution by peaceful means, Castro-type revolutions may rock and wreck country after country south of the border."[4] The point was to bring real change at the local level, to produce development projects that would in turn create political support both for capitalism and for the United States. That sort of idea had never been on Batista's radar. Because of his role in fighting against Batista, Fidel Castro enjoyed support in the United States, as reporters like *The New York Times'* Herbert Matthews wrote sympathetic articles about his movement.

As should be quite obvious, the arguments we've been discussing throughout this book on presidentialism do not hold in Cuba, because it has been almost continuously authoritarian and has very little historical experience with democracy at all. The legislature played a minimal role in Cuban politics, and the judicial system was corrupt. Even after the revolution, Fidel Castro did not always hold the official office of "president." Nonetheless, Cuban politics has always been characterized by a very high degree of executive power, at the expense of other state institutions. Hypotheses about democracy therefore have not applied well to Cuba.

The Revolution: Remaking the Nation

On January 1, 1959, the revolution finally triumphed, using the guerrilla techniques that Che Guevara would later publish as a book for others to copy. Guevara defeated government troops in Santa Clara, and Fulgencio Batista fled to the Dominican Republic. Fidel Castro soon marched on to Havana, and by the next day from afar installed a president, Manuel Urrutia, a judge who had fled the Batista regime two years earlier. José Miró Cardona became prime minister. It soon became clear, however, that all power emanated from Fidel Castro regardless of what official title he happened to have (in February 1959 he took the title of prime minister). After a year, only nine of the original twenty-one cabinet members remained as Castro forced their resignations. From the beginning of the revolutionary movement, its platform had included elections, but within a few months the government announced there would be none.

Indeed, from the beginning there was neither horizontal nor vertical accountability in Cuba. The revolution had an initial façade of representation and was popular across a broad swath of political tendencies in Cuba. Batista was extremely unpopular at the time of his overthrow, and Cubans clamored for change. The movement was clearly radical but ideologically vague, which assured a honeymoon period as the new government settled in. But by the end of 1959, disenchantment had begun to set in because Fidel Castro had no intention of sharing power.

International Factors: The Role of the Soviet Union

The government moved quickly on agrarian reform in 1959, expropriating large estates and offering long-term bonds as compensation. Che Guevara became president of the Central Bank, and the economy lurched in the direction of state planning. The rhetoric of the revolution fit perfectly with what would become dependency theory, and in the postrevolutionary period many theorists viewed the Cuban model as the ultimate solution for economic dependency. Only by breaking away completely from the core of capitalist economies could a developing economy have the opportunity to flourish on its own. Cuba could therefore be seen as a test case for the theory. A critical problem, however, was that instead of becoming economically independent, Cuba just gradually shifted its dependence from the United States to the Soviet Union.

Initially, Fidel Castro was careful not to align himself immediately with the USSR. To what degree he already embraced Marxist principles by 1959 is a matter of some debate (Raúl Castro and Che Guevara were both openly committed to Marxism). Regardless, Castro waited at least six months before engaging in dialogue with the Soviets. In early 1960, the Soviets agreed to purchase large amounts of Cuban sugar and to provide loans, and shortly thereafter announced they were selling weapons to Cuba as well. Relations with the United States spiraled down quickly. When the Soviets shipped oil to Cuba, the U.S.-owned companies refused to refine it, which then led to their nationalization. The Eisenhower administration cut Cuba's sugar quota, and the Soviets responded that they would purchase any sugar the United States refused to buy. Meanwhile, the Cuban government ordered the seizure of any property owned by U.S. citizens (and then of all private interests regardless of nationality). In 1960, the United States began a partial **embargo** on the island, excluding a number of essential items such as medicine.

Not long after Castro took power, the U.S. Central Intelligence Agency (CIA) began examining possible ways to overthrow him (and later to assassinate him) just as it was doing in a wide range of other countries around the world as part of the overall U.S. strategy of fighting the Cold War. The basic plan was to organize the many Cuban exiles coming to the United States, then train and equip them for an amphibious assault on the island. There was no shortage of potential fighters, as emotions rode very high about the socialist direction that Fidel Castro was taking. The CIA itself was quite confident of victory, for two main reasons. First, the agency believed that the invasion would parallel the successful model of Guatemala in 1954, where internal opposition crumbled in the face of even a relatively small fighting force. Second, the CIA believed incorrectly that the revolution was really unpopular and so Cubans would welcome the opportunity to overthrow the Castro regime. Ultimately, the attack took place in April 1961 at the Bay of Pigs, where the ships ran aground and then came under intense fire from Cuban forces. The Cuban military took over 1,200 prisoners. Despite its efforts to maintain "plausible deniability" (which included refusing to provide air cover), the Kennedy administration was immediately implicated and thoroughly embarrassed by the failure.

After the invasion, Fidel Castro officially proclaimed himself to be Marxist-Leninist and moved even closer to the Soviet Union. Logically, his fear of more U.S. intervention increased to the point that he requested help from the Soviets, who obliged with nuclear missiles. For Soviet Premier Nikita Khrushchev, it was an opportunity to extend his reach into the Western Hemisphere and thereby to demonstrate the power of the USSR. He expected that the young and inexperienced President Kennedy would likely back down from any potential conflict. But when Kennedy was given photographic proof, he insisted the Soviets remove the missiles. The conflict moved perilously close to nuclear war as both the United States and the Soviet Union refused to yield. It took thirteen days for the two sides to come to agreement, and the USSR removed the missiles while the United States agreed not to invade Cuba and later also to remove its nuclear missiles from Turkey. Throughout, Fidel Castro was largely a peripheral figure. He advocated preemptive nuclear strikes on the United States but was told that was inadvisable for a number of reasons, one of which was that Cuba itself would bear the greatest brunt of the counterattack. The negotiation to end the dispute took place between the two great powers, and Fidel Castro was alerted to the missile's removal by a reporter. Just as in 1898, Cuban political leaders were excluded.

In 1962, President Kennedy expanded the scope of the economic restrictions to all Cuban goods. One goal was to strangle the Cuban economy sufficiently that it would lead to an armed rebellion against the Castro government. Another was, as a Department of State memorandum put it, "to reduce the economic capacity of the Castro government to engage in acts of aggression, subversion, or other activities endangering the security of the United States and other nations of the hemisphere."[5] These measures would collectively become known as the "embargo" on Cuba, and 2012 marked its fiftieth anniversary.

International Factors: The United States Embargo

The embargo prohibited U.S. companies from conducting business with Cuba. It had an immediate economic impact, particularly because Cuban vehicles and machines needed American parts, and the Soviet Union could not replace them. Many industrial inputs also vanished, which made it difficult to produce rubber, paint, or even pharmaceuticals. As historian Lou Pérez puts it, "improvisation became the hallmark of early Cuban development efforts."[6] Many factories simply had to shut due to lack of spare parts, but others were consolidated and continued producing. Cuban roads were dotted with American-made cars, and their owners found new and ingenious ways of keeping them running even when parts were unavailable. As the United States had been Cuba's primary trading partner, the embargo was a long-standing economic shock, contributing to widespread and lasting shortages. The average Cuban found it difficult to find essential goods as international influence had a huge impact. After all, the entire economy was designed for trade with the United States.

The political effects are less obvious. Although the intent of the embargo has always been to damage the regime, in many ways it has become a useful foil for Fidel Castro. Regardless of their true origin, economic problems can be (and routinely are) blamed on the United States. When Cubans could not obtain meat or milk, did they blame Fidel? Not necessarily. Fidel Castro has called the embargo "genocide" for its adverse effects, though of course shortages are also attributable to the inefficiencies of a planned economy. Still, supporters of the embargo argue that its removal would benefit the regime economically. The debate has raged for so long that President Barack Obama presides over a policy put in place when he was an infant.

In 1963, President Kennedy added travel restrictions as well, so that U.S. citizens must obtain special permission for travel to the island. Thus, for decades it has been closed to all but those who receive special permits (such as for educational purposes), which can be difficult to obtain. There were periods of relative relaxation, such as during the Carter administration, but in general business and tourism were cut off. In 2000, the U.S. Congress passed the Trade Sanction Reform and Export Enhancement Act, which allows for food exports as long as they are conducted in cash. Cuba has been taken advantage of this opportunity to the tune of about $700 million in 2008, but it remains limited given the country's shortage of hard currency.

It is not easy to disentangle the national and international influences on the Cuban revolution during this period. The failed U.S. actions made Castro more popular than ever, both at home and abroad, as David defeated the immense Goliath. U.S. efforts to invade, assassinate, or sabotage served to promote a sense of revolutionary unity. This did not necessarily derive from support for all aspects of the revolution, but rather from a feeling of nationalist pride that went down to the most local level. At the same time, Castro was popular in his own right. He seemed ever-present, giving speeches that lasted for hours, going into the sugarcane fields himself to help with harvesting, and constantly calling on Cubans to work and to resist counterrevolutionary temptations. He also continually reorganized the government, even entire ministries, in an ongoing effort to maintain state control while avoiding overcentralization. That balance, naturally, was no easy task.

▬▬▬ CUBA'S POLITICAL INSTITUTIONS ▬▬▬

Last constitution: 1992

Unitary system of fourteen provinces plus municipality of the Isle of Youth

Executive: President of the Council of State, elected by the National Assembly

Legislative: Unicameral National Assembly with 609 members (majority vote). Candidates chosen by the Community Party

Judiciary: People's Supreme Court

Contemporary Cuban Politics

In the years immediately following the revolution, the most notable socioeconomic advances came in the areas of health and education, and these had both immediate and long-lasting impacts on the local population. By the 1970s, malnutrition was essentially eliminated. The average Cuban diet was not necessarily varied, but it was guaranteed. The state worked quickly to address the serious illiteracy problem. In 1958, almost half of Cuban children aged 6 to 14 years had not received education.[7] After an intense campaign of volunteers, within a few years Cuba had the highest literacy rate in Latin America. Schools appeared in remote areas that had never seen them before. But the state also centered attention on higher education, and eventually Cuba produced a large number of doctors, technicians, engineers, and other highly trained individuals who at times became part of international missions. Education focused strongly on technology to produce concrete benefits for the revolution.

Fidel Castro worked to create a command economy that in theory would be driven by the needs of the people, but also sustained by their selfless hard work. Government officials even talked about eliminating money altogether. If the revolutionary ideal of self-sacrifice was real, then money would no longer be necessary. That idyllic dream eventually gave way to the reality that incentives of some sort were necessary to keep production levels up. By the 1970s, wages became tied to output. That made bonuses possible, but also pay cuts if the quota was not met. Workers who did well could also obtain consumer goods that otherwise might be too difficult or expensive to purchase. Economic growth was strong and steady during this period. Between 1971 and 1980, the economy grew by an average rate of 5.7 percent.[8]

Dependency theory posits that less-developed countries are tied to wealthier core countries, providing raw materials and importing finished goods in a manner that does not allow for independent development. That was certainly the case with prerevolutionary Cuba, which was tightly bound to the U.S. economy and investors. The most radical advocates of dependency theory called for Marxist revolution, and so the Cuban revolution represented a perfect example of theory transformed into practice. The net effect, however, was not economic independence. Instead, the Cuban economy switched dependence from the United States to the Soviet Union, which filled the vacuum when the United States created the embargo. For example, not only did Cuba rely on heavily subsidized delivery of Soviet oil, but it actually reexported some of that oil, thus bringing in badly needed revenue without actually producing anything.

Politically, the Cuban revolution was almost immediately repressive. There was (and is) vertical control rather than vertical accountability. The Ministry of the Interior was in charge of domestic surveillance and security, which literally went down to the most local levels. The Committees in Defense of the Revolution (CDR) are local spying networks formed by the government to ensure that no counterrevolutionary activities could get going. The CDRs are important conduits between the government and the local population, with the "block captains" having the responsibility of knowing all the goings-on of their particular area. They provide key connections between the national and the local.

Under the leadership of Raúl Castro and with Soviet funding and training, the Revolutionary Armed Forces (FAR) became the backbone of the regime and the center of national political power as well. Of course, it was responsible for protecting the country from invasion, but it was also involved in internal security. Further, the FAR increasingly became involved in economic activities, particularly in joint ventures (such as hotels and tourist airlines) when the Cuban economy liberalized in the 1990s. Although he lacked the same charisma as his brother, Raúl Castro excelled at organization and discipline, so that the FAR has always been a loyal defender of the revolution.

Cuban political institutions maintain a façade of democracy but do not challenge Fidel or Raúl Castro's authority. Since 1976, the unicameral National Assembly of People's Power is the national legislative body in Cuba, and its members are elected for five-year terms. It then elects the thirty-one member Council of Ministers, which includes the president. The outcome of these elections is not in doubt, and the candidates routinely win well over 90 percent of the vote. The entire legislature meets twice a year, but it represents only a rubber stamp while providing an aura of representative legitimacy to decisions made by the Council of Ministers.

In a similar vein, the Supreme Court's members are elected by the legislature. In name, the court is independent of the executive branch, but it must answer to the National Assembly of People's Power, which includes the president and vice presidents. The 1992 constitution provides for considerable authority in name as justices "only owe obedience to the law." In practice, however, the courts accede to the executive's will and have not been a force for horizontal accountability. Since very early on in the revolution, no one doubted where the real political power resided.

As the regime consolidated, it also moved closer to the Soviet Union, on which it depended economically, so international influence remained very strong. Cuba moved closer to the East European Council for Mutual Economic Assistance (CMEA) to export primary products, which provided essential markets but increased dependency on the Soviet bloc. Politically, the 1970s saw the increase of power of the Cuban Communist Party, built along the same lines as the Soviet model. One price of dependence was supporting Soviet foreign policy, which included applauding the invasion and occupation of Czechoslovakia in 1968 and Afghanistan in 1979, both of which were the types of imperialist policies Fidel Castro typically condemned.

The Post-Cold War: Local and National Economic Collapse

In the 1980s, the Soviet economy was grinding to a halt. A reformer named Mikhail Gorbachev took power in 1985 and initiated a process of major political and economic change. He advocated for "glasnost" (openness) and "perestroika" (restructuring) of the Soviet Union. For the first time, people came out into the streets to protest, while Gorbachev encouraged debate over how to save the socialist economy from its shortcomings. Part of this effort included cutting the aid that had kept countries like Cuba afloat (other Communist countries, like North Korea, also suffered as a result). The Soviet Union ceased to exist in late 1991, and by 1992 all the subsidies, military aid, and preferential trade relationships with Cuba had disappeared. The U.S. government pressured Gorbachev's successor Boris Yeltsin to cut all those ties as a precondition for receiving assistance. As the ideological link between Russia and Cuba no longer existed, Yeltsin opted for the pragmatic solution of ending the long-standing relationship. There was also support within the Russian government for that decision, since many viewed Cuba as a drain on resources without sufficient political or economic payoffs. The end of Soviet assistance was disastrous for the highly dependent Cuban economy. In 1991 the government announced that the country had entered the "Special Period in Peacetime" (See Box 7.1) The essence of the Special Period was sacrifice, as there were shortages of virtually everything, from oil to electricity to food.

BOX 7.1

The Special Period: How International Factors Impact the Local Level

International: Fidel Castro announced the Special Period in Peacetime in 1991 in response to radical changes taking place in the Soviet Union. The Soviet Union had been propping up the Cuban economy for years, most critically in terms of providing very cheap oil and gasoline and buying sugar. In 1990 and 1991, however, Soviet Premier Mikhail Gorbachev began cutting economic and military assistance to Cuba. The Council of Mutual Economic Assistance (CMEA), which was the trade bloc of socialist countries, fell apart. It had accounted for 85 percent of Cuba's trade, and so its dissolution hurt badly.

National: Between 1990 and 1993, Gross Domestic Product plummeted 35 percent, and imports fell by 88 percent.[9] Rationing of food became the order of the day. Production in all sectors of the economic fell, and the drop of food production really hit Cubans hard, as basic foodstuffs were difficult to obtain unless one had dollars to spend in the black market. The government worked to maintain jobs, but unemployment rose. Those who remained employed, however, often made little money. Net salaries dropped 42 percent in those three years. Women were especially hard hit, as by necessity they had to find ways to obtain basic goods while still managing their households. It sparked ingenuity (and illegality) as people had to do anything they could to survive.

Local: The Special Period also included formal political reform that affected local politics. The government promulgated a new constitution in 1992 that codified some of the new changes,

such as economic decentralization and allowance for some measure of property rights (such as joint ventures) that would spur foreign investment. Lastly, the Special Period sparked mass emigration. So-called *balseros* ("rafters") launched from Cuban beaches and risked the shark-infested and hurricane-prone waters of the Florida Straits. In 1994, some 50,000 Cubans left the country. Not until the latter half of the 1990s would the economy finally stabilize.

Discussion Questions

- Can you think of ways that international and local factors come together to convince individuals to leave their country, even if it means risking their lives?
- Why might the national economic crisis lead to more local autonomy?

The Special Period also sparked an increase in migration to the United States. In 1994, a number of Cuban boats were hijacked and taken to Miami. Domestic tensions increased, including demonstrations, and as in the past Fidel Castro responded by abruptly announcing that anyone could leave. Similar circumstances had arisen in 1965 and 1980, with protests against the regime followed by an abrupt announcement that any Cuban could leave the country if he or she desired. Mass migration was used both as a political tool to exile the discontented and a foreign policy tool to force concessions from the U.S. government, which did not want the influx of migrants. The so-called Mariel Boatlift of 1980 was a disaster for the United States, with 100,000 Cubans—some of them criminals—arriving in Florida.

Economic deprivation meant that people who previously felt more connected to the national economy had to scramble to make ends meet in any way. The Special Period set into motion a flotilla of homemade rafts, risking the treacherous Florida Straits to reach the United States. The Clinton administration was taken by surprise, and in 1994 responded by implementing a new immigration policy for Cuba alone. It became known as the "wet foot, dry foot" policy. Instead of accepting any Cuban migrant, the United States would only accept those who had arrived on land. In other words, if a Cuban hijacked a boat that was then intercepted by the U.S. Coast Guard, they would be deported back to Cuba. The Castro regime, in turn, promised that anyone deported would not be penalized for the mere fact of migrating, though anyone who had committed a crime such as hijacking would still face Cuban justice. The United States also agreed to accept up to 20,000 Cubans to migrate legally, though that ceiling is not often met.

At the time, it seemed entirely possible that the regime might collapse under the weight of the crisis. As one CIA analyst notes, U.S. intelligence agencies concluded in 1993 that there was "a better than even chance that Fidel Castro's government will fall within the next few years."[10] That idea perhaps even reached the status of conventional wisdom, at least outside of Cuba. The argument was that crisis at the local level—no jobs, no food—combined with more international demands would cause national uprisings. Of course, odds are just that. Instead, as we discuss, Fidel Castro demonstrated more of the improvisation that had served him well in the past.

Political Support: The Role of Women and Afro-Cubans

Part of the regime's durability lay in its policies toward women and Afro-Cubans. The Cuban revolution was transformative for women's political activism, but it built on an already existing base. After years of struggle, women gained the right to vote in 1934. The 1940 constitution also enshrined gender equality and the right of women to be financially independent from men. When Batista assumed dictatorial power in 1952, women took on important opposition roles and joined a large number of groups, including the 26th of July. Fidel Castro made a point of acknowledging the importance of women in the revolutionary struggle, and in 1958 created an all-female platoon in the Sierra Maestra. In 1960, he created the Federation of Cuban Women, which has been a central vehicle for women's issues since then. Interestingly, it was established as a nongovernmental organization (NGO) without formal ties to the government. It seeks to connect women from the local to the national levels, focusing especially on education. The vast majority of Cuban women are members.

There was immediate impact on the local level. The revolution put women to work in agricultural brigades (particularly in sugarcane fields) and as teachers going to remote areas of the country. Rural women in particular were also beneficiaries of the latter program, as literacy became a vehicle for greater political participation. In urban areas, women moved into the workforce, and by the 1980s there were about 1,000 day care centers across the country to alleviate the burden on families. Broad cultural patterns of machismo and male domination still remain obstacles to equality, however, and have never disappeared. In 1974, the government enacted the Family Code, which outlined male responsibility for the households. However, it remained more of an aspiration than an accomplishment.

Later, the economic crisis that exploded in the late 1980s hit women disproportionately hard. They were expected to be active workers, but with food scarcity they also needed to become entrepreneurs to utilize the black market to obtain necessary goods. On top of that, they were expected to maintain the same household responsibilities as in the past. Tradition compounded with necessity stretched women to the limit. Since then, whenever the Cuban economy moves more toward capitalism, older patterns of discrimination once again become apparent as the state has fewer resources to provide for childcare and other local-level necessities.[11]

Afro-Cubans have also been major beneficiaries of the revolution. Race relations in prerevolutionary Cuba were conflict-ridden, marked by massacres, lynchings, and other less violent but still discriminatory practices. Black Cubans had always been more poverty-stricken than the rest of the population, and so the revolution offered something that no government had before. Fidel Castro addressed racial discrimination directly, and for that has always been popular with the black population. After the revolution, that population was immediately granted access to the beaches, restaurants, and other areas that before had been denied them. Indeed, only a very small percentage of emigrants to the United States are black.

In a 1994 poll, 73 percent of blacks and 62 percent of whites agreed that blacks would be worse off without the revolution.[12] Large majorities of blacks believed the revolution had enjoyed "great success" in providing education (93 percent), health care (94 percent), and job opportunities (77 percent). At the same time, however, 77 percent believed that it had only provided moderate success in eliminating racial discrimination and prejudices. Economic and social inequalities still exist. Privatization and legalization of dollars benefit whites more, because blacks had less access to dollars in the first place, and fewer connections to reap the full benefits of any market reforms.

Race relations are still a matter of complex public discussion, which goes down to the local level, even to walking on the street. Afro-Cubans feel they are stopped by the police more than whites. Housing segregation also persists, so that blacks are more likely to live in crowded tenements, while the shantytowns around Havana and Santiago de Cuba are predominantly black as well.[13] Overt racial discrimination is illegal, but more subtle forms still take place. The essential problem is how to address the divisions in Cuban society while also maintaining revolutionary unity for the regime. For Afro-Cubans the issue of race is also connected to the perception of race relations in the United States, especially in the exile communities of Miami, which are viewed as very racist. Thus, despite concerns about the Castro government's treatment of race, support for the revolution continues because it is still seen as superior to any alternative.

Cuba's International Influence

Although Cuba's political and economic development was shaped in important respects by international influences, Fidel Castro also positioned the country to have its own international impact. Under the direction of Raúl Castro, the military became a well-trained force that evolved into another Cuban export in defense of fellow revolutionaries in Latin America and Africa. In 1965, Che Guevara himself traveled to the Congo, hoping to make contact with rebels and lead anti-imperialist forces, though he left the continent without achieving much success. Approximately 36,000 Cuban soldiers were central to the

Marxist government's victory against insurgents in Angola in 1975 and 1976, and Cuba was involved in some manner all around Africa. In Latin America, Cuba assisted the Sandinista rebels in Nicaragua, and also a Marxist government in Grenada, where a Cuban force of approximately 700 could not withstand a U.S. invasion in 1983 to overthrow it. Cuba's commitment to helping Marxist movements around the world solidified Castro's personal stature as well. At the same time, Castro was pragmatic and did not support insurgencies against governments that recognized his government. Ideology thus did not always take priority when determining who to fund and support logistically.

Armed conflict was indeed not the only strategy in the Cuban playbook. Fidel Castro allied himself with disparate organizations and peoples who similarly felt threatened by U.S. foreign policy. For example, he was a vocal supporter of the Palestine Liberation Organization as well as the African National Congress in South Africa. Cuba became an active member of the Non-Aligned Movement, created by India in 1955 to bring together states that professed not to be on one side or another in the Cold War. Since Cuba relied heavily on the Soviet Union, it was by no means nonaligned, but the organization provided another platform for Fidel Castro to articulate his anti-U.S. message.

Cuba's international influence declined rapidly in the late 1980s as Soviet aid decreased. The government did not have the resources to fund revolutionary movements, and in any case many key battlegrounds, especially in Central America, were engaged in the protracted process of peace negotiation. Yet even as Cuba's international reach found strict limitations, the United States exerted ever more pressure, so as always international influence was significant.

The thrust of U.S. policy did not change with the end of the Cold War. Indeed, it intensified. Convinced that the revolutionary government would fall at any moment, members of Congress passed legislation intended to hasten the process. The 1992 Cuban Democracy Act sought to punish foreign subsidiaries of U.S. companies for trading with Cuba, while the 1996 Helms-Burton Act (formally named the Cuban Liberty and Democratic Solidarity Act, but more commonly known by the names of its sponsors, Senator Jesse Helms and Representative Dan Burton) went a step further by punishing foreign companies that were utilizing property in Cuba that previously was owned by U.S. citizens before expropriation. The overall rationale was that tightening the embargo would crush the Cuban economy to the extent that Cubans themselves would demand change. This was really only an extension of the embargo's original logic. Helms-Burton Act is unique because it actually moves foreign policy decision making from the White House to Congress, stipulating that only Congress can rule whether Cuba has moved sufficiently toward democracy to allow open trade and travel.

These policies were cheered on by exile groups in Miami. The most powerful was the Cuban American National Foundation (CANF) under the leadership of Jorge Mas Canosa. Mas Canosa modeled the organization on other successful lobbyist groups, using money and votes as leverage to pressure policy makers. For years, the Cuban American community could be counted on to vote on the narrow issue of U.S.-Cuba relations, which had the effect of forcing presidential candidates to court it. Florida's electoral votes have often proved critical for presidential races, so CANF and its allies were ignored at the candidate's peril.

Cuba's Economic Transformation

The Castro regime looked to new trading partners to find economic footing. Relaxed joint venture laws brought in foreign investment from around the world. Foreign companies invested in agriculture, mining, construction, light manufacturing, and tourism. The last in particular became a new focus for revenue. The Cuban government entered into agreements that built new hotels, restaurants, and clubs that would once again make Cuba a popular tourist destination. Yet the influx of tourists highlighted the widespread deprivation of the population. Tourists enjoyed many goods and services (even as basic as soap and shampoo) that were either unavailable or difficult to find for the average Cuban. There was also a large disparity between the peso and dollar economies.

One important international factor for the Cuban economy's recovery was the election of Hugo Chávez as president of Venezuela in 1998. He had always admired Fidel Castro and started providing oil to relieve the shortage in Cuba. By 2009, Venezuela exported 100,000 barrels of oil a day to Cuba, at a 40 percent discount. Overall, trade between Venezuela and Cuba reached about $7 billion a year by 2007. With Venezuela, Cuba also cofounded the Bolivarian Alternative for the Americas (commonly known by its Spanish acronym ALBA), an organization of countries with leftist governments aimed at strengthening trade ties and mutual assistance. Through ALBA, Cuba agreed to send doctors to Venezuela in exchange for oil. In addition to ALBA, Cuba reestablished long dormant trade ties across all of Latin America.

Cuba has also strengthened its weakened ties to Russia. The government of President (and then Prime Minister) Vladimir Putin once again viewed Cuba as important from a geostrategic perspective given its proximity to the United States. For Russia, military exercises and an increase in trade relations and investment served to send a message that if the United States were involved in Eastern Europe, then Russia could do the same in the Western Hemisphere. But Latin America also serves an economic purpose, as in 2009 Russia overtook the United States in the amount of arms sales in the region as a whole.

Despite its socialist orientation, the Cuban economy resembles some of its capitalist Caribbean and Central American counterparts in terms of reliance on remittances, which reach upward of $1 billion a year. Although many, if not most, Cuban Americans hope for the fall of the Castro regime, they want to help their relatives, and so dollars flow in. The Cuban government responded in turn, running dollar-only stores that become a vehicle for bringing dollars into the treasury. In 2004, the administration of George W. Bush restricted the sending of remittances to immediate family members and only to $300 for people traveling to the island, though President Obama subsequently relaxed them.

Like other Latin American countries, Cuba also experienced severe debt problems, which still plague it. Because of its inability to repay, Cuba has one of the worst credit ratings in the world. It has defaulted on debt to Japan, Spain, and other developed countries. Cuba has also run up debt with China, which then enabled it to buy Chinese goods, and in 2008 the Chinese government put off repayment for ten years. Cuba still owes over $20 billion to Russia (most of it Soviet-era) and is increasingly indebted to Venezuela.

As the economy started to grow again, Fidel Castro moved to recentralize economic control. In 2004, he mandated that dollars should be converted into a local (and nonconvertible) currency. That decision, however, also suggested that the government was concerned about its own lack of hard currency, which was needed to continue servicing the country's sizeable external debt. The government reduced the number of permits for self-employment, which had the effect of moving back in the direction of a command economy. The revolutionary ideal of providing Cubans with all basic needs was obviously no longer viable. Despite these types of policy reforms, life in Cuba was more oriented than ever in finding ways—legally or not—to obtain essential goods, from food to soap or toothpaste. Cuba also moved away from a reliance on sugar, which had long been a core part of the economy. An increase of production in other countries, such as Brazil, lowered the price of sugar, while sugar substitutes such as high-fructose corn syrup further damaged the market. It became cheaper to import some sugar for domestic consumption rather than produce it locally.

The Evolution of Political Control

The regime became less repressive than in the past, in part because it lacked the same capacity. One author has labeled the change as "charismatic post-totalitarianism."[14] Despite the fact that the revolution was clearly not living up to its professed ideals, Fidel Castro's own charisma and connection to the Cuban people served to stabilize the regime. Nonetheless, the military was given control over the Interior Ministry in 1989, which further militarized internal security. That came after a high-profile purge of senior army officers and some Interior Ministry officials as well, serving the purpose of firming up government control.

Political opposition did emerge at the local level, building to take on national and even international significance. The most influential was the Varela Project, created in 1998 by Osvaldo Payá, a political activist with strong religious convictions. He helped found the Christian Liberation Movement in 1988, and at times was imprisoned for his opposition to the dictatorship. The Varela Project took a novel and nonviolent root, based on the Cuban constitution, which allowed for a referendum on the proposal of new laws (to be ultimately considered by the Cuban legislature) as long as proponents obtained at least 10,000 signatures. The proposed law would allow freedoms (such as speech, association, religion, and even the right to own businesses). Despite receiving the necessary signatures in 2002, the initiative was denied by the government, which claimed it was a subversive effort, aided by the United States, to destroy the revolution. Within a year, twenty-five Varela Project members were arrested and imprisoned. Fidel Castro then reformed the constitution to state that the revolution was permanently Marxist, unchangeable by any vote.

The limits of the state's tolerance are exemplified by the blogger **Yoani Sánchez**, whose blog "Generación Y" has received attention across the world. She writes sometimes stinging critiques of the regime, highlighting economic deprivation and political repression. She has been assaulted by Cuban authorities and prohibited from traveling around the island. After repeated attempts, in 2013 she was finally given permission to travel briefly outside Cuba. In fact, her blog reaches a much greater international than domestic audience, since the Internet is not widely available and is controlled.

The lessons of the Soviet Union had not been lost on Fidel Castro. He had been very critical of Gorbachev's glasnost, which he correctly believed would destroy Marxism by allowing too much dissent and uncontrolled questioning of government policies. Any restructuring in Cuba would therefore be carefully controlled. Too much freedom of speech would create cracks into which the United States and other counterrevolutionary forces could force themselves. The Cuban revolution would not suffer the same fate. Indeed, the core issue for Cuba has been how the revolution will be altered when Fidel Castro dies or is otherwise incapacitated. Cuba's institutional structure has been remarkably durable, but it has always been driven by Fidel Castro.

In 2006, he announced he was sick. He provided few details, though it was subsequently known that he had intestinal surgery to address internal bleeding, quite possibly for diverticulitis, a serious intestinal inflammation. He then informed Cubans and the world that he was stepping down temporarily from all of his many positions of leadership and that Raúl Castro would assume power, which became official in 2008. He noted that he had to carefully control the power shift because of the threat from the United States, and ended with a typical exhortation: "I do not harbor the slightest doubt that our people and our Revolution will fight until the last drop of blood to defend these and other ideas and measures that are necessary for safeguarding this historical process." Speculation became rampant about the state of his health. Rumors of his illness or even death were nothing new, but always exaggerated.

Of course, the other important question was how smoothly the transfer of power to Raúl would progress. Fidel's younger brother was widely considered an efficient administrator (he had firm control over the armed forces) but not a charismatic leader. Over time, his views were also more pragmatic than Fidel's, so that he was much more open to economic liberalization instead of ideological purity. This is ironic, since the brothers had opposite views at the time of the revolution. Given the secrecy that always surrounds the highest echelons of power in Cuba, we have nothing but rumors to help us understand the transition. From the outside, however, it appeared to go off without a hitch. Fidel left the public eye, though occasionally the state published his picture, or he met with visiting foreign leaders. Eventually he even began writing his own periodic column in the state newspaper *Granma*, on topics ranging from politics to history to baseball. He also gradually made public appearances, belying the near constant predictions of his death.

Economic Policy Under Raúl Castro

Politics has changed relatively little under Raúl, but important economic shifts are underway. In particular, economic policy has slowly transformed in the direction of limited capitalism. In 2008, he used decree powers to allow Cubans access to computers and cell phones. He also granted Cubans the right to farm up to 99 acres of unused land, and to profit from the sales of produce after fulfilling the government quota. That policy was a response to the fact that Cuba was importing upward of $1.5 billion in food annually. One consequence was a rise in prices, because scarcity in state-run stores kept demand very high. In 2009, therefore, the government announced price controls on sales of produce. Raúl repeatedly made the point that he was not going to restore capitalism to Cuba, but in 2009 he also announced spending cuts in education and health care, which had long been touted as some of the most important achievements of the revolution. He argued that the current rate of spending was unsustainable in the face of the global recession that began in 2008. Perhaps the most capitalist-oriented move came in 2010, when the government announced it would cut 500,000 state jobs and encourage the development of small businesses. In an interview, Fidel Castro himself said, "The Cuban model doesn't work for us anymore."

Raúl Castro's ascent to power highlights once again the essential role of the Cuban military within the revolution. In the early days, it was the only institution that Fidel Castro considered capable and loyal enough to undertake the necessary tasks of institution-building and economic reform. The Special Period sparked dramatic cuts in the military budget, which went from $1.1 billion in 1990 to $537 million in 1998, recovering a bit to $879 million in 2000.[15] Although this has reduced its size and firepower, the armed forces remain a major source of foreign exchange. They are involved in tourism, taxis, airlines, construction, shopping centers and even discotheques. As mentioned, through these roles it has also entered into joint ventures with foreign companies. The armed forces therefore have consistently been a central player in the Cuban economy. But perhaps even more importantly, Raúl Castro's forces still represent the backbone of the revolution, protecting it both from internal and external enemies.

Another development that emerged after Raúl Castro took power was acceptance of criticism of the socialist model. With echoes of Mikhail Gorbachev's glasnost (which Fidel had strongly rejected), the government's goal was to determine the optimal ways to address the country's core economic problems without engendering political change. High-level Cuban officials occasionally also began referring to problems with the socialist model, as it was increasingly unable to fulfill its stated goals of providing sufficient food, employment, and other essentials.

Overall, the shift toward capitalist reforms has fostered noticeable economic changes at all levels of Cuban society. Inequality has increased, particularly because those with access to dollars have a much greater ability to make effective use of the black market. That means an advantage for families with relatives living abroad (and less for the Afro-Cuban population, as fewer live abroad). Social problems such as crime and prostitution have also increased. Divorce rates have risen, while the quality and availability of health care has deteriorated. The Cuban state can no longer afford the same services that it provided with assistance from the Soviet Union, and so Cubans often have to look elsewhere for what they need.

These changes have also transformed the local level. The country had a centrally planned economy, but the Special Period prompted decentralization. The existing Municipal Administrative Council was intended to provide a forum for local problems, but generally did not tackle the most serious, particularly if there was no obvious solution available. Further, local issues had to be adapted according to national priorities, which might or might not mesh well. This was exacerbated by a lack of funding. Neighborhood Transformation Workshops and People's Councils were therefore created and offered a measure of local autonomy for policy making. This involves economic decisions, such as homes with rooms for rent or small private restaurants. But it can also involve public policy, like addressing problems with trash collection, as residents work with government officials, NGOs, academics, and others. The "local" level in Cuba can mean a neighborhood, since the municipalities are large.[16] The People's Councils in particular marked a new era of neighborhood transformation. They must operate within the confines of the dictates of the central government, but at least have offered new ways of solving local needs that grew dramatically after the end of Soviet subsidies.

International Influence: The United States After the Cold War

The policy of the United States toward Cuba has been very resistant to change. Laws such as Helms-Burton clearly did not accelerate the collapse of the Castro regime. In many ways, tightening the embargo contributed to its continuation, as the Special Period and other economic ills were blamed on the United States. If anything, Fidel and Raúl became more entrenched, buoyed by the vocal and material support of Hugo Chávez. Even the Organization of American States reconsidered its rejection of the Castro government.

But there have been signs that the once monolithic Cuba lobby in the United States is shifting. When Barack Obama was running for president in 2008, he gave a speech to the CANF in which he advocated for diplomacy. That message was received with applause, and in fact when presidential candidate Senator John McCain gave a more hardline speech, CANF president Francisco "Pepe" Hernández (who succeeded Jorge Mas Canosa after his death) expressed his disappointment that McCain was not more open to rethinking Cuba policy. After his election, President Obama made some changes, such as increasing the amount of allowed remittance money and liberalizing travel for family members, along with granting telecommunications firms the right to do business in Cuba. More and more voices are calling for an end to the embargo, including from businesses that view Cuba as a source of profit, but the current restrictions to cash-only agricultural trade do not offer much opportunity. Substantive change, however, will require congressional action, which has yet to occur. Reforms to Cold War–era laws have been extremely slow and cautious.

TABLE 7.1 Cuban Economic Indicators, 1991–2011

Year	GDP Growth	Inflation	Unemployment	Poverty Rate (Not Available)	Human Development Index
1991	−10.9	—	—	—	0.769
1992	−11.2	—	—	—	0.666
1993	−14.7	—	—	—	0.726
1994	0.6	—	—	—	0.723
1995	2.4	—	—	—	0.729
1996	7.8	—	—	—	—
1997	2.5	1.9	7.0	—	0.765
1998	1.5	2.9	6.6	—	0.783
1999	6.3	−2.9	6.3	—	—
2000	6.1	−3.0	5.5	—	—
2001	3.0	−0.5	4.1	—	0.806
2002	1.5	7.0	3.3	—	0.809
2003	2.9	5.0	2.3	—	—
2004	4.5	2.9	1.9	—	—
2005	11.2	3.7	1.9	—	0.838
2006	12.1	5.7	1.9	—	—
2007	7.3	10.6	1.9	—	—
2008	4.3	−0.1	1.6	—	—
2009	1.4	−0.1	1.7	—	—
2010	1.9	1.7	2.5	—	0.775
2011	2.7	1.4	3.2	—	0.777

Sources: Unemployment: *GDP and Inflation: Preliminary Overview of the Economies of Latin America and the Caribbean*, 1994–2012.
Poverty rate: Social Panorama of Latin America. Economic Commission for Latin America, 1990–2012.
Human development index: United Nations, *Human Development Report*, 1990–2013.

Conclusion and Comparative Perspective

Fidel Castro's talks with Herbert Matthews way back in 1957 still resonate. The Castro regime seems sure of itself, while international factors—both positive and negative—are ever present. The only predictable aspect of the revolution's future is unpredictability. For so many analysts, the death of Fidel Castro and the downfall (or at least reform) of the revolutionary reform has been imminent for years. International influence has been central, with economic dependence, a prominent place for Cuba in the Cold War, and a constant effort by the United States to overthrow the government. Yet for over fifty years, through assassination attempts, illness, economic depression, invasion, and covert operations, Fidel and Raúl Castro still rule Cuba, and we can only speculate about what will happen when they eventually pass from the scene. It is still too early to know whether history will absolve him.

Yet it is clear at the national level that Raúl Castro's style of governance is more pragmatic and less ideological than his brother's. This shift includes more recognition of the limitations of the socialist model to provide for all citizens, and the need for some measure of input and criticism from the Cuban people to address those shortcomings. Nonetheless, such changes should not be taken to mean a transition toward democracy, such as occurred in Nicaragua—also an avowedly revolutionary government—in 1990. There is neither horizontal nor vertical accountability in Cuba, and the elections do not provide real political alternatives. Freedoms such as speech, association, and movement remain limited, even as the regime shifts economic power down to the local level. In short, Cuba is still an authoritarian state, even though the contours of the dictatorship have evolved over time. A central question for Cuba's political future is what mode of transition the country eventually follows toward a more democratic system.

Cuba is a unique case given its unusually antagonistic relationship with the United States since the revolution. Mexico is also closely tied to the United States given its geography and history, but relations tend not to get quite as personal. The level of personal animosity from some policy makers in the United States is analogous to Hugo Chávez in Venezuela. At the same time, though, Cuba shares a number of characteristics with other countries in Latin America. Although its particular ideological brand of authoritarian rule has not been copied elsewhere, the questions both of human rights and the prospects for political transition are similar to those posed during the era of dictatorships in other parts of Latin America.

Economically, the Cuban economy relies heavily on remittances from its migrants abroad, primarily in the United States. This makes it no different from, say, Guatemala or the Dominican Republic. Like those and other small Central American and Caribbean nations, Cuba also needs to find markets for a relatively small number of primary products while developing a tourism industry to benefit from the disposable income held by citizens of more developed countries. Its economic future, then, is bound very tightly to international factors.

Key Terms

- Fidel Castro
- Platt Amendment
- Fulgencio Batista
- Raúl Castro

- Embargo
- Special Period in Peacetime
- Yoani Sánchez

Discussion Questions

- There is a long-standing debate about whether U.S. policy drove Fidel Castro toward the Soviet Union, or whether he had already been planning that move. Which argument appears to be more compelling about this international effect, and why?
- What kinds of economic reforms might Cuba have to undergo before it can be called *capitalist*?
- Discuss the effects of the Special Period in Cuba. Given the widespread belief that the Castro regime would fall as a result of economic collapse, explain the key reasons why it did not.
- Assess how critical the Cuban revolution is to an understanding of Latin American politics during the Cold War. In what ways did it contribute to political change across the region?
- In what ways has the revolution improved the socioeconomic status of Afro-Cubans, and how has it fallen short of the changes it promised?

Further Sources

Books

Brenner, Philip, Marguerite Rose Jiménez, John M. Kirk, and William M. LeoGrande (eds.). *Reinventing the Revolution: A Contemporary Cuba Reader* (Lanham: Rowman and Littlefield Publishers, Inc., 2008). This is a very useful overview of Cuban politics, economics, foreign policy, society, and culture. A total of forty-nine separate essays by noted scholars offer a broad panorama of the Cuban revolution and its effects.

Erikson, Daniel. *The Cuba Wars: Fidel Castro, the United States, and the Next Revolution* (New York: Bloomsbury Press, 2009). Erikson examines how the transfer of power from Fidel to Raúl Castro has been perceived in both the United States and in Cuba. In particular, Raúl Castro has created an entirely new set of expectations that may drastically change the status quo.

Latell, Brian. *After Fidel: Raúl Castro and the Future of Cuba's Revolution* (New York: Palgrave Macmillan, 2005). The author is a former CIA analyst, and so the book provides not only an interesting account of the past and future of the Cuban revolution, but it also provides insights into how intelligence professionals in the United States view the Castro brothers and Cuban politics more generally.

Pérez, Louis A. Jr. *Cuba: Between Reform and Revolution*, 3rd edition (New York: Oxford University Press, 2005). This is an indispensable source on Cuba by the most prominent historian of Cuba in the United States. It includes an extensive annotated bibliography at the end.

Schoultz, Lars. *That Infernal Little Cuban Republic: The United States and the Cuban Revolution* (Chapel Hill: University of North Carolina Press, 2009). A meticulously researched book on the long-time efforts by the United States to control Cuba, focusing mostly on the period after 1953. It offers a detailed analysis of how policy makers viewed Cuba and how in many ways they have not changed over the past century and more.

Web sites

Association for the Study of the Cuban Economy (http://www.ascecuba.org/). The ASCE is a nonpartisan organization that studies the dynamics of the Cuban economy and holds an annual conference. It includes links to articles and scholarly papers on the topic.

Castro Speech Database (http://lanic.utexas.edu/la/cb/cuba/castro.html). This is a fascinating searchable database that includes speeches, interviews, and other similar statements by Fidel Castro from 1959 until 1996. All are translated into English.

The Cuban Rafter (http://balseros.miami.edu/). The University of Miami's digital library uses maps and photos along with timelines and history to explain the plight of the Cuban rafters who seek asylum in the United States.

Granma (http://www.granma.cu/ingles/index.html). This is the official state newspaper of Cuba, which is published online in Spanish, English, French, Portuguese, German, and Italian. It is updated constantly and includes both current events and commentary about the revolution and U.S. policy. It also includes Fidel Castro's periodic column in English.

United States Interests Section (http://havana.usint.gov/index.html). This is the Web site of the Interests Section, which operates in the absence of an embassy. It includes overviews of U.S. policy toward Cuba, information about immigration policy, and also a lengthy list of links to nongovernmental Web sites dedicated to Cuba.

Endnotes

1. Quoted in DePalma, Anthony. *The Man Who Invented Fidel: Castro, Cuba, and Herbert L. Matthews of the New York Times* (New York: Public Affairs, 2006), 86.
2. Quoted in Schoultz, Lars. *Beneath the United States: A History of U.S. Policy Toward Latin America* (Cambridge: Harvard University Press, 2008), 139.
3. Gunther, John. *Inside Latin America* (New York: Harper and Brothers, 1941), 469.
4. Eisenhower, Milton S. *The Wine is Bitter: The United States and Latin America* (New York: Doubleday and Company, Inc, 1963), 12.
5. *Foreign Relations of the United States* 1961–1963, Vol. X, Cuba 1961–1962. http://history.state.gov/historicaldocuments/frus1961-63v10.
6. Pérez, Jr., Louis A. *Cuba: Between Reform and Revolution* (New York: Oxford University Press, 1995), 346.
7. Pérez 1995, 354.
8. Pérez 1995, 354.
9. Carranza Valdés, Julio, Juan Valdés Paz, and Raúl J. Rosales. "Institutional Development and Social Policy in Cuba: The 'Special Period.' " *Journal of International Affairs* 58, 1 (Fall 2004): 175–188.
10. Latell, Brian. *After Fidel: Raul Castro and the Future of Cuba's Revolution* (New York: Palgrave Macmillan, 2005), 239.
11. Jennissen, Therese and Colleen Lundy. "Women in Cuba and the Move to a Private Market Economy." *Women's Studies International Forum* 24, 2 (2001): 181–198.
12. De la Fuente, Alejandro and Laurence Glasco. "Are Blacks 'Getting Out of Control'? Racial Attitudes, Revolution, and Political Transition in Cuba." In Miguel Angel Centeno and Mauricio Font (eds.), *Toward a New Cuba? Legacies of a Revolution* (Boulder: Lynne Rienner Publishers, 1997).

13. Sawyer 2005, 121.
14. Mujal-León, Eusebio. "Tensions in the Regime." *Journal of Democracy* 20, 1 (January 2009), 20–35.
15. Klepak, Hal. "Cuba's Revolutionary Armed Forces: Last Bulwark of the State? Last Bulwark of the Revolution?" In Philip Brenner, Marguerite Rose Jiménez, John M. Kirk, and William M. LeoGrande (eds.), *Reinventing the Revolution: A Contemporary Cuba Reader* (Lanham, MD: Rowman and Littlefield Publishers, Inc., 2008), 66–67.
16. Uriarte, Miren. "Rediscovering *Lo Local*: The Potential and the Limits of Local Development in Havana." In Alexander I. Gray and Antoni Kapcia (eds.), *The Changing Dynamic of Cuban Civil Society* (Gainesville: University Press of Florida, 2008), 90–115.

CHAPTER 8

Bolivia, Ecuador, and Peru

LEARNING OBJECTIVES

- Identify how the three levels of analysis interact in Bolivia, Ecuador, and Peru

- Use theoretical propositions to understand political and economic development in Bolivia, Ecuador, and Peru

- Explain how and why political and economic development in Bolivia, Ecuador, and Peru differs from other Latin American countries

TIMELINE

1821	Peru becomes independent
1822	Ecuador becomes independent
1825	Bolivia becomes independent
1952	MNR begins revolution
1964–1982	Military governments in Bolivia
1968–1980	Military governments in Peru
1972–1979	Military governments in Ecuador
1980	Shining Path forms
1990	Alberto Fujimori elected
1992	Self-coup in Peru
2000	Fujimori resigns and leaves the country
2000	Economy dollarized; Jamil Mahuad overthrown in Ecuador
2003	Gonzalo Sánchez de Lozada resigns
2006	Evo Morales takes office

(Continued)

2007	Rafael Correa takes office
2008	New constitution ratified in Ecuador
2009	New constitution ratified in Bolivia
2011	Ollanta Humala takes office

Bolivian President Evo Morales often faced a balancing act. He was of indigenous descent and was elected twice with the critical support of major indigenous groups in the country. But different indigenous leaders have different priorities, so governing at the national level means sometimes alienating local organizations, even ones he normally supported. In 2010, for example, major protests broke out to pressure the government to increase investment in certain regions, and also against changes in fuel subsidies. In 2011 he faced indigenous protestors who opposed his plan to build a highway through their land and argued that it damaged the environment. Both his defense and interior ministers resigned because of the government's harsh response to the protestors.

This put President Morales between the proverbial rock and a hard place, where local demands conflicted with national priorities. The government viewed the development as essential to both regional and national development, but had clearly not anticipated the ways in which those affected at the local level would respond. The overall result was that his approval rating began moving downward.

The Andean countries of Bolivia, Ecuador, and Peru share some essential features. In the colonial era, they were an important source of wealth for Spain. All have large indigenous populations that have historically been marginalized politically, economically, and culturally. Approximately 71 percent of Bolivia's population is of indigenous descent, the largest proportion in Latin America. Peru (47 percent) and Ecuador (43 percent) are third and fourth (second in the region is Guatemala with 66 percent). In all, political rule has been oligarchic and exclusionary. They all have troubled political histories, with few eras of democratic rule. Finally, since the 2000s, all three countries have been experiencing democracy after serious political conflicts, but also face obstacles in keeping those democracies intact. For these reasons, we can fruitfully consider them together analytically.

All three countries have also dealt in different ways—and varying degrees of success—with economies that are based almost entirely on commodities. Dependence on those commodities has not produced equal results. More so than the others, Bolivia has nationalized industries. Ecuador, meanwhile, fully dollarized its economy and produces oil, which has brought in much needed revenue. Peru relies heavily on mining and has welcomed foreign investment, a strategy that brought impressive gross domestic product (GDP) growth.

ECUADOR
Population: 14.8 million
Size: 109,000 square miles
Capital: Quito
Currency: U.S. Dollar

PERU
Population: 29.5 million
Size: 496,000 square miles
Capital: Lima
Currency: Nuevo Sol

BOLIVIA
Population: 10.9 million
Size: 424,000 square miles
Capital: Sucre
Currency: Boliviano

Map of Bolivia, Ecuador, and Peru

Historical Roots of Political and Economic Development

Spain created the Viceroyalty of Peru in 1542 to govern much of South America (including both Bolivia and Ecuador) and to administer the large-scale extraction of gold and silver. In 1717, Ecuador would be shifted to a new Viceroyalty of New Granada. When the wars of independence broke out, Peru was a bastion of royal resistance and became independent in 1821 (though, in fact, Spain did not recognize that fact until 1879). Ecuador became independent in 1822 as part of Gran Colombia (with Colombia and Venezuela) and then its own republic in 1830. Named for the liberator Simón Bolívar, Bolivia declared independence in 1809 and finally won it in 1825.

The economies of all three countries depended on primary products. In the Peruvian case, there was even an economic boom in the mid-1800s based on guano, which you might better recognize as bird droppings. Until a synthetic substitute was discovered later in the century, it was a popular product in

Europe as a fertilizer. Bolivia had tin and silver, while Ecuador had little mining but instead produced cacao, coffee, and seafood products. These were then exported largely to more developed countries.

Political instability was pervasive. In the first fifty years after independence in Peru, there were thirty-three different presidents, and twenty-seven of them were military officers.[1] In Ecuador, after 1925 there have been eleven governments taking power as a result of a coup. Bolivia has experienced 193 coups since 1825. Weak economies contributed, as did long-standing conflict between political and economic elites on the one hand, and large indigenous populations on the other. National and local conflicts simmered on a more or less constant basis.

■■■ BOLIVIA'S POLITICAL INSTITUTIONS ■■■
Last constitution: 2009

Unitary state with nine departments

Executive: President with five-year term; one reelection

Legislative: Bicameral with 130 member Chamber of Deputies (77 from single-member districts and 53 through party-list proportional representation) and 36-member Senate (elected by proportional representation)

Judicial: Supreme Court; Constitutional Tribunal judges constitutionality of legislation

Bolivia

In Bolivian political history, there is little that compares in importance to the **War of the Pacific** (1879–1884). In that war, the country lost its access to the ocean to Chile. There was disagreement about how long to continue fighting the war, which led to the formation of Liberal and Conservative parties. After the war until 1920, they devised a power-sharing agreement for control over the national government. The leadership was largely affluent and white, and only about 2 to 3 percent of the population could vote. It controlled natural resources, as during the colonial period the main exports were minerals, such as tin and silver.

The predominant indigenous group in Bolivia is the Aymara, a group that dates back hundreds of years to the pre-Inca period in the highlands (or "altiplano"). The indigenous population was effectively excluded from political participation until the revolution of 1952. In 1941, Víctor Paz Estenssoro cofounded the reformist **Revolutionary Nationalist Movement (MNR)** and in 1951 won as its presidential candidate. Deeming his government too radical, the military overthrew him. A popular uprising returned him to power in 1952, and he initiated a period of extensive reforms that enfranchised all Bolivians, nationalized the major tin mines, and enacted redistribution of land. The MNR took on a corporatist model to bring together the military, workers, and peasants under its control. The model proved untenable, though, and in 1964 the army once again overthrew Paz Estenssoro, who had been reelected in 1960. The military then ruled for over twenty years. The international context of the Cold War also played a prominent role in Bolivia. It was during this period that Che Guevara traveled to Bolivia, hoping to create a guerrilla force that could defeat the government just as in Cuba. In 1967, however, he was captured and executed.

Imperfect National, Political, and Economic Reform

Between 1977 and 1980, there were failed efforts at democratization, which meant elections, military overthrow (some very bloody), and a succession of interim governments. The military was split internally, while worker and/or peasant protests periodically rocked the country. Bolivia underwent a pacted transition in 1982, and the military stepped down from power, but as is the case with such transitions retained considerable political power. However, the armed forces were so divided, and the short-lived dictatorships so unpopular, that the leadership ultimately decided that respecting elections was in its own best interests. Congressional elections were actually held in 1980, then presidential elections two years later. Hernán Siles Zuazo, a former president (1956–1960), was once again elected.

The MNR returned to power in 1985, but Paz Estenssoro proved unable to combat inflation, which ran at an average of 8,000 percent during his presidency. Ironically, he had been an architect of Bolivia's state capitalist model decades earlier, yet his presidency was characterized by the dismantling of that very system. Decree 21060 began a process of public sector layoffs and other cuts with the goal of finally taming runaway inflation. Also in 1985, Evo Morales became leader of a union of coca growers. This local organization gradually grew in national prominence.

The economic crisis of the 1980s highlighted the continued dependent nature of the economy, an international reality that creates conflict. The export of primary products such as silver, zinc, and tin has always been a hallmark of Bolivian exports, and changes in government did little to alter it. The United States is Bolivia's largest trading partner, which in practice means Bolivia exports primary products and imports finished goods. It has, however, also increased trade with regional partners through membership in the Andean Community (with Colombia, Ecuador, Peru, and Venezuela). In recent years, a newly prominent commodity is natural gas. Its development has in turn caused domestic conflict, centering on whether it should be in private or public hands, how the benefits of gas revenue should be distributed throughout the country, where it should exported (such as Chile, its old enemy), and how much should be exported versus consumed domestically. These disputes were intense enough to lead to the ouster of a president in 2003 and nationalization in 2005.

Bolivia is an example of what has been called *hybrid presidentialism*, meaning that its version of presidential rule incorporates elements of parliamentary systems.[2] If no presidential candidate receives an absolute majority of votes (as has often been the case), then Congress has the responsibility of voting for the winner. That injects a dose of parliamentarism into the political system, although once elected the president does not have to retain the confidence of his supporting coalition to remain in office. The main difficulty, however, lies in the fact that there have been so many different political parties, at times as many as twenty-seven in the legislature. Especially when presidents won only a small plurality of the population, Congress asserted its dominance over the executive branch.

If hybrid presidentialism has been a challenge for Bolivian political development, it is nothing compared to the demands placed on the unitary system. As Bolivia has deep political divisions that run (though not perfectly) along geographical lines, there has been a constant struggle over political control. Until 1994, local governments had virtually no resources. At that time, the Popular Participation Law created 308 municipalities, allowed for mayoral elections, and provided them with extensive power to enact development policies (a total of 20 percent of the national budget). The law also recognized local grassroots organizations and provided a framework within which they could interact with the local government and ensure that their interests were taken into account. The impetus for decentralization was that the MNR had worked hard to increase its support at the local level, and to increase its rural presence. It therefore calculated that decentralization would actually give the party more influence in the long run.[3] In fact, as political scientist Donna Lee Van Cott has argued, enhanced democracy at the local level in both Bolivia and Ecuador has meant that local actors (such as mayors) have the flexibility to create their own institutions, free of too much central control.[4]

Economic Source of Local Discontent

The decentralization process was accompanied by initial efforts to formally recognize the role and importance of indigenous groups. President **Gonzalo Sánchez de Lozada** took office in 1993, and during his administration, the constitution was amended to label Bolivia as a "multiethnic and plurinational" state. He had even chosen a vice president of Aymara descent as a way to demonstrate his commitment to indigenous rights. At the same time, though, Sánchez de Lozada deepened the market reforms that had been launched in the 1980s. His policies included large cuts in government expenditures, privatization of some of the large state-owned industries, and increased taxation. Inflation had reached levels upward of 60,000 percent, and foreign debt had soared. The measures helped macroeconomic stability, and the president took great pride in telling the world how Bolivia had beaten the odds and resolved its problems. What he didn't note that was that it took a heavy toll on the poor, and a growing number of Bolivians felt excluded.

Simultaneously, the U.S. government had been exerting pressure on Bolivian governments to participate more actively in antinarcotics operations. In 1988, the Paz Estenssoro administration passed Law 1008, which asserted that a small amount of coca (12,000 hectares a year) could be cultivated for traditional use, but the rest would be eradicated. The goals were difficult to reach, however, which led the United States to decertify Bolivia several times. That meant Bolivia, as also occurred several times in Colombia, was deemed not to be living up to expectations of the U.S. government and therefore aid would be cut. By the end of the Sánchez de Lozada administration, coca represented roughly half of Bolivia's export earnings. In 1997 President Hugo Banzer (himself a former dictator) created Plan Dignidad ("Dignity Plan"), which was an aggressive eradication effort. Banzer subsequently declared victory in the war on drugs, as coca cultivation had dropped by 40,000 hectares. That success, however, had two important consequences. First, the "balloon effect" (whereby if you squeeze a balloon in one place, it expands in another direction) spread coca cultivation to Colombia. Second, eradication came at an increasing socioeconomic cost. Policy makers paid insufficient attention to providing alternate means of local economic development, and already were cutting government spending. Therefore, resentment toward the programs (and toward U.S. policies) spread and fostered more political instability.

During the late 1980s and early 1990s, disparate local groups began to organize in opposition, but remained largely isolated from each other. By the late 1990s, however, their leaders began to seek each other out to a much greater degree. In particular, there was a growing connection between rural and urban political activists.[5] In fact, the coca growers had already been activated by the drug war, and so by virtue of their organization were in a good position to make connections with urban movements that had similar—if not identical—political goals.

In 2000, for example, the privatization of water and sewer—which entailed a sudden and large rise in rates—in the city of Cochabamba sparked violence. That was followed by a general strike and the spread of protests to other cities. The so-called Water Wars reflected the growing schism between the state and its citizens. It is within this context that **Evo Morales**—whom we met in the first chapter of the book— first ran for the presidency in 2002, and narrowly lost to Sánchez de Lozada (22.5 percent to 20.9 percent). According to the constitution, a failure to achieve a majority meant Congress had to vote between the two top vote getters, and in that vote Sánchez de Lozada won decisively (84–43 percent).

Sánchez de Lozada would not be in office long. By early 2003 protests grew, especially in response to economic reforms and to the continuation of anticoca policies. They grew when Sánchez de Lozada reportedly favored exporting natural gas through a Chilean port. That was enough to stoke nationalist fervor and intensify calls to nationalize hydrocarbons. The president ordered the use of force to break through roadblocks, which led to dozens of deaths. Sánchez de Lozada resigned and fled the country. His vice president, Carlos Mesa, became president until he too was forced to resign in 2005, and the subsequent interim president called for new presidential elections. The dizzying pace of presidential turnover was like that of Argentina from 2001 to 2003. In that election, Evo Morales won 53.9 percent of the vote, a decisive victory that made a second round unnecessary, and the revolving presidential door stopped swinging. In his inauguration speech, he was highly critical of past governments as well as economic elites, comparing Bolivia to South Africa: "Threatened, condemned to extermination, we're here, we're here."

ANALYZING DOCUMENTS

As the first Bolivian president of indigenous descent, Evo Morales' inauguration was an historic event. He emphasized how the indigenous population had never been integrated into national policy except in terms of exclusion, and how he would work to correct the mistakes of past administrations. Avoiding local resistance to national policies, however, has been difficult.

Evo Morales' Inauguration Speech (2006)

To remember our predecessors with permission from the President of the National Congress, I ask a moment of silence for . . . many of my fallen brothers, cocaleros of the tropical zone of Cochabamba, for the fallen brothers in defense of the dignity of the alteño people, of the miners, of millions of human beings that have fallen all across the Americas and them, Mr. President, I ask a moment of silence. Glory to the martyrs of liberation!

. . .

This morning, early, I saw with much happiness some brothers and sisters singing in the historic plaza of Murillo, the Plaza Murillo, also in the Plaza San Francisco, where forty or fifty years ago we did not have the right to enter the Plaza San Francisco or the Plaza Murillo. Forty or fifty years ago our predecessors did not have the right to walk on the sidewalks. This is our history, our experience.

Bolivia is like South Africa. Threatened, condemned to extermination, we're here, we're here. I want to tell you that these people who are enemies of the indigenous peoples still have bad habits. We want to live in equal conditions as them, so we're here to change our history, this original indigenous movement is not a concession from anyone, nobody gave it to us, it is the conscience of my people, of our people.

I want to tell you, so that the international press knows, that the first Aymaras and Quechuas that learned to read and write had their eyes taken out, they cut their hands so they could never again learn to read and write. We have been repressed, and now we are searching for a way to resolve this problem, but not with vengeance because we are not malicious.

. . .

It is not possible for basic services to be privatized. I cannot understand how the ex-rulers privatized basic services, especially water. Water is a natural resource, and without water we cannot live. Therefore water cannot be a private business, because the moment it is a private business you have violated human rights. Water should be a public service.

The struggles for water, for coca, and for natural gas have brought brothers and sisters here. We have to recognize that these mistaken, erroneous, and self-interested policies, the auctioned natural resources, and privatized basic services obliged them to be the conscience of the Bolivian people. We are obligated to change these policies. Constitutionally, the latifundia is unconstitutional. Unfortunately because of powerful interest groups there are latifundia. How is this possible? How is it possible that when some people plant, they need 20, 30, 40, 50 hectares to raise a cow, that you need to be a cow to have 50 hectares? This is all part of the economic model.

. . .

Because of these classes of injustice was born the so-called political instrument for sovereignty, a political instrument of the people, a political instrument to search for equality and justice, a political instrument for the Movement Toward Socialism, that wants to live, with peace and social justice, this is called unity in diversity.

Discussion Questions

- What does Evo Morales suggest the proper way the national government should connect to the local population?
- How does he seem to view the role of international influence on the Bolivian indigenous population?

Source: Bolpress Web site: http://www.bolpress.com/art.php?Cod=2006012301

Conflict Between Different Levels Under Evo Morales

In 2009, voters approved a new constitution, which had been an important part of Morales' platform. He praised it as a proindigenous document, as it guaranteed indigenous seats in the legislature and sought to democratize landholding by placing limits on the size of any future land purchases. The new Bolivian constitution also allows for the popular election of judges, a practice that is unique in Latin America. It allowed Morales to run for reelection in 2014, but there is a two-term limit. It also continued the process of decentralization to departmental, regional, municipal, and indigenous levels. This is an especially delicate process in Bolivia because the Media Luna (referring to the wealthier eastern part of Bolivia) is rich in natural gas, and therefore decentralization often teeters perilously close to secession and national disintegration.

After Morales was reelected in 2009, the Media Luna consistently lobbied for greater freedom from central authority. In 2010, President Morales signed a new "Transition Law" that began a process of granting more autonomy to regions and departments. He announced the dawning of a new "era of autonomies." In 2010 and 2011 he ran into serious opposition—even from supporters—when he decreed the end of some fuel subsidies, which would have driven up prices. He argued that the subsidies had prompted rampant smuggling to neighboring countries with higher gas prices. The national and international contexts thus collided. Protests against what became known as the *gasolinazo* forced him to back down, and in the wake of the controversy his approval ratings dropped sharply. These events serve to emphasize the tenuous nature of his support, and how social movements do not subside simply because there is a sympathetic figure in the presidency.

One of Morales' most successful reforms to date has been in institutionalizing water rights, addressing a serious point of contention within many local indigenous movements. One of Morales' first moves after taking office was to create a Water Ministry to oversee the registry of legal claims to water and ensure indigenous communities, peasants, and small farmers access to water in their ancestral territories. The 2009 constitution formalizes the state's policy, stating that, "Access to water and sewers constitutes human rights. They are not an object of either concession or privatization and they are subject to a system of licenses and registrations, in accordance to the law." The new law does represent a dramatic shift in Bolivian policy, but it is important to note that much of the success in its implementation has been because of the Commission for Integral Management of Water in Bolivia (CGIAB), a network of nongovernmental organizations, research organizations, and civil society groups that have been active since 2000, when privatization first became an issue.

Although the government has demonstrated pragmatism with regard to nationalization policies, internal polarization and unpredictable regulation have damaged the investment climate. Annual FDI averaged $452 million between 1990 and 2000, but by 2007 was $204 million. A slowdown in investments has generated doubts regarding Bolivia's ability to fulfill contracts with many of its major gas consumers, most notably Argentina, which has begun to secure gas supplies from other sources. In addition, the global economic crisis adversely affected Bolivia's economy through declines in remittances and commodity prices. By 2009, this caused a significant drop in real GDP growth rates. Trade with the United States also slowed after President George W. Bush suspended Bolivia's participation in the Andean Trade Promotion and Drug Eradication Act, which offered preferential treatment to imports from Andean countries who are fighting drug trafficking. The Bush administration argued that the Bolivian government was not combating drug trafficking sufficiently, thus ending Bolivia's special access to the U.S. markets.

The cultivation of coca has been the source of long-standing tensions with the United States. Coca is chewed as part of cultural practice by the Aymara, though a majority of coca grown in Bolivia is processed into cocaine for export. The Morales administration adopted a "zero cocaine but not zero coca" position, but has also taken steps such as the deportation of a U.S. Drug Enforcement Agency officer, and the U.S. response has been increased distrust and the public airing of doubts about Morales' commitment to combating drug trafficking. By 2010, however, the Bolivian government itself expressed concern that the cocaine trade was on the rise, and also accompanied by the types of violence evident in Colombia and Mexico. In 2012 Brazil announced a new antinarcotics plan with Bolivia, which included the use of drones.

Bolivia and Chile continue to have a shaky relationship, as Bolivia has been trying unsuccessfully to negotiate formal access to the ocean. In 1978 the military leaders of each country began talks that soon included Peru, but could not find common ground. As a result, Bolivia broke relations and since then they have only consular rather than full diplomatic relations. With the election of Evo Morales the relationship warmed, but no solution has been reached. Verbal sparring periodically occurs, even including Peru, for example, in 2009 when he cracked that President Alan García's obesity affected his judgment when the latter argued that Bolivia had already given up its claim to the sea. With his administration, Bolivia's key regional ally has been Venezuela under Hugo Chávez, a relationship that has included establishing joint ventures, aid packages, and participation in the Bolivarian Alternative for the Americas (ALBA).

Despite the polarization evident in Bolivia, the Morales government has not been threatened by the military. Morales has made the armed forces part of his developmentalist project and has been very skillful in rooting out high-level officers who might oppose him, while also emphasizing nationalism rather than ideology when employing the military in activities such as seizing gas fields for the state. The armed forces have remained loyal to the central government in the face of regional demands for autonomy. This augurs well for democracy in a country that has suffered so many overthrows of democratically elected governments.

ECUADOR'S POLITICAL INSTITUTIONS

Last constitution: 2008

Unitary State with twenty-four provinces

Executive: President with four-year terms; limit of two terms

Legislative: Unicameral National Congress with 124 members, elected through party-list proportional representation

Judicial: National Court of Justice, also a Constitutional Tribunal if the president or Congress believes legislation is unconstitutional

Ecuador

Like Bolivia, Ecuador is split along geographic and racial lines. The highlands are populated primarily by indigenous, while the coasts are more mestizo and white (with a small Afro-Ecuadorian population as well). Ethnic conflict has been a mainstay of politics since the military left power in 1979. The fact that there have been 35 different administrations since 1925 provides a sense of the chronic instability.

The major political figure of the twentieth century was José María Velasco Ibarra. He was president five separate times from the 1930s until the 1970s and was ousted by the military in four of them. He initiated a period of import substitution industrialization and emphasized a state capitalist economic strategy that sought to incorporate marginalized groups into Ecuador's economy. In his last term, his overthrew ushered in seven years of dictatorship. Similar to the Peruvian military government of the time, the army had a nationalist and reformist platform, and was less repressive than many of its South American counterparts. As oil is a major export and routinely funds about half of the national budget, relative harmony was facilitated in the 1970s by very favorable oil prices. Nonetheless, the army has been highly politicized and politically active even when not formally in power. The military junta (called the Supreme Council) held democratic elections in 1979, which began a wave of democratization across Latin America.

Although Ecuador was once again democratic, the party system was fragmented (by 2010, ten parties had some level of representation in the legislature). Parties are heavily regionalized, and tied closely to individuals, and therefore come and go with personalities rather than becoming institutionalized at either the local or national levels. As in Brazil and Guatemala, party switching is common, and elected officials see it as a way to make bargains and receive payoffs. In some cases, as with Sixto Durán Ballén in 1992, a presidential candidate successfully created a party expressly for the elections. A chaotic political system was unfortunately accompanied by budget problems. The economy stagnated throughout the 1980s, as the debt crisis was too overwhelming for any president to address. Per capita income in 1994 was less than in 1981 because annual GDP growth remained behind population growth.[6] Although exports rose, low prices for commodities such as oil brought in less revenue than in the 1970s.

In the context of economic crisis, human rights abuses also became a problem. In 2010, the Ecuadorian Truth Commission issued a report that, especially between 1984 and 1988, the administration of León Febres Cordero routinely used extrajudicial killings, torture, and illegal arrests. Of the 456 people who suffered such abuses between 1988 and 2008, 78 percent took place during those four years. Certainly, these numbers are pale in comparison to the pervasive political violence in military dictatorships but are indicative of the ways in which economic collapse can go hand in hand with political repression, even in polyarchies.

The Political Consequences of National Economic Collapse

Economic collapse was also a catalyst for various simultaneous developments. This included the creation of women's organizations, which responded to the local vacuum left by the state to provide necessary services in poor areas. These first appeared in Quito and then spread throughout the country. At the same time, there are significant splits that pose an obstacle to a unified movement. Furthermore, there is a certain amount of tension between ethnic and gender identity. Ethnic movements like the **Confederation of Indigenous Nationalities of Ecuador (CONAIE)** rose to prominence in a way that women's organizations did not, and they did not pay much attention to gender. In fact, indigenous women suffer disproportionately more violence and have less access to educational opportunities than other groups. The Confederation of Indigenous Women of Ecuador (CONMIE) was formed in 1996 but was opposed by CONAIE and remained weak. As in many Latin American countries, Ecuadorian women bore the brunt of economic deprivation but gained little political power.

Populism resurfaced in 1996, when Abdalá Bucaram won the presidency. Of Lebanese descent, he had married President Roldos' sister, and founded the Ecuadorian Roldista Party. His nickname "El Loco" (the crazy one) provides a glimpse into what became an erratic style of governing that initially appealed to the masses, but this style became problematic when corruption charges arose and when Bucaram embarked on market-oriented reforms after promising the opposite. He was faced first by massive protests from all sides of the political spectrum, and then by a congressional vote of "mental instability." Within a few months of his inauguration, he was forced to resign.

Bucaram's presidency also marks the rise of the left-wing Pachakutik Party, formed in 1995. It came out of CONAIE, created in 1986 to articulate the political demands of Ecuador's indigenous population. Given its high level of organization, CONAIE has routinely launched marches and protests that at times have virtually shut down parts of the country, including the capital of Quito, and have taken over local governments. In fact, until 1995 CONAIE rejected participating in electoral politics at all. Because CONAIE was being courted by national politicians, ultimately its leadership decided it could achieve its goals more effectively by participating formally.

Bucaram's overthrow ushered in a period of extended political disarray, with the armed forces taking on the role as political arbiter, a persistent problem across Latin America. After a dispute about who should become president, Fabián Alarcón assumed office, and in 1997 elections Jamil Mahuad won. In 1998, the country approved a new constitution, which provided more recognition of the indigenous population (e.g., labeling Ecuador as "multiethnic"). In the face of spiraling inflation and economic stagnation, Mahuad froze $400 million in assets and abruptly announced that he was dollarizing the economy as a way to stabilize the economy. Dollarization means just that: adopting the U.S. dollar as the national currency. As noted in Chapter 4, it can bring about exchange rate stability, but at the same time it means losing seignorage as well as control over the money supply.

The response to dollarization was intense opposition, as the government was blamed for creating the crisis and there was precious little confidence it was capable of finding a solution. As Eduardo Silva has argued, disparate groups were able to agree on the need to decommodify labor and land and reinsert the state more forcefully into the economy.[7] In 2000 CONAIE allied with junior officers in the army, led by Lucio Gutiérrez, to overthrow Mahuad and install a short-lived junta. The coup leaders handed power to Vice President Gustavo Noboa. In 2003, indigenous leaders threw their support behind Gutiérrez (he gave Pachakutik four cabinet seats in return), who was elected just three years after overthrowing the government. His penchant for market policies, however, soon made him unpopular. He responded to demonstrations in Quito by calling for a state of emergency and dissolving the Supreme Court, which in 2005 prompted Congress to vote for his removal and name Vice President Alfredo Palacio in his place. When the military made clear it supported that decision, and Pachakutik members had left his government, Gutiérrez resigned.

The Era of Rafael Correa

Into this political turmoil came an economist with a PhD from the United States. **Rafael Correa** briefly held the position of Minister of Economy and Finance under President Palacio, but resigned when the president did not support his proposed statist reforms. Aside from that experience, he was an outsider and became known for his populist, antiestablishment views. He won the 2006 presidential election against Alvaro Noboa, the wealthiest man in Ecuador, and the campaign highlighted the ideological split in the country, as Noboa labeled Correa as a communist and Correa referred to Noboa as a conceited elitist. Correa lost the first round of voting to Noboa (26 to 22 percent), but then he won a subsequent runoff. He thus became the seventh president in a decade.

In 2007, Correa called for a referendum to hold elections for a new constituent assembly and won with 82 percent of the vote after a sometimes violent dispute with Congress over the powers of that assembly (which included dissolving the legislature itself and thereby superseding it, which obviously angered the opposition). His coalition then proceeded to win 80 of the 130 seats in that body. He won reelection in 2009 with 52 percent of the vote. Former president Lucio Gutiérrez came in a distant second with 28 percent.

Correa developed what has been called a *plebiscitary presidency*.[8] This means he routinely appeals to his supporters directly rather than working with the legislature or other political institutions. He noted that he was running a "permanent campaign" and the traditional political parties represented an obstacle to getting things done (see Box 8.1). Unlike his predecessors, Correa was at least initially successful in obtaining legislative support. Although the Ecuadorian president is quite powerful on paper, since 1979 that has not necessarily translated into achieving political goals easily. Further, because the legislature can censure cabinet members, there is often rapid turnover. For example, between 1979 and 1998, economic ministers lasted less than a year on average.

BOX 8.1

The Presidency of Rafael Correa

International: President Rafael Correa has defied easy ideological categories and exemplified the limitations of the broad term *leftist*. In a 2010 interview, he expressed admiration for the United States and even Anglo-Saxon culture, saying that Latin American culture focused too much on lying. He participated in UNITAS exercises with the United States and governments like Colombia's with much more conservative views. Domestically, he has also shown a willingness to side at times with business over indigenous groups. But he also harshly criticizes U.S. foreign policy—particularly regarding trade and drugs—and joined the Bolivarian Alternative for the Americas (ALBA). Further, he is a self-proclaimed socialist.

National: Rafael Correa is an atypical Latin American president. His governing style has clear populist leanings, with considerable attention to indigenous rights, yet he has also shown himself willing to pursue sometimes unpopular policies during his presidency. He obtained a PhD in Economics in the United States, yet is critical both of U.S. foreign and economic policies.

He served briefly as economic minister, but his background is more technocratic than political. He emerged at a time of serious upheaval in Ecuador, as protests and coups ousted one president after another. His outsider status proved to be an asset, and he successfully ran for president in populist style, denouncing the traditional parties and politicians and winning on the basis of

his direct appeal to the voters. He has a difficult relationship with the media, to put it mildly.

Local: Although Correa's approval rating dipped below 50 percent by 2010, he has enjoyed far greater popularity and stability than any president in decades. Nonetheless, in 2010 he did face a police rebellion (based on Correa's policy regarding bonuses) that became serious enough that many, including Correa himself, argued that it constituted a coup attempt. Longer-term stability will depend on his ability to build a coherent organization at both the national and local levels that can carry on without him. Populist movements tend to crumble without the charismatic leader.

Discussion Questions

- What about Correa's background suggestion that international influence is not easy to predict?
- How might his views of international actors contribute to his national popularity?

The mere fact that President Correa has worked on behalf of the indigenous population does not mean that its support is unconditional. A key point of tension between the national government and local indigenous organizations stems from the fact that historically the latter have become politically active against neoliberal policies that allowed foreign companies to enter their territory without consent, causing social, cultural, and environmental degradation through unregulated and unsupervised extraction methods. Because of deep-rooted struggles such as this, indigenous movements and activists tend to view Correa's policy through the same lens. Acción Ecológica, an organization that has been active in Ecuador for decades, asserted that the Mining Law was written in a way that favored corporations over the legitimate concerns of the people affected by the law. Meanwhile, Correa faced large protests against a proposed law that would put political control over water in the executive branch rather than a collective entity. As in Bolivia, having a left-leaning president does not mean that civil society becomes passive or overly accommodating to government. At the same time, Correa must deal with traditional tensions with the security forces, including a major confrontation in 2010 with police regarding pensions. Correa even claimed that it represented a coup attempt, though the army sided with him.

Economic Growth and International Factors

Economic growth has been solid, though not spectacular, and Ecuador managed the global economic crisis reasonably well, with GDP growth over 7 percent in 2008 and at least positive growth afterward. Especially given dollarization, inflation has remained low—generally under 6 percent—despite a spurt in 2009. Export earnings are still concentrated in primary products. Of course, petroleum products are central, but so are bananas and cut flowers, as well as seafood such as shrimp.

Oil remains a key source of export earnings, and Ecuador once again became a member of Organization of the Petroleum Exporting Countries (OPEC) in 2007 (it had pulled out in 1992 because it resisted paying the $2 million membership fee and did not like what it believed was a low production ceiling). Roughly half of the national budget is funded by oil. In turn, foreign companies run about half of the production process, which has led to disputes about environmental degradation and spills. On behalf of local indigenous groups, the Ecuadorian government charged Texaco (which was later bought by Chevron) with dumping 18.5 billion gallons of oil, a case that remains pending. Further, in recent years the government has threatened expropriation if foreign oil companies did not increase the revenue amount allotted to the state.

To sustain the generous social spending necessary for continued political support, Correa declared he would break from reliance on traditional lenders and seek out external financing from political allies. In December 2008, the government defaulted on an interest payment of Ecuador's $10 billion in international debt, accusing foreign officials and bankers of profiting irresponsibly from bond deals. Correa announced that "as president I couldn't allow us to keep paying a debt that was obviously immoral and illegitimate."[9] By 2009, the government had softened its policy, agreeing to buy back 91 percent of its defaulted bonds, but under a more favorable agreement that would save the government approximately $300 million a year in interest payments. To expand its budget on social spending, the government has sought out financial agreements with Iran and Venezuela, and in 2009 began negotiating $1 billion in financing with China. By late that year, however, Correa ended the talks, stating that negotiating with China was worse than negotiating with the IMF and claiming that the agreement threatened Ecuador's sovereignty.

It is noteworthy that although dollarization encountered stiff resistance initially, not even Correa—a vocal critic of U.S. economic policy—has advocated dismantling it. The combination of macroeconomic stability (particularly with regard to keeping inflation in check) and international investor confidence has prompted governments since 2000 to accept its indefinite existence. Over time, dollarization has also slowly become more popular because of that stability despite the ways in which it restricts the government's ability to make economic decisions such as devaluation.

Strong international influences for Ecuador go well beyond economic ties. Its border with Colombia has become a source of serious conflict because of the presence of the Revolutionary Armed Forces of Colombia (FARC). Historically, the FARC has moved back and forth across that border with frequency and impunity. Their activity has also created a constant flow of Colombian refugees into Ecuador, at a rate the government can barely handle. Over 135,000 Colombians have fled to Ecuador, and since 2000 approximately 40,000 of those have applied for asylum status. In 2009, the Colombian government bombed Ecuadorian territory to destroy an encampment, which killed an important guerrilla leader and yielded FARC laptops. What Colombia viewed as a military success, however, was considered to be an act of belligerence by the Ecuadorian government. Diplomatic ties were broken and have been strained since.

Along these lines, one important difference Ecuador enjoys from its neighbors (and from Colombia) is that it never faced a "drug war" or even any sort of armed insurgency. Interestingly, Ecuador has almost no coca cultivation. The colonial economy moved in other directions, and chewing coca was not as central to indigenous culture, as was the case in Bolivia. By 1990, moreover, the government developed a hard-line policy intended to make sure that the profits reaped by traffickers in neighboring countries did not become a temptation for native production. That fact has helped Correa in his efforts to bring political stability to a country that has not enjoyed it much.

▬▬ PERU'S POLITICAL INSTITUTIONS ▬▬

Last constitution: 1993

Unitary system with twenty-five regions

Executive: President with five-year term; no immediate reelection but former presidents can run again after leaving power at least one term

Legislative: Unicameral Congress with 120 members (elected through proportional representation)

Judicial: Supreme Court, with Constitutional Court to decide constitutionality of legislation

Peru

Political instability was the norm for Peru during most of the nineteenth century. Rapid successions of government, accompanied by rewriting of the political rules of the game, meant that solid political institutions could not form. In the latter half of the century, Peru lost the War of the Pacific (and consequently some of its southern territory) and the guano boom ended. This led to political collapse and military rule. Not until the beginning of the twentieth century did a civilian government last for a sustained amount of time, when Nicolás de Piérola was president from 1895 to 1919 (with a brief removal through a coup in 1914) as part of the so-called Aristocratic Republic. The economy remained dependent on primary products, but within that there was more diversification, to goods like cotton and sugar. The populist Augusto Leguía ruled from 1919 to 1930, and during that time (in 1924) Raúl Haya de la Torre founded the **American Revolutionary Popular Alliance (APRA)**. That party would be at the center of Peruvian politics for much of the century.

Haya was categorically anti-Marxist but attracted support from the working class and the poor with a radical reformist platform. As a result, the party became a target for political elites, and between 1930 and 1968, APRA was only allowed to offer a presidential candidate twice. By the late 1960s, deep political schisms combined with slowing economic growth prompted gridlock and then a military coup in 1968, led by Juan Velasco Alvarado. The resulting authoritarian government, however, was reformist rather than conservative. Its rhetorical goal was a new participatory democracy, and its main achievement was extensive agrarian reform that included much of the peasantry that the state had essentially ignored or repressed since independence. Nonetheless, its lofty goals did not come to fruition, and instead there was internal dissent within the military as well as continued economic crisis. Women's groups began to organize in large numbers in the late 1970s as the dictatorship was drawing to a close. Women took an active role in protesting against the military government, though it was not as repressive as elsewhere. However, leaders of such organizations suffered at the hands of guerrillas, which accused them of collaborating with the government.

The Challenges of Democratic Transition

Velasco eventually was forced out, and his replacement (General Francisco Morales Bermúdez) called for a transition to democracy. Through this pacted transition, a Constituent Assembly was elected in 1978, and a new constitution went into effect in 1979. In 1980, a presidential election brought Fernando Belaúnde Terry to office, who had been overthrown twelve years prior. He proved unpopular, and the young Alan García was viewed within APRA as the symbol of generational change in the party, and that change was indeed important for Peruvian democracy, as there had been no democratic handover of power since Manuel Odría left office in 1956.

Peruvian democracy, however, faced a serious challenge. One of the most important differences in Peru compared to Bolivia and Ecuador was the genesis of brutal guerrilla forces that emerged alongside democracy. The Túpac Amaru Revolutionary Movement was active in the 1980s and 1990s, though remained relatively small. Much more dangerous, and infamous, was the **Shining Path** (*Sendero Luminoso* in Spanish). Shining Path was a local creation, established in Ayacucho, the poorest of Peru's departments, by philosophy professor Abimael Guzmán. In 1980, there were scattered reported acts of violence, which finally reached Lima in the form of dead dogs hung from lamp posts. That would then expand to terrorizing both rural and urban Peru. The ideology was Marxist, specifically Maoist, viewing the country as similar to China in the 1930s, mostly feudal and ripe for revolution. In practice, it meant targeting large segments of the population as counterrevolutionary. As Guzmán once argued, "the mass have to be taught through overwhelming acts so that ideas can be pounded into them."[10] He had no interest in allying with organized labor or local peasant organizations, and his actions (such as strikes) sometimes worked against their material interests. If they were part of the system at all, then they were the enemy.

The Peruvian government was slow to respond to Shining Path. In 1982, it called a state of emergency in Ayacucho, but the Belaúnde administration made no effort to address the socioeconomic problems that had given rise to the movement in the first place. Its ultimate response added to violence in the countryside. The army organized peasant militia ("civil defense committees") and adopted a hard-line counterinsurgency strategy that attacked anyone believed to be sympathetic to the guerrillas. This put many peasants in the impossible position of being killed by the army if they refused to fight the guerrillas, or being killed by the guerrillas if they did. The local population was therefore most affected by a guerrilla war waged on a national scale.

Peruvian political institutions, already no models of legitimacy, were further threatened by Shining Path, and the situation was exacerbated by economic mismanagement. The APRA presidency of Alan García (1985–1990) was very unpopular because of economic instability. Inflation soared over 7,000 percent, and the rate of poverty shot up as well. When he left office, 70 percent of the economically active population was unemployed or underemployed, while GDP had fallen 28 percent.[11]

The Era of Alberto Fujimori

Public fears about guerrillas and economic uncertainty paved the way for the successful candidacy of **Alberto Fujimori,** a relatively unknown who ran against the famous (and later Nobel Prize-winning) novelist Mario Vargas Llosa. In very populist fashion, Fujimori portrayed himself as above politics, a technocrat who knew how to get things done and who rejected the orthodox economic policies that Vargas Llosa advocated. Fujimori won the 1990 presidential election in a landslide. When he took office, however, he enacted many of those same policies, even as he launched an assault on Shining Path. The latter involved sending the legislature a series of proposals that would strengthen the executive and increase the militarization of the fight against Shining Path. He did not enjoy the support of a majority in the legislature, which posed a major obstacle to his political goals. In 1992, Fujimori announced the dissolution of Congress, which became known as an *autogolpe,* or *self-coup* (though the name is not entirely apt because Fujimori certainly did not overthrow himself). A so-called

Government of National Emergency ruled the country, with Fujimori of course in charge.

Under international pressure, Fujimori called for a Constituent Assembly to write a new constitution. The traditional political parties, including APRA, refused to participate, which meant the new charter reflected Fujimori's own goals, emphasizing both neoliberal policies and a strong military. Abimael Guzmán was captured in several months after the self-coup, which greatly boosted Fujimori's popularity, as did his economic strategy of opening the country up to foreign investment while simultaneously increasing spending. He decisively won a second term in 1995 (64.4 percent of the vote versus 22.8 percent for former United Nations Secretary General Javier Pérez de Cuéllar).

The war against Shining Path took a terrible toll. The Peru Truth Commission issued a report in 2003, noting the deaths of 69,280 people from 1980 until 2000. More than 40 percent were from Ayacucho, where Shining Path started, and 75 percent spoke Quechua as a first language (compared to 16 percent of the population). The guerrillas were responsible for 54 percent of the victims, and the report indicated that this was a far greater percentage than for other rebel groups in Latin America, where the government was typically more violent. The war ravaged the Peruvian countryside, as 79 percent of the victims were engaged in agriculture. In short, local populations suffered horribly. Fujimori also bore much responsibility, as he had instituted broad antiterrorist measures after taking office that eroded civil liberties, including such dramatic examples as the institution of hooded military tribunals. He would later be convicted and imprisoned for abuses committed during his presidency.

ANALYZING DOCUMENTS

The sheer brutality of the Shining Path is unsurpassed by any other Marxist guerrillas in Latin America. The report of Peru's Truth Commission details the destruction at the local level, where Peru's poor were caught in the middle, slaughtered in particular by the Shining Path.

Peru Truth and Reconciliation Commission Final Report (General Conclusions) (2003)

As the result of its investigation into the process of violence of political origin that was experienced in Peru between the years 1980 and 2000, the Truth and Reconciliation Commission [TRC] has come to the following conclusions:

I. The Dimensions of the Conflict

1. The TRC has established that the internal armed conflict experienced by Peru between 1980 and 2000 constituted the most intense, extensive and prolonged episode of violence in the entire history of the Republic. It was also a conflict that revealed deep and painful divides and misunderstandings in Peruvian society.
2. The TRC estimates that the most probable figure for victims who died in the violence is 69,280 individuals. These figures are greater than the number

of human losses suffered by Peru in all of the foreign and civil wars that have occurred in its 182 years of independence.

3. The TRC affirms that the conflict covered a larger share of the national territory than any other conflict, caused enormous economic losses through the destruction of infrastructure and deterioration of the population's productive capacity, and came to involve the society as a whole.

4. The TRC has established that there was a significant relationship between poverty and social exclusion and the probability of becoming a victim of violence. More than 40 percent of the deaths and disappearances reported to the TRC are concentrated in the Andean department of Ayacucho. These victims taken together with those documented by the TRC in the departments of Junin, Huanuco, Huancavelica, Apurimac and San Martin, add up to 85 percent of the victims registered by the TRC.

5. The TRC has established that the peasant (campesina) population was the principal victim of the violence. Of the total victims reported, 79 percent lived in rural areas and 56 percent were engaged in farming or livestock activities. These figures contrast with those of the 1993 census, according to which 29 percent of the population lived in rural areas and 28 percent of the economically active population worked in the farming/livestock sector.

6. The TRC has been able to discern that the process of violence, combined with socioeconomic gaps, highlighted the seriousness of ethno-cultural inequalities that still prevail in the country. According to analysis of the testimonies received, 75 percent of the victims who died in the internal armed conflict spoke Quechua or other native languages as their mother tongue. This figure contrasts tellingly with the fact that, according to the 1993 census, on a national level only 16 percent of the Peruvian population shares that characteristic.

7. The TRC has shown that, in relative terms, the dead and disappeared had educational levels far inferior to the national average. While the national census of 1993 indicates that only 40 percent of the national population had failed to attain secondary school education, the TRC has found that 68 percent of the victims were below this level.

8. The TRC concludes that the violence fell unequally on different geographical areas and on different social strata in the country. If the ratio of victims to population reported to the TRC with respect to Ayacucho were similar countrywide, the violence would have caused 1,200,000 deaths and disappearances. Of that amount, 340,000 would have occurred in the city of Lima.

9. The TRC has established that the tragedy suffered by the populations of rural Peru, the Andean and jungle regions, Quechua and Ashaninka Peru, the peasant, poor and poorly educated Peru, was neither felt nor taken on as its own by the rest of the country. This demonstrates, in the TRC's judgment, the veiled racism and scornful attitudes that persist in Peruvian society almost two centuries after its birth as a Republic.

10. The TRC has found that the conflict demonstrated serious limitations of the State in its capacity to guarantee public order and security, as well as the fundamental rights of its citizens within a framework of democratic action.

(Continued)

11. The TRC has also found the constitutional order and the rule of law to be precarious, and breached in those moments of crisis.

II. Responsibilities for the Conflict
A. The Partido Comunista del Peru-Sendero Luminoso
[Communist Party of Peru-Shining Path, PCP-SL]

12. The TRC believes that the immediate and fundamental cause of the unleashing of the internal armed conflict was the PCP-SL's decision to start the armed struggle against the Peruvian State, in opposition to the will of the overwhelming majority of Peruvians, men and women, and at a time in which democracy was being restored through free elections.

13. In the TRC's view, based on the number of persons killed and disappeared, the PCP-SL was the principal perpetrator of crimes and violations of human rights. It was responsible for 54 percent of victim deaths reported to the TRC. This high degree of responsibility on the part of the PCP-SL is an exceptional case among subversive groups in Latin America, and one of the most notable unique features of the process that the TRC has had to analyze.

Discussion Questions
- What does the report tell us about the impact of the guerrilla war on the local population?
- What does the report suggest about how divided Peru is between urban and rural areas?

Source: Truth and Reconciliation Web site: http://cverdad.org.pe/ingles/ifinal/conclusiones.php

The Peruvian economy recovered as the Shining Path threat receded. Inflation dropped into the single digits and the economy grew. At the same time, however, those successes barely made a dent in poverty and unemployment. The bloom gradually came off the rose of the Fujimori administration also because of his authoritarian tendencies. The National Intelligence System (SIN) was run by his close ally, the shadowy Vladimir Montesinos, who spied on the opposition and supporters alike and used extortion and blackmail to achieve political ends. Under his direction, the legislature ruled that Fujimori could run for a third term. Although the constitution dictated a two-term limit, his supporters argued that because he had been in office at the time of its ratification, the first term did not count.

For the 2000 election, Alejandro Toledo ran as part of "Perú Posible" (Possible Peru). Fujimori won with just under 50 percent of the vote (49.8 percent), but Toledo refused to participate in a second round, citing evidence of voting fraud. Even so, Fujimori managed only 51.2 percent in the second round. The SIN scandal broke and his presidency very quickly unraveled. Later in 2000, he traveled to Japan and from there announced his resignation. After a brief interim presidency, a new election was held in which Toledo defeated García. In 2007 Fujimori traveled to Chile, and eventually was extradited to Peru, where he was convicted of kidnappings and murders that he had ordered. His daughter Keiko Fujimori was elected to the legislature in 2006 and quickly became a presidential contender, a sign that the Fujimori brand still retained some popularity.

National Recovery From the Fujimori Era

The Fujimori era effectively fragmented the already fractious party system in Peru. APRA continues to function, and in 2006 Alan García won the presidency for the party. However, both he and the party's candidates in Congress only attained just over 20 percent of the vote. Electoral volatility in the legislature is 51.9 percent since 1978, one of the highest levels in the world.[12] In addition, Peruvian presidents and their governments have not been able to attain better than mediocre approval ratings. Ollanta Humala, a highly controversial army lieutenant colonel who led an unsuccessful coup attempt against Fujimori in 2000, launched a populist campaign for the presidency with the Union for Peru party. He won the first round with 30.1 percent in 2006 but lost to Alan García in the second round. The 2011 presidential election revealed again the severe party fragmentation, as parties tended to be only reflections of individuals. Humala ran again with the Gana Perú (Peru Wins) coalition. He garnered the highest percentage of votes (32 percent) but went to a runoff with Keiko Fujimori, who had created a party, Fuerza 2011 (Strength 2011), expressly for the election. Humala won that runoff with 51.5 percent. As in Venezuela, a former coup plotter became a democratically elected president with his own personalized party.

On the surface, the Peruvian economy is one of the strongest in Latin America, with GDP growth dipping in 2009 but then roaring back to life with commodity exports. Yet the long-standing conundrum still stands, because growth does not correlate to presidential popularity and seems to affect only a minority of the population. Peru is still highly dependent, as it exports primary products like fish products (which means its maritime disputes, especially with Chile, have very high stakes), copper, and gold, not too unlike its traditional colonial roots. It imports finished goods from abroad, particularly the United States. The Gini index is high, steady at about 0.50 and the indigenous population, which is largely rural, has yet to enjoy many of the fruits of macroeconomic success. As long as commodity prices are robust, Peruvian economic growth will still be the envy of the developed world, but beyond that there is fragility behind the success.

Humala pledged to address the plight of the poor and indigenous. Despite the political vacuum that opened in Peru, unlike Bolivia and Ecuador its large indigenous population has not organized and mobilized with success. Instead, crosscutting identities have become obstacles for a common identification, so that someone who self-identifies as "indigenous" also views him- or herself as some combination of peasant, Andean, mestizo, native, or other labels that come and go over time.[13] As a result, there is no Peruvian equivalent to CONAIE. Some organizations of this type have periodically emerged, but have struggled to gain legitimacy. Another critical reason is that the presence of a guerrilla war prevented broad participation in protests. The state was extremely sensitive to anything that smacked of instability, and made much greater efforts to block them.

Like many other Latin American countries, Peru underwent a process of decentralization that began in 2003, granting more administrative and economic autonomy to local government, such as in Colombia, but that process was both corrupt and inefficient. Thus, the process of moving budgeting responsibilities to regional authorities has been difficult. Further, one unexpected consequence has been the rise of subnational nationalism, where regional leaders adopt critical attitudes toward transnational capital in a way that does not occur at the national level.[14] A proposal to reduce the number of regions in the country and thereby ostensibly make governance more efficient was put to a national vote in 2005 but defeated.

At the national level, there is considerable party fragmentation. Humala's coalition won only 47 of 130 seats (36.1 percent) in the unicameral legislature. That still represented a plurality, because five other coalitions split up the remaining seats. The executive-legislative divide that contributed to Fujimori's autogolpe are therefore still in evidence, because a lack of a majority makes it much harder for the president to pass legislation. That is further complicated by the rise of the subnational nationalism mentioned earlier. Humala, already a controversial figure, faced immediate obstacles to effective governance.

Conclusion and Comparative Perspective

Despite all the very serious protests he has faced, the administration of President Evo Morales is still one of the most stable in recent Bolivian political history. The irony, though, is that he has found himself in a similar position as so many past presidents on the opposite side of the ideological spectrum. In other words, he has forged policies aimed at achieving national goals, but which alienate vocal local constituencies. He therefore either has to back down, or possibly face the same consequences as some of his predecessors, who left power early and involuntarily. President Rafael Correa is in a very similar position, walking the same narrow line. President Ollanta Humala began dealing with the same types of issues, balancing commitment to the large and historically underrepresented indigenous population with the need to boost economic growth in the context of a weak international economy.

There has been a crisis of representation in these three Andean countries for decades. In all three, this has led to the cracking of the traditional national party system and emergence of populist leaders who have generated considerable support (winning elections by margins not often seen in those countries) but also opposition, which is most intense in Bolivia. This echoes similar developments in Venezuela, and in fact both Ollanta Humala and Hugo Chávez are retired military officers who previously tried to overthrow the government. There has been a serious lack of connection between the national government and local populations, especially in rural areas. Peru is the only country that has emerged from populism (in its case more right wing), but the parties are still very weak. All three countries continue the struggle to generate not only economic growth but greater equality and less poverty, goals that have long been elusive.

At the extreme, inequality has led to civil war. That has been the most severe by far in Peru with Sendero Luminoso and the Fujimori government's response, but both Bolivia and Ecuador have also experienced periods of authoritarian rule and/or civil unrest. In Bolivia and Peru this is exacerbated by the international influence of drug trafficking, which seeps down to the local level. These multiple and simultaneous challenges make political stability all the more elusive. Colombia has suffered from similar problems, but the consensual

TABLE 8.1 Bolivian Economic Indicators, 1991–2011

Year	GDP Growth	Inflation	Unemployment	Poverty Rate	Human Development Index
1991	5.4	14.5	5.8	—	0.588
1992	1.7	10.5	5.4	—	0.530
1993	4.2	9.3	5.8	—	0.584
1994	4.8	8.5	3.1	45.6 (urban)	0.589
1995	4.7	12.6	3.6	—	0.593
1996	4.4	7.9	4.2	—	—
1997	4.2	6.7	4.4	62.1	0.652
1998	5.0	4.4	6.1	—	0.643
1999	0.4	3.1	7.2	60.6	—
2000	2.5	3.4	7.5	—	—
2001	1.7	0.9	8.5	—	0.672
2002	2.5	2.4	8.7	62.4	0.681
2003	2.7	3.9	9.2	—	—
2004	4.2	4.9	6.2	63.9	—
2005	4.0	4.9	8.2	—	0.557
2006	4.6	4.9	8.0	—	—
2007	4.6	11.7	7.7	54.0	0.729
2008	6.1	11.8	6.7	—	—
2009	3.4	0.3	7.9	—	—
2010	3.8	5.6	6.5	—	0.668
2011	5.2	9.9	5.8	—	0.671

Sources: Unemployment: *GDP and Inflation: Preliminary Overview of the Economies of Latin America and the Caribbean,* 1994–2012.
Poverty rate: Social Panorama of Latin America. Economic Commission for Latin America, 1990–2012.
Human development index: United Nations, *Human Development Report,* 1990–2013.

party system that emerged after 1957 allowed for the development of stronger political institutions.

As in so many other Latin American countries, all three countries remain heavily dependent on primary products, which has meant highly uneven growth rates. That strong international factor has been a constant. Internationally

TABLE 8.2 Ecuadorian Economic Indicators, 1991–2011

Year	GDP Growth	Inflation	Unemployment	Poverty Rate	Human Development Index
1991	5.0	49.0	8.5	—	0.784
1992	3.0	60.2	8.9	—	0.718
1993	2.2	31.0	8.9	—	0.764
1994	4.4	25.4	7.8	52.3	0.775
1995	3.0	22.8	7.7	—	0.767
1996	2.3	25.6	10.4	—	—
1997	3.3	29.9	9.3	49.8	0.747
1998	2.1	43.4	11.5	—	0.772
1999	−6.3	60.7	14.4	58.0	—
2000	2.8	91.0	14.1	—	—
2001	5.3	22.4	10.4	—	0.731
2002	4.2	9.4	8.6	49.0	0.735
2003	3.6	6.1	9.8	—	—
2004	7.9	2.0	11.0	51.2	—
2005	4.7	3.1	10.7	48.3	0.772
2006	4.1	2.9	10.1	43.0	—
2007	2.0	3.3	7.6	42.6	0.806
2008	7.2	8.8	6.9	42.7	—
2009	0.4	4.3	8.5	42.2	—
2010	3.5	3.4	8.0	—	0.719
2011	8.0	4.5	6.0	—	0.722

Sources: Unemployment: *GDP and Inflation: Preliminary Overview of the Economies of Latin America and the Caribbean,* 1994–2012.
Poverty rate: Social Panorama of Latin America. Economic Commission for Latin America, 1990–2012.
Human development index: United Nations, *Human Development Report,* 1990–2013.

inspired market reforms have then prompted the development of populist leaders. Future economic and political development will hinge in large part on whether these new styles of governing in Bolivia and Ecuador foster lasting political institutions that can outlive their current leadership, and then alternate in power democratically with the opposition. For long-term stability, increasing

TABLE 8.3 Peruvian Economic Indicators, 1991–2011

Year	GDP Growth	Inflation	Unemployment	Poverty Rate	Human Development Index
1991	3.2	139.2	5.9	—	0.709
1992	0.2	56.7	9.4	—	0.642
1993	5.7	39.5	9.9	—	0.694
1994	14.7	15.4	8.8	—	0.717
1995	10.0	10.2	8.4	—	0.729
1996	2.3	11.8	7.9	—	—
1997	7.4	7.1	9.2	47.6	0.739
1998	−0.7	6.0	8.5	—	0.737
1999	0.9	3.7	9.2	48.6	—
2000	3.0	3.7	8.5	—	—
2001	0.2	−0.1	9.3	54.8	0.752
2002	5.2	1.5	9.4	—	0.752
2003	3.9	2.5	9.4	54.7	—
2004	5.2	4.1	9.4	48.6	—
2005	6.4	1.5	9.6	48.7	0.773
2006	8.0	1.1	8.5	44.5	—
2007	8.9	3.9	8.4	39.3	0.806
2008	9.8	6.7	8.4	36.2	—
2009	0.9	0.2	8.4	34.8	—
2010	8.6	2.2	8.0	—	0.733
2011	6.9	3.4	7.7	—	0.738

Sources: Unemployment: *GDP and Inflation: Preliminary Overview of the Economies of Latin America and the Caribbean*, 1994–2012.
Poverty rate: *Social Panorama of Latin America*. Economic Commission for Latin America, 1990–2012.
Human development index: United Nations, *Human Development Report*, 1990–2013.

social demands must be channeled through democratic institutions rather than individuals.

There are important points of comparison to Central America, which also has dealt with marginalized indigenous populations, inequality, a major disconnect between the national and local levels, as well as periods of violence marked by guerrilla warfare and counterinsurgency. Both subregions also have strong militaries that periodically intervene in politics as moderating powers (such as Ecuador in 2000 and Honduras in 2009). From an economic perspective, both Ecuador and El Salvador are dollarized, exemplifying the importance of the U.S. economy and how a foreign currency can contribute to national economic growth. Central America depends much more on the United States to buy exports, but Andean countries are also strongly tied to their northern neighbor.

Key Terms

- War of the Pacific
- Revolutionary Nationalist Movement (MNR)
- Gonzalo Sánchez de Lozada
- Evo Morales
- Confederation of Indigenous Nationalities of Ecuador (CONAIE)
- Rafael Correa
- American Revolutionary Popular Alliance (APRA)
- Shining Path
- Alberto Fujimori

Discussion Questions

- In what ways can a guerrilla movement like Shining Path pose a threat to democracy?
- Why would a government find it difficult to eliminate dollarization?
- How has the president tended to treat the legislature in these Andean countries?
- What are the similarities and differences between right-wing and left-wing populism?
- What kinds of political challenges do presidents like Evo Morales and Rafael Correa face from indigenous groups even when they are largely sympathetic to those groups?

Further Sources

Books

Crandall, Russell, Guadalupe Paz, and Riordan Roett (eds.). *The Andes in Focus: Security, Democracy and Economic Reform* (Boulder: Lynne Rienner Publishers, 2005). Readable collection that analyzes the countries of the Andean region and the impact of U.S. policy. It focuses on the three different themes, with particular attention to economic reform.

De la Torre, Carlos and Steve Striffler (eds.). *The Ecuador Reader: History, Culture, Politics* (Durham: Duke University Press, 2008). This is a very useful edited volume with different articles on historical development, nation-building, international influences, indigenous issues, and identity.

Dunkerley, James. *Bolivia: Revolution and the Power of History in the Present* (London: Institute for the Study of the America, 2007). James Dunkerley is a long-time observer of Bolivian politics, and this book is a collection of essays he has written over the years. They cover both political history and a lengthy discussion of the rise to power of Evo Morales.

Kenney, Charles D. *Fujimori's Coup and the Breakdown of Democracy in Latin America* (Notre Dame, IN: University of Notre Dame Press, 2004). The book examines Alberto Fujimori's *autogolpe* in detail, with extensive but accessible discussion of Peru's political institutions, parties, and personalities. It also provides a comparative context to democratic breakdown in other Latin American countries.

Van Cott, Donna Lee. *Radical Democracy in the Andes* (New York: Cambridge University Press, 2009). Van Cott studies municipal-level political institutions in Bolivia and Ecuador to understand the connection between political parties and indigenous organizations. She argues that democracy is enhanced when local governments are led by indigenous leaders.

Web Sites

Andean Information Network (http://ain-bolivia.org/). Focused in particular on the drug war and human rights in Bolivia, the AIN publishes analyses of current political events.

Andina (http://www.andina.com.pe/ingles/Inicio.aspx). This is the Web site of the Peruvian News Agency, which has English-language articles on current political events, but also on economics and culture. It includes links to the main English-language Peruvian government Web sites as well.

Bolivia Weekly (http://www.boliviaweekly.com/bolivian-press/). This Web site provides updated news on Bolivian politics, with links to Spanish-language stories in the Bolivian media. It also includes a list of all major online sources of Bolivian news Web sites, both English and Spanish.

Ecuador News (http://www.ecuadornews.com/). The Web site is a news aggregator, compiling links to English-language news sources on stories related to Ecuador, which also allows readers to submit story links and make comments.

Peruvian Times (http://www.peruviantimes.com/). This is a source of English-language news about Peru. These stories include extensive hyperlinks to other news sources as well, and can be followed on Twitter.

Endnotes

1. McClintock, Cynthia. "Peru: Precarious Regimes, Authoritarian and Democratic." In Larry Diamond, Juan J. Linz, and Seymour Martin Lipset (eds.), *Democracy in Developing Countries: Latin America* (Boulder: Lynne Rienner Publishers, 1989), 338.

2. Gamarra, Eduardo A. "Hybrid Presidential and Democratization: The Case of Bolivia." In Scott Mainwaring and Matthew S. Shugart (eds.), *Presidentialism and Democracy in Latin America* (New York: Carmbridge University Press, 1997).

3. O'Neill, Kathleen. "Decentralization in Bolivia: Electoral Incentives and Outcomes." In Alfred P. Montero and David J. Samuels (eds.), *Decentralization and Democracy in Latin America* (Notre Dame, IN: University of Notre Dame Press, 2004), 35–66.

4. Van Cott, Donna Lee. *Radical Democracy in the Andes* (New York: Cambridge University Press, 2009).
5. Stefanoni, Pablo and Hervé Do Alto. "The Emergence of Indigenous Nationalism in Bolivia." In Francois Polet (ed.), *The State of Resistance: Popular Struggles in the Global South* (London: Zed Books, 2007), 29–34.
6. Vélez, Fredy Rivera and Franklin Ramírez Gallegos, "Ecuador: Democracy and Economy in Crisis." In Russell Crandall, Guadalupe Paz, and Riordan Roett (eds.), *The Andes in Focus: Security, Democracy and Economic Reform* (Boulder: Lynne Rienner Publishers, 2005), 126.
7. Silva, Eduardo. *Challenging Neoliberalism in Latin America* (New York: Cambridge University Press, 2009).
8. Conaghan, Catherine M. "Ecuador: Correa's Plebiscitary Presidency." In Larry Diamond, Marc F. Plattner, and Diego Abente Brun (eds.). *Latin America's Struggle for Democracy* (Baltimore: The Johns Hopkins University Press, 2008), 199–213
9. Quoted in BBC News, "Ecuador Defaults on Foreign Debt," December 13, 2008.
10. Quoted in Degregoria, Carlos Iván. "The Origins and Logic of Shining Path: Two Views." In David Scott Palmer (ed.), *Shining Path of Peru* (New York: St. Martin's Press, 1992), 40.
11. Orias Arredondo, Ramiro. "Peru: The Trauma of Postdemocratic Consolidation." In Russell Crandall, Guadalupe Paz, and Riordan Roett (eds.), *The Andes in Focus: Security, Democracy & Economic Reform* (Boulder: Lynne Rienner Publishers, 2005), 69.
12. Mainwaring, Scott. "The Crisis of Representation in the Andes." In Larry Diamond, Marc F. Plattner, and Diego Abente Brun (eds.), *Latin America's Struggle for Democracy* (Baltimore: The Johns Hopkins University Press, 2008), 21.
13. Lucero, José Antonio and María Elena García. "In the Shadows of Success: Indigenous Politics in Peru and Ecuador." In A. Kim Clark and Marc Becker (eds.), *Highland Indians and the State in Modern Ecuador* (Pittsburgh: University of Pittsburgh Press, 2007), 234–247.
14. Eaton Kent. "Subnational Economic Nationalism? The Contradictory Effects of Decentralization in Peru." *Third World Quarterly* 31, 7 (October 2010): 1205–1222.

CHAPTER 9

Colombia

LEARNING OBJECTIVES

- Identify how the three levels of analysis interact in Colombia

- Use theoretical propositions to understand political and economic development in Colombia

- Explain how and why political and economic development in Colombia differs from other Latin American countries

---

TIMELINE

1819	Independence declared
1899–1902	War of the Thousand Days
1948	Jorge Eliécer Gaitán assassinated; La Violencia begins
1957	Sitges Agreement ends La Violencia
1964	Revolutionary Armed Forces of Colombia (FARC) is formed
1974	Official power-sharing agreement ended
1991	New constitution ratified
1998	FARC given demilitarized zone
2000	Plan Colombia goes into effect
2002	Alvaro Uribe elected
2003	Paramilitary demobilization began
2006	Alvaro Uribe reelected
2010	Juan Manuel Santos elected

As Defense Minister in 2008, **Juan Manuel Santos** organized the bombing of Colombian guerrilla camps in neighboring Ecuador, which killed a key rebel leader and yielded laptops with intelligence but also froze relations with the Ecuadorian government. The same year, he also worked on Operation Jaque, which freed fifteen prisoners inside Colombia held by guerrillas, including the former presidential candidate and longtime hostage Ingrid Betancourt. Later as president he vowed to work at the local level to restore land that had been taken violently from peasants or abandoned as the war against guerrillas and drug traffickers raged in the country. For years, the local population was terrorized. In recent decades, political violence has been a constant challenge in Colombia, and Santos' own responses show how international, national, and local factors must all be viewed to understand Colombian politics.

Colombia has the distinction of being viewed for years as a model of political stability and modernization and then shortly thereafter as an example of pure disaster. Not unlike Venezuela, what appeared to be an equitable

Map of Colombia

distribution of power frayed at the edges and ultimately began to lose legitimacy while the party system fractured. Until the latter half of the twentieth century, Colombia's economy was heavily dependent on the export of coffee, though oil did also bring in important revenue. It has since become more diversified, though still largely reliant on primary products.

Particularly in the 1980s and 1990s, Colombia's global image was not positive. Anecdotally that was evident given the plethora of movies in the United States depicting the country as a drug-infested wasteland. Given the firepower of Marxist guerrillas, paramilitary groups, and drug traffickers, sovereignty in many parts of the country seemed in doubt. Unlike many other Latin American countries, Colombia had not experienced dictatorial rule for decades, but the level of violence had begun displacing Colombians and making many fear for their lives, which also seriously disrupted local politics. The phrase *failed state* was used with more regularity. In the first decade of the twenty-first century, that situation had improved significantly. The government made inroads into disarming the paramilitaries and had won important military victories against the guerrillas. The economy was not only stable, but growing.

Historical Roots of Political and Economic Development

Simón Bolívar declared Colombia independent in 1819 after nine years of warfare, and it required two more to defeat Spanish forces. Initially "Gran Colombia" (which had been the colonial viceroyalty) included Ecuador, Panama, and Venezuela, though Bolívar's experiment with unification was short-lived, as Venezuela and Ecuador became independent in 1830. Panama, on the other hand, would not be separated until U.S. intervention in 1903. Politically the country split quite evenly into liberal and conservative camps, which by 1850 had coalesced into strong Liberal and Conservative parties. They were oligarchic and decentralized, because the country's mountainous geography made centralization initially difficult. At the same time, they were multiclass enough that they absorbed peasants and workers to an extent that other parties did not form, or were co-opted and/or intimidated.

Local and National Legacies of Violence

There were seven civil wars in the nineteenth century, and so Colombia seemed an example of a country that was unable to achieve "modern" status. Between 1830 and 1876, 24,600 Colombians were killed as a result, and 100,000 more during the War of the Thousand Days (1899–1902).[1] Liberals dominated from 1863 to 1885, followed by Conservatives from 1886 to 1930. Political competition was marked by violence, which ended with the construction of consociational arrangements to find solutions that might prevent future outbreaks. Consociationalism refers to power-sharing agreements (whether formal or informal) that prevent political groups from being completely excluded and therefore resentful. It serves as a bridge between major divisions in a country, and in Colombia has traditionally been utilized to end bouts of conflict. Colombia became an unusual combination of elite domination and political openness. Suffrage was expanded, moderate political opposition organized freely, and dictatorship was largely avoided.

Violence With Economic Development

Coffee was the main export in the nineteenth century, and a price boom in the late nineteenth through the early twentieth century fuelled the economy. Small landowners multiplied, which has often been cited as a source of political stability. Radical ideas (such as Marxism) were less likely to take hold because relatively few felt exploited by large latifundia owners or foreigners. The economy was clearly dependent on the developed world, receiving finished goods in exchange for its raw materials. It would become more diverse in the mid-twentieth century, as Colombia embarked on import substitution industrialization precisely to reduce its dependence and to industrialize. That would lead to such industries as petrochemicals, machinery, vehicles, and glass.

However, Colombian ISI was less state-driven than elsewhere, with more of an eye toward export promotion. That meant the state was not saddled with so many inefficient industries after the debt crisis, as was the case in Mexico. Modernization theory would suggest that Colombia was moving in the "correct" direction in virtually all regards, ready to finally start moving upward into developed status. As two historians put in 1922, "Colombia's citizens seem to have become aroused to the damage wrought their country by fierce civil wars and to have settled down to an era of regular, constitutional government."[2] That assessment turned out to be completely wrong.

This goal was deferred because political conflict intensified after the global economic crash of 1929. Elections in 1930 and 1931 were marred by violence. Reforms implemented by Liberal President Alfonso López Pumarejo (1934–1938) were met with resistance, as landowners fought agrarian reform and industrialists resisted unionization, to the point that he publicly agreed not to move forward. Although López became president again in 1942 (with assistance from electoral fraud), he faced a coup attempt in 1944 and resigned the following year. Political unrest was accelerating, and the 1946 presidential election only increased polarization.

Colombia exploded in 1948, when charismatic Liberal populist presidential candidate Jorge Eliécer Gaitán was assassinated. His death sparked massive riots in the capital Bogotá (and therefore became known as the *Bogotazo*) and then civil war between Liberals and Conservatives. This war would last roughly a decade (1948–1958) and would take over 100,000 lives. It was characterized by such vicious tactics—dismemberment, crucifixion, bayoneting, and so on—that it became known simply as "**La Violencia**," or "The Violence." That outbreak of national violence left a deep imprint on Colombian politics, guiding it for several decades. In 1953, General Gustavo Rojas Pinilla overthrew the Conservative Laureano Gómez and installed a dictatorship. The only silver lining was that his repressive rule served to bring the two parties together in opposition, and Rojas was forced out in 1957. An interim government served while the two sides determined the formation of a new political system.

▬ COLOMBIA'S POLITICAL INSTITUTIONS ▬

Last constitution: 1991

Unitary system with thirty-two departments and one capital district

Executive: President with two five-year terms

Legislative: Bicameral with House of Representatives (166 members) and Senate (102 members) both elected by party-list proportional representation

Judicial: Supreme Court of Justice, also Constitutional Court of Colombia with power of judicial review

Contemporary Politics in Colombia

Contemporary politics dates specifically to the Sitges Agreement of 1957, which ended La Violencia and established a formal power-sharing agreement. The National Front guaranteed power and representation to both sides as a way to end the killing. Liberal and Conservative elites agreed that the two parties would rule together, alternating the presidency every four years and guaranteeing that each party split other major administrative offices. Women were also granted the right to vote that year, but the political system was still restrictive. New political parties were not allowed to form until 1968, and legislation had to be passed with a two-thirds majority, which was intended to ensure consensus and compromise. That arrangement lasted until 1974, at which time elections became more competitive and open. Colombia was gradually held up as a model for democratization in the developing world. Despite the extreme polarization of the 1940s and 1950s, it had consolidated a polyarchy and had avoided authoritarianism of either the right or the left while many other South American countries were succumbing to dictatorship. The political ice was thin, however, and elites were periodically concerned about fresh outbreaks of violence related to presidential elections, such as when retired General Rojas managed to garner 39 percent of the vote in 1970 and came close to winning, which generated fear about popular uprisings in opposition.

Constitutional reform in 1968 allowed parties to put together multiple candidate lists for elections, which increased competition at the local level. Regional power brokers were freer from national central control, but simultaneously helped legitimize the state by providing clientelistic local benefits. At the same time, however, the reform served to splinter the National Front even further, as its constituent parties moved in different directions. Nonetheless, until the 1980s presidents sought to provide some measure of parity in the cabinet with the opposition to keep up the basic idea of national cooperation.

But the 1968 constitution also increased executive power, particularly with regard to economic policy. Although its intent was to foster (or really force) cooperation, one effect of the National Front was to emphasize presidentialism. The very nature of Colombian consociationalism, which included ensuring no party held large legislative majorities and a two-thirds majority to get laws passed, produced gridlock. The presidential response was to use decree power under a state of siege, which could be selectively used in different parts of the country. In practice, the decrees remained in place for years if the president could not convince the legislature to pass the desired law. States of siege also became more common as a way for the executive to curb labor or student unrest. As a result, laws intended to produce partisan parity ended up reducing horizontal accountability.

Into the 1970s Colombia also began moving away from the import substitution model, even joining the General Agreement on Tariffs and Trade in 1975, which opened up the economy. The government pushed for some economic liberalization, though this was limited when the price of coffee rose in the mid-1970s, as that filled state coffers and provided latitude for more spending without the pain of allowing more foreign competition. More attention was also paid to agricultural exports, and oil remained (and remains) an important export. Overall, Colombia's economic policies have remained moderate and changes have been gradual regardless of who was in the presidency. Colombian leaders refrained from borrowing too much until a fall of coffee prices compelled them to do so in the 1980s. From 1957 to 1981, it had some of the highest growth rates in Latin America, at an average of 5.15 percent.[3] Nonetheless, sustained growth did not improve income equality, which has consistently been among the worst in the region. Within that context, the political model no longer corresponded to the demographic change and urbanization taking place in the country, which meant greater numbers of Colombians felt alienated. That, in turn, affected national politics.

In the 1980s, moreover, this model was threatened by the effects of the drug trade and guerrilla war. Very weak currency controls meant it was quite easy to launder drug money. At the same time, during the 1970s the consumption of drugs—especially cocaine—in the United States fuelled a dramatic increase in their production within Colombia. Wide swaths of the country are ideal for growing coca, the plant from which cocaine is derived. Not only is it a hardy plant, making it relatively easy to cultivate, but there are extensive areas in Colombia that are remote and therefore free from any government intrusion. As international demand grew, supply was perfectly able to meet it.

International Influence: The Drug Trade

Drug trafficking had a huge impact on Colombian politics. It helped to hasten the end of the National Front agreement, as the corruption caused by drug money served to further delegitimize a regime that was increasingly being viewed as unresponsive to the needs of average Colombians. Urbanization had led to new social demands, which political elites were very slow to address, and so abstentionism ran high. Why vote if it seems to have no impact? Participating on some level of the drug trade therefore became more attractive to many people who felt they had little choice in the formal economy. Meanwhile, the power of drug cartels grew exponentially because of the massive profits they made.

The 1970s and 1980s also marked an increase in activity by the **Revolutionary Armed Forces of Colombia,** or FARC. This guerrilla group formed in 1964 in the wake of the Cuban revolution to combat the National Front, though for years it was less powerful than some of its guerrilla counterparts, such as the National Liberation Army (ELN). As the drug trade spread throughout rural areas, however, the FARC began to "tax" it, which really meant extortion. That revenue allowed it to obtain weapons—even very high-tech—and other supplies, and its ranks swelled. The FARC's goal was to emulate the Cuban revolution by destroying the government and establishing a Marxist system in its place. Unlike the Cuban revolutionaries, however, the FARC was largely unable to gain widespread popularity. Therefore it remained a serious threat but not to the point of winning a revolutionary war.

Although the military stayed out of power, it became much more repressive as it fought on multiple guerrilla fronts. The so-called M-19 was initially the only primarily urban guerrilla force but would be joined by the ELN, which even launched a bold attack on the Palace of Justice in Bogotá. In response, the army sent troops along with a tank to take the building, and in the process killed over 100 people, including 10 of 12 Supreme Court justices. It is important to note, however, that in the aftermath of that disaster, the Betancur administration successfully negotiated the M-19's demobilization and transformation into a democratic political party, a process completed several years later.

Violence spiraled during the presidency of Julio César Turbay (1978–1982). As historian Marco Palacios puts it, "every group in Colombia with even a modicum of organization seemed to take the law into its own hands during the Turbay years."[4] Indeed, it was during this time that Pablo Escobar, the infamous leader of the Medellín drug cartel, ran and won a seat in Congress in 1982 with the Liberal Party. That same year, the cartel created its own death squad called *Death to Kidnappers* (known as *MAS*) whose aim was to destroy the M-19. It received training support and weapons from the Colombian military and police, and would establish a long-standing formula by which the state could assist illegal operations as a way to fight common enemies. The MAS was implicated in hundreds of deaths.

Liberal and conservative unity began to crack in 1982, as the populist Belisario Betancur won the presidency and pushed for negotiations with the guerilla movements. Under the continued guerrilla assault, there was no longer a united party response about what to do. Betancur's effort in 1984 to establish a national dialogue was not broadly popular, especially with the armed forces. Nonetheless, he set an important precedent by convincing the M-19 to lay down its arms and eventually became a political party. Yet Colombian consociationalism was still coming apart.

Betancur was also responsible for the initiation of political and economic decentralization in Colombia, which mirrored much of the rest of Latin America. Although Colombia remained a unitary state, mayors were elected for the first time and had their own budgets. Fiscal decentralization increased accountability at the local level, because mayors dealt directly with their constituents. Unfortunately, the strength of the FARC (and later paramilitary groups as well) meant that mayors sometimes faced perhaps even more intense challenges than politicians at the national level. Extortion and intimidation remained a problem for years. In 1991 there were 28,284 murders in Colombia, compared to 10,713 in 1981.[5] During the same period, kidnappings rose from 99 to 1,550. By any measure, human rights were simply not being respected or protected in Colombia during the 1980s and into the 1990s. Presidents Virgilio Barco Vargas (1986–1990) and César Gaviria Trujillo (1990–1994) both acknowledged the need to do something about guerrilla and drug violence, but were ineffective at doing so.

The 1990 presidential election was especially brutal, as three presidential candidates were killed. This helped spark popular pressure—initiated by those candidates' upset supporters—to reform the constitution as a way to address the inequalities in the country and promote solutions that might reduce the violence. The basic idea was to incorporate human rights in specific ways and to guarantee the rights of minorities. Those reforms changed the electoral system, eliminating the traditional emphasis on rural areas (and therefore rural-based politicians) and increasing urban seats in the legislature. To break the dominance of the two main parties, senatorial elections became national, rather than regional. To increase horizontal accountability, Congress was given broader powers vis-à-vis the president, including the ability to censure cabinet ministers. Reforms also fostered the transfer of money from the central government to local counterparts, thus accelerating decentralization.

International influence was a critical factor in the 1990s, as Colombian governments faced intense and public criticism from the U.S. government, similar to the scrutiny in Bolivia. The low point was during the administration of Ernesto Samper (1994–1998) who was accused of having ties to the Cali drug cartel, which allegedly helped pay for his presidential campaign. As Russell Crandall has put it, U.S. policy was "narcotized," so that virtually all aspects of U.S.-Colombian relations boiled down to how well the fight against drug production and trafficking was progressing.[6] As a result, Colombia was "decertified" in 1996 and 1997, meaning the U.S. Congress did not believe it was participating effectively with the war on drugs (which entailed losing aid) and even had Samper's U.S. visa revoked. Samper was dogged by accusations of drug connections throughout his presidency, and some of his political allies were indicted, though he was never formally charged. Samper discussed negotiating with the FARC, but nothing concrete ensued. But he did make strides, perhaps in response to U.S. pressure, because the Cali cartel was effectively dismantled in the mid-1990s with the arrests, extradition, and later conviction of key members of its leadership. The torrential flow of drugs continued, however, as smaller drug organizations replaced the large cartels (the Medellín Cartel met a similar fate).

So what to do? Samper's successor, Andrés Pastrana (1998–2002), who was a vocal critic of Samper for those alleged drug ties, took a similar tack with the FARC. He was elected in large part because of his campaign promise to begin serious negotiations with the guerrillas. That included the *despeje* (roughly translated as *clear area*), a demilitarized zone about the size of Switzerland that was ceded to the FARC in exchange for peace talks. It soon became clear, though, that the guerrillas had no intention of fulfilling their side of the bargain, and the net effect was to strengthen the FARC's hold on the Colombian countryside, which meant even greater violence and disconnect at the local level. But Pastrana also proposed a new plan to the Clinton administration and to the European Union, which would combine funding for security and economic development as a comprehensive strategy for combating drug trafficking. For the time being, it did not include funding for the guerrilla war, which the United States insisted was a domestic rather than international problem.

By that point, the guerrillas were effectively sovereign in large parts of Colombia. They filled a vacuum in remote rural areas where the Colombian state did not reach. With the money it was making from drug trafficking (or the "taxes" on drug traffickers), the FARC provided local-level services that the national government did not provide, such as rudimentary schools (with, of course, Marxist and antigovernment messages) and basic medical care. Such connections, combined with fear, consolidated the FARC's control over large jungle areas. Pastrana, and then Uribe after him, eventually shifted the government's response in a more military and police direction to dislodge the guerrillas.

Political Violence and Economic Development

No amount of strong law enforcement, however, could effectively address the economic roots of Colombian instability. Economically, Colombia is highly unequal in numerous ways. Its Gini index is consistently one of the highest in Latin America and indeed among the highest in the world (0.56 in 2006). There is also an urban–rural divide. In rural areas poverty afflicts 80 percent of the population, with about 42 percent in extreme poverty. An absence of land reform has meant that ownership of land remains in the hands of a small elite. The Colombian state has been notably absent from the countryside, which also helps to account for why the guerrilla war has lasted so long. That conflict, in turn, increases the number of displaced, which exacerbates poverty.

When Pastrana took office, the Colombian economy was in recession and unemployment had risen above 20 percent. He devalued the currency as a way to boost exports, and then in 1999 let it float as the peso became impossible to shore up. The peso had already been under attack by investors, who were particularly leery because neighboring Ecuador had also just announced it was defaulting on its debt. As had occurred in many other countries, Pastrana then negotiated IMF loans and embarked on structural adjustment policies to cut spending and boost productivity. This made inequality worse but stabilized the economy, which began to grow again by 2000.

In large part for these economic reasons, political scientist (and longtime Colombia observer) Harvey Kline has written—paraphrasing the writer Gabriel García Márquez—that Pastrana's peace process was a "chronicle of a failure foretold."[7] The country is divided into so many different constituent parts that coordinated economic growth and peaceful coexistence have yet to occur. Colombia has never been integrated, which distorts economic growth and exacerbates existing inequalities.

The National Front excluded the left, and Colombian politics was a top-down affair, which added to local disaffection and opened the door further for young people to be attracted to illegal activities as a way to make a living. The intent of the 1991 constitution was to initiate change in that regard, but it was minimal. No matter what institutional reform was implemented, the fundamentals of the Colombian economy did not augur well for the inclusion of poor youths, especially in rural areas. There were too many illegal opportunities available for those who felt politically and economically isolated from their national government.

One illegal activity that literally exploded was participation in **paramilitary** groups, which refers to armed organizations that operate apart from the military. Although often unofficially sanctioned, they are typically illegal. There was an alphabet soup of different paramilitaries, but the most important was the United Self-Defense Forces of Colombia (known most commonly by its Spanish acronym, AUC), which formed in 1997. Paramilitary groups had existed for years, formed and funded by local elites who were threatened by guerrilla activity (e.g., Chiquita Brands International was found guilty of paying off paramilitaries). The government was aware of them but considered them useful in the fight against the FARC. A 1989 decree ordered prison sentences for anyone (civilian or military) who participated in or funded them, but it was not well enforced. The AUC became an umbrella group for these disparate organizations, and soon became the source of more human rights abuses than the government or the FARC. Led by Carlos Castaño, the AUC moved into the drug trade, which created a permanent funding stream and broadened the group's political influence. By the 1980s, narcotraffickers owned large parcels of land, which required armed protection. Similar to the FARC, paramilitaries deliberately targeted young Colombians, using a combination of enticement and force to compel them to take up arms.

Paramilitary leaders defended their groups' right to exist, publicly presenting themselves as "a political-military movement which uses the same irregular methods as the guerillas. Its members are not terrorists, nor common criminals, but rather persons who have found it necessary to violate the law because the Colombian state penalizes the legitimate right of self-defense even though it is incapable of providing that defense."[8] In other words, they break the law because the law is broken to begin with. That entailed not only protection of land but also forced displacement of people, particularly those who were deemed to be guerrilla sympathizers. In many areas, these groups became de facto law enforcement.

As the state seemed unable to fight on its multiple fronts, popular support for a hard-line national government response grew. This is particularly important because the Colombian executive is strong. The president can declare a state of siege, which provides de facto legislative powers. From 1958 until the abrogation of the constitution in 1991, the country was governed under a state of siege 75 percent of the time.[9] In 1991, the measure became known as a State of Internal Commotion and some restrictions were applied, such as placing a 90-day time limit. However, the president can call for a 90-day extension on top of that—only a second extension requires consent from the Senate. Reforms have allowed Congress to revoke emergency decrees and require adherence to human rights norms, but it remains a powerful presidential tool. This followed the long tradition of including regimes of exception in Colombian constitutions.

Congressional fragmentation has served to solidify presidential power. As mentioned, reforms have been crafted to rectify the problem, but the executive maintains the upper hand. Congress has historically been both unwilling and unable to pursue major initiatives on its own. Members of Congress who wish to advance a particular issue look instead to the executive branch to get it done. The flip side of this situation is that the president can often find it difficult to get legislation passed at all. As in Brazil, the multiplicity of interests and party factions can stymie action. The result is a powerful president who nonetheless cannot necessarily run roughshod over the legislature given the limits of decrees.

The judicial system has gradually increased horizontal accountability. The two main judicial institutions in Colombia are the Constitutional Court and the Supreme Court. As its name suggests, the charge of the Constitutional Court is to ensure that all laws and policies conform to the constitution. It has become a powerful player and has routinely overturned legislation, including economic policies. That is an important exception to the otherwise executive-dominant system. The Supreme Court acts as the highest court for all civil and criminal cases, but it cannot rule on the law. Judges in both courts have proved willing to make rulings that contradict the interests of the government in power, which have created a reputation for independence and reinforced horizontal account-ability. At the same time, the law very clearly does not extend to all parts of the country, and so local judicial reality is very different. Citizens in rural areas have little chance to have their grievances addressed, and even existing cases face a massive backlog that makes long delays inevitable. Indeed, the sheer number of new laws and reforms has placed large burdens on judges, who are therefore slower to make rulings. One improvement for transparency has been a shift from the traditional Napoleonic system to an accusatorial one in which people have the right to a public trial decided by a judge or jury. Public prosecutors no longer have judicial powers.

A serious problem for the Colombian judiciary at all levels is fear. This includes fear of reporting crimes (especially those that might implicate members of organized crime), of acting as witness, or even for judges to prosecute. The growth of private militia reflects in part the privatization of justice. If for whatever reason a desired settlement was not reached by legal means, then the extralegal became more common.

National and International Implications of Political Violence

Reforms in 2003 required all parties to submit a single list in each district, which was intended to increase party unity and reduce fragmentation. In the past, each party had multiple lists in each district, which had the effect of pitting candidates from the same party against each other. The Liberal and Conservative parties had already splintered badly, echoing other countries like Peru and Venezuela. **Alvaro Uribe** ran for president in 2002 without a party label, though he had strong ties to the Liberal Party. He would never return to the party, however, and instead would create his own vaguely defined electoral coalition, "Colombia First." His supporters, particularly former members of the Liberal Party, coalesced around the Party of National Social Unity (known as *la U*). He advocated a hard-line response to guerrilla violence, and soon after taking office decreed a "State of Internal Commotion," which granted him broad powers that circumvented Congress. He maintained it for nine months until the Constitutional Court finally struck it down. The hard-line approach also involved encouraging citizens to become informers as a way to provide intelligence to the government.

By 2006, the traditional two-party system was gone. President Uribe successfully lobbied for a constitutional amendment to allow consecutive reelection, which was approved by the Constitutional Court in 2005. Uribe handily won a second term with 62 percent of the vote, while the Conservative Party did not even run a candidate. The Liberal Party candidate garnered only 12 percent of the vote. In the 2006 elections in the Chamber of Deputies, twenty-three different parties were represented, fourteen of which won only one or two seats. The Liberal Party did have the most seats at thirty-five, but that was only 21 percent of all seats.

The 2010 legislative elections saw the rise of a new phenomenon, the Party of National Integration (PIN). Because of ties to paramilitary groups, a number of political parties had been deemed illegal and some of their members jailed. Their members re-coalesced in the PIN, whose newly elected legislators had strong connections (in some cases relatives) to those imprisoned former members. The PIN then won nine seats in the legislature. The two parties most closely tied to Uribe, the Party of the U and the Conservatives, won fifty seats. Along with other parties of the right, including the PIN, the government maintained a comfortable majority.

There was also a new movement on the left. The Independent Democratic Pole (PDI) formed in 2003. Perhaps its most controversial platform is a negotiated settlement with the FARC to end the guerrilla war. For the 2006 presidential election, the PDI allied with another small party of the left, Democratic Alternative, to create the Alternative Democratic Pole (PDA). Their candidate, Carlos Gaviria (a former judge of the Constitutional Court, no relation to the former president), won 22 percent of the vote. The coalition won nine seats in the lower house and eleven in the Senate. The moderate left faces a particularly difficult challenge in Colombia, as the radical left still remains committed to a violent overthrow of the government and a Marxist vision for the country. It is therefore more difficult for the left to win support because it becomes tainted in the public eye as a result.

The International Politics of Economic Reform

In the 1990s, when the administration of César Gaviria began liberalizing the economy and dismantling the state-led development model, Colombia experienced generally sluggish or even negative growth compared to three percent gross domestic product (GDP) growth in the 1970s. The high level of violence disrupted economic activity all across the country. The reduction of violence in the 2000s, however, opened the door for more investment and trade. Manufacturing (such as chemicals), textiles, and mining in particular have become stronger, as well as some areas of agriculture.

Growth in exports was enhanced by the United States' Andean Trade Promotion and Drug Eradication Act (ATPDEA). Begun in 2002, the ATPDEA provides tariff-free access for many Andean exports. Colombia, Bolivia (though it was eventually removed), Peru, and Ecuador all benefit from the agreement, which must be reconfirmed by the U.S. Congress, sometimes as often as six months at a time. In 2006, the U.S Trade Representative signed a free trade agreement with Colombia, which was ratified by the U.S. Congress in 2011. For the Colombian government, a free trade agreement provides access to more goods in the U.S. market and is permanent, thus eliminating the need to continue approving the ATPDEA.

Exports are still focused largely on agriculture, and so the country faces a dependency dilemma for international trade. However, Colombia diversified away from such heavy reliance on coffee, which means the economy is no longer tied to its price, which was the case for decades. By the 1980s, in addition to oil Colombia was also producing cut flowers (paying specific attention to the U.S. market, where demand surges for Valentine's and Mother's Days), cotton, corn, bananas, and sugar. Economic growth after 2002 has been strong, while both inflation and unemployment declined. The decrease of violence during that time has been central to growth. A rise in commodity prices even prompted the government to begin buying dollars in 2011 as a way to curb the appreciation of the peso, which was threatening exports. Nonetheless, the informal economy is still very large, so as always the overall growth numbers obscure the plight of a large proportion of the Colombian population.

The economic program of the Uribe government and that of his successor Juan Manuel Santos has been pro-market and export oriented. Colombia produces about 700,000 barrels of oil a day (and is the ninth largest supplier of oil to the United States). It exports about half of that. There is a state-owned oil company, Ecopetrol, which is the largest producer in the country, though unlike Mexico's Pemex it has been partially privatized and also competes with private companies. Oil constitutes 25 percent of the state's revenue and pipelines have thus also become popular targets for guerrillas, as it is relatively easy to disrupt the flow in remote areas. Nonetheless, production grew in the 2000s because increased security limited the number of pipeline attacks.

Colombia has not faced the same inflationary pressures as some of its neighbors, particularly Venezuela. Inflation was over 20 percent in the mid-1990s, but dipped into single digit even before Uribe took office. By 2013, it was around 2 percent. Monetary policy helped explain this, as the Central Bank kept interest rates stable and there was a floating exchange rate. The Central Bank, in fact, aggressively purchased foreign exchange to keep the domestic currency down and avoid any inflationary pressures. Along with increased security, the investment climate has therefore become more favorable.

Political Development: The Local Level

The political crisis engendered by drug-related and ideological violence often overshadowed the important process of decentralization, which began in earnest after the adoption of the 1991 constitution. It gave new functions to departments and municipalities, such as decision-making autonomy and fiscal responsibilities. These local institutions now exert extensive influence over agricultural policies, education, health, and infrastructure.

Roughly 50 percent of the national budget was eventually shifted to local and state governments.[10] This effort was implemented unevenly and imperfectly, as the transfer of resources was not accompanied by the institution-building necessary to coordinate it. As a result, a lot of money was wasted or used inefficiently. Individual departments are generally not well-equipped to administer and distribute the funds they receive. In practice, this has meant that departments have gone into debt providing services, assuming that they would eventually be bailed out by the central government.

More scholarly attention is being paid to the position of Colombian mayors, who have become the main face of the government for many citizens who, especially amidst the collapse of the traditional parties, otherwise view the parties as disconnected from them. The constitution allowed for their direct election, and since 2004 their terms are four years with no immediate reelection. Because they are not in office a long time, the qualities they bring immediately to office are critical. The educational level of the mayor, for example, correlates to administrative effectiveness, particularly in terms of improved tax collection and spending on social programs.[11] Not surprisingly, the presence of illegal armed groups harms effectiveness, as mayors are forced to abandon certain policies or are extorted, both of which are obstacles to the mayor being able to do his or her job well.

International Influences: The Drug Trade

The drug trade relates to basic supply and demand on an international level, which then greatly affects both national and local levels. In the 1970s, the use of cocaine in the United States grew rapidly. Given the immense profit to be made, supply rose to meet the demand. People like Pablo Escobar organized large-scale production and trafficking organizations. The level of violence increased dramatically as well, both in Colombia and in the United States. The origins of the drug trade also have local elements, such as the lack of a government presence in the countryside where coca is grown and processed, but the ultimate demand for drugs comes overwhelmingly from abroad, and mostly from the United States (though the European market is also being tapped).

In the late 1990s, President Pastrana proposed a new "**Plan Colombia,**" the purpose of which was to attract aid from both the United States and Europe. It would have both military and social components to combat coca cultivation and promote economic development projects that would lead Colombians away from the drug trade. With little interest in Europe, Plan Colombia's final form was heavily militarized and funded by the United States. By 2010, the United States had spent approximately $10 billion, and Colombia was the third largest recipient of U.S. aid, behind only Israel and Egypt. Determining the effects of the plan is complex. Given the continued flow of cocaine to the United States, it has not achieved a core objective because the movement of drugs has simply shifted to more remote parts of Colombia and/or to other countries, which is the so-called balloon effect. The aerial spraying of coca fields has proved unpopular because the pesticides kill fields of legitimate crops, thus leaving the rural poor in an even worsened condition.

On the other hand, Plan Colombia meshed well with President Uribe's military-oriented Plan Patriota, created in 2004 with the support of the United States to fight the FARC and the ELN. The guerrilla groups are far weaker than they were at the beginning of Uribe's first term. The FARC is much more on the defensive, and its ability to terrorize rural areas has likewise diminished. One of the FARC's key leaders, Raúl Reyes, was killed in 2008 just over the border with Ecuador, which raised a serious diplomatic dispute with the Ecuadorian government but served as an example of how the Colombian military was succeeding in tracking and attacking the guerrillas. Intelligence work also led to the rescue of a number of hostages, including U.S. citizens. Thus, Plan Colombia was successful from Colombia's point of view, even though fighting guerrillas was not its original objective. Over time it has transformed into the "National Consolidation Plan," which is intended to provide more of a nonmilitary government presence in the country (which, in fact, had been the original intent of Plan Colombia).

Despite the heavily securitized nature of Colombian antiguerrilla and antidrug policies, the armed forces remain outside politics. Political scientist William Avilés has argued that in Colombia, as in Peru, the widespread violence greatly weakened civil society's ability to contest market reforms.[12] This weakened statist or populist elements in the military as well, and opened the door for reduction in military prerogatives. The armed forces have remained content to play a critical role in fighting insurgencies rather than challenging democratic leaders.

In 2009, the administration of Barack Obama negotiated a new defense pact with Colombia, which provided access to seven Colombian military bases. The agreement was forged in response to the decision of the Ecuadorian government not to renew a lease at its Manta airbase, which was used for drug interdiction. The pact sparked regional controversy, with Venezuelan President Hugo Chávez likening it to war, while Brazilian President Lula emphasized the lack of transparency and failure to anticipate the concerns that neighboring countries might have. The FARC responded with a blistering communiqué that emphasized its continued, though seemingly fruitless, hope of gaining adherents from the armed forces to fight against the perceived loss of sovereignty and to "halt the threatening flight of the eagle of the Monroe Doctrine over the skies of Our America."

The overall emphasis on security has raised questions about the effects on the population. Both in and out of office President Uribe has faced considerable criticism for human rights in Colombia (both at home and abroad), which he clearly disliked. He gave a speech in 2009 to the General Assembly of the United Nations, in which—as in many other instances—he emphasized the reduction of violence and displacement. He argued that fighting terrorism did not have to mean compromising democracy. Colombia was fighting a "heroic battle" against narcoterrorism and it was winning.

▬▬▬ ANALYZING DOCUMENTS ▬▬▬

Alvaro Uribe's two terms in office marked a substantial change from the past. He obtained international support (from the United States) to fight the national and local problems of guerrilla violence. His hard-line policies were both popular and controversial, which prompted speeches like this one to defend them.

Alvaro Uribe, Speech to the United Nations (2009)

I would like to begin by congratulating you, Mr. President, and by reiterating to the United Nations the recognition for its beneficial presence and collaboration with the people of Colombia. The Government that I preside has the objective of increasing the confidence of the national and international community in our Country.

We support that search for confidence on three pillars: security with democratic values, promotion of investment and entrepreneurship with social responsibility, and social cohesion with freedoms. We continue to make progress in security but also with pending challenges. I would like to highlight intangible achievements that validate the democratic credentials of our security project:

- We have recovered two monopolies that we never should have lost: the monopoly of institutional forces to combat criminals and the monopoly of justice that terrorists once wanted to displace. Paramilitarism, a term that emerged to describe private criminal gangs whose objective was to combat drug trafficking guerrillas, has been dismantled. Today, the State is the only one that combats all criminals. These, in all their forms, drug-trafficking guerrillas, criminal gangs, are brought together in a mafia-style relationship that unites them or pits them against each other to share or fight over the profits of the criminal drug enterprise. Justice, with the Supreme Court assassinated in 1985 in an assault by drug traffickers and guerrillas, tormented by the threat and assassination of judges and displaced in many regions by terrorists leaders of guerrillas and paramilitaries that attempted to replace it, has recovered in the entirety of the Country its full effectiveness.
- Victims did not stand up out of fear of retaliation or belief that it would be useless. Now, thanks to the recovery of security, 239,758 victims have been registered, and we are carrying out a determined reparation effort with them, that is never complete, but that will lead to reconciliation as it advances, by cancelling spirits of vengeance and hatred.
- We have recovered the independence of decentralization and of political exercise. Terrorism had displaced 30% of mayors, stolen and corrupted large amounts of municipal and departmental budgets and coerced political sectors. Mayors have

recovered the security for the free exercise of their mandates and the transparent management of resources. Politics are freely exercised in the expression of all forms of thought.

- This terrorist threat has been confronted without martial legislation, with full civil and political guarantees and absolute respect for the liberties that we promote through security.

- We work towards both the effectiveness of the Public Forces and the respect for human rights. We do not hesitate to punish those who violate them nor do we back away from defending our soldiers and policemen, sometimes victims of a dirty legal war. Colombia has voluntarily presented itself to the United Nations human rights review. Furthermore, in spite of suffering caused by the anti-personnel landmines planted by terrorist groups, the State destroyed those in possession of the Public Forces for training purposes. Our country is one of the leaders of the Ottawa Convention for the destruction of such landmines and will host its next meeting in Cartagena.

- We combat terrorism with wholehearted determination and we practice democracy with full devotion. That is why Colombia's doors have been open without restrictions to international vigilance. We deliberate and disagree, but impartial observers and biased critics alike have had guaranteed spaces in Colombia.

- Our interest is not the fanatical confrontation between left and right, which is dangerous as it is obsolete, we are betting on a modern democracy, safe, free, builder of social cohesion, with independent institutions, with confidence derived from the transparency that is based on a high degree of citizen participation.

- We have not been able to completely overcome displacement but we have multiplied by 12 the budgetary resources allocated to provide assistance to displaced persons. We promote confidence links between state forces and communities so that operations against drug-trafficking are not frustrated by the displacement provoked by drug-traffickers. 51,783 members of terrorist groups have demobilized and the size of these groups has been reduced from nearly 60,000 to less than 8,000. We have shown complete generosity with the demobilized and full severity with the 7% who have relapsed into criminal behavior. The Justice and Peace Law that covers them has allowed for the revelation of 29,555 criminal acts, the confession of 12,104, the discovery of 2,492 corpses in 2,043 graves, the identification of 708 bodies and the return of 581 to their families. The participation of the victims and new procedures for the restitution and redress of their rights are a determining component of this demobilization process. Terrorism cannot be ignored in the name of good international relations. On the contrary, multilateralism and diplomacy must lead to collaborative actions among States to overcome this drama and its accomplices like trafficking in arms, illicit drugs, money and asset laundering, terrorist havens, among others. We reiterate our commitment to multilateralism, in all its legitimate expressions, from the organizations of neighboring countries to the most global, but believe that multilateralism has to demonstrate effectiveness in defeating international crime.

(Continued)

- Colombia has recognized the internal problem of narco-terrorism, has led a heroic battle that will ultimately prevail, cooperates with the international community and requests more effective cooperation. We cooperate with Mexico, Guatemala, Panama, Costa Rica, Haiti, the Dominican Republic, Peru, Afghanistan and other countries. We recognize the efforts of the United States to work jointly with us in dismantling narco-terrorism. We ask for more cooperation from more countries and from the international community.
- Our objective is recovering domestic security, never participating in the arms race for the bloody game of international war. Our tradition is one of respect for the global community.

Discussion Questions
- In what ways did President Uribe acknowledge the importance of international influence in Colombia?
- How does he envision the connection between the national government and the local population?

Source: http://www.un.org/ga/64/generaldebate/pdf/CO_en.pdf

Critics point to the scandals that have broken out with regard to security. Many members of the government and the armed forces have been found to have ties to paramilitary groups. Since 2008, the military has also been implicated in the case of so-called false positives, where civilians were killed and their bodies put in FARC uniforms as a way to increase the body count of the guerrilla war. Over 500 officers have been implicated, and the death toll is estimated to be at least 2,000. Human rights activists also point to the high number of trade unionists killed (51 were murdered in 2010, though that was down from 184 in 2002 as Uribe took office), as Colombia is one of the more dangerous countries in the region for union leaders. The Uribe government repeatedly referred to various human rights groups as potential subversives, perhaps linked to the FARC, which raises the specter of making them into targets.

Supporters of security-oriented policies point to the decreased rate of murder and kidnappings, arguing that such an entrenched problem cannot be solved overnight. Homicides dropped over time. There were 29,000 in 2002, and 16,000 in 2008, a 45 percent decrease. Kidnappings fell 73 percent from 2002 to 2005. Eventually, Mexico took over the ignominious crown of the country with most kidnappings. Supporters also argue that the country is far more secure than in the not-too-distant past when many Colombians were fearful of traveling even short distances because of the possibility of coming into contact with paramilitary and/or guerrilla forces. The government also points to the successful campaign against the FARC, which yielded important military victories and extended the state's presence more into remote areas of the country. This in turn has also prompted higher levels of foreign investment. Thus, local, national, and international are tightly intertwined.

Beginning in 2002, the government also organized the large-scale demobilization of the AUC. By the completion of the process in 2006, roughly 20,000 members—representing the vast majority—had laid down their arms. More than a dozen have been extradited to the United States to stand trial. In 2006 the government created the High Council for the Social and Economic Reintegration of Disarmed People and Groups to organize the disarming process, under the auspices of the Administrative Department of the Presidency. There have been a number of obstacles, the most pressing of which was disillusionment on the part of the participants, who felt the government did an inadequate job providing jobs and they were not given sufficient protection from still armed combatants who targeted them for betrayal.[13] There remains a strong incentive to return to a life of violence, which is much more lucrative.

Questions related to reparations, information about murders, and justice for crimes committed remain also unanswered, and new groups have appeared (such as the so-called Black Eagles) that carry out the same types of violent activities of the AUC. Similarly, the ELN has demobilized considerably, though it has resisted a formal agreement with the government, and currently has only around 1,000 members. It has become weakened to the point that its members have been much more likely to defect than the FARC.

The cost of these successes has been considerable. According to the Colombian Defense Ministry, between 2002 and 2010 there were a total of 20,915 combat deaths.[14] This includes individuals identified as "subversives," members of illegal militia and criminal gangs, as well as the Colombian security forces (of which 4,571 were killed). Of course, a body count does not take into consideration the millions of people whose lives were permanently affected one way or another as a result of the guerrillas, paramilitaries, drug traffickers, and government security forces. Local disruption is a continuing and serious problem.

Understanding the dynamics of human rights in Colombia is therefore complicated. The issue of human rights has spilled over into international relations, especially with regard to passing a free trade agreement with the United States. Opponents in the United States, particularly in the Democratic Party, argued that a free trade agreement should not be ratified until the Colombian demonstrated more progress with improving its human rights record. Quantifying that can be a slippery and imperfect process.

The growth of organizations dedicated to human rights is a relatively recent phenomenon in Colombia. In the 1980s, the political left learned from the Southern Cone countries how to incorporate human rights ideals into their discourse and to create formal groups to counteract politically motivated violence. As the problem worsened, human rights became more mainstream and institutionalized. The 1990s saw the creation of the Defensoría del Pueblo, which coordinates ombudsmen to inform citizens of their rights, as well as a number of different human rights initiatives within government agencies and ministries, including the Ministry of Defense. President Uribe created the Vice President's Human Rights Program, though it has little political influence. Nonetheless, the combination of nongovernmental organizations (NGOs) and government agencies has raised the profile of human rights to an unprecedented degree.

Regardless, throughout his two terms President Uribe maintained some of the highest approval ratings of any Latin American president, even topping 80 percent in 2008. His predecessors, Pastrana and Samper, had average ratings of 20 and 33 percent, respectively. Even the various scandals did not puncture that popularity to a large degree, and he left office as one of the most popular presidents in Colombian history.

As his second term progressed, supporters of President Uribe floated the possibility of amending the constitution once more to allow for a third term. Uribe himself remained largely close-lipped about the matter, though periodically he made comments indicating he would welcome the development. After extensive discussions, Colombia's Constitutional Court ruled in 2010 that a draft referendum on the issue was unconstitutional, and therefore could not be put to a vote, which was a sign of horizontal accountability. Uribe then made it clear that his preferred candidate was Defense Minister Juan Manuel Santos, who won a plurality in the first round of the 2010 presidential election against Green Party candidate Antanas Mockus, a dark horse former mayor of Bogotá who rose rapidly in the polls. Santos then won convincingly in the second round. A key question for a Santos presidency was how much he would maintain Uribe's policies, particularly with regard to security. He sent mixed signals, on the one hand emphasizing continuity as a way to garner votes, but on the other asserting that he was not simply a carbon copy. That issue became most evident when, just before leaving office, Uribe accused the Venezuelan government of harboring the FARC. Hugo Chávez responded that he would not hold a dialogue with Colombia until Santos had assumed power. One in office, the two met and Santos announced—how seriously or not is open to question—that Chávez was his new best friend. He also worked to reestablish diplomatic ties with Ecuador, which had not appreciated being bombed, and the two countries once again exchanged ambassadors.

Although he had been central to the security-oriented strategies of the Uribe government and was often portrayed as essentially carrying on Uribe's legacy, Santos' overall tone tended to be more moderate than his predecessor. He has been more open to returning peasant land stolen by paramilitary groups, for example. Their differences led to Uribe criticizing Santos' decisions publicly, even through Twitter. Nonetheless, he maintained an aggressive counterinsurgency strategy intended to keep the FARC on the run and kill its leadership, while starting negotiations in Cuba without a ceasefire.

National Meet Local: Indigenous, Racial, and Gender Issues

Insecurity in Colombia has greatly affected underrepresented groups. Yet especially when compared to other countries in the region, Colombia has a relatively positive record in addressing the needs of its indigenous population, which is approximately 3.4 percent of the total population and is composed of 85 different groups. Such efforts have aimed at increasing local autonomy. Between 1960 and 1990, the state established more than 200 local reserves, or *resguardos*, a concept that dated back to colonial times, and in 1989 created special rights for Indians living in the Amazonian area.[15] About two-thirds of the indigenous population lives on such a reserve. Within the *resguardos*, native languages are official, whereas outside them Spanish is the official language. There has been encroachment on these lands, however, as well as controversy over whether the central government should be allowed to spray herbicides there as part of its anticoca efforts.

Activism increased after 1991, including a blockade of the Pan-American Highway in 1999 that involved 12,000 people and lasted eleven days, followed by others of even greater scope. Not only were these mobilizations intended to advance indigenous rights but also to remind the government that the indigenous deserved the same type of attention that the FARC was receiving simply because it was so violent. That stance became more difficult when the peace talks failed and the government pursued a more military-oriented policy toward the guerrillas. So, for example, when large protests were held in 2006 in southwestern Colombia, they were met with helicopters and tear gas.

Indigenous activists expressed fear that they were being targeted as part of the government's focus on destroying subversion in the country, as activists sometimes used land seizures as a protest strategy. In fact, the government openly accused activists of being tied to the FARC, and people of indigenous descent account for 7 percent of the displaced in Colombia, a disproportionate share. This led in 2004 to increased attention to broadening the scope of protests to connect better to both national and international actors. One result has been the "minga," a word that means *collective work* in Quechua. In 2008, 40,000 people came together for six weeks of protests against the Uribe's government economic and security policies. They marched from southwest Colombia to Bogotá, and even had a debate with government ministers.

With regard to race, Colombia has the second largest black population in Latin America, after Brazil, though political leaders have been overwhelmingly white. Estimates range from 15 to 35 percent of the entire population of 44 million, with the highest concentration living on the Pacific Coast.[16] Afro-Colombian student groups began organizing in the 1970s and became particularly active in the debate over drafting the new constitution which, although mentioning race only briefly, emphasizes equality. Further, groups like the Process of Black Communities (PCN) emerged at the local level and have been successful in interpreting existing laws related to race in ways that benefit poor black communities.

This activism has been especially relevant for the implementation of Law 70, which provides collective ownership of land for Afro-Colombians on the Pacific Coast. The passage of Law 70 focused national attention on the economic plight of the rural black population, while also sparking the creation of new local NGOs aimed at addressing the problems faced by Afro-Colombians while also preserving their culture. Although complaints have surfaced about how few land titles have actually been granted, the existence of the law provides a basis for further activism and increased vertical accountability. At the same time, political violence in rural areas has hit black populations hard. Roughly one-third of displaced people in Colombia are black. That entails an increase of urban poor, because internal refugees avoid the conflict by making their way to cities.

A certain growth of vertical accountability is also apparent with regard to gender. Colombian women first began organizing politically in the 1930s, primarily to achieve suffrage, which took twenty years to pass. The 1991 constitution guarantees equality before the law, but in practice discrimination is still a problem. The government has made efforts to provide economic opportunities for women, such as microcredit. The Women's World Bank in Colombia has been successful in this regard, funding tens of thousands of women. Women have been entering the workforce in greater numbers, and the gender wage gap slowly narrowed from the 1990s onward. It should be noted that the growing workforce was not always positive, as at times it reflected greater internal migration prompted either by local violence or by a lack of opportunities in rural towns.

Women face unique problems in Colombia because rape and other types of abuse (such as forced abortions) have become common for both guerrillas and right-wing paramilitaries. More women (and, of course, children) than men make up the population of the displaced, and Colombia's human rights ombudsman estimated that 40 percent are subject to sexual violence. On the flip side of the conflict, women attempting to flee the violence must face serious risks as they migrate internally to find refuge. The United Nations High Commissioner for Human Rights has documented that women are often not taken seriously and find it difficult to convince officials to investigate, much less prosecute, human rights abuses. Meanwhile, women are also involved, on the other side, in the rebel movements themselves. They play prominent roles within the FARC (see Box 9.1).

BOX 9.1

Local Connections Women in the FARC

International: As in other revolutionary forces in Latin America (such as the Cuban revolution or the FMLN in El Salvador), women play an important role in the Revolutionary Armed Forces of Colombia (FARC). Marxist guerrilla groups have often welcomed women, ostensibly offering them the opportunity to fight not only the capitalist system but also gender discrimination at both the local and national levels. At least on the surface, they provide something that women cannot obtain otherwise—money, some type of education, belonging,

and respect.[17] Many women find attractive the idea that they can challenge existing social conventions through membership in the FARC.

National: Formally, the FARC enforces gender equality as part of its ongoing struggle to "free" the Colombian people. Women play the same roles as men, including combat, and can move up the leadership ranks, though the Secretariat is entirely male. Women make up approximately 30 percent of the FARC, which is a larger proportion than most conventional armies. They are expected to perform the same tasks as men, which are often very arduous given their life as an illegal fighting force in the jungle.

Local: Thus, the FARC works at the local level to find new recruits for its national war, which in turn has important international consequences. Conditions for the poor in small towns and rural areas create a ripe environment, as it is not difficult to find a receptive audience for an antigovernment message.

From a practical standpoint, however, there is considerable discrimination. Women who become pregnant, for example, are sometimes forced to have abortions in very primitive conditions

(or they desert, an option that has become increasingly popular in recent years for both men and women as the Colombian government has had more successful military campaigns). There is also harassment and rape. The FARC recruits young girls, in their early teens, and despite the official declarations of equality, discrimination is common.

Discussion Questions
- Why would it be important for the FARC to present an image of gender equality?
- Can you think of reasons why women at the local level might be attracted by the FARC's gendered message?

Conclusion and Comparative Perspective

Like so many of his predecessors, Juan Manuel Santos came to office promising his fellow citizens and the international community to reduce the level of political violence in a country that has suffered from it for much of its history. That promise, though, did come from someone who had coordinated the bombing of a neighboring country. It is notable that, as one political scientist has put it, Colombians continue to "vote amid violence." [18] Despite all the international pressures, local intimidation (especially in rural areas), urban violence, paramilitary scandals, and even questions about reelection at the national level, electoral democracy perseveres. Violence remains a major problem, and tens of thousands are displaced, yet both horizontal and vertical accountability persist and the armed forces remain in the barracks, while Colombians are less afraid than in the past. Nonetheless, the state still does not extend effective rule of law or even infrastructure in all parts of the country. The national and local levels are often not well-connected, which creates a power vacuum filled by guerrillas and paramilitaries.

Economically, Colombia still faces the age-old problem of extending opportunity to rural areas where collaboration with drug traffickers and/or the FARC remains a profitable alternative. Rural land remains both badly underutilized and highly concentrated in the hands of a relatively small elite. Inflation has remained low, and before economic contraction in 2008, GDP growth was very favorable. Unfortunately, many of the benefits of macroeconomic stability have not reached a large proportion of the population. Primarily because of the security threat, unlike other Latin American cases, Colombians have not voted for a candidate of the left.

Colombia is an unusual case where a tremendous amount of political violence occurs in the context of electoral democracy. In that sense it is unlike Central America in the 1980s or Peru in the 1990s, but more like Mexico after 2006. The particular mix of drug trafficking and guerrilla warfare yields an especially vicious type of internal conflict. Yet it also shares characteristics with

TABLE 9.1 Colombian Economic Indicators, 1991–2011

Year	GDP Growth	Inflation	Unemployment	Poverty Rate	Human Development Index
1991	1.6	26.8	10.2	50.5	0.836
1992	3.9	25.1	10.2	—	0.813
1993	4.5	22.6	8.6	—	0.840
1994	6.3	22.6	8.9	47.3	0.848
1995	5.4	19.5	8.8	—	0.758
1996	2.1	21.6	11.2	—	—
1997	3.0	17.9	12.4	44.9	0.768
1998	0.6	16.7	15.3	—	0.764
1999	−4.2	9.2	19.4	48.7	—
2000	2.9	8.8	17.3	—	—
2001	2.2	7.6	18.2	—	0.779
2002	2.5	7.0	17.6	51.5	0.773
2003	4.6	6.5	16.6	—	—
2004	4.7	5.5	15.3	51.1	—
2005	5.7	4.9	13.9	46.8	0.791
2006	6.8	4.5	12.9	46.8	—
2007	7.7	5.7	11.4	—	0.807
2008	3.0	7.7	11.5	—	—
2009	0.8	2.0	13.0	45.7	—
2010	4.0	2.6	12.4	—	0.714
2011	5.9	3.4	11.5	—	0.717

Sources: Unemployment: GDP and Inflation: Preliminary Overview of the Economies of Latin America and the Caribbean, 1994–2012.
Poverty rate: Social Panorama of Latin America. Economic Commission for Latin America, 1990–2012.
Human development index: United Nations, Human Development Report, 1990–2013.

Venezuela because both countries suffered a period of intense violence in the middle of the twentieth century, followed by a stable pacted transition that excluded a large proportion of the population. Unlike other countries where party systems fell apart, populism did not emerge in Colombia. Politicians have fairly smoothly shifted into new parties and coalitions, and the military has stayed out of politics.

From an economic perspective, Colombia is very similar to other countries that rely heavily on the export of commodities. It does have oil, which provides it more of cushion at a time when oil prices are high, and successive governments have endeavored to diversify the primary products being exported. Similar to Mexico, it has a strong economic relationship with the United States and for years actively lobbied for completing of a free trade agreement. Unlike many other South American countries, in recent years its international orientation has been much more toward the United States than to its neighbors.

Key Terms

- Juan Manuel Santos
- La Violencia
- Revolutionary Armed Forces of Colombia
- Paramilitary
- Alvaro Uribe
- Plan Colombia

Discussion Questions

- In what ways has Colombian consociationalism after 1957 contributed to or hindered the long-term development of democracy?
- Colombia has suffered tremendous violence, yet remains a polyarchy. How has it avoided dictatorships?
- Discuss the evolution of counterinsurgency strategies in Colombia. What has seemed to be most effective against guerrillas and why?
- How well have Colombia's efforts to promote racial equality succeeded in achieving their goals? Have they been different from those employed in other countries?
- What has driven economic growth in Colombia? In what ways have governments succeeded in diversifying its economy?

Further Sources

Books

Palacios, Marco. *Between Legitimacy and Violence: A History of Colombia, 1875–2002* (Durham: Duke University Press, 2006). An excellent English translation of a detailed but easy to read history of Colombia. Of particular interest is Palacios' discussion of the breakdown of the National Front and the implications of the simultaneous rise in violence.

Russell, Crandall. *Driven by Drugs: U.S. Polict Toward Colombia*, 2nd edition (Boulder: Lynne Rienner Publishers, 2008). Given the strong influence of U.S. policy, this book provides a good analysis of how the emphasis on narcotics has affected Colombian politics. In particular, it offers a good framework for understanding the dynamics of Plan Colombia.

Tate, Winifred. *Counting the Dead: The Culture and Politics of Human Rights Activism in Colombia* (Berkeley: University of California Press, 2007). Rooted in an anthropological analysis, the book examines the development of human rights activism in Colombia. It also includes the perspectives of the armed forces and international NGOs.

Taylor, Steven L. *Voting Amid Violence: Electoral Democracy in Colombia* (Boston: Northeastern University Press, 2009). This book provides a very clear overview of Colombian politics, focusing in particular on the formal institutional elements of democracy. Taylor argues that Colombia is an electoral democracy seeking to become a liberal one.

Welna, Christopher and Gustavo Gallón (eds.). *Peace, Democracy, and Human Rights in Colombia* (Notre Dame, IN: University of Notre Dame Press, 2007). This edited volume offers a comprehensive look at Colombian politics, broken into sections on peace, democracy, and human rights. Chapters range from the peace process to political reform.

Web Sites

The Central Bank of Colombia (http://www.banrep.gov.co/en). The Central Bank maintains a useful Web site in English, including many different statistics, reports, speeches, and press releases. Particular attention is paid to prices, inflation, and interest rates.

Colombia Reports (http://colombiareports.com/). A useful English-language news organization based in Medillín, Colombia. It has articles on a broad range of topics (including culture, travel, and sports), but it focuses particularly on political news.

Washington Office on Latin America (http://www.wola.org/country/colombia). This is a nonprofit with extensive analysis and commentary on Colombian politics, with a focus on human rights.

Endnotes

1. Hartlyn, Jonathan. "Colombia: The Politics of Violence and Accommodation." In Larry Diamond, Juan J. Linz, and Seymour Martin Lipset (eds.), *Democracy in Developing Countries: Volume 4, Latin America* (Boulder: Lynne Rienner Publishers, 1989), 297.
2. Robertson, William Spence. *History of the Latin-American Nations* (New York: D. Appleton and Company, 1922), 383.
3. Hartlyn 1989, 311.
4. Palacios, Marco. *Between Legitimacy and Violence: A History of Colombia, 1875–2002* (Durham: Duke University Press, 2006), 199.
5. Kline, Harvey F. *State Building and Conflict Resolution in Colombia: 1986–1994.* (Tuscaloosa: The University of Alabama Press, 1999), 186.
6. Crandall, Russell. *Driven By Drugs: U.S. Policy Toward Colombia*, 2nd edition (Boulder: Lynne Rienner Publishers, 2008).
7. Kline, Harvey. *Chronicle of a Failure Foretold: The Peace Process of Colombian President Andrés Pastrana* (Tuscaloosa: University of Alabama Press, 2007).
8. Quoted in Hristov, Jasmin. *Blood & Capital: The Paramilitarization of Colombia* (Athens, OH: Ohio University Press, 2009), 72.
9. Archer, Ronald and Matthew Soberg Shugart. "The Unrealized Potential of Presidential Dominance in Colombia." In Scott Mainwaring and Matthew Soberg Shugart (eds.), *Presidentialism and Democracy in Latin America* (New York: Cambridge University Press, 1997), 126.

10. Cepeda Ulloa, Fernando. "Colombia: The Governability Crisis." In Jorge I. Domínguez and Michael Shifter (eds.), *Constructing Democratic Governance in Latin America*, 2nd edition (Baltimore: The Johns Hopkins University Press, 2003), 193–219.
11. Avellaneda, Claudia N. "Mayoral Quality and Local Public Finance." *Public Administration Review* 69, 3 (2009): 469–486.
12. Avilés, William. "Despite Insurgency: Reducing Military Prerogatives in Colombia and Peru." *Latin American Politics and Society* 51, 1 (2009): 57–85.
13. Denissen, Marieke. "Reintegrating Ex-Combatants into Civilian Life: The Case of the Paramilitaries in Colombia." *Peace and Change* 35, 2 (2010): 328–352.
14. http://www.mindefensa.gov.co/descargas/Sobre_el_Ministerio/Planeacion/ResultadosOperacionales/Resultados%20Operacionales%20Ene%20-%20Mar%20 2010.pdf
15. Brysk, Alison. *From Tribal Village to Global Village: Indian Rights and International Relations in Latin America* (Stanford: Stanford University Press, 2000), 267.
16. Dixon, Kwame. "Transnational Black Social Movements in Latin America: Afro-Colombians and the Struggle for Human Rights." In Richard Stahler-Sholk, Harry E. Vanden, and Glen David Kuecker (eds.), *Latin American Social Movements in the Twenty-First Century: Resistance, Power, and Democracy* (Lanham: Rowman and Littlefield Publishers, Inc., 2008), 181–195.
17. Taylor, Steven L. *Voting Amid Violence: Electoral Democracy in Colombia* (Boston: Northeastern University Press, 2009).
18. Gonzalez-Perez, Margaret. *Women and Terrorism: Female Activity in Domestic and International Terror Groups* (New York: Routledge, 2008), 41.

Venezuela

TIMELINE

1821	Independence from Spain
1908–1935	Dictatorship of Juan Vicente Gómez
1914	First oil well tapped
1945–1948	Democratic government of Rómulo Betancourt increases role of the state
1948–1958	Dictatorship of Marcos Pérez Jiménez
1958	Pact of Punto Fijo reached
1977	Nationalization of oil companies
1989	"Caracazo" riots
1992	Two failed coup attempts
1998	Hugo Chávez elected
2002	Coup briefly removes Chávez from power
2004	Recall referendum against Chávez defeated
2006	Chávez reelected
2007	Constitutional referendum defeated
2009	Indefinite reelection approved
2013	Hugo Chávez died

With exclamations, impromptu singing, finger wagging, and other theatrics, President **Hugo Chávez** conducted his television show, *Aló Presidente* (Hello President) every Sunday. Following a populist model, he connected to Venezuelans by allowing them to make their local concerns heard by the highest national officials. With his cabinet sitting around him, he took phone calls and made instructions to solve problems that callers describe, from housing problems to the effects of natural disasters. Without political parties or any other intermediary, the president took care of the issue personally in an almost textbook definition of clientelism. That led to a hard core of supporters, which has helped carry him in elections and cheer his policies of "twenty-first century socialism." After his death from cancer in 2013, his supporters pledged to keep his model alive.

Venezuela's political transformation in recent years has been nothing short of stunning. The country had long been described as the very model of stability and democracy because for decades after the late 1950s, it was free of military intervention or dictatorship. Elections were held regularly and Venezuelans enjoyed more freedom than many of their Latin American counterparts, particularly during the Cold War. Prosperity also seemed more evident, the result of tremendous oil reserves. In so many ways it appeared "modern" in economic

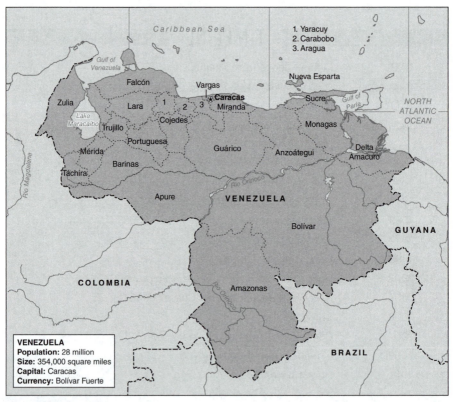

Map of Venezuela

and political terms. Under the veneer of stability, however, was a strong current of disaffection and discontent, which manifested itself in the rise of Hugo Chávez, an army Lieutenant Colonel who led an unsuccessful coup attempt in 1992 and then was elected president in 1998. As president, he embarked on reforms that reshaped the country's economy and political institutions, and in the process became a symbol of hope, resistance, and democracy to his followers and the embodiment of personalism and caudillismo to his opponents.

In terms of development, Venezuela has immense oil reserves, but it has struggled to translate oil revenue into sustainable development. Periods of economic boom, fuelled (no pun intended) by high oil prices have been bracketed by collapses, in large part because during the good times, there was not enough growth in the non-oil sectors of the economy. Juan Pablo Pérez Alfonzo, a prominent Venezuelan who was instrumental in creating the Organization of Petroleum Exporting Countries (OPEC), once famously referred to oil as the "devil's excrement" in the 1970s because the economy relies so heavily on it even while it generates corruption and clientelism. The phrase "**Dutch disease**" also captures a key problem with oil, as it refers to how a currency gets stronger when a country exports a primary product, which then means manufacturing exports are too expensive in foreign markets. In the Venezuelan case, manufacturing has been shrinking while reliance on oil has become the centerpiece of the economy.

Historical Roots of Political and Economic Development

Hugo Chávez was famous for invoking Simón Bolívar, the hero of Latin American independence. In 1821, Bolívar proclaimed independence for Gran Colombia, which included not only present-day Venezuela but also Colombia (including present-day Panama) and Ecuador, and roughly coincided with the colonial viceroyalty of New Granada. Bolívar's enduring popularity can be ascribed in large part to his professed desire to help the poor and enslaved, and also to his dream of a unified Latin America that could stand strong against the United States, whose governments he did not trust. Bolívar admired U.S. political institutions but felt correctly—that U.S. policy would center on creating its own sphere of influence.

With separation from Gran Colombia in 1830, Venezuela's borders began to take shape. By the 1830s, under the leadership of General José Antonio Páez, Venezuela began exporting coffee, and until the 1850s the country experienced its only period of relative peace until the twentieth century. When the price of coffee fell, both political and economic stability evaporated. As with much of Latin America during the eighteenth century, dependency theory has considerable explanatory power. Venezuelan economic elites established coffee plantations with foreign credit, exported the coffee, and then imported finished goods from the United States and Europe. As a result, the economy became entirely dependent on the indefinite continuation of high prices, which of course was unsustainable.

Dependency theory, however, tells us less about politics. Although the economy depended heavily on the more developed world, politics in Venezuela in the nineteenth century was a local and national affair, with much less foreign involvement than other Latin American countries. In large part, this was due to the relative lack of profitable industry. In the pre-petroleum era, Venezuela had relatively little to offer to investors.

The Federal War (1858–1863) stemmed from discontent among Liberals regarding Conservative domination of the government and the patronage that went with prominent government positions. It took the form of a fight for provincial autonomy, and Liberals won after five years of devastating warfare that killed upward of 100,000 Venezuelans.

Thereafter caudillo politics would characterize the country, with military strongmen such as Antonio Guzmán Blanco, who dominated the country between 1870 and 1888. In fact, no civilian president would stay in power more than a short time until Rómulo Betancourt was elected in 1945 (and even he was overthrown after three years). In practice, the ideal of regional autonomy was transformed into corrupt local leaders who owed personal allegiance to Guzmán but whose interests in enrichment precluded any coherent national plan for development.

One other caudillo in particular, Ezequiel Zamora, would later capture the attention of Hugo Chávez as an example of a leader who rallied the peasants and challenged the national oligarchy. Chávez's great-great grandfather fought alongside Zamora, who eventually was killed by his own troops in 1860, as they were fearful of his populist pronouncements.[1] Chávez viewed himself as the continuation of a line of Venezuelan patriots, starting with Bolívar and continuing with Zamora.

Juan Vicente Gómez ruled Venezuela (at times with puppet presidents) from 1908 until his death in 1935. He had been former dictator Cipriano Castro's choice to lead the military, but eventually overthrew him. Gómez brought some of the appearances of modernity to Venezuela, particularly to Caracas, with infrastructure (such as highways), a professionalized military, and a focus on reducing debt. Only a few years earlier, in 1902, Great Britain, Germany, and Italy bombarded the country until the government repaid debt, so Gómez's rule—despite being marked by corruption and dictatorship—was a watershed for the country's economic development. However, only after 1935 would Venezuela slowly begin to democratize.

During Gómez's reign, Venezuela embarked on the state-building project that had so eluded it in the nineteenth century, as the central government established more control and local caudillos were brought to heel. He accomplished this in part by ruthlessly crushing political opposition, and outlawing labor unions and political parties. He also continued Cipriano Castro's initial efforts to professionalize the military, whereas before each caudillo had his own regional force. Nonetheless, centralization may well have contributed to the stability (and eventually democracy) that Venezuela experienced after the discovery of oil, an experience not shared by Mexico.[2]

During the Gómez regime, author Rómulo Gallegos (who would serve briefly as president in 1948) published *Doña Bárbara* (Lady Barbara), a critique of the Gómez era that became the most celebrated Venezuelan novel of all time. It also had the memorable character William Danger, an American who had come to Venezuela:

> The country pleased him because it was as savage as his own soul, a good land to conquer, inhabited by people he considered inferior because they did not have light hair and blue eyes.[3]

That image would later be borrowed by President Chávez, who referred to President George W. Bush as "Mr. Danger."

The Politics of International Influence: Venezuela and Oil

For the most part, until World War I Venezuela received relatively little attention from the more developed world, both in scholarly and political terms. With the advent of the automobile, oil companies began exploring in Venezuela, and in 1914 the first commercially viable wells were struck; a much larger well was found in 1921. Juan Vicente Gómez immediately seized the opportunity for profits, both for the nation and for himself, through selling concessions to oil companies. In terms of economic development, oil has consistently represented a dilemma because it entails dependence.

Very quickly, oil overcame coffee as the main source of export earnings. In 1921, coffee earned almost nine times oil, whereas in 1936 earnings from oil were 21 times those of coffee.[4] The depression of the 1930s decimated the coffee industry and ensured that petroleum would be the dominant export indefinitely.

The National Politics of Oil

In the post-Gómez era, Rómulo Betancourt became a key player in the construction of a Venezuelan polyarchy. In 1928, along with many other students (the so-called Generation of 1928, which produced several prominent political leaders) he was sent into exile for leading protests. He dabbled in Communism, but on his return to Venezuela he formed the Democratic Action Party ("Acción Democrática," or AD) in 1941. The party's clearly left-leaning tendencies included criticizing the foreign control of oil and advocating for economic reform that would benefit the masses. Despite its democratic rhetoric, Betancourt was first put in power in 1945 by a short and very violent coup d'etat led by junior officers disillusioned with the political fragmentation of the times.

During Betancourt's first term, the Venezuelan state increased taxes on oil companies, following AD's nationalist electoral promises. He would write in his memoirs that, "The villain of this piece is that great god of the mechanical age, petroleum."[5] This sentiment was no doubt inspired in part by the fact that foreign oil companies reacted strongly to the AD regime, and they joined other business elites fearful of radical change in opposing the government.

Major Marcos Pérez Jiménez (who had helped bring Betancourt to power) was at the epicenter of military discontent, which rapidly escalated. In 1948 Betancourt was overthrown, and the coup was framed in terms of protecting the country from communism. Under the military regime, oil production rose, and Pérez Jiménez, who became unelected president in 1952, viewed himself as the modernizer of the Venezuelan economy, and in fact expanded the country's infrastructure. Economic growth, however, was highly unequal and generated resentment. Further, it was largely dependent on injections of oil revenues into the economy. Over the 1950s, his government became more unpopular and his repressive tactics, not to mention bribery and extortion, increased as a result.

In 1954, President Dwight Eisenhower bestowed the Legion of Merit on Pérez Jiménez, thus infuriating many Venezuelans chafing under the yoke of the dictatorship, but economic expansion and scattered organized opposition ensured that he would remain in power several more years. In 1957, a coup launched by dissident military officers failed, but demonstrated that support for the regime was crumbling. By early 1958, popular opposition (even among some elites) led to mass protests and riots, and the general fled the country (first to the United States, but he was later extradited, prosecuted for embezzlement, jailed in Venezuela, then later exiled to Spain).

▮ VENEZUELAN POLITICAL INSTITUTIONS ▮

Last constitution: 1999

Federal system with twenty-three states

Executive: Presidential, six-year term, indefinite reelection

Legislative: Unicameral National Assembly (167 members); 60 percent single-member district, first-past-the-post voting; 40 percent closed-list proportional representation

Judicial: Supreme Judicial Tribunal with a wide range of powers including reviewing constitutionality of laws

Contemporary Politics in Venezuela

Free elections were held later in 1958, and Betancourt won once again. The major parties, AD, the Democratic Republican Union (URD), and the Social Christian Party (COPEI), agreed to share power in what became known as the "Pact of Punto Fijo," named after the Caracas house of Rafael Caldera, head of COPEI (and a future president). Caldera had formed COPEI in 1946 in the aftermath of the 1945 coup, and it had grown to be the second dominant political party in the country. The pact assured agreement between the parties for any reforms and effectively blocked any other, more radical groups from entering the political system to any significant degree. The pact assured neutrality from the United States, which viewed it as a bulwark against communism, and after a shaky start, the military was similarly assuaged by the agreement's moderation and commitment to military autonomy.

This became the basis for a very stable political system, which weathered the violent political storms that battered most other South American countries during the Cold War (with the notable exception of Colombia). Unlike so many of its regional counterparts, a presidential election was held every five years. However, the high level of domination was ultimately counterproductive, as it created what has been called a *partyarchy*, a system in which parties have absolute control over representation.[6] For years, the democratic surface masked sometimes acute discontent with the political rules of the game.

In Congress, the elite consensus that emerged from Punto Fijo spread to executive-legislative relations. Depending on the distribution of seats, Congress could potentially either force policies down the opposition's throat (if the president's party had a majority) or create total gridlock (if the opposition had a majority). However, those situations were relatively rare, as party leaders consulted with one another before enacting major policies. At times, though, the country did suffer from a different type of problem, namely, Congress forcing policies onto the president, who had no veto power. Article 173 of the constitution gave Congress authority to pass legislation by simple majority even if the president disapproved (though the president did have the opportunity to send it back to Congress one time for reconsideration). But only the president could execute the law, so stalemate sometimes ensued when a law was passed and the president sat on it.

Oil was part of Betancourt's modernization project. He spearheaded the creation of OPEC in 1960, joining with four Arab countries in an effort to protect the price of Venezuelan oil. OPEC's purpose is to influence prices by coordinating oil output, which became more feasible as governments nationalized their oil industries. Despite problems with coordination, at times OPEC has wielded considerable power, and later Hugo Chávez would revive the institution.

From the perspective of modernization theory, Venezuela after the 1960s would seem to be a clear success story. The country was very much "westernized" in the sense of absorbing the cultural values of capitalist consumption to go along with democratic rule. The trappings of consumerism, such as beauty pageants, would at least superficially suggest a Western mentality that ultimately should lead to enduring prosperity. To be sure, Venezuela's brand of modernity was elitist, but given oil revenue the country appeared to have a highly successful economic strategy. Despite some bumps, it was on that linear path toward prosperity.

Cracks in the National Political System

Nonetheless, just as stability masked disputes over party domination, it also served to obscure divisions within both AD and COPEI. Movements within the parties based on class and/or race were blocked. The parties were often successful in bringing state resources to areas of the economy where private companies were not meeting the public's needs, but at the same time the parties were unwilling to allow the development of grassroots movements that they could not control.[7] Although most foreign observers saw a "model" democracy, the reality was quite different.

The price of oil jumped in 1973 as a result of the Middle East crisis (whereby Arab countries in OPEC sought to punish countries that supported Israel in the Yom Kippur War that year). This provided Venezuelan presidents with a wide range of options to increase social spending. But it also highlights a problem that Venezuela has yet to overcome, regardless of who is in power. Without adequate investment in economic sectors beyond petroleum, the economy is dependent in large measure on the international price of oil, over which, of course, the government has no control.

Riding high on nationalist sentiment and oil revenue, Carlos Andrés Pérez nationalized the oil industry. Pérez entered politics at a very young age (even acting as secretary to President Betancourt) and was a founder of the Democratic Action party. He was therefore a symbol of the entire structure of Venezuelan politics. His nationalization project was conducted in a unique manner. The government created a new company, Petroleum of Venezuela (known by its Spanish acronym, PDVSA), that would coordinate all activities related to petroleum, but it also created three separate holding companies that were controlled by the government while operating independently (thus, Citgo, which has gas stations all over the United States and elsewhere, is a wholly owned subsidiary of PDVSA). This would, its planners hoped, maintain the spirit of capitalist competition within a state-controlled context. The law went into effect in 1976. He nationalized other industries as well, such as steel, and embarked on a number of infrastructure projects.

Yet by the 1980s, what seemed the Latin American model for democracy finally showed clear signs of strain. Like other Latin American countries, Venezuela had taken on large amounts of debt and, like Mexico, was hit hard by declining oil prices. As a result, the government of Luis Herrera imposed market-oriented reforms in 1983. As the economy sputtered in the 1980s, the elitist nature of the pact proved a major part of its undoing.

The Caracazo and the Political Aftermath

The 1961 Venezuelan constitution allowed for reelection after ten years of being out of power. As one scholar has put it, "former leaders do not disappear, but grow weak and then reappear."[8] Carlos Andrés Pérez was thus eligible for reelection in 1988. He won and took office in 1989. Almost immediately he announced that only draconian measures could save the economy because of severe fiscal deficits, and thus did an entire about-face of economic policy. The reform package included devaluation and spending cuts, yet the most immediate and controversial measure was the lifting of most price controls, which the president argued were being held at artificial and unsustainable lows. The price of food, public transportation, and utilities skyrocketed. Caracas, where approximately 70 percent of the population was considered poor, with many living precariously on hills surrounding the city, exploded in February 1989.

What became known as "Caracazo" (the "blow to Caracas") consisted of riots that lasted for three days and left at least 300 people dead, with some estimates even higher. It began as a protest against a sharp increase in public transportation fares, and by later in the day engulfed the entire capital. Using the emergency powers found in most Latin American constitutions, Andrés Pérez called a state of emergency and the armed forces were then responsible for most of the deaths that ensued, a situation that incensed many junior officers who identified with the protestors. In the aftermath, Andrés Pérez created a "Plan to Confront Poverty," the purpose of which was to provide subsidies to the poor as a way to alleviate the immediate effects of neoliberal reforms. This was part of an overall neoliberal package that he called the *Great Turnaround* (*el gran viraje*) that was supposed to put Venezuela back on its economic feet.

Because the political link between AD and COPEI and the urban poor was clientelist, and therefore based on reciprocity (the granting of state resources in exchange for political support), the reforms in the 1980s broke the party-constituent link. Thereafter party loyalty dissolved quickly. The fact that Pérez ignored his own party greatly exacerbated the crisis. In Argentina around the same time, President Menem shifted his strategy from "party excluding" to "party accommodating," meaning that he responded to his own party's concerns about neoliberal reforms.[9] That kept the political system more stable.

As a consequence, the rest of his term was characterized by political disintegration. In 1992, dissident members of the army launched two unsuccessful coup attempts. The first (from which the president barely escaped) was led by army Lieutenant Colonel Hugo Chávez Frías, who had been organizing like-minded officers disgusted with the corruption of the Puntofijista era but also with what they saw as an assault on the poor. Even though he surrendered and was later imprisoned, Chávez famously told a national television audience that his movement was defeated only "for now," which became the mantra for his supporters. Chávez had no political experience of any kind, but he was connected in a very powerful way with millions of disaffected Venezuelans who responded viscerally to his call for radical political and economic change. His charisma was unmistakable.

The era of Carlos Andrés Pérez then came to an abrupt end in 1993 when he was impeached for corruption, removed from office, and imprisoned for misappropriation of funds. After his release in 1998, he went in exile to Miami, which rapidly became the Mecca of disaffected Venezuelans. The mighty had fallen in a fairly short amount of time, and before long Venezuelan politics would center not on parties or pacts but on Hugo Chávez himself.

Prior to the Caracazo, the foundations of Venezuelan democracy were oil wealth, very strong parties, and an apolitical military. Unlike Mexico, where the PRI alone dominated for decades, in Venezuela the two major parties ensured a much better approximation of representative democracy. Their influence went very deep into society. Beginning in the 1960s, virtually all social organizations were tied to parties, and their elections went along party lines. This went from bar associations all the way down to dentists, architects, and perhaps even the beauty contests.[10] Given their reach, the party unraveling that took place was even more traumatic.

The Failure of Presidentialism

Despite macroeconomic stability in the wake of the Caracazo, the political underpinnings of the Pact of Punto Fijo were buckling, and Venezuelan presidentialism contributed to that process. Venezuela's "partyarchy" started at the top, and the president—along with his party—was instrumental in determining how the benefits from oil revenue would be distributed. Once those benefits dried up, the president felt compelled to resort more often to force. This was coupled with long-standing and deeply entrenched corruption, which was rarely convicted in a complicit judicial system.

By the 1998 presidential election, the party collapse in Venezuela was complete. In 1993, Rafael Caldera abandoned COPEI, running and winning the presidency through an independent "National Convergence" coalition while AD and COPEI combined won 46 percent of the vote, down from 94 percent in 1988. Political polarization ensued, because voters wanted neither major party to rule, and in their place came a wide variety of coalitional movements and regional parties. Caldera's term was therefore tumultuous because he simultaneously needed to balance popular discontent with traditional parties while also working with those parties (particularly AD) to pass legislation. In practice, this prompted Caldera to use presidential decree power extensively, and emergency powers to maintain order.

In 1998, Hugo Chávez had no formal party organization. Indeed, his rhetoric was always harshly antiparty, because he blamed the traditional political parties for the Venezuela's disastrous economic situation. Rather, his supporters coalesced within the Fifth Republic Movement (MVR) party ("*Movimiento Quinto República*," with the Roman numeral V for *fifth*) as part of the "Patriotic Pole" coalition. Neither AD nor COPEI could muster enough support even to run their own candidates. Instead, they threw their support to an independent candidate, Henrique Salas, who garnered 40 percent of the vote. Chávez won the election with 56.2 percent. He minced no words in his inaugural address: "We are being called to save Venezuela from this immense and putrid swamp in which we have been sunk during 40 years of demagoguery and corruption."[11]

The opposition to Chávez, already badly splintering after 1993, underwent bitter internal conflict, which continues to prevent it from forming a broad coalition or offering many unity candidates in major political races. The primary opposition has slowly joined as a coalition (with shifting names) but even now fights to gain political traction. This lack of political influence is partly self-inflicted, as the coalition, joined by AD, COPEI, and several other parties, boycotted the 2005 legislative elections, arguing that the National Electoral Council (CNE) might be able to decipher individual's votes through the fingerprint scanners used at polling places. The government argued that they were backing out only because they knew they would lose. No matter the reason, the parties ceded legislative power to Chávez allies.

The Fifth Republic

Chávez sought nothing less than a complete overhaul of Venezuelan political and economic institutions, what he called the *Bolivarian Revolution*, involving the birth of the "Fifth Republic." One of Chávez's first priorities was to write a new constitution. In his own words, "My idea was not to swear allegiance to that constitution but rather to kill and bury it."[12] Soon after taking office, he held a referendum to allow for the election of a commission to draft a new charter. The vast majority of that commission's members were from Chávez's

Patriotic Pole party (120 of 131). The new constitution went up for a vote on December 15, 1999, and was approved by 72 percent of voters. Until the new constitution took effect on January 31, 2000, the National Constituent Assembly voted itself the power to dissolve the legislature and Supreme Court, and for the next six weeks passed laws and used the power of appointment to pack government posts with pro-Chávez appointees.

ANALYZING DOCUMENTS

Hugo Chávez made it very clear that he did not respect the Venezuelan constitution and that one of his main priorities was to draft a new one. He argued that the new constitution better addressed the rights of the oppressed, down to the most local level, while his opponents responded that it was intended to enhance his political power.

Constitution of the Bolivarian Republic of Venezuela (1999)
Article 1
The Bolivarian Republic of Venezuela is irrevocably free and independent, and bases its moral heritage and values of freedom, equality, justice, and international peace on the doctrine of Simón Bolívar, the Liberator. Independence, liberty, sovereignty, immunity, territorial integrity and national self-determination are irrevocable rights of the Nation.

Article 6
The government of the Bolivarian Republic of Venezuela and of the political entities comprising it, is and shall always be democratic, participatory, elective, decentralized, alternative, responsible, pluralist, and with revocable mandates.

Article 112
All persons may dedicate themselves freely to the economic activity of their choice, save only for the limitations outlined in this Constitution and those established by law for reasons of human development, security, health, environmental protection or other reasons of social interest. The State shall promote private initiative, guaranteeing the creation and fair distribution of wealth, as well as the production of goods and services that meet the needs of the population, freedom of work, enterprise, commerce, industry, without prejudice to the power of the State to dictate measures to plan, rationalize and regulate the economy and promote the overall development of the country.

Article 119
The State recognizes the existence of indigenous peoples and communities, their social, political and economic organization, their cultures, ways and customs, languages and religions, as well as their habitat and original rights to the lands they ancestrally and traditionally occupy, and that are necessary to develop and guarantee their way of life. It falls to the National Executive, with the participation of the indigenous peoples, to demarcate and guarantee the right to collective ownership of their lands, which shall be inalienable, irrevocable, unseizable, and nontransferable, in accordance with this Constitution and the law.

(Continued)

Article 299

The socio-economic regime of the Bolivarian Republic of Venezuela is based on the principles of social justice, democracy, efficiency, free competition, protection of the environment, productivity and solidarity, with the goal of ensuring overall human development and a dignified and beneficial existence for the collectivity. The State, together with private initiative, will promote the harmonious development of the national economy, with the end of generating sources of employment, a high rate aggregate national value, raising the standard of living of the population and strengthening the economical sovereignty of the country, guaranteeing judicial integrity; the solid, dynamic, sustainable, permanent and equitable growth of the economy to ensure a just distribution of wealth through democratic, participatory, and consultative strategic planning.

Discussion Questions

- How does the constitution seem to view local political and economic development?
- What does the role of the national government seem to be?

Source: *Gazeta Oficial de la República Bolivariana de Venezuela*, No. 5908, February 19, 2009. (Translation by author).

The constitution is long (350 articles) and complex. According to Article 6, the government "is, and will always be, democratic, participatory, elective, decentralized, alternative, responsible, pluralist, and with revocable mandates." It details a wide range of rights, including life, speech, non-discrimination, association, due process, as well as education, health, housing, employment, and even sports recreation. Not surprisingly, given the amount of government spending required to fulfill all such rights, many remain goals rather than accomplishments (unemployment, e.g., is not zero). Supporters, however, contend that the constitution is much more inclusive and, unlike examples around the hemisphere (even the U.S. constitution, which is minimalist), it makes the government a positive force in people's lives.

More contested is the power of the executive branch. Of particular importance has been Article 236, which grants the president the right to create decrees with the force of law. This means that the president can request that the legislature delegate its authority and give the president the right to use decrees to make laws. The constitution also extended the presidential term from four to six years, and allowed two presidential terms in office.

Once the constitution was ratified, the next step was to have fresh presidential elections, held in 2000. Similar to 1998, Chávez won a solid majority (59.8 percent) while the opposition was in disarray (the main candidate, Francisco Arias, a disaffected former ally, garnered 37.5 percent). His coalition, the MVR won 44 percent of the seats in the National Assembly (91 out of 165).

In 2001, Chávez passed 49 special "enabling" laws (the concept is discussed later in the chapter), which ensured the government would have a majority stake in companies engaged in oil extraction. They also facilitated expropriation of land if the owners were not growing sufficiently on it (known as "idle land"). In general, the laws were intended to begin reversing the entire process of both decentralization and market-oriented reforms that had been taking place for a decade, but which had become highly unpopular. Their passage prompted a strong negative response from the business community.

The opposition, concentrated among the middle and upper classes, which controlled many media outlets, lashed out at Chávez, calling him a Communist and often even insulting him with racist comments because of his darker skin. The PDVSA remained under conservative opposition control (in contrast to Colombia, where the oil workers union is considerably to the left of the government ideologically) and in 2002 oil workers went on strike to protest Chávez's proposal to shift oil revenue from PDVSA to the state. Chávez responded by firing members of PDVSA's Board of Directors. That pushed a coup plot into motion, which removed Chávez from power very briefly in April 2002, blackened the reputation of many opposition leaders, and ironically solidified Chávez's popularity and hold on power (see Box 10.1). No matter what they thought about their president, a majority of Venezuelans did not support a coup d'etat.

It was obvious that the military was not yet firmly controlled by the president, so in the wake of the coup Chávez worked even more diligently to ensure that only loyal officers made their way to positions of leadership. He also created a military reserve, comprised of civilian volunteers who would ostensibly protect the country from internal and/or external threats. It took orders directly from the president, and Chávez touted it as an essential aspect of defense. His overall goal was to provide some measure of protection from another coup. Indeed, coup rumors surfaced periodically, and even a former close ally, General Raúl Baduel, began criticizing the government publicly. Meanwhile, Chávez also symbolically brought the armed forces into the revolutionary fold by compelling them to say "Fatherland, Socialism or Death" with salutes, especially before a superior officer.

In December 2002, the opposition organized a general strike, which ran into 2003 (lasting 63 days), to force Chavez either to resign or to accept a recall referendum. The strike damaged the economy, as gross domestic product was –7.8 in 2003, but Chavez was able to withstand it by forcing the resumption of oil production and by employing the military to continue distributing goods to poor areas. Given how central oil is to the economy, the opposition could not deal a crippling blow once it flowed again.

BOX 10.1

Ideology and Political Conflict: The 2002 Coup

International: On April 11, 2002, President Hugo Chávez was overthrown by a military coup and arrested, while Pedro Carmona, the president of the Venezuelan Federation of Chambers of Commerce (*"Fedecámaras"*), was named provisional president. The international influences for the coup remain a matter of debate. The administration of George W. Bush immediately recognized the Carmona government and blamed Chávez for

(Continued)

the crisis. It is also clear that the U.S. government had intelligence suggesting a coup was imminent, though there is no evidence it actively encouraged it. Nonetheless, the rebellious factions of the Venezuelan military believed they had the U.S. government's support. According to Rear Admiral Carlos Molina Tamayo, "We felt we were acting with US support. We agree that we can't allow a communist government here."[13]

Ultimately, the coup understandably left Chávez wary of further U.S. support for his overthrow. That possibility became a staple of his speeches, as he criticized the Bush administration for interfering in Venezuelan affairs.

National: Although the opposition had long wanted him ousted, the immediate cause was Chávez's efforts to purge the PDVSA of his opponents. He fired numerous top officials of the state oil agency. That prompted Fedecámaras to call for a national two-day strike in protest. A rally was held in Caracas, and the plan was to march to the PDVSA offices, but then shifted and made its way to Miraflores, the presidential palace. There it clashed with Chávez supporters, which led to twenty shooting deaths. The opposition claimed that government officials acted as snipers. Video, later proven to be manipulated, was shown on television, which seemed to show Chávez

supporters firing into crowds. Anti-Chávez sentiment swelled, and even senior military officers, such as the head of the army, publicly stated they no longer supported the president.

Carmona became the civilian leader of the coup as military rebels ordered Chávez to resign. On April 11, the military surrounded Miraflores and took Chávez into custody. Subsequent events would become legend for Chávez and his supporters. Carmona was sworn in as president, and his first actions were to issue decrees dissolving the legislature, the Supreme Court, and to fire *Chavista* public officials.

Local: Meanwhile, word began spreading that Chávez had not resigned, which made the new government unconstitutional and illegal. People therefore poured from poor neighborhoods to call for Chávez's return. Large public protests against the coup combined with loyalist military officers to force Carmona to flee the presidential palace, and eventually rescued Chávez and brought him back.

Discussion Questions
- Why might members of the military feel that it was important to have the support of the United States?
- How did the response to the coup demonstrate local support for Hugo Chávez?

Chávez subsequently sought to deepen his reforms, and in 2005 officially proclaimed his revolution to be socialist. That culminated in the draft of a new constitution, put up for a national vote in 2007. There were various centralizing revisions, such as giving the president power over the Central Bank, but the most controversial aspect was abolishing presidential term limits. Chávez lost the vote by a slim margin, and therefore had to wait for another opportunity to pursue the reforms. The ability to remain in power longer has been a persistent theme for Chávez, such that a year after losing the constitutional referendum, he requested that his supporters launch a new petition drive to eliminate term limits. Unlike the 2007 effort, there would be nothing else on the ballot. The vote took place in February 2009, and Chavez won with 54 percent of the vote.

The other part of the "Bolivarian Revolution" entails an expanded state presence in the economy. Control over oil revenue became even more critical after September 11, 2001, because of the dramatic rise of oil prices. When Chávez was elected in 1998, the average price of a barrel of oil was about $12. A decade later, in January 2008, the price hit $100. As a result of the economic crisis in the United States, in September 2008, the price plummeted, an issue to which we return later in the chapter.

Chávez envisioned "*twenty-first century socialism*," a term that has never been defined precisely, but which centered on vastly increasing the state's commitment to the poor, rejecting free-market capitalism, and nationalizing industries if they failed to contribute sufficiently to the government's economic program. Nationalization does not necessarily involve total state ownership, as in some cases (such as oil) it means majority state ownership, with minority stakes (and, of course, profits) for private companies.

The pace of state takeovers accelerated after the 2006 presidential election, which Chávez won resoundingly with 62.8 percent of the vote. His main opponent was Manuel Rosales, the governor of Zulia state and a prominent opposition leader (he had supported the Carmona government) who won only 36.9 percent. Understandably, Chávez viewed the election as a clear mandate, and accordingly initiated policies intended to deepen his political project, including nationalization.

Chávez first ordered the nationalization of selected small farms and businesses, then moved to a number of larger companies, including oil (an incremental strategy completed in 2007, with expansion to oil services in 2009), telecommunications and electricity in 2007, then the largest steel company (owned by a company in Luxembourg), as well as Swiss, Mexican, and French cement companies in 2008.

Chávez placed nationalization in the contest of using the state to advance the well-being of the people. Along the same lines, the government imposed price controls on a wide range of essential goods. It also established a state-run chain of supermarkets, called MERCAL, which are located in poor communities. Because private supermarkets continue to operate, MERCAL represents a parallel structure, albeit in parts of the country where markets tended not to operate.

Another important initiative after the 2006 presidential election was the creation of the **United Socialist Party of Venezuela** (PSUV), which would replace the MVR and include the other *Chavista* parties under one umbrella. The PSUV would also serve as a vehicle for centralization, because it coordinated the relationship between the central government and local communities.

All of these initiatives were centered on improving the economic outlook for the country's poor. There is vociferous disagreement about Chávez's successes in this endeavor. For example, Francisco Rodriguez, former Chief Economist of the National Assembly, argued that the reduction in poverty rates (from 54 percent in 2003 to 27.5 percent in the first half of 2007) is because of the drastic increase of oil prices, and not due to any structural reforms that will keep poverty down in the future.[14] Further, the Gini index was 0.44 in 2000, but 0.48 in 2005, and other indicators—such as the percentage of underweight babies—have worsened since Chávez took office. Bernardo Alvarez, the Venezuelan Ambassador to the United States, responded that Rodriguez failed to incorporate all social spending, such as that by PDVSA, and that he ignored all the advances being made, such as lives saved (over 47,000) because of expanded access to doctors for the poor, increased school attendance, and in general the massive reduction of people in poverty (down 18.4 percent between 2002 and 2006).[15]

Not under dispute is the rise of inflation, which according to the Central Bank has usually been over 20 percent. This is a natural consequence of increased cash transfers between the government and the poor, who were putting that money back into the economy and thereby pushing prices up. The rate of inflation was lower than in the troubling times of the 1990s, but still a matter of some concern for the government. One measure the government took was to replace the old currency, the "bolívar," with the "bolívar fuerte," or "strong bolívar," beginning in January 2008. It meant taking away three zeroes (so that something that cost 10,000 would now cost 10).

In 2003, the government created the National Exchange Control Administration (CADIVI), a currency control board to regulate the exchange rate. It pegged the bolívar (then later the strong bolívar) to the dollar, but the real exchange rate has been much weaker. But it also stipulated that foreign exchange could be transacted only through the Central Bank, which placed limits on how many bolívars could be exchanged for dollars. As we saw in Chapter 4, regulations on foreign exchange can create unintended consequences. In this case, because people cannot always get as many dollars as they want legally, a black market emerged to meet demand, requiring far more bolívars than the government relative to the dollar. More affluent Venezuelans can leave the country, get dollar advances on their credit cards (the amount of which is also regulated by the government) then return to Venezuela, get bolívars through the black market, and pay off their credit cards at the official rate, thus making a profit. Figure 10.1 shows how the local, national, and international levels all converge.

Nonetheless, it is important to keep in mind that Chávez and his policies were popular. According to the 2011 Latinobarómetro regional poll, Venezuelans strongly supported democracy, as at 77 percent they were the highest in the region. Chávez's approval numbers dipped at times—down to around 50 percent—but a hard core of support remained solid for years.

Here we encounter a confusing connection between theory and practice. Hugo Chávez's style of governing once again raises the issue of populism, which is part and parcel of a collapsed party system. He saw himself as an individual working against strong structural constraints. The combination of weak institutions and a strong personality are clearly negative for democracy, but Venezuelans believe their democracy is quite strong. Although he called for the creation of the PSUV, it clearly centered on him as an individual, and he alone—through speeches, his radio and then television program *Hello President*, and other means—determined the nature of the Venezuelan variant of socialism. One key is that he reached out to the average person, even attempting to solve their specific problems when they call into his show. This is a hallmark of "delegative democracy," in which, as we've discussed in particular for the Central American

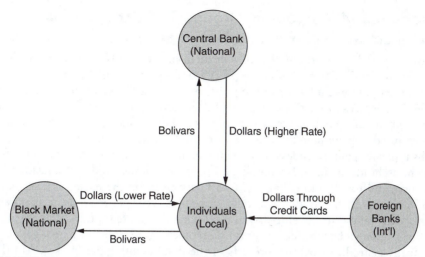

FIGURE 10.1 Currency Exchange in Venezuela

and Andean countries, citizens elect a leader who then takes it on his- or herself to define the common good and to do whatever necessary to achieve it, without much horizontal accountability.

These same qualities, which many Venezuelans view in positive terms, potentially pose long-term problems for democracy. Some of the challenges Chávez faced underscore the dilemma inherent in the combination of presidential government and a weak—almost nonexistent—party system which, ironically, had greatly helped his rise to power. The government's defeat in the 2007 constitutional referendum demonstrated the persistence of democracy in national elections even when the government doesn't get the result it wants, but in the absence of parties there is far less democracy within the government, where all major decisions were made by Chávez himself. Policy making thus acquired a very ad hoc flavor. How it will be handled after Chávez is a critical question.

For example, in 2007 Chávez used his television program to call for tanks to be mobilized and sent to the Colombian border in response to Colombia's bombing of a FARC rebel camp in Ecuador. Similarly, in 2008 Chávez expelled the director (a Chilean citizen) of the human rights group Human Rights Watch after the organization issued a report highly critical of his government. Without benefit of any legal process or judicial order (thus violating Article 44 of the constitution), he was charged with interfering with the internal affairs of Venezuela and expelled from the country.

Because *Chavistas* are by no means a homogeneous bloc, there is considerable debate between soft- and hard-liners about the direction the revolution should take, how radical reforms should be, and where state resources should be directed. However, these debates are generally informal, and therefore reach formal channels only indirectly. There is often disagreement with decisions the central government makes, and dissent is tolerated, but it does not necessarily translate into political action that influences policy. We can see some of these dynamics by examining women and the indigenous population, both of which have been natural allies.

Women and Indigenous Groups: The Struggle for Activism at the Local and National Levels

Women first began organizing in Venezuela in the 1930s, and won the right to vote in 1947. The high level of party domination of politics, however, left women largely excluded from the political process. Effective organizing outside the auspices of parties was difficult. The economic crisis of the late 1990s hit women very hard, as was the case across Latin America. By 1990 women constituted approximately 30 percent of the Venezuelan workforce, and their jobs typically paid much less than men. Further, they were often responsible for the household's income. Nationally, 25 percent of households were headed by women, and for the poor that rose to 50 percent.[16] Yet the pacted transition of 1958 effectively demobilized women, viewing a women's movement as potentially detrimental to the elite-driven (and male-dominated) political consensus. Reforms that did arise, such as granting women equal rights in marriage, were typically geared toward the interests of the middle and upper classes.[17] In the wake of the 1992 coup attempts, poorer women were very receptive to Chávez's message of social justice.

Women lobbied to include gender issues in the 1999 constitution, and so it guarantees equality and labels housework as befitting social security benefits (Article 88). The constitution also contains gender neutral language (referring to a "presidente o presidenta" because Spanish words specify gender). In 2000, the Chávez administration created the National Institute for Women (INAMUJER), which has sought to reach out to poorer women and increase female representation in elected officers. After Chávez took office, women began organizing Popular Women's Circles, which in part sought to democratize gender relations. The Chávez government also created the Women's Development Bank (Banco de Desarrollo de la Mujer, or BDM) in 2001 as a way to facilitate microfinance loans to women while also spreading the ideals of the Bolivarian Revolution. Both during the 2002 coup and the 2004 recall election, poor women came into the streets to support Chávez, and registering new voters in the barrios.

Community leaders in poor neighborhoods still tend to be men, but women have become both more politically and socially active, with Chávez as their political hero. Much of the activism, therefore, originates at the local level, though is mediated by national-level political actors in the government. Important questions for the future include whether such movements can continue to flourish even without Chávez and to what degree women can successfully carve out autonomous political spaces that depend to a lesser degree on men.

The indigenous population of Venezuela, which constitutes approximately 1.5 percent of the population, was equally energized by the Bolivarian Revolution. The Pact of Punto Fijo was not conducive to demands from below, and so the rise of Chávez promised a significant shift. Throughout his 1998 campaign, Chávez emphasized his indigenous roots. The 1999 constitution recognized Venezuela's cultural and linguistic diversity (native languages have official status for those who speak them), incorporation of native culture into political practices, collective ownership of indigenous lands, and a guarantee of representation in the National Assembly. In a symbolic move,

Chávez also renamed Columbus Day (October 12) as "Indigenous Resistance Day," including a revision of textbooks to include the role of indigenous peoples.

Decentralization and the Dynamics of Local and National Political Power

The way in which Chávez appealed to such underrepresented groups demonstrates how expansion of executive authority coexists with examples of greater local autonomy. In fact, decentralization is alive and well in Venezuela. Strange as it may sound, in a number of ways this process has enhanced Chávez's influence.

Even before Chávez came to power, the Venezuelan government had started a process of decentralization, primarily as a way to reconnect at the local level to disillusioned constituents in the midst of economic crisis. For the first time, elections were held for regional and municipal offices (such as mayors) in 1988, and then for governors in 1989 (previously, AD and COPEI had appointed them on the basis of patronage). In 1988, the Laws on Decentralization and Transfer of Responsibilities and the Law on the Municipal Regime laid out the different responsibilities to be held by different levels of government (the central government, the states, and the municipalities).[18] Subsequent laws delineated how the resources would be shared. However, the process of decentralization has been slowed by the increase in centralization of power by the Chávez government (discussed in the following paragraphs).

Nonetheless, one important consequence of the decentralization process in the 1980s was that governors gained a much higher political profile, and their importance in national politics grew, which was an important development for more local political power. They were able to seize the opportunity at a time when the central government was weak.[19] As the economy strengthened during the Chávez administration, gubernatorial independence became a bone of contention.

Other initiatives aimed at the local level proved more controversial. The government launched what it labeled *Bolivarian Missions*. The guiding principle of these local organizations was to allow workers and activists to take a more direct role in addressing social ills, such as illiteracy, malnutrition, and lack of housing, as well as environmental problems like deforestation and overuse of energy. As the name suggests, each has a particular mission to accomplish. Supporters of the government view them as essential for engaging the disadvantaged and giving them the resources necessary to advance themselves. Opponents consider them highly politicized and an extension of Chávez's personal power. For example, the "Florentine Mission" was established to support Chávez in the 2004 recall referendum, while "Mission Miranda" (named after Francisco de Miranda, a favorite hero of Chávez's) brings together a militia to defend the country from invasion, which according to Chávez would come from the United States. Chávez was open about the mix of social improvements and military training: "We have to be on guard, we have to train the people to defend our country, but we also have plans to use the half [of unused land] for cattle breeding."[20] The latter includes distribution of weapons. Opponents resented the strong Cuban role, as many of the doctors, teachers, books, and other supplies came from Cuba.

Decentralization in Venezuela, though, certainly has its limits. Local elected officials have also been stripped of some power. In 2009 the legislature approved a measure that took control of the Caracas budget away from the opposition mayor and placed it in a new federal authority, leaving the mayor with only about 10 percent of his normal funding. Control over all ports and airports have also been transferred to the federal government. The question for Venezuelan democracy is how much the president exerts sole authority to direct political and economic policy at all levels of government.

Political Institutions and Horizontal Accountability

For all the centralization, there is also a strong plebiscitary flavor to Bolivarian presidentialism. For example, the constitution allows for a publicly prompted presidential recall. To go to a national vote, the recall petition must gather signatures equaling 20 percent of registered voters. If the president does not receive majority support, then new elections must be held within thirty days. Beginning in 2003, the opposition began organizing a recall against President Chávez, and by early 2004 claimed they had 3.4 million signatures, well more than the 2.4 million needed. The CNE claimed fraud and rejected 1.8 million of them. A second submission was accepted, and after well-organized campaigning, Chávez won with 59 percent of the total vote. It was an important victory for Chávez, reaffirming not only the legitimacy of his election, but also demonstrating his ability and willingness to win democratically. There has been a considerable amount of vertical accountability, as Venezuelans have ample opportunity to offer their opinions on the president.

The legislature is unicameral, partly first-past-the-post and partly proportional representation. Because the opposition to Chávez was so disorganized and many boycotted the legislative elections, the 2005 elections yielded a strong majority for Chávez supporters. The MVR, which later became part of the United Socialist Party, won 60 percent of the seats. Periodically, and first in mid-2000, Chávez convinced the legislature to cede authority to him. According to article 203 of the constitution, with a 3/5 vote the legislature can vote to grant decree power to the president, allowing Chávez to craft and enact his own legislation without putting it to any vote. Chávez utilized these "enabling laws" in a wide range of areas, from expropriation to creation of civilian militia. We need to keep in mind, however, that such enabling laws were a fixture in Venezuelan politics after 1958. Pérez Jiménez was the most active in that regard, as during his 1974–1979 term in office, he once issued 830 decrees in one year.[21] The difference is that under the 1999 constitution, the scope of potential presidential authority is broader, going beyond the economic and financial issues prescribed in the 1961 constitution.

As a practical matter, therefore, especially after 2005 the legislature has played a minimal role in terms of horizontal accountability. That changed after the 2010 elections, when the opposition united to a much greater degree than before. The Coalition for Democratic Unity won 64 of 165 seats, short of a majority but sufficient to ensure that anything requiring a supermajority would necessitate government–opposition negotiation.

Nonetheless, the opposition has been unable to garner a majority. The 2012 presidential election pitted Chávez against Henrique Capriles, a governor from

Miranda who led the united opposition coalition. Capriles emphasized the need for change while also maintaining many of the popular *Chavista* social programs, but ultimately was decisively defeated 55 to 44 percent.

The judiciary has also become a point of debate. The constitution asserts that the judiciary is entirely independent, but in 2004 a law passed that expanded the size of the Supreme Court from 20 to 32 members. Further, it gave the National Assembly the right to choose the extra 12 members, and to remove judges, both by a simple majority vote. Particularly after the opposition failed to run campaigns in the 2005 legislative elections, the result has been a court packed with Chávez supporters. As the Supreme Court has considerable power over lower courts (including the ability to remove judges), there has been an impact across the entire judiciary. Courts and judges were widely viewed as corrupt and politicized in the "puntofijista" period, and this perception persists.

It has been argued, in fact, that "Chavismo" in general bears resemblance to the puntofijista era. As one scholar put it, "There has been a revolutionary shift in the distribution of power, but a remarkable permanence in the art of its practice."[22] The pattern is one of choosing who will be included and excluded from state generosity, and Chávez generally inverted the previous winners and losers. A major difference, however, is that politics revolved around the person of Hugo Chávez, which created considerable uncertainty about how the system will function without him. That became particularly relevant in 2011, when after an extended absence from the public eye he announced that he had a cancerous tumor removed. In late 2012 he left for Cuba and was never seen in public again. He died on March 5, 2013.

The Bolivarian Revolution: International Influences

The notion that Venezuela should have an independent-minded foreign policy did not originate with Hugo Chávez. Even during the Cold War, oil revenue provided Venezuela with a unique opportunity in that regard. In the 1970s, Carlos Andrés Pérez reestablished diplomatic relations with Cuba and trade ties with the Soviet Union. He also employed the rhetoric of national sovereignty for all Latin American countries, putting him at odds with the U.S. government, which considered many leftist movements to be the puppets of the Soviet regime.

Hugo Chávez took a very active international role, but unlike Pérez his rhetoric was anti-imperialist and revolutionary, which put him on a collision course with the United States. In some cases, this has meant open confrontation, such as his now-famous speech to the United Nations in 2006 when he referred to President George W. Bush as "the devil," saying that the podium still smelled of sulfur.

Various members of the Bush administration (most notably former Secretary of Defense Donald Rumsfeld) and President Chávez exchanged a wide range of insults over the years. Because of the U.S. government's support for the 2002 coup, Chávez also worked to ally himself with countries similarly deemed rivals or enemies of the United States, such as Russia, Iran, and Syria (in addition to Cuba). From an economic standpoint, his most important strategy was to revive OPEC and to argue successfully that the organization should limit production as a way to increase prices, rather than bow to U.S. pressure for greater production and therefore lower prices. As a result, the price of oil rose from $11 per barrel in 1998

◼◼◼◼   ANALYZING DOCUMENTS   ◼◼◼◼

Hugo Chávez genuinely relished the opportunity to criticize the policies of the U.S. government, which he argued are destructive and create misery worldwide. He employed some political theater in a United Nations speech, comparing President George W. Bush to the devil.

Hugo Chávez's Speech to the United Nations General Assembly (2006)

Madam President, Excellencies, Heads of State and Government, and high ranking representatives of governments from across the world. A very good day to you all.

First of all, with much respect, I would like to invite all of those who have not had a chance to read this book, to do it. *Hegemony or Survival: America's Quest for Global Dominance* is one of the most recent work of Noam Chomsky, one of the most famous intellectuals of America and the world. An excellent piece to help us understand not only what has happened in the world during the 20th century, but what is happening today, and the greatest threat looming over our planet: the hegemonic pretension of U.S. imperialism that puts at risk the very survival of humankind itself. We continue to warn the world of this danger, and call on the people of the United States and worldwide to halt this threat, which is like the sword of Damocles…

I believe that the first to read this book should be our brothers and sisters of the United States, because the main threat is on their homeland. The devil is here. The devil; the devil himself is in their homes.

The devil came here yesterday. Yesterday, the devil was here in this very place. This rostrum still smells like sulfur. Yesterday, ladies and gentlemen, from this podium, the President of the United States, whom I refer to as the Devil, came here talking as if he owned the world. It would take a psychiatrist to analyze the speech he delivered yesterday.

As the spokesperson for imperialism, he came to give us his recipes for maintaining the current scheme of domination, exploitation and pillage over the peoples of the world. His speech perfectly fit an Alfred Hitchcock movie, and I could even dare to suggest a title: "The Devil's Recipe." That is to say, the U.S. imperialism, as stated by Chomsky in a very clear, evident and profound manner, is making desperate efforts to consolidate its hegemonic system of domination. We cannot allow this to happen. We cannot allow a world dictatorship to be installed or consolidated.

…

Yesterday, the United States President said in this same hall the following. I quote: "Wherever you look at, you hear extremists telling you that violence, terror and torture can help you escape from misery and recover your dignity." Wherever he looks he sees extremists. I am sure he sees you, my brother, with your skin color, and he thinks you are an extremist. With his color, the Honorable president of Bolivia, Evo Morales, who came here yesterday, is also an extremist. Imperialists see extremists everywhere. No, we are not extremists, what happens is that the world is waking up, and people are rising up everywhere. I have the feeling, Mister Imperialist Dictator, that you are going to live as if in a nightmare the rest of your days, because no matter where you look at, we will be rising up against the U.S. imperialism. They call us extremists, since we demand total freedom in the world, equality among the peoples, and respect for sovereignty of nations. We are rising up against the Empire, against its model of domination.

…

[I]in a few days it will be the 30th anniversary of ... the terrorist attack when a *Cubana de Aviación* airplane was blasted and 73 innocent people died. And where was the worst terrorist of this continent, the one who admitted being the intellectual author of the Cuban airplane blasting? He was convicted in Venezuela for years and he escaped with the complicity of CIA officials and the Venezuelan government of that time. Now, he is living here in the US, protected by the U.S. government. He confessed and was imprisoned. Evidently, the U.S. government has double standards and protects terrorism.

...

I mentioned Cuba, we went happily to Havana ... We have relaunched the Non Aligned Movement, and if there is anything I may ask of you all, my friends, brothers, and sisters, is to please lend your support to strengthen the Non Aligned Movement, which has a paramount importance in the birth of a new era, to prevent hegemony and imperialism. Moreover, you all know that we have designated Fidel Castro, as President of the NAM, for a three-year term and we are convinced that our friend, Fidel Castro, will lead it with much efficiency. For those who wanted Fidel Castro to die, they remained frustrated, because he is once again wearing his olive green uniform, and is now not only the President of Cuba but also President of the Non Aligned Movement.

...

I believe the United Nations must be located in another country, in some city of the South. We have proposed this from Venezuela. You all know that my medical personnel had to remain inside the airplane as well as my Chief of Security. They both were denied to enter the United Nations. This is another abuse and an outrage, Madame President, that we request to be registered as a personal abuse by the Devil, it smells like sulfur, but God is with us.

Discussion Questions
- In what specific ways does Hugo Chávez consider the international influence of the United States to be negative?
- What does Hugo Chávez believe is the local response to the international influence of the United States?

Source: United Nations Web Site: http://www.un.org/webcast/ga/61/pdfs/venezuela-e.pdf

---

to $27 in 2000, which was critical for funding his social projects.[23] Approximately 15 percent of oil consumed in the United States comes from Venezuela, and so particularly after September 11, 2001, and the 2003 invasion of Iraq, oil-producing states became even more critical to the U.S. economy than ever before.

But aside from antagonism with the United States, the Chávez government has worked to advance regional integration. Indeed, Article 153 of the 1999 constitution states that "the Republic will promote and favor Latin American and Caribbean integration." This effort is aimed explicitly at reducing the role of the United States and international financial institutions like the International Monetary Fund (IMF), and harkens back to Simón Bolívar's own goals of integration. It rests on the assumption, long advanced by dependency theorists, that strong connections to the developed capitalist world are ruinous for less developed countries. Chávez spearheaded the Union of South American Nations

(UNASUR), an organization that uses the European Union as a model for integration, including a common currency, free movement of people, and a regional legislature. The Bank of the South is a UNASUR initiative, and its purpose is to allow Latin American governments to borrow for development projects without going through the IMF. Most South American countries contributed funds. Given the size of its economy, Brazil is critical to the future of the bank, and its future depends heavily on whether Brazil continues to support it, because it already has its own development bank operating around the region (the National Bank of Social and Economic Development, or BNDES).

Chávez also launched and promoted ALBA, the Bolivarian Alliance for the Americas, which was intended to counter the (failed) effort by the United States to establish Free Trade Areas of the Americas (FTAA). Its goal is economic integration that focuses more on social welfare than strictly on profit. Members include Bolivia, Cuba, Ecuador, Honduras, and Nicaragua, in addition to small states in the English-speaking Caribbean. Especially given the absence of the largest economies of the region, its influence remains limited.

Finally, Chávez signed agreements around the world to provide oil at heavily discounted prices for the poor. This effort even included the United States, where the Venezuelan government worked with elected officials in Massachusetts to give discounted heating oil to low-income households. The obvious intended irony was that a developing country was providing aid to the poor in a developed country. Chávez consciously made an effort to spread Venezuela's independent international influence to as many countries as possible, even to the heart of the "empire."

Conclusion and Comparative Perspective

The rise of Hugo Chávez raises important questions about the very definition of democracy. The highly personal nature of his rule is perfectly captured by the hours and hours he has spent on *Aló Presidente*, solving the problems of the common Venezuelan and establishing a closer link between the national and local levels. That style polarized the country. It has been paradoxically labeled "authoritarian, though formally democratic."[24] Along similar lines, his government simultaneously enjoys "popular sovereignty based on popular sovereignty" while sacrificing "democratic legitimacy based on liberal democratic principles."[25] These seemingly strange dichotomies reflect the paradoxes of the government itself. Free and fair elections take place in Venezuela, and Chávez accepted losing the 2007 constitutional reforms, which demonstrates at least some level of vertical accountability, yet horizontal accountability has gradually shrunk.

As has so often been the case in Venezuela, the question of economic development rests on the question of whether the government has sufficiently nurtured the non-oil sectors of the economy. From a theoretical perspective, at least on the surface Venezuela has modernized, yet remains highly dependent on international demand for a single primary product for export. In 2008, the price of oil dropped dramatically, from a record high of $147 per barrel in July to around $50 in the wake of the economic crisis in the United States. It rebounded, but commodity prices can be volatile. Over the long term, the

TABLE 10.1 Venezuelan Economic Indicators, 1991–2010

Year	GDP Growth	Inflation	Unemployment	Poverty Rate	Human Development Index
1991	10.2	31.0	8.7	—	0.859
1992	6.9	31.9	7.1	—	0.820
1993	−0.4	45.9	6.6	—	0.859
1994	−3.0	70.8	8.7	42.1	0.861
1995	4.8	56.6	10.3	—	0.860
1996	0.0	103.2	11.8	—	
1997	6.9	37.6	11.4	42.3	0.792
1998	0.6	29.9	11.3	—	0.770
1999	−5.5	20.0	15.0	44.0	
2000	3.7	13.4	13.9	—	
2001	3.4	12.3	13.3	—	0.775
2002	−8.9	31.2	15.8	48.6	0.778
2003	−7.8	27.1	18.0	—	
2004	18.3	19.2	15.3	—	
2005	10.3	14.4	12.4	37.1	0.792
2006	10.3	17.0	10.0	30.2	0.826
2007	8.4	22.5	8.7	28.5	—
2008	4.8	31.9	7.3	27.6	—
2009	−3.3	26.9	7.8	—	—
2010	−1.6	26.9	8.6	—	0.744
2011	4.2	27.1	8.3	—	0.746

Sources: Unemployment. GDP and Inflation: *Preliminary Overview of the Economies of Latin America and the Caribbean*, 1994–2012.
Poverty rate: *Social Panorama of Latin America*. Economic Commission for Latin America, 1990–2012.
Human development index: United Nations, *Human Development Report*, 1990–2013.

most pressing question for the Bolivarian Revolution is whether it can persevere without the same level of oil revenue it previously enjoyed.

Although the country was more stable than others for much of the second half of the twentieth century, the rise of populism in Venezuela is akin to many other examples across Latin America. In Argentina under Juan Perón, Bolivia under Evo Morales, or Ecuador under Rafael Correa we see similar situations in which existing political institutions suffer a legitimacy crisis and pave the way for a charismatic leader to take over. Perón is an exception, because he successfully created a political party that continued after his death, but Venezuela is similar to its contemporary counterparts in that the national party system essentially disintegrated.

Nonetheless, Venezuela has been much more stable than many other South American countries. Only in Colombia do we see a similar political context, where political elites forged agreements that ended political violence and dictatorship. Those agreements ultimately served to avoid coups but over the long term did foster resentment from those who felt excluded from the political system.

From an economic perspective, the populist response also shows how economic crisis in Venezuela bears similarity to other countries. The debt crisis hit Venezuela very hard, and its dependence on oil demonstrated the drawbacks of relying on the price of a single commodity. Although economic policy in Chile and Venezuela is very different, for example, both are greatly impacted by the price of copper and oil, respectively. The prospect of Dutch disease raises important questions about the sustainability of economic growth and the long-term viability of the Chávez model, especially without the presence of the man himself.

Key Terms

- Hugo Chávez
- Dutch disease
- Pact of Punto Fijo
- Caracazo
- PDVSA
- United Socialist Party of Venezuela (PSUV)

Discussion Questions

- Why did support for the two strongest Venezuelan political parties sour so much in the 1980s?
- What aspects of President Chávez's rule conformed to the definition of populism? Do these seem problematic for democracy?
- To what degree was political power in Venezuela under Hugo Chávez more centralized than during the puntofijista period?
- What were the primary goals of Venezuelan foreign policy under Hugo Chávez, and to what degree have those goals been achieved?
- What is the impact of oil revenue on Venezuela's overall economic growth?

Further Sources

Books

Ellner, Steve. *Rethinking Venezuelan Politics: Class, Conflict, and the Chávez Phenomenon* (Boulder: Lynne Rienner Publishers, 2008). This book challenges traditional notions about Venezuela's "exceptional" democracy and focuses on the underlying class (as well as racial) divisions that were always present in Venezuelan politics. Ellner argues that too much attention is paid to personalities rather than to key socioeconomic factors that influence politics.

Friedman, Elisabeth J. *Unfinished Transitions: Women and the Gendered Development of Democracy in Venezuela, 1936–1996* (University Park, PA: The Pennsylvania State University Press, 2000). Friedman challenges the idea that Venezuelan political parties were essential for democratization by showing how women were marginalized more under democracy because the major parties were male dominated. The time frame of the book also provides a good overview of twentieth-century Venezuelan politics.

Jones, Bart. *¡Hugo! The Hugo Chávez Story from Mud Hut to Perpetual Revolution* (Hanover, NH: Steerforth Press, 2007). It is very difficult to write about Hugo Chávez's life without coming down in favor or opposition to his political career, but this book offers a generally balanced, though clearly sympathetic, view. It is a well-researched and thorough account of his life.

McCoy, Jennifer L. and David J. Myers. *The Unraveling of Representative Democracy in Venezuela* (Baltimore: The Johns Hopkins University Press, 2004). A good collection of chapters that focus on political actors (such as the urban poor, the military, and entrepreneurs) and policy making. It is more critical of the Chávez government, and concludes with a number of hypotheses stemming from the Venezuelan experience.

Trinkunas, Harold. *Crafting Civilian Control of the Military in Venezuela: A Comparative Perspective* (Chapel Hill: The University of North Carolina Press, 2005). The book analyzes the evolution of civil-military relations in Venezuela, focusing on the decrease in oversight that contributed to the two military rebellions in 1992 as well as the politicization of the armed forces after the 1999 constitution went into effect.

Web Sites

Bolivarian News Agency (http://www.avn.info.ve/english). The official news agency of the Venezuelan state offers a version of its Web site in English. It is a very good source for understanding how the government interprets and views current events. It also provides constant updates of news from around Venezuela.

U.S. Embassy in Venezuela (http://caracas.usembassy.gov/?lang=en). The U.S. embassy in Venezuela provides a counterpoint to the Bolvarian News Agency, focusing on the positive aspects of U.S. foreign policy toward Venezuela and toward Latin America in general.

El Universal (http://english.eluniversal.com/). This long-standing Venezuelan newspaper publishes articles online in English. In the world of the Venezuelan press, it is no easy task to be balanced, but El Universal is more balanced than most.

The Revolution Will Not Be Televised (http://video.google.com/videoplay?docid=5832390545689805144). In April 2002, Irish filmmakers happened to be at Miraflores Palace when the coup took place. As a result, they were able to film events from a participant's perspective, which in many cases contradicted official versions of what occurred. The film is available for viewing free online.

Endnotes

1. Jones, Bart. *¡Hugo! The Hugo Chávez Story from Mud Hut to Perpetual Revolution* (Hanover, NH: Steerforth Press, 2007), 27.
2. Rodríguez, Francisco and Adam J. Gomolin. "Anarchy, State, and Dystopia: Venezuelan Economic Institutions before the Advent of Oil." *Bulletin of Latin American Research* 28, 1 (2009): 102–121.
3. Gallegos, Rómulo. *Doña Bárbara* (translated by Robert Malloy) (New York: Peter Smith, 1948), 139.

4. Hellinger, Daniel C. *Venezuela: Tarnished Democracy* (Boulder: Westview Press, 1991), l38.
5. Betancourt, Rómulo. *Venezuela: Oil and Politics* (Boston: Houghton Mifflin, 1979), 368.
6. Coppedge, Michael. "Venezuela: Democratic despite Presidentialism." In Juan J. Linz and Arturo Valenzuela (eds.), *The Failure of Presidential Democracy: The Case of Latin America*, Volume 2 (Baltimore: The John Hopkins University Press, 1994), 2.
7. Ellner, Steve. *Rethinking Venezuelan Politics: Class, Conflict, and the Chávez Phenomenon* (Boulder: Lynne Rienner Publishers, 2008), 56.
8. Tanaka, Martín. "From Crisis to Collapse of the Party Systems and Dilemmas of Democratic Representation: Peru and Venezuela." In Scott Mainwaring, Ana María Bejarano, and Eduardo Pizarro Leongómez (eds.), *The Crisis of Democratic Representation in the Andes* (Stanford: Stanford University Press, 2006), 56.
9. Corrales, Javier. "Presidents, Ruling Parties, and Party Rules: A Theory on the Politics of Economic Reform in Latin America." *Comparative Politics* 32, 2 (January 2000): 127–149.
10. Coppedge 1994, 328.
11. Quoted in Coppedge, Michael. "Venezuela: Popular Sovereignty versus Liberal Democracy." In Jorge I. Domínguez and Michael Shifter (eds.), *Constructing Democratic Governance in Latin America* (Baltimore: The Johns Hopkins University Press, 2003), 175.
12. Quoted in Guevara, Aleida. *Chávez, Venezuela and the New Latin America: An Interview with Hugo Chávez* (Melbourne: Ocean Press, 2005), 35.
13. Quoted in Jones 2007, 312.
14. Rodriguez, Francisco. "An Empty Revolution." *Foreign Affairs* 87, 2 (March–April 2008): 49–62.
15. Alvarez, Bernardo. "How Chávez Has Helped the Poor." *Foreign Affairs* 87, 4 (July–August 2008): 158–160.
16. Friedman, Elisabeth J. *Unfinished Transitions: Women and the Gendered Development of Democracy in Venezuela, 1936–1996* (University Park: The Pennsylvania State University Press, 2000), 235.
17. Fernandes, Sujatha. "Barrio Women and Popular Politics in Chávez's Venezuela," *Latin American Politics & Society* 49, 3 (Fall 2007): 97–127.
18. De la Cruz, Rafael, "Decentralization: Understanding a Changing Nation." In Jennifer L. McCoy and David J. Myers (eds.). *The Unraveling of Representative Democracy in Venezuela* (Baltimore: The Johns Hopkins University Press, 2004): 181–201.
19. Penfold-Becerra, Michael. "Electoral Dynamics and Decentralization in Venezuela." In Alfred P. Montero and David J. Samuels (eds.), *Decentralization and Democracy in Latin America* (Notre Dame: University of Notre Dame Press, 2004): 155–179.
20. Quoted in Guevara 2005, 55.
21. Coppedge 1994, 334.
22. Buxton Julia. "Venezuela's Contemporary Political Crisis in Historical Context." *Bulletin of Latin American Research* 24, 3 (2005): 329.
23. McCoy, Jennifer L. "From Representative to Participatory Democracy? Regime Transformation in Venezuela." In Jennifer L. McCoy and David J. Myers (eds.), *The Unraveling of Representative Democracy in Venezuela* (Baltimore: The Johns Hopkins University Press, 2004), 263–295.
24. Tanaka 2006.
25. Coppedge 2003, 175–176.

CHAPTER 11

Brazil

TIMELINE

1821	Independence from Portugal
1889	Monarchy replaced by Republic
1937–1945	Estado Novo under Getúlio Vargas
1964	Military coup
1980	Worker's Party (PT) formed
1985	End of military government
1988	New constitution passed
1992	President Collor de Mello resigns after being impeached
1994	Real Plan implemented; Fernando Henrique Cardoso elected president
2002	Lula elected president
2006	Lula reelected president
2009	Brazil becomes creditor to the IMF
2010	Dilma Rousseff elected

Born into poverty in a small town in the state of Recife, Luiz Inácio Lula da Silva, or **Lula,** became part of local workers' unions as a teenager. The injustices he saw all around him prompted him to work his way up to be president of a metalworkers' union. From there he helped create the new, and eventually very powerful, national political party, the Workers' Party. Because of his background, both inside and outside Brazil, many considered him radical. With that party as a platform, he ultimately became president of the country, where he worked to benefit Brazil's poor with a strong global economic presence combined with poverty reduction programs at home. In 2005 he spent 70 days of the year in twenty-eight other countries, always emphasizing the importance of using foreign relations as a way to increase prosperity.[1] Probably no president in the country's history had a more keen sense of how the local level could connect nationally and internationally. He left office as one of the most popular presidents in Brazilian history.

Brazilians have long joked that theirs has always been the country of the future. It is the largest country in Latin America both in terms of area (3.3 million square miles, fifth most in the world) and population (about 194 million, also fifth largest) and is abundant in natural resources. Yet it suffers tremendous economic inequality, which is tied to racial discrimination. Brazilian presidents have sought to make the country a world power, but that status has been very slow in coming. Economically, the combination of growth with inequality is a constant part of the debate over Brazilian development.

Brazilian politics is a sprawling, messy affair that involves the power of regional elites in a federal system, strong presidential powers, and a wide diversity of different political parties, but also the growing strength of civil society, which has often sprouted from the local level. After the end of a long military dictatorship in 1985, the challenge of Brazilian democracy has been to harness its incredible economic potential while also bringing more Brazilians into the political system. Although those goals are very similar to other Latin American countries, Brazil's origins were quite different.

In the recent past, though, Brazil has begun to pose a theoretical challenge. Through years of state capitalism, it has developed a thriving and diverse economy, with both heavy industrial and agricultural sectors. Once far more dependent on the developed world as an export market and source of finished goods, Brazil now has a large domestic market and exports its industrial products globally. Yet it has also retained its cultural characteristics, both good and bad. Brazilians refer to *jeito,* or the ability to get around rules, which entails an ambivalent relationship with the rule of law. Brazil is thus neither dependent nor a carbon copy of the developed world.

Historical Roots of Political and Economic Development

Brazil is distinct from its Latin American counterparts because it remained an empire until 1889. When Napoleon Bonaparte invaded Portugal, the royal family fled to Brazil (by contrast, no Spanish monarch ever visited the Spanish

Map of Brazil

American colonies). This experience with self-rule led Brazilian elites to resist when Portugal declared that Brazil should once again become a colony after Napoleon's defeat. King João's son (and regent) Pedro I refused to leave Brazil and instead created a new government. With the help of foreigners hired to assist a naval effort to fight Portuguese forces, in 1825 Brazil convinced Portugal to recognize Pedro I as Emperor of Brazil. International factors were therefore paramount. The first constitution had gone into effect in 1824 and stipulated a presidential government with the emperor acting as a balance between the different branches of government. It was also unitary, which over time generated resistance from regional leaders who chafed at centralized authority. Pedro I ruled until 1831, when in the midst of political crisis (especially regarding his desire to abolish slavery) he chose to abdicate in favor of his young son, Pedro II, who would rule until the end of the empire.

The End of Empire

The issue of slavery remained a bone of contention throughout the nineteenth century, and still now the question of race in general is central to Brazilian politics in many ways. The abolition of slavery in 1888 with the so-called Golden Law was the culmination of a gradual process of emancipation and restriction of the slave trade. The end of slavery had a devastating effect on many rural elites who depended on forced labor, and set in motion a civil-military movement to overthrow the emperor.

Thus, Brazilian independence bears virtually no resemblance to the experiences of other Latin American countries. In particular, it was much less violent. Nonetheless, by the end of the century, the country faced many of the same challenges. By virtue of the War of the Triple Alliance in the late 1860s (pitting Argentina, Brazil, and Uruguay against Paraguay), which culminated in the occupation of Paraguay's capital Asunción, the military became an important political actor. Further, the Brazilian state embarked on ambitious economic development projects, which raised national expectations about the future of the country's economy. This in turn would spark calls for industrialization.

The National and Local Implications of Political Institutions

When the empire dissolved, the Brazilian liberals and military officers who controlled the transition established presidentialism with a federal system. Brazilian politics were oligarchic and stable for four decades, characterized by some elite disputes but no major armed conflict. The president worked in tandem with governors, with a quid pro quo arrangement that ensured support for the executive in exchange for noninterference in state affairs. One unfortunate long-term effect was that governors developed their own strong party bases, which fostered regionalism at the expense of national unity. The local level clashed with the national.

That became evident by the late 1920s, as discontent grew regarding the traditional elite's ability to manage the economy and the political dominance of the state of São Paulo. In particular, the national economy depended heavily on *paulista* export of coffee, the international price of which plummeted after 1929. President Washington Luís was overthrown in 1930, and the military placed Getúlio Vargas, a former governor and failed presidential candidate, into the presidency. Vargas moved quickly to consolidate his power, successfully defeating a secessionist movement in the state of São Paulo and then creating a Constituent Assembly to draft a new constitution, which went into effect in 1934. Although the constitution centralized political power, it provided broad new suffrage rights, including for women. Nonetheless, political power remained largely concentrated in the same large landowners as the pre-1930 period, as coffee and ranching received preferential treatment.

Vargas nationalized the largest natural resources (such as mining), thus increasing the size and scope of the state. Opposition to Vargas' populist and corporatist projects led in 1937 to his dissolving the legislature, abolishing political parties, and declaring a "New State" (**Estado Novo**). He wrote yet another constitution that essentially legalized dictatorship, characterized by extensive decree power and censorship laws. Anticommunism was a thread that ran across all of his policies. He implemented a number of programs aimed at elementary education, public health, and workers, with the expectation that they would appreciate these measures without involvement in the decision-making process. Opposition once again mounted, especially within the armed forces. Vargas promised a presidential election for 1945, but concern he would renege led the military to force him from office. The election was held, and General Eurico Gaspar Dutra, his minister of war, won the presidency. Dutra and his successors were perhaps even more openly populist than Vargas, offering benefits to specific groups in return for political support and votes.

BRAZIL'S POLITICAL INSTITUTIONS

Last constitution: 1988

Federal system with twenty-six states plus the Federal District

Executive: President with four-year term, one consecutive reelection allowed (but can be elected again nonconsecutively)

Legislative: Bicameral with 81 senators (majority vote) and 513 deputies (proportional representation)

Judiciary: Superior Justice Tribunal and Supreme Federal Tribunal, with judicial review

Contemporary Politics in Brazil

In his classic work, political scientist Alfred Stepan argued that between 1945 and 1964, the Brazilian military played a "moderator" role, stepping in when civilian elites deemed it necessary or when senior officers believed civilians were not governing well. This moderating role also entailed at least one military officer running in every presidential election after 1945: "coups could be considered not merely as a unilateral response of an arbitrary and independent military institution acting on behalf of its own institutional needs and ideology, but as a dual response of both military officers and civilians to political divisions in the society."[2] Civilians were too deeply divided to rule democratically.

National Factors in the Breakdown of Brazilian Democracy

In general, at the national level there was high political drama. Vargas returned as a democratically elected president, but then committed suicide in 1954 amidst a sagging economy and charges of corruption. There was a crisis in 1955 as a faction of the military sought to prevent Juscelino Kubitscheck from assuming the presidency. The political crisis deepened in 1961, when President Jânio Quadros resigned, hoping that it would prompt an outpouring of popular and military support for his return to power (and cut through the existing political Gordian knot in the country), but instead his resignation was accepted and his vice president, João Goulart, became president. A well-known leftist, Goulart was allowed to assume office only after the military created a new position of prime minister to dilute his power and called for a plebiscite to be held in 1965 about whether Brazil should utilize a presidential or parliamentary form of government. Knowing his presidency was in jeopardy, Goulart attempted to placate the military, but his strategy of appealing to different military factions only angered the leadership more. In the face of widespread strikes and disorder, the armed forces informed Goulart that he would face civil war if he did not resign. Goulart was unable to garner popular support to stay in power, and in 1964 fled to Uruguay.

Economic development, then, had most certainly not led Brazil in the direction of either modernity or democracy. As Guillermo O'Donnell points out, Brazil imported capital and intermediate goods, referring to goods that are used to produce something else (such as metals that then used for the production of cars, tractors, etc.).[3] This in turn led to a foreign exchange shortage because the finished industrial exports were not garnering sufficient profit. In short, the economy was becoming much too reliant on imports, which increasingly became a drag on reserves. Because consumer demand remained high, inflation soared. This represented a problem that neither military nor civilian governments could solve for decades given the potential political costs involved.

With the 1964 coup, the military moved into direct rule. At the same time, however, the military government never considered itself permanent. So, for example, it allowed Congress to continue functioning, albeit only with members it considered acceptable and a legally mandated two-party system until 1979. Local elections were still held to provide at least the image of democratic rule, though the political system remained solidly authoritarian, with restrictions on civil liberties, free speech, and an absence of accountability, which meant it lacked even the basic characteristics of a polyarchy. Labor was strictly controlled and the main labor organization was abolished. The progovernment party was the National Renovating Alliance, while the opposition party was the centrist Brazilian Democratic Movement, founded in 1965. It would later become the Brazilian Democratic Movement Party. The institutional foundations for Brazil's future democracy were therefore in place.

The dictatorship was not as repressive as its neighbors, though a government report eleven years in the making (entitled *The Right to Memory and Truth*) published in 2007 detailed the deaths of 475 victims. An amnesty passed in 1979 has placed obstacles to bringing those responsible to justice. The most repressive years were under General Emilio Médici (1969–1974) during which the military had an active counterinsurgency program to defeat guerrilla uprisings. The question of justice is far less public and politically pressing than in Argentina or Chile.

Creating a New National Economic Policy

Despite sometimes drastic political change, the economic strategies of civilians and generals alike centered on import substitution, with heavy state involvement in the economy. Brazil's sheer size provided unique opportunities because it had a large domestic consumer market for goods as well as its own natural resources to contribute to industrialization. As the country stabilized politically under the dictatorship, foreign capital became plentiful, and the military government placed heavy emphasis on economic growth. Brazil experienced impressive growth rates. Between 1968 and 1974, gross domestic product (GDP) growth was never under 8.2 percent, and hit a high of 13.9 percent in 1973. The share of industry in GDP rose from 24.1 percent in 1950 to 40.9 percent in 1980.[4] From the perspective of modernization theory, Brazil seemed once again to be taking off, moving forward toward developed status.

Economic policy included a "crawling peg" (meaning a system that allows for small, gradual changes in the exchange rate), tax incentives for large projects, a focus on infrastructure, and in general a strong role for the state. Between 1967 and 1973, manufacturing grew by 12.0 percent.[5] In the same time period, GDP grew at an average rate of 11.5 percent. Exports grew rapidly, from $1.9 billion in 1968 to $6.2 billion in 1973. But by the 1970s that growth was increasingly financed with loans. By 1979, external debt accounted for 27 percent of gross national product.[6] Further, by 1981 Brazil was paying $10 billion in interest because interest rates had risen so much throughout the 1970s. That situation was made worse by the rise of oil prices, which brought inflation up to 50 percent in 1979 as firms raised prices to keep up with the costs of production. Further, there was strong geographic inequality, as the north and northeast of the country remained far behind. Yet overall growth numbers looked impressive, so that Brazil seemed always to be on the verge of emerging as a global economic power.

One particularly important initiative launched by the military government in 1975 was the National Alcohol Program, which produced ethanol fuel from sugarcane. The oil crisis of the early 1970s had been a shock for much of the world, so the government began working to reduce Brazil's dependence on petroleum. By law, gasoline in Brazil must be blended with ethanol. Ethanol also became a major export, and as oil prices once again rose in the 2000s, ethanol production skyrocketed and now constitutes a critical part of the Brazilian economy, combining both agricultural and industrial sectors.

The spending associated with all these projects, however, added to debt. As in so many other countries, the Brazilian government responded to the debt crisis by reducing internal demand. The state retreated from the economy by reducing spending and eliminating subsidies, accompanied by tax increases. Strikes then became a real political problem. To encourage exports, the government devalued the currency, but public fears of currency instability led consumers to spend while they could, which made inflation even worse. When the global recession hit in the early 1980s, Brazil required renegotiation of its debt. As elsewhere creditors no longer loaned as they had been during the boom years of the 1970s.

Brazil's Political Transition

In the context of economic troubles, Brazil once again became a polyarchy. The transition from authoritarian rule in Brazil was pacted and protracted. By the early 1970s, the original rationale for the coup, such as combating guerrilla groups and Communist influence, no longer applied. Further, the regime's economic record was decidedly mixed, thus opening the door to moderate political opposition. General Ernesto Geisel became president in 1974, and announced a policy of "distensão," or "decompression." His rationale was likely that liberalization would increase support for the military regime, particularly because Brazil had experienced a so-called economic miracle. He did not achieve that outcome, because the opposition made advances in the 1974 congressional elections, increasing from 87 to 160 seats in the lower house. Liberalization also included loosening electoral rules in 1979 to allow for new parties to form, which was intended to divide the opposition. By the 1980s, it expanded into "**abertura**," or "opening." The impetus for these political changes was entirely national.

The military government controlled the pace of this pacted transition. One key feature of such a transition is that the armed forces have significant leverage over the protection of their prerogatives once elected civilian governments returned. Even as they negotiated the end of military rule, senior military officials ensured that they even directly influenced the drafting of a new constitution. So, for example, the military still retains the role (through article 142) as guarantor of "law and order," although as yet it has not chosen to exert that right, which is vague and therefore open to interpretation (and abuse). The result was a democracy constrained by military power, though it should be noted that particularly after 1990, the military was not viewed by any significant political sectors as a viable ruler. Progress on reducing military prerogatives has been slow, though steady at least in recent years. Expansive military court jurisdiction was reformed only in 2004 (meaning that if a member of the military commits a crime against a civilian, he or she must now face a civilian court). Further, civilians were finally put in charge of intelligence, which like in many other Latin American countries had been controlled by the armed forces.

The constitution stipulated an indirect presidential election, but in anticipation of the 1985 presidential election, the Brazilian Democratic Movement Party (PMDB), which originated as one of the two legal opposition parties, organized the "direitas ja" ("direct elections now") movement that brought millions of people to the streets. A proposal to that effect reached the legislature, where the military's political allies successfully blocked it. The transition included explicit discussions between Tancredo Neves (who would win the election) and military leaders. As we would expect from a pacted transition, the process was relatively peaceful but placed important restraints on accountability and participation. Unfortunately, Neves became ill the night before he was to be sworn in, and he died soon thereafter of intestinal complications. His vice president, José Sarney, took office instead. Sarney was associated with the military government, and the negotiated transition ensured, at least for the short term, that the political structure constructed by the military would remain. This included censorship laws, military prerogatives, laws against strikes, and a military presence in the presidential cabinet. The process of creating a new polyarchy therefore took years after the initial opening.

Sarney enjoyed early support, particular with the short-lived success of his Cruzado Plan in 1986, which fought inflation. The plan involved freezes on prices, wages, and even rent payments as a way to reduce the amount of capital in the economy. The plan enjoyed initial success, but it did not address the structural sources of inflation. By the presidential election of 1989, inflation had soared close to 1,000 percent and the political race was wide open. This would mark Luiz Inácio Lula da Silva's first attempt at the presidency, and he barely lost (53–47 percent) in a runoff with Fernando Collor de Mello, the governor of Alagoas. Collor had a difficult relationship with the legislature, and his own party had only 5 percent of the seats, so like many other Latin American presidents he felt compelled to implement policies (particularly market reforms) by decree. He issued 163 in his first year alone.

Collor was dogged by charges of corruption, and in 1991 was accused by his own brother of being paid millions of dollars in bribes through his campaign treasurer. A congressional commission took up the case, and the following year Collor was impeached, convicted, and forced from office. Although he lost his right to run for office for eight years, in 2006 he was elected senator of his home state. His removal from office showed that Brazilian presidentialism was sufficiently flexible to avoid the breakdowns that are often ascribed to presidential governments. It also demonstrated that although the Brazilian executive does enjoy broad powers, there is still a strong dose of horizontal accountability in a way that parallels Colombia. During this period, the debate over presidential and parliamentary forms of government once again arose, and what was a matter of academic discussion became a concrete political matter. In 1993, Brazilians went to the polls to decide whether they preferred to continue with a presidential system or to shift the country toward parliamentarism. They chose to retain presidentialism. In all, these events were a boon to Brazilian democracy, which endured and became stronger even within the context of executive-legislative disagreement.

The International Influence on Economic Transition

After Mexico's crash in 1982, Brazil found it difficult to access international credit, and the recession deepened. Also problematic was that the anti-inflationary measures did not work as intended, with inflation remaining persistently in triple digits. The economy stabilized under the direction of **Fernando Henrique Cardoso**, who became minister of finance in 1993, and in 1994 implemented the "Plan Real." In the 1960s he had been a proponent of dependency theory, which is highly critical of international capitalism, but by the 1990s he had revised those views and argued that the Brazilian economy could recover only if economic liberalization measures were taken. In other words, Brazil should embrace economic globalization and open its economy to competition, while retaining a role for the state. That has been the stance of every Brazilian government since then.

In March 1990, Congress passed the National Privatization Program, which then formed a committee to oversee the process of privatizing state-owned enterprises. This included mining, public utilities, telecommunications, and even roads, bridges, sanitation, and railways.[7] Between 1991 and 2005, the privatization of 120 companies yielded $87.8 billion at both the state and federal levels.

The stabilization measures generated support for their main proponent, as Cardoso was elected president in 1994. As finance minister, earlier in the same year he had initiated the "Real Plan," which was intended to stabilize the Brazilian currency as way to combat inflation. It created a nonmonetary currency, the "Real Unit of Value" (URV), which existed alongside a new currency, the *real*. As Brazil had become so integrated into the global economy, it was important to avoid drastic exchange rate swings. The new *real* was initially set one-to-one with the URV, which reduced what is known as "intertial inflation." Intertial inflation involves a constant adjustment of prices, where the expectation of future inflation fuels ever-increasing price increases. If, for example, someone signs a contract, he or she would adjust the value according to the forecast of future inflation. The Real Plan therefore served to end the public expectation of constantly rising inflation.

However, there were limits to its success. In particular, the Russian and Asian economic crises of 1997–1998 hit Brazil hard because they prompted capital flight, a critical problem for many developing countries at the time as investos became skittish. The government had kept a fixed exchange rate with the dollar, but the *real* had become overvalued. Over time this had created a trade deficit of about $4 billion a year. Consequently, in 1998 the government devalued approximately 30 to 40 percent. As we shall see, that devaluation was devastating for Argentina, whose currency remained pegged to the dollar. In Brazil, devaluation led to a rise of inflation, but the Real Plan still served to avoid the hyperinflation that had occurred in the past. In general, the government was successful in convincing the public and investors alike that it was working to create a budget surplus and to avoid the inflationary spirals of the past.

National Transformations of the Underrepresented

As Brazil changed economically, it also underwent change politically. Similar to the Chilean case, the Brazilian dictatorship politicized women and prompted them to organize in ways they had not in the past. As in Chile, the Catholic Church played an important role in this process, as it connected women activists to poor and working-class women's groups.[8] The families of lower-class women were most adversely affected by repression, so they were the first to come together in organized protest against the military government. The church did not support feminist goals that challenged traditional views of the family, but it did provide a mass base that otherwise would not have existed. By the early 1980s, the political opposition had made a concerted effort to reach out to women's groups, which further solidified their political influence.

When the military left power, Brazilian women were left in a similar position to their counterparts in other postauthoritarian contexts. The original purpose of democratization was complete, and women's groups found it difficult to remain united and bring demands into the formal political arena. There was little agreement on which demands to make, and what priorities to set for the first legislative elections in 1982.

Nonetheless, there has been reform at the national level. In 1995, the legislature passed a law establishing quotas for mayoral races and positions for Municipal Chambers. In 1997, that was extended to state legislatures and the Chamber of Deputies. The law stipulates that 30 percent of total candidacies must be women, but not all 30 percent of candidacy vacancies must be filled. In practice, parties often leave the vacancies unfilled. As a result, quotas have had only a minimal effect on the number of women elected. In 1998, the number of women in the Chamber of Deputies dropped from 1994 (6.2 percent to 5.7 percent) and rose only slightly to 8.2 percent in 2002.[9] Over time, however, party leaders do seem to be recruiting women they feel will be competitive. In the short term, parties chose not to fill vacancies with female candidates who were not competitive, because that requires resources for little electoral benefit. The question for the long term, then, is whether women become more prominent within the parties and the number of competitive female candidates increases.

The gradual increase of women in politics has not translated into significant policy reforms with regard to gender issues, such as maternity leave or legalized abortion. Interestingly, the attitudes of individual legislators have become more progressive over time, but the laws remain quite conservative.[10] The essential problem is that party fragmentation makes any type of reform problematic, and gender issues have not been prioritized by either the party leaders or the president. The government has, however, worked to recognize the realities of domestic violence. For example, it passed the 2006 "Maria da Penha" law, named after a woman who was severely beaten over a period of years, which increased the penalties for abuse and allowed for special courts.

Workers have also enjoyed electoral success. Lula worked in factories from a very young age and eventually became involved in union organizing. He helped to found the Partido dos Trabalhadores (**Workers' Party, or PT**) in 1980 and the Central Única dos Trabalhadores (United Workers' Center, or CUT), the main labor association in Brazil. The PT itself was the result of local grassroots organization, and its constitution asserts the right of political autonomy for local actors, as opposed to the traditionally more elitist nature of Brazilian politics. Therefore it rejected the more establishment PMDB. Lula and other PT candidates explicitly noted the importance of class divisions and the need to express the demands of the poor and disenfranchised. In 1986 he won a seat in Congress for the PT, and in 1989 made his first run for the presidency, which he narrowly lost after a runoff with Fernando Collor de Mello.

The PT has had striking political success. It has successfully balanced the need to maintain central party authority for discipline while also ensuring that local interests always have the opportunity to channel their concerns upward. In other words, its internal structure fostered vertical accountability, with dialogue going both up and down.

The party's fortunes progressively improved after Lula's first run for the presidency. The traditional political elite was disappearing, and political discourse was moving leftward. The PT's message was therefore becoming more mainstream. The PT itself had become less radical and more willing to work with its historic enemies, particularly corporations and wealthy investors. Lula did not advocate socialism, but rather a new focus on the poor within the existing market system. In that sense, he was similar to Presidents Ricardo Lagos and Michelle Bachelet in Chile. Even in his inaugural speech, he clearly stayed away from radical change: "We are going to change, yes. We are going to change with courage, but carefully. We will be humble and daring. We will change, but at the same time we know that it is a gradual and continuous process and not just a simple expression of will."

ANALYZING DOCUMENTS

Lula's inauguration was an important moment in Brazilian political history. In his inauguration speech, he outlined the type of policy strategy he planned to follow, which involved pushing for change, especially for the poor and for Afro-Brazilians. But he also emphasized that such change should not be too radical.

Lula Inauguration Speech (2003)

Change. That is the key word. That was the grand message from Brazilian society in the October elections. Hope finally defeated fear and Brazilian society decided the time had come to tread new roads...

And here I am, on this day many generations of fighters that came before us dreamed of, to reassert my deepest and most essential commitments, to reiterate to all citizens of my country the meaning of each word I said during the campaign, to imprint change with practical intensity, to say that Brazil has reached the hour to become the nation that we always dreamed of—a sovereign and dignified nation, aware of its own importance in the international arena, and at the same time capable of housing, welcoming, and treating all of its children with justice.

We are going to change, yes. We are going to change with courage, but carefully, with humility and audacity. We will change, but at the same time remain aware that it is a gradual and continuous process and not just a simple act of will...

This is a country that never ceases to be young and nee, with people who know the meaning of suffering, but at the same time know the meaning of happiness, who believe in themselves and in their own strength. I believe in a great future for Brazil because our happiness is bigger than our pain, our strength is bigger than our misery, and our hope is bigger than our fears.

This is a country that has so much fertile land and so many people who want to work that there is no reason to talk about hunger. However, millions of Brazilians in the countryside and in cities, in the most remote rural and in the urban periphery, lack food right now. They survive, miraculously, under the poverty line, if they do not die of misery while begging for a piece of bread. This is an old story.

Brazil is great. In spite of acts of cruelty and discrimination, especially against indigenous and black communities, and all the inequalities and pain we should never forget, the Brazilian people have achieved an admirable endurance and national construction ... This is a nation that speaks the same language, shares the same fundamental values and it feels Brazilian...

Today we are starting a new chapter in the history of Brazil, not as a submissive nation that gives away its sovereignty or as an unjust nation that watches passively as the poor suffer, but as a noble and proud nation that courageously affirms its role without discrimination based on class, ethnicity, sex or beliefs...

What we are living right now, my comrades, my brothers and sisters from all over Brazil, can be summarized in a few words: today is the day when Brazil finds itself again. I thank God for having arrived where I am...

I ask God for the wisdom to govern, discretion in judgment, serenity to administrate, courage to make decisions, and a heart the size of Brazil so I can feel united to each Brazilian citizen each day during the next four years. Long live the Brazilian people!

Discussion Questions
- According to Lula, what priorities should the national government have?
- For Lula, what are the national and international sources of national "dignity"?

Source: The Brazilian Presidential Web page: http://www.biblioteca.presidencia.gov.br/ex-presidentes/
luiz-inacio-lula-da-silva/discursos-de-posse/discurso-de-posse-1o-mandato/view

---

Unlike Chile, however, in Brazil there is no significant party on the right. The Demócratas Party is in the center, with a platform modeled on that of the Democratic Party in the United States. To its right are only small parties with little political power. In the postauthoritarian era, it seems not to be politically advantageous to be considered conservative. Parties on the right have gradually moved toward the center (though, it should be noted, leftist parties have similarly edged toward the center). This was a phenomenon known as the "ashamed right," as conservatives became hesitant to self-identify with the right in the years immediately after the transition. These politicians routinely portray themselves as further to the left than their own party.

Lula's moderate political stance alienated many of his supporters on the left. He forged congressional alliances with the opposition, including José Sarney, the former president who became president of the Senate. Civil society organizations began to distance themselves in response. For example, both the CUT and MST formed a new organization, the Coordination of Social Movements, which did not include the PT. Lula's willingness to work with more conservative members of the legislature and his vocal support for market mechanisms did not resonate with many political actors on the left, who believed that market-based solutions were not feasible or desirable.

The strength of democracy is also evident in the 2010 election of **Dilma Rousseff** of the Workers' Party for president, defeating Jose Serra in a second round runoff, 56 to 44 percent. Rousseff had once been a member of a guerrilla organization, fighting against the military government, and was imprisoned for it. She later became active in both provincial and national politics, and eventually became an important part of Lula's cabinet. She is the first female president in Brazilian history, and also underlines the strength of the Workers' Party in a fragmented party system. Despite the many obvious challenges that remain, polyarchy is alive and well in Brazil.

Many reforms initiated under Cardoso or Lula, then continued under Rousseff, have greatly benefited the disadvantaged. Some of the most prominent are Bolsa Família ("Family Grant") and Fundef (Fund for Maintenance and Support of Basic Education). Bolsa Família provides cash (through a debit card) for families who can document that their children are attending at least 85 percent of their classes. By 2011, it had reached 12 million families and benefited approximately 55 million family members, at a cost of about $2.2 billion. It should also be noted that by no means did civil society entirely desert Lula. For example, the Brazilian Association of Non-Governmental Organizations remains a close partner of the Workers' Party, and continues to channel concerns to the government. The same is true of the National Conference of Brazilian Bishops.

Inequality remains a pressing problem. By so many measures, Brazil is industrial and economically modern. By the twenty-first century, Brazil produced millions of vehicles, cell phones, televisions, refrigerators, and even airplanes (EMBRAER is the world's fourth largest aircraft manufacturer).[11] By contrast, across the country, only 55.3 percent of Brazilians were connected to a sewage system, and just less than 90 percent had access to a water supply system. In poorer regions, such as in the north, these numbers are worse. Brazil has indeed been developing, but the fruits of that progress have always been concentrated within a relatively small elite. Brazil's Gini coefficient is extremely high, at 0.53 in 2010. That was up from 0.493 in 1979. Fortunately, that was down from 0.602 in 1997, but still put it around the same level as much poorer countries like Haiti, Botswana, and Paraguay.

Inequality is also reflected in racial terms. Indeed, Brazil did not abolish slavery until the very end of the empire, in 1888. Blacks and "pardos" (referring to mixed race) now constitute about 45 percent of the population. Blacks in Brazil earn only 48 percent of what whites make for the same job.[12] Interestingly, many Brazilians consider their country to be a "racial democracy," where difference in skin matters little. This idea was bolstered when the 1988 constitution finally allowed illiterates to vote, a category that was disproportionately black. Fernando Henrique Cardoso was the first Brazilian president to openly acknowledge racism and to forge social programs to address racial inequality. But racial inequality has remained virtually unchanged for years.

One obstacle to addressing racial inequality is the fact that Afro-Brazilians do not share enough group identity to organize effectively for political reform. There are organizations, most notably the Unified Black Movement (MNU), which formed in 1978 and gained momentum in the 1990s, lobbying for equal rights. Further, in 2003, Lula created a Special Secretariat for the Promotion of Racial

Equality. Its work has included the promotion of affirmative action plans, particularly in higher education. Such policies have gradually been puncturing the long-held "myth of racial democracy" by raising questions about the lack of progress Afro-Brazilians have made in socioeconomic terms. It has also highlighted the complexities of race in Brazil, where not all people of African ancestry necessarily self-identify as "black." There are many different self-classifications for people of color, which further complicates both policy making and political organization.

Presidentialism and National Fragmentation

Difficulty in organizing civil society is exacerbated by political institutions. The Brazilian party system is quite fragmented, meaning that there are many different parties with divergent goals, and a high level of competition within the parties themselves, which reduces coherence. A major reason for this situation is the use of open-list proportional representation. When Brazilians cast votes for the legislature, they make a choice for an individual, but the seats are allocated according to the proportion of the total vote the party receives. The party then assigns the seats to the candidates who received the most votes within the party list. Each state must have at least eight seats in the lower house (out of a total of 513), and no more than seventy. In the Brazilian case, proportional representation both increases the number of parties and creates fierce competition within them to garner the most votes. This personalizes politics, since voters can focus on individuals rather than parties, while the individual candidates are actually opposed to each other even when they belong to the same political party.

Another factor in fragmentation is the ease with which politicians can change parties. The military government had prohibited the practice, and once the laws were removed, switching occurred at a dizzying pace. Between 1987 and 1995, there were 459 defections from one party to another, meaning that one in three federal legislators changed parties.[13] Politicians rely much more on name recognition and clientelist networks than on party affiliation. Parties therefore become vehicles for their particular interests, rather than coherent institutions with clear loyalties. Legislators also tend not to stay in office long, often for only one term. Instead, they leapfrog to federal offices that offer more power and access to resources. Overall, this generates distrust of the legislature (and politicians in general) among the public.

Clientelism is an enduring feature of Brazilian politics. That has a negative effect on vertical accountability, because state officials operate according to the dictates of their own networks. As politicians do not stay in office long, they are much less likely to take the needs even of their own constituents into consideration. Even as individuals take different positions within the government, their patron–client networks remain strong. Currying favor is a more important goal than efficiency.

The result is a political system that remains very oligarchic. The connection between parties and voters is weak. The PT is an exception to a certain degree, but Lula's move to the center reduced party discipline and created schisms. These have been made worse by political scandals. Even before Lula was elected, a kickback scandal emerged that led to the murder of a PT mayor in 2002. Two years later, members of the PT were implicated in extortion. The worst, however, was in 2005 when a high-level PT official admitted buying political support with monthly payments. Hundreds of millions of dollars were funneled to fake government contracts, and everyone around Lula was implicated.[14] The rise to power of a leftist party was certainly historic, but in many ways Brazilian politics was still business as usual, which contributes further to greater distance between politicians and their constituents.

The fragmentation is quite obvious when considering the distribution of seats in the legislature. In the 2010 election, the PT won the most seats in the Chamber of Deputies with 88 out of 513, but that represented only 17 percent of all seats. The PMDB came out with the second most, at 79. An astonishing 22 different parties gained seats in that election, some with only one or two. After the 2010 elections, the Senate was in a similar situation. A total of 15 parties occupied the 81 seats, with no party obtaining more than 19 (or 24.6 percent of the seats). For a more panoramic view, since 1990 no political party has managed to win more than 20 percent of the vote in the Chamber of Deputies. By necessity, then, the immediate job of every Brazilian president is to forge the necessary coalition partners to get any bill passed, which in practice means doling out money in a clientelist fashion. Of course, the difficulty of that task is precisely one reason why the use of decrees can be so tempting.

Fragmentation has also meant that presidents rely more on exerting their constitutional powers than on building and maintaining partisan coalitions. The president can veto legislation (or even just parts of the legislation), and an override requires a majority of the legislature. A combination of absenteeism (i.e., members who do not attend sessions) and fragmentation mean that overrides are not easy to muster. The constitution also grants the president, rather than the legislature, the right to initiate legislation in certain areas, such as job creation, the budget, administrative organization, or the size of the armed forces. The executive therefore sets the agenda in important respects, including forcing special sessions of Congress, where only the president's issue can be debated. Even more importantly, the president can enact provisional laws for 30 days without congressional approval. If Congress then rejects them, the president can issue them again. This decree power has been used extensively by presidents after 1988.

Traditionally, Brazilian presidentialism has also been associated with corruption, as the party in power benefits from its position. The PT campaigned on an anticorruption platform, arguing that it would transform politics as usual, but it didn't. That has hit the PT in a very serious way. As mentioned, high-level party officials, including some who were very close to Lula, were implicated in 2005 for using illegal funds in the 2002 elections and for buying votes from the opposition in the lower house. The fallout has forced resignations from legislators and cabinet reshufflings and has prompted wide-ranging investigations into tax fraud, embezzlement, and other crimes but has thus far not damaged Lula's own popularity significantly.

Nonetheless, there are signs of greater political institutionalization. More and more Brazilians identify with political parties and can discern differences between them. There are more coherent party coalitions, so that even though there may be a number of different parties, they are arraying themselves in clear blocs. In particular, the PT and the PSDB have forged alliances that are critical to their electoral success. The strategy includes providing cabinet seats for coalition partners. There has also been a trend over time of legislators favoring nationally oriented legislation rather than just particularistic bills. This means they are focusing less on their local clientelist ties and more toward universal policies. All of these developments make Brazilian politics more stable. But they are in the early stages.

Democracy in Brazil: The Local Level

As the process of democratization accelerated in the early 1980s, more Brazilians than ever became involved in "participatory institutions," particularly as a result of the same economic crises that were hitting the rest of Latin America. These are organizations at the local level (even neighborhood associations) that work with political parties to advance the interests of their members, who generally had been peripheral to the political system in the past. Thus, by 2004 over 400,000 people were involved in participatory budgets, and over 400,000 people were in health and social assistance councils.[15]

Yet not even these associations guarantee true representation. A study of São Paulo found that many such organizations have "assumed representation," meaning that their claims to representation are not necessarily shared by their constituency.[16] For example, there is not necessarily any formal membership. In practice this means there may not be much accountability, or ways to determine whether people's views of such organizations change.

One of the most famous examples of a grassroots organization in all of Latin America is the **Brazilian Landless Workers' Movement** (Movimento dos Trabalhadores Rurais Sem Terra, or MST). The MST began as a group of several thousand people who occupied unused land in the state of Rio Grande do Sul in 1980. By the end of the military dictatorship, it became a formal organization that now boasts some 1.5 million members. It became more powerful during the administration of President Cardoso, who believed that land reform was a necessary component of economic development. His vision was to combine market-based reform with redistribution. The MST continued to occupy land, sometime resulting in violent reprisals by local authorities. Cardoso did expropriate land (with repayment) and redistributed it to small farmers who were required to pay off the titles over time. In this manner, some 500,000 families received plots of land between 1995 and 2002.[17]

This market-based approach did not appease the MST, which issued a manifesto in 2000 outlining its grievances and singling out Cardoso for blame: "But since 1994, with the neoliberal policies of Fernando Henrique Cardoso's government, the problems have become even more acute. This economic policy represents only the interests of the banks and of multinational companies." He had excluded the MST leadership from the planning process, and so the land occupations continued.

■ ANALYZING DOCUMENTS ■

Given its size and coordinated ability to act, the Landless Rural Workers' Movement could not be ignored. In 2000 the movement released its manifesto, which was intended to explain its actions and increase its popular support throughout Brazil.

MST Manifesto to the Brazilian People (2000)

Dear companheiros and companheiras, throughout our immense and beloved Brazil,

We have been camped out in Brasília, with more than 11 thousand delegates from 23 states of the nation—men, women, children, youth and adults, from the rural areas, sharing sacrifices, joy and hopes. We have been reunited for the 4th National Congress of the Movimento dos Trabalhadores Rurais Sem Terra, MST (Landless Rural Workers' Movement).

Our country is experiencing a grave crisis. But this crisis does not affect everyone. The wealthiest continue to earn a lot of money through exploitation. The large multinational corporations continue to send billions of dollars abroad. The banks have never earned as much money as now. But for those who survive from their sweat, living conditions have become increasingly precarious; those who have work earn very little; young people lack quality schools; and universities are no longer public and free. Many people have been forced to leave the rural heartland to live on the periphery of the large cities. There, they find misery and violence.

What is the cause of this?

It is true that our society has always been unjust. Like any capitalist society, the poor have always been exploited and humiliated. And the rich class, earning more and more all the time, has always repressed the people and submitted it to the interests of international capital.

But since 1994, with the neoliberal policies of Fernando Henrique Cardoso's government, the problems have become even more acute. This economic policy represents only the interests of the banks and of multinational companies. For these, the government guarantees high interest rates and financial help. Suffice to say: last year the government spent 64% of the national budget servicing the interest on internal and external debt. Despite all the social problems, the government of the Brazilian elites has the nerve to send 50 billion dollars to the rich countries every year. That is why there is a lack of money for education, health, public transport, popular housing, and employment generation.

In agriculture the situation is more grave still. The Cardoso government wants to "modernize" the rural areas stimulating large export-orientated estates; handing control of the agricultural market over to the multinational corporations; and allowing agro-industries to control the storage of food products.

...

In politics, every day sees the proliferation of news about corruption and embezzlement of the public funds and property. There is a sector, increasing in size all the time, of dominating classes that is enriching itself merely through the diversion of public money, through narco-trafficking or contraband. These sectors are so powerful and influential that they include high court judges, commanders of the Military Police, deputies, senators, newspapers owners, bankers, military personnel—it has even reached the ex-secretary of the Planalto (presidential palace). The latter, considered the right arm of the government, is alleged to belong to the group responsible for the theft of 169 million reais, destined to the construction of the São Paulo's Industrial Tribunal.

Is our country a lost cause?

We don't believe so. However, the Brazilian people must rise up, organise itself, and take to the streets, in order to struggle for their historic rights. It is, indeed, possible to build another project for Brazil—a Popular Project that tends to the needs of the people. Radical changes are needed, however. We must prevent the banks, the multinationals and the thieves of the people from enriching themselves.

The repayment of foreign debt must be suspended. The financial system and interest rates must be controlled. We must ensure that banks use capital to finance production, and not speculation. Foreign debt must be renegotiated and the public budget prioritised towards education, health and agriculture. We should retake the reigns of economic policy so that it be administrated by Brazilians in favour of our people—thus, breaking the agreement with the IMF. Agrarian reform, associated with a new agricultural model, should be implemented. An agrarian reform that can guarantee income for farmers and a future for those that live in the rural areas.

With the resources that will no longer be sent to the banks and oversees, a national fund of social investments should be established, in order to create jobs and increase the purchasing power of the population.

Finally, there is no economic or social reason that impedes every Brazilian having access to land, work, dignified housing, quality public schools, and food. But we need to have the courage to change our government, rethink economic policy and challenge the profits of the powerful.

The following months and years will be decisive for the future of our country. Either we regain our national sovereignty or we will be condemned to be a new colony of the US government, which even has its eye on the Amazon region.

That's why, as a social movement of landless rural workers, we urge all Brazilian popular organisations to organise themselves and fight for these changes.

...

And we must continue struggling, always.

Every social conquest has been the result of massive, popular struggles. Together with the Brazilian people, we hope to construct a Popular Project—a project that will regain our national sovereignty, our dignity and the well being of all the population.

Discussion Questions

- What types of effects does the MST believe that national and international factors have on the local level?
- Does the MST seem to think that international influences have a positive or negative effect on Brazilian workers?

Source: http://www.mstbrazil.org/manifesto.html

After Lula took office, the protests organized by the MST and other groups actually increased. Their goal was to provide him political leverage to pass progressive reforms by demonstrating the power of civil society that was firmly behind him. They did, however, shift their tactics away from disrupting government (such as protesting in or around government buildings). But Lula's ambivalent relationship with the MST increased the gap between them, and increasingly the organization made specific demands of the government to speed up the passage of reforms. In particular, Lula resisted the sweeping land reform that the MST calls for, asking instead for patience as he carefully navigated the political waters.

Many Brazilians were participating in some form of association, but life at the local level is not always so positive. Poverty has spawned large "favelas," or slums, that teem with illegal activity (see Box 11.1). In many case they are beset by organized crime syndicates and offer little hope of advancement. In Rio de Janeiro, the world famous Copacabana and Ipanema beach communities are right next to the favelas, which are perched up on the steep hills of the city. Many residents have also become the victims of police abuse. Crime is such a problem that in 2010 the army occupied some favelas in Rio for several months as a way to restore order (as well as to create a high-profile assurance to potential visitors to the 2014 World Cup and 2016 Olympics). Those troops augment the Police Pacification Units in Rio that sought to connect the police more closely to community leaders.

The favelas are not new. In 1960, the remarkable favela resident Carolina María de Jesus published *Child of the Dark*, which was soon translated into English. She wrote of the extreme difficulties of life in the slums: "Hard is the bread that we eat. Hard is the bed on which we sleep. Hard is the life of the *favelado*."[18] The Brazilian state has been very slow in addressing the problems inherent in such slums, and so organized crime has moved in where the government fears to tread. More Brazilians are being lifted out of poverty, which in the 1980s was nearly half the population, so government efforts have borne fruit, but currently still over 25 percent remain impoverished, with many more on the edge.

National Insecurity and the Judiciary

Insecurity is a central social and political issue, and goes well beyond the favelas. Surveys consistently show that public security is one of the top concerns of Brazilian voters. One problem is coordination among disparate agencies. In 1998, President Cardoso created the National Secretariat for Public Security within the Ministry of Justice (SENASP). Its purpose was to bring different state agencies together under one umbrella. Otherwise a wide range of police forces, intelligence organizations, and other law enforcement act with little idea what the others are doing. Of course, this hampers any effort to track criminals or to set up operations against them. For the first several years of its existence, SENASP had many different directors and little continuity, but it gained new prominence after Lula's election.[19] This included increased funding for data collection and training. There has also been a shift of emphasis away from traditional police work to greater focus on crime prevention and youth education.

BOX 11.1

The National and International Politics of Poverty
Children of the Favelas

International: Favelas are slums, characterized by shanties built by the tenants themselves, often without title, that often lack basic services like sewage or electricity (though obtaining electricity illegally has become more common). Favelas in Brazil have a long history, dating over a century, but their growth exploded in the 1970s after a wave of urbanization. The national economic emphasis on industrialization and export prompted rural residents to find work in the burgeoning cities. Indeed, economic policies were aimed specifically at improving agricultural output at low costs, which meant mechanization, and providing a base of low-wage workers for industry. The country's insertion into international markets contributed to the swelling of favela populations.

National: The government is paying increasing attention to the children who live in the favelas. As mentioned, Lula's Bolsa Família is aimed specifically at encouraging the poor to keep their children in school, but favela children still suffer from neglect as their parents do what they can to make a living. All too often, the children turn to crime, either petty or violent. They also become involved in drugs, both in terms of consumption and selling. Children become involved in drug activities as young as 10 or 11, though typically the street dealers are in their late teens.[20]

Local: The government views them as a threat to tourists and businesses alike. The military government periodically sought to remove people from the favelas, as they were viewed as a blight in cities like São Paulo and Rio de Janeiro. Since then, the police have been implicated in numerous cases of abuse and murder. One very highly visible case occurred in 1993 when police shot eight street children sleeping at a church; the official police response to favela children becomes quite obvious.

Perhaps nowhere else is the inequality in Brazil more evident. Despite Herculean efforts by the Catholic Church, nongovernmental organizations, and residents alike, favela children face a grim future. In the 2002 Brazilian movie *Cidade de Deus* (*City of God*, the name of a favela created in the 1960s), we see a young man who manages against all odds to leave the slums. He watches (and chronicles with his camera) as everyone else he knows is drawn into a cycle of violence through which children freely circulate.

Discussion Questions

- What kinds of incentives does Lula's national economic policy offer the poor in Brazil?
- In what ways can international economic pressures affect poverty at the local level?

Further, it is not possible to enact economic policy in Brazil without close consultation with state-level politicians. The federal system spawned local political machines that could derail national initiatives. Thus, when President Cardoso enacted land reform he was compelled to involve local interest groups by funneling state funds in their direction. Without that clientelist back scratching, resistance to reform would have been too much to overcome. Conversely, however, it also led to a more watered-down policy with considerable obstacles for poor farmers, such as a complicated system of land title transfers and limited state assistance to help peasants once they obtain the land.

The judicial branch is a key player in the political system as well. The 1988 constitution sought to ensure independence from political influence, to the point of even giving budgetary authority to the Supreme Federal Court. But it goes well beyond simple judicial review, and injects the courts in political areas. For example, lower courts can challenge the implementation of legislation. The eleven-member Supreme Federal Court can also rule on legislation and has been active in doing so. For example, over 200 years the U.S. Supreme Court ruled 135 federal laws to be unconstitutional. By contrast, after only 15 years of existence the Brazilian court debated over 1,000 such cases and altered over 200.[21] This stands in contrast to most Latin American countries, where the courts are often less adversarial with both the legislative and executive branches.

At the same time, the decisions of that highest court are only references for other courts and can also be challenged by lower courts, making the entire process very cumbersome. At the extreme, it has led to disputes in which defendants are ordered detained by one judge and freed by another. This decentralization mirrors the decentralized political system, and fosters a climate of delay and indecision.

Although the courts have important influence at the national level in terms of affecting policy, the legal system is problematic at the local level, where there are only 6,000 judges for the entire country.[22] Citizens find it difficult to have their concerns addressed because the system is complex and confusing. There are also fewer judges in rural areas (such as in the north and northeast) than in the cities. Especially in those more remote areas, the judges have close ties to local politicians and landowners, which results in relatively few convictions against local elites. Judges have resisted reform of the judicial system, such as forcing lower courts to accept the summary judgments of the Supreme Federal Court. That would speed up the decision-making process by eliminating the ability of local judges to make their own decisions. Currently, appeals can delay cases for years. In fact, in 2008 the court received 100,000 cases! There is even a drive-through window so lawyers can drop off their cases without having to leave their cars.

Nonetheless, the strong institutional role of the judiciary vis-à-vis the other branches is a positive sign of horizontal accountability. When viewed in light of the impeachment of President Collor, it is clear that Brazil has democratized in important ways since the end of the dictatorship. Corruption in particular is pervasive, but political institutions are slowly becoming stronger in a manner that might serve to combat the problem more effectively. For example, twenty-five defendants, including high-profile members of the PT and members of Congress, were found guilty of vote buying in 2012.

Brazil at the International Level

Dilma Rousseff has followed the long-standing presidential pattern of advancing Brazil as both a regional and global power. For example, Brazilian presidents have long championed a permanent seat on the United Nations Security Council. The so-called G4 group of Brazil, Germany, India, and Japan has worked together in tandem for that purpose. In 2010 the administration of Barack Obama publicly supported India's bid, which suggested that future change may occur. Brazil is a central part of Mercosur, as well as newer initiatives like the Union of South American Nations (UNASUR) and the Bank of the South. Lula also emphasized Brazil's military position. In 2009, he announced the purchase of 36 high-tech Rafale fighter jets from France, arguing that Brazil was destined to be a great power in the twenty-first century. That same year, he successfully landed a bid for Rio de Janeiro to host the 2016 Olympic games. Brazil is one of the so-called BRIC countries (Brazil, Russia, India, and China) that are considered the most important emerging economic powers.

This conscious international projection even extends to economics. In the face of the global recession that hit in 2008, the International Monetary Fund asked its members to buy its bonds as a way to increase the funds available for the IMF to act as a lender of last resort. Lula agreed to lend $10 billion to the IMF. Brazil had paid off its previous debt to the IMF in 2005 (two years ahead of schedule) and for the first time acted as creditor to the fund rather than debtor. Economic growth improved despite the recession. Inflation has dropped and has stayed well below 10 percent. All of these results have enhanced the Brazilian government's ability to forge trade agreements and invite investment.

Brazilian leaders have been adept diplomatically, successfully at maintaining positive relationships with different countries—such as the United States and Venezuela—while maintaining policy independence. For example, Lula became deeply involved in the 2009–2010 crisis in Honduras, after President José Manuel Zelaya was overthrown and exiled (discussed in Chapter 6). He secretly made his way back into Honduras and appeared at the Brazilian embassy. Lula agreed to allow him to stay there, despite criticism from the de facto Honduran government. Historically, Brazil has shown little interest in Central America, so this represented a new direction in foreign policy.

As part of a global-oriented strategy, Lula became active in Middle East diplomacy. Working with the Turkish government in 2010, he presented a plan to address the issue of Iran's nuclear program. Although the plan was never implemented, it demonstrated the newly active nature of Brazilian foreign policy. In 2010, Brazil recognized the Palestinian state, one of very few Latin American countries to do so, which was clearly aimed at increasing Brazil's visibility in the Middle East. Rousseff has not followed Lula's orientation exactly, but he still pays close attention to the Middle East, such as voting in the United Nations to send human rights observers to Iran.

Conclusion and Comparative Perspective

Looking over the span of his life, Lula's story is one of rags to political riches. The signs of change in Brazil were further emphasized by his successor, a woman and former guerrilla. As in Chile since 1990, Brazil has come a very long way since the military dictatorship ended in 1985. By 2002, Lula's election demonstrated that all sectors of Brazil were willing to accept the political rules of the game. He demonstrated that it was certainly hard, but by no means impossible for someone to work their way from the local level to the heights of national power. Horizontal and vertical accountability are fragile but improved. In the twenty-first century, there is no fear of a military coup. Lula's own image went from radical reformer to moderate leftist. From a macroeconomic perspective, Brazil had improved considerably. The tiger of inflation had been tamed, exports were varied and competitive, poverty had been reduced from previous astronomical levels, and the country was running a budget surplus. Given these strong indicators, Brazil was able to weather the global recession that began in 2008. This puts the country in a better position to achieve its lofty goals.

Nonetheless, from a socioeconomic perspective Brazil still faces critical challenges that its leaders have never fully addressed. Poverty is still high and inequality remains high by any standard, indeed worse than in most of Latin America, which is already the most unequal region of the world. In the longer term, the question remains whether the social programs initiated under Lula will succeed in relieving poverty and reducing inequality. The latter is negatively correlated with economic development, so is a constant drag on economic growth. Brazil may always be a country of the future, but realizing its potential is no simple task. The pressing problem of race parallels countries like Bolivia or Peru, where a large indigenous population and geographic inequalities make the work even of reformist governments very difficult.

Brazil's political development and institutions share other similarities with its South American neighbors. Indeed, the breakdown of democracy in 1964 marked the beginning of a wave of coups in the region, and the pacted transition in 1985 was similar to Chile and Uruguay. As democracy has become more consolidated, Brazil's federal system shows similar strains to that of Argentina, where regional elites wield a lot of political power and require intense negotiation. Thus, even in the context of fairly strong presidentialism, the executive must constantly bargain to pass national-level policies.

Like Venezuela, Brazil has worked to raise its international profile, becoming more vocal about Middle Eastern politics, for example. This is a relatively new development. During the Cold War, Cuba was the main country actively engaged in the politics of distant countries. Also new is Brazil's interest in mediating regional political conflict, which also mirrors Venezuela. This expansion of its international horizons may mean that Brazil could someday achieve its goal of being the country of the future.

TABLE 11.1 Brazilian Economic Indicators, 1991–2011

Year	GDP Growth	Inflation	Unemployment	Poverty Rate	Human Development Index
1991	1.0	475.1	4.8	—	0.804
1992	−0.3	1149.1	5.8	—	0.756
1993	4.5	2489.1	5.4	45.3	0.796
1994	6.2	929.3	5.1	—	0.783
1995	4.2	22.0	4.6	—	0.738
1996	2.9	9.1	5.4	35.8	—
1997	3.0	4.1	5.7	—	0.739
1998	0.0	1.7	7.6	—	0.747
1999	0.3	8.9	7.6	37.5	—
2000	4.3	6.0	7.1	—	—
2001	1.3	7.7	6.2	37.5	0.777
2002	2.7	12.5	11.7	—	0.775
2003	1.1	9.3	12.3	38.7	—
2004	5.7	7.2	11.5	37.7	—
2005	3.2	5.7	9.8	36.3	0.800
2006	4.0	3.1	10.0	33.3	—
2007	5.7	4.5	9.4	30.0	0.813
2008	5.9	5.9	7.9	25.8	—
2009	−0.6	4.3	8.1	—	—
2010	7.7	5.6	6.8	—	0.727
2011	2.7	6.6	6.0	—	0.728

Sources: Unemployment: *GDP and Inflation: Preliminary Overview of the Economies of Latin America the Caribbean*, 1994–2012.
Poverty rate: *Social Panorama of Latin America*. Economic Commission for Latin America, 1990–2012.
Human development index: United Nations, *Human Development Report*, 1990–2013.

Key Terms

- Lula
- Estado Novo
- Abertura
- Fernando Henrique Cardoso

- Workers' Party
- Brazilian Landless Workers' Movement
- Dilma Rousseff

Critical Thinking Questions

- To what degree did Lula seem to be following similar economic policies as his predecessors despite his leftist political background?
- Compare the experience of federalism in Brazil to other Latin American countries with federal systems. What accounts for different levels of political fragmentation?
- In what ways have Afro-Brazilians entered Brazilian politics? How effective have they been in promoting racial equality?
- Discuss the changing patterns of Brazil's efforts to establish itself as a global leader. What changes have occurred and why?
- Analyze the effects of open-list proportional representation on the executive's ability to get bills passed. How does this compare to other Latin American countries?

Further Sources

Books

Avritzer, Leonardo. *Participatory Institutions in Democratic Brazil* (Baltimore: The Johns Hopkins University Press, 2009). This book analyzes the ways in which Brazil has increased popular participation in politics after the transition to democracy. It examines the specific issues of budgeting, health councils, and city master plans to analyze the successes of local level participatory institutions.

Baer, Werner. *The Brazilian Economy: Growth and Development*, 6th edition (Boulder: Lynne Rienner Publishers, 2008). A highly readable but also comprehensive look at the Brazilian economy throughout its history, but focusing on the post-1945 era. In addition to analysis of economic policy, it includes separate chapters on such issues as environmental degradation, health care, and inequality.

Kingstone, Peter R. and Timothy J. Power (eds.). *Democratic Brazil Revisited* (Pittsburgh: University of Pittsburgh Press, 2008). This edited volume is broken into sections on the PT, political institutions, inequality, and democratization viewed from below. The authors are all acknowledged experts on Brazilian politics, and they offer insights into what has changed and what has remained the same as a result of Lula's presidency.

Montero, Alfred P. *Brazilian Politics: Reforming a Democratic State in a Changing World* (Cambridge: Polity Press, 2005). A concise and well-written introductory survey of Brazilian politics, analyzing state-building, representation, democratization, civil society, and international political economy.

Vidal Luna, Francisco and Herbert S. Klein, *Brazil Since 1980* (New York: Cambridge University Press, 2006). This is an accessible introduction to contemporary Brazilian politics and economics. It pays special attention to education, demography, and inequality.

Web Sites

Brazil News (http://www.brazilnews.com/). This is a useful aggregator for news on Brazilian politics and economics, all in English. It is also possible to sign in and join groups that focus on specific topics.

Chamber of Deputies (http://www2.camara.gov.br/english/). This is the chamber's official English-version Web site. It provides descriptions of the legislature's functions and structure. It also includes the latest version of the Brazilian constitution in English.

Landless Worker's Movement (http://www.mstbrazil.org/). The MST maintains an official Web site in English. Its primary purpose is to provide updated news stories on issues of interest to the organization.

Library of Congress Guide to Brazilian Law Online (http://www.loc.gov/law/help/guide/nations/brazil.php). The U.S. Library of Congress maintains an extensive list of links to sources on Brazilian law, and many of them are in English. There are links to information on the executive, legislative, and judicial branches, as well as specific Web sites on such issues as children's rights, labor laws, and human rights legislation.

OECD: Brazil (http://www.oecd.org/brazil). The Organization of Economic Cooperation and Development has statistics about the Brazilian economy. There are more 100 different economic indicators.

Endnotes

1. Bourne, Richard. *Lula of Brazil: The Story So Far.* (Berkeley: University of California Press, 2008), 155.
2. Stepan, Alfred. *The Military in Politics: Changing Patterns in Brazil* (Princeton: Princeton University Press, 1971), 85.
3. O'Donnell, Guillermo. "Human Development, Human Rights, and Democracy." In Guillermo O'Donnell, Jorge Vargas Cullell, and Osvaldo M. Iazzetta (eds), *The Quality of Democracy: Theory and Applications* (Notre Dame, IN: University of Notre Dame Press, 2004), 9–92.
4. Abreu, Marcelo de P., Afonso S. Bevilaqua and Demosthenes M. Pinho. "Import Substitution and Growth in Brazil, 1890s–1970s." In Enrique Cárdenas, José Antonio Campo, and Rosemary Thorp (eds.), *An Economic History of Twentieth Century Latin America*, volume 3 (New York: Palgrave, 2000), 162.
5. Roett, Riordan. *Brazil: Politics in a Patrimonial Society*, 3rd edition (New York: Praeger, 1984), 167.
6. Lunda, Francisco Vidal and Herbert S. Klein. *Brazil Since 1980* (New York: Cambridge University Press, 2006), 49.
7. Baer, Werner. *The Brazilian Economy: Growth and Development* (Boulder: Lynne Rienner Publishers, 2008), 230–232.
8. Alvarez, Sonia E. "The (Trans)formation of Feminism(s) and Gender Politics in Democratizing Brazil." In Jane S. Jaquette (ed.), *The Women's Movement in Latin America: Participation and Democracy*, 2nd edition (Boulder: Westview Press, 1994), 13–63.
9. Miguel, Luis F. "Political Representation and Gender in Brazil: Quotas for Women and their Impact." *Bulletin of Latin American Research* 27, 2 (2008) : 202.
10. Htun, Mala and Timothy J. Power. "Gender, Parties, and Support for Equal Rights in the Brazilian Congress." *Latin American Politics & Society* 48, 4 (2006): 83–84.

11. Baer 2008, 1.
12. Montero, Alfred P. *Brazilian Politics* (Cambridge, MA: Polity, 2005), 75.
13. Montero 2005, 58.
14. McCann, Bryan. *The Throes of Democracy: Brazil Since 1989* (London: Zed Books, 2008), 42–43.
15. Avritzer, Leonardo. *Participatory Institutions in Democratic Brazil* (Baltimore: The Johns Hopkins University Press, 2009).
16. Houtzager, Peter P. and Adrian Gurza Lavalle. "Civil Society's Claims to Political Representation in Brazil." *Studies in Comparative International Development* 45, 1 (March 2010): 1–29.
17. McCann 2008, 85.
18. De Jesus, María Carolina. *Child of the Dark* (New York, Signet Books, 1962), 42.
19. Pereira, Anthony W. "Public Security, Private Interests, and Police Reform in Brazil." In Peter R. Kingstone and Timothy J. Power (eds.), *Democratic Brazil Revisited* (Pittsburgh: University of Pittsburgh Press, 2008), 190–191.
20. Arias, Enrique Desmond. *Drugs and Democracy in Rio de Janeiro* (Chapel Hill: University of North Carolina Press, 2006), 32.
21. Taylor, Matthew M. *Judging Policy: Courts and Policy Reform in Democratic Brazil* (Stanford: Stanford University Press, 2008), 13–14.
22. Montero 2005, 40.

CHAPTER 12

Argentina

LEARNING OBJECTIVES

- Identify how the three levels of analysis interact in Argentina

- Use theoretical propositions to understand political and economic development in Argentina

- Explain how and why political and economic development in Argentina differs from other Latin American countries

TIMELINE

1816	Independence declared
1829–1852	Rule of Juan Manuel de Rosas
1946	Juan Perón elected president
1955	Juan Perón overthrown
1966–1973	Military rule
1976	Military coup launches dictatorship and "dirty war"
1982	War with Britain over Malvinas/Falklands
1983	Democratic rule resumes
1989	Carlos Menem elected
1990	Final of four military rebellions
2001	Economic crisis and end of the dollar peg
2003	Néstor Kirchner elected president
2007	Cristina Fernández de Kirchner elected president
2011	Cristina Fernández reelected

By 2013, inflation in Argentina had been creeping upward for several years. It got to the point that some shopkeepers did not bother posting prices outside their stores because they kept changing so rapidly.[1] Nonetheless, two successive governments denied that inflation was a problem, which generated considerable controversy. Inflation is reported at the national level, and when it's high, the national government gets the blame. But the most serious effects are felt at the local level, where the poor in particular struggle to keep up with rising prices, especially if their wages do not keep up. Even wealthier citizens feel it if they have bought the government's inflation-indexed bonds, as their return is lower if inflation is underreported. In Argentina, many analysts argue that inflation is at least double what the government reports, and so the mere reporting of the percentage becomes politicized. This affects the international level as well, as foreign investors look closely at economic indicators (Table 12.1) to determine the risk involved in putting their money into the Argentine economy. Given Argentina's truly turbulent economic situation in the not too distant past, which was much worse, the government managed to maintain a solid base of support.

From the perspective of modernization, Argentina is a unique case because it is a country that supposedly already arrived more than a hundred years ago. As the twentieth century began, the cattle trade was booming and many observers considered Argentina on a par with Europe. The connection with Europe was further enhanced by a large immigrant population, especially from Italy. Today, the broad avenues of the capital Buenos Aires and buildings like the magnificent opera house (the Teatro Colón, which opened in 1908) are testament to the belief that Argentina had already arrived in both material and cultural terms.

Modernization theory would therefore confidently predict that democracy and stable political institutions would follow, but they have not. In fact, Argentina is the wealthiest country to suffer a military coup and, as two political scientists have noted, Argentine politics have been characterized by a "Hobbesian world of extreme uncertainty, short time horizons, and low levels of trust and cooperation."[2] That political context has left Argentina struggling with political crises that affect the economy and, at time, threaten democracy itself. Grand theory does little to advance our understanding of Argentine politics, and instead we have to take a closer look at issues like populism as well as the interaction of political institutions, particularly the nature of the federal system.

Historical Roots of Political and Economic Development

Argentina declared independence in 1816, and General José de San Martín successfully defeated Spanish troops two years later. The Vice Royalty of Rio de la Plata was an important part of the Spanish Empire, but it chafed under the crown's mercantilist policies. But independence did nothing to unify the country, as efforts to centralize authority were defeated, and it slid toward anarchy. The provinces did manage to come together and form a confederation, where

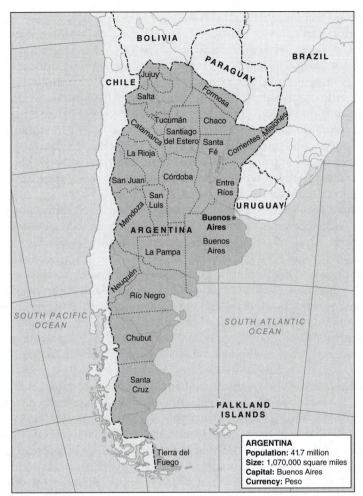

Map of Argentina

they held primary power, and there was virtually no central authority. It is notable that during this period, in 1825, Argentina supported its neighbor Uruguay's fight to become independent from Brazil, which had annexed it several years earlier. The two countries have had close—though sometimes difficult—ties ever since.

The Importance of Federalism

There has always been tension between the capital of Buenos Aires and the outlying areas of the country's interior. Those disputes are still present, and under a federal system the states and the central government are in a more or less constant struggle for political power. The power vacuum ended when caudillo and dictator Juan Manuel de Rosas forced authority on the regions with a vengeance, ruling from 1829 until 1852. His political opponents (of which there were many) succeeded in overthrowing him in 1852, and he lived in Great Britain until his death. His legacy, however, was considerable. Until the 1916 elections, Argentine politics was characterized by oligarchic stability and enough elite consensus to avoid prevent internal disputes from becoming civil war. A new constitution in 1853 formally established a federal system, the structure of which remains largely in place today. During much of the nineteenth century, there was contestation about the relative power of the central government and the provinces, but there were also a fight for power between the provinces themselves, especially in terms of weaker provinces coming together to counter Buenos Aires, by far the most powerful.

Relative stability brought economic development. Argentina is a very large country, with enormous "pampas" (plains) ideal for cattle. Successive liberal governments attracted foreign capital and established infrastructure to facilitate international trade. By the end of the nineteenth century, in comparison with much of the world the Argentine population was relatively well-educated, well-fed, and industrious. Waves of European immigrants also contributed, trying to find employment opportunities, and the Argentine government responded by liberalizing immigration laws to facilitate their arrival. The government actively encouraged this immigration for both economic and racial reasons, as it served to populate the *pampas* while also whitening the population in general. Buenos Aires began to resemble European cities. Argentina had only a very small indigenous population—always minuscule and currently less than 1 percent of the population—and so it consciously borrowed many high cultural characteristics from Europe instead. What this also means is that Argentina has faced far less indigenous conflict than most Latin American countries, and national identity has been greatly affected by its European immigrants. The same is true of Uruguay.

British investment in particular spurred growth. Infrastructure such as railroads built by the British facilitated connection between the pampas and ports. The so-called Conquest of the Desert entailed subsidies for cultivating land in distant regions. By the turn of the century, not only were meatpacking, wool, and other cattle industries booming (even today, Argentina far exceeds all other Latin American countries in consumption of animal protein), but so was production of wheat, corn, and linseeds. Land was concentrated into a small number of hands, and the landed oligarchy became politically powerful both in rural areas and in cities, where the state embarked on large public works projects. Argentina seemed to have achieved the types of growth that would qualify it as "modern." On the other hand, it relied heavily on one set of commodities and imported finished goods from Europe and the United States.

The Perils of National Political Competition

Argentine politics shifted for good in 1916, when Hipólito Yrigoyen won the presidency. He was from the **Radical Civic Union Party (UCR)**. The UCR emerged in the 1890s in opposition to the elitist nature of national politics, opening the door for a shift toward polyarchy. Universal male suffrage had just been

ARGENTINA'S POLITICAL INSTITUTIONS

Last constitution: 1994

Federal system with twenty-three provinces plus the Federal District (formally known as an "autonomous city") of Buenos Aires

Executive: President with four-year term, one reelection allowed

Legislative: Bicameral with 72 senators (plurality vote) and 256 members of the Chamber of Deputies (proportional representation)

Judicial: Supreme Court with judicial review

granted in 1912 (immigrants and women still could not vote) and so Yrigoyen was able to appeal to many newly enfranchised voters. Because the legislature was still controlled by conservatives, he found it difficult to get much passed, but the very fact that free and fair elections became a norm was critical for Argentine democracy. Until the mid-1940s, Argentina had divided government, so political competition was high as no single party was able to establish monolithic control. However, the global depression that struck in 1929 devastated the economy. Meanwhile, urbanization and immigration had created an urban working class whose demands were not being met. Yrigoyen had been reelected in 1928 but was overthrown in 1930 by retired General José Uriburu.

From then on, the military expanded its political influence and the country grew more polarized. As one Argentine historian puts it, politicians "reduced all their enemies to one: high finances and imperialism combined with the Communists, the foreigners responsible for national disintegration, and also the Jews, all united in a sinister conspiracy."[3] The army was given a privileged position in terms of budgeting and clientelist connections and professional issues became subsumed by political ones. During this period, the state also embarked on import substitution industrialization, for although World War II created markets for both meat and grains, the economic crash had made clear that relying on primary products alone was not sustainable.

Contemporary Politics in Argentina

The armed forces took power again in 1943, and Colonel **Juan Domingo Perón** served both as vice president and as minister of war. Sympathy for fascism was evident from the fact that the government refused to declare war or break relations with Germany until the war was nearly over (breaking relations only in 1944 and declaring war in 1945). Perón was jailed by fellow members of the army fearful of his growing popularity, but protests led to his release and then new elections. In 1946 he organized his own political party and won the presidential election, with reelection in 1951. His government wrote a new constitution in 1949 that further expanded presidential power. He went after his radical opponents, including a 1950 law aimed at their direction that broadly prohibited slander against public officials. His authoritarian style, combined with his mobilization of the working class, made him dangerous in the eyes of many political elites.

The Role of Peronism in Argentine Politics

What became known as Peronism (though the party itself was officially named the **Justicialist (Peronist) Party**) was based on a populist appeal to the masses, and Perón connected with unions in particular and they became his political base. In practice this meant the construction of corporatist institutions, such as the General Confederation of Labor (CGT) that would establish central control over unions, and channel benefits—such as raises—downward all the way to the local level. Peronism can be difficult to pin down precisely, because even Perón himself was not always consistent. But the state is the driving force of the economy in conjunction with private business. Peronism was antagonistic toward both socialism and communism, and instead was oriented more toward state capitalism. As elsewhere, import substitution was intended to propel the country forward from its focus on the export of primary goods. In the context of the Cold War, Perón drew an ideological line between a command economy on one side, and a market economy on the other. Unfortunately, that line satisfied nearly no one.

As a result, he (and his movement even after his death) generated very complex responses. Large industries, especially those oriented toward export and connected to foreign capital, tended to oppose him. Other industries, particularly those producing for the domestic market, shifted according to whether his policies at any given time benefited them. For example, Perón's policies increased levels of domestic consumption, which was favorable to business, but his policies of protectionism hurt companies that imported much of their raw materials. As Perón developed the idea of a "social economy," he encountered opposition from businesses that argued they were unable to raise wages while remaining competitive. As many business sectors turned against him, they found support from the armed forces. Still, his style of state capitalism and support for labor provide him with a large and fervent base of support. Even so, in 1950 a prominent history of Latin America argued that "Argentina is basically one of the richest and most progressive of the American Republics."[4]

Evita Perón became an integral part of her husband's political success. Only 26 when she married Juan Perón, she quickly became a core symbol of his populist policies. Her 1951 autobiography perfectly summarizes the image they were trying to create. It had a conscious religious flavor to it, and even compares the era of Peronism to the time of Jesus Christ's birth, and suggests that the Christmas cider and spiced loaves they handed out were similar to the wine and bread of communion. At its height, the populism of Peronism reached that level of idolatry. She died in 1952 (only 33 years old) of cervical cancer, and although Peronism would live on, it did not regain that same semi-mythical quality (and in her case real life is far more interesting than the movie version with Madonna). Perón himself never reached that level of idolatry again.

President Juan Perón's wife Evita has become famous across the world, still known many years after her death and even the inspiration for a fairly bad Hollywood movie. She was instrumental in cementing support for Perón's populist government. Her memoir gives many examples of how she successfully made Argentines feel connected personally to her.

Evita, My Mission in Life (1951)

Reason, with me, often has to give way to emotion; and so, to explain the life I lead today, that is to say, what I am doing now out of motives that spring from the bottom of my heart, I have to go back and search through my earliest years for the first feelings that make sense, or at least explain, what to those severe critics is "an incomprehensible sacrifice," but which to me is neither sacrifice nor incomprehensible.

I have discovered a fundamental feeling in my heart which completely governs my spirit and my life. That feeling is my indignation when faced with injustice.

Ever since I can remember, all injustice has hurt my soul though something were stabbing it. Memories of injustice against which I rebelled at every age still rankle.

I remember very well how sad I was for many days when I first realized that there were poor and rich in the world; and the strange thing is that the fact of the existence of the poor did not hurt me so much as the knowledge that, at the same time, the rich existed.

...

Why didn't the humble men, the workers of my country, take the same attitude as the "ordinary men," instead of understanding Perón and believing in him?

There is only one explanation: that one needs only to see Perón to believe in him, in his sincerity, in his loyalty and in his openness.

They saw him, and believed.

What happened in Bethlehem nearly two thousand years ago was repeated here. The first to believe were not the rich, not the wise, not the powerful, but the humble.

For almost always the rich, the wise, and the powerful are hedged in by egoism and selfishness.

On the other hand, the poor, as at Bethlehem, live and sleep in the open air, and the windows of their simple souls are almost always open to out-of-the-ordinary things.

That is why they saw and believed. They also saw that a man was risking all for them. I know well how many times he risked all for his people on one single throw.

Happily, he won. Otherwise he would have lost everything, including his life.

I, meanwhile, kept my promise to "be at his side."

I held the lamp that lighted his darkness; I kept it burning as best I knew how, guarding his flank with my love and my faith.

Often I saw him from a corner in his office in the loved Secretariat of Labor and Welfare, listening to the humble workingmen of my country, speaking to them of their problems, giving them the explanations they had been craving for many years. Never will those first pictures of our life together be erased from my memory.

...

And when I saw him clasp the hard and horny hands of the workers I could not help thinking that in him and by him my people, for the first time, were shaking hands with happiness.

...

Today is Christmas, Christmas of 1950. Last night, in five million Argentine homes, toasts were drunk in the cider, and the spiced loaves from "Perón and Evita" were eaten.

This, too, our adversaries have severely criticized.

They have told us that we throw crumbs onto the tables of the Argentines so as to buy the good will of the people.

...

But the average person does not realize that our cider, and our spiced loaves, are nothing more than a symbol of our union with the people.

It is our hearts (mine and Perón's) that wish to be united on Christmas Eve with all the hearts of the country's *descimisados* in an immense, fraternal, affectionate embrace.

Discussion Questions

- How can populism contribute to a strong sense of nationalism?
- How did Evita connect so effectively to the local level?

Source: Eva Perón, *My Mission in Life* (translated from the original by Ethel Cherry) (New York: Vantage Press, 1951), 5–6, 24–25.

The pursuit of import substitution industrialization was a hallmark of Perón but was also later followed by anti-Peronist governments even as they purged Peronists from the government and from unions, so there was consensus that the model was an appropriate step toward greater prosperity. Argentina was the primary case for Guillermo O'Donnell's famous work on bureaucratic-authoritarianism. The number of large state enterprises increased in the 1940s and 1950s, such as in energy, telecommunications and transport, which led to growth. However, this also led to large budget deficits. Perón was overthrown in 1955 by a group of both civilians (particularly business, the Catholic Church, and the middle class) and military officers. They all had different gripes, but all felt threatened by the Peronist movement and Perón's use of presidential power against them and their economic interests. Economically, after the coup successive governments maintained similar economic policies focused on machinery and chemical industries, while also providing incentives for farmers to mechanize.[5] In 1955, the combination of cereals and meats constituted 54 percent of total exports, but over time dependence on those primary resources decreased, down to only 14 percent in 1990.

Between 1955 and 1966, the country was split between Peronists and anti-Peronists. The Peronist Party was alternatively outlawed and legalized, and Perón himself sometimes exiled (at various moments to Paraguay, Spain, or Venezuela) and other times allowed in the country. President Arturo Frondizi was overthrown by the military in 1962 for legalizing the party, as well as for showing too much sympathy for the Cuban revolution. Arturo Illia of the UCR was then subsequently elected in 1963, but his policies, such as once again legalizing Peronism as well as the Communist Party, soured the military. Perón unsuccessfully tried to enter the country in 1965, though he sent his wife María Estela (known more commonly as Isabel) to provide support for Peronist legislative candidates, and amidst that political conflict Illia was overthrown in 1966.

Argentina's Dirty War

General Juan Carlos Onganía took control, and the military ruled until 1973. The state capitalist model was finally challenged as the government enacted economic austerity policies (such as wage freezes) intended to address the deficits and inflations plaguing the country. To suppress dissent, the government dissolved the legislature, cracked down on unions, stifled university freedoms, and imposed censorship (even to the point of forbidding signs of culture excess like the miniskirt). However, a weak economy and growing political violence, along with disagreement among factions within the armed forces, prompted the military to plan for a return to democracy, and elections were held in 1973. Although Perón was not allowed to run, he was soon allowed to return. Once he was back in Argentina, the president changed the electoral rules, resigning to allow new elections, which Perón won.

The populism embodied by Perón, however, was coming to an end. As O'Donnell puts it, "The effects of modernization were visible in increased social differentiation, which expressed itself in political pluralization, in the emergence of deep inter-industry cleavages, in further penetration (in scope and density) of technocratic roles, and increased political activation of the popular."[6] Perón's corporatist model no longer functioned, as there was little to redistribute, and he could not control leftist guerrilla groups like the Montoneros that launched attacks against the government. There was, in fact, a quite literal explosion of guerrilla groups in the late 1960s and early 1970s. Some were nationalist, others tied to Cuba. Some were urban, while others were more rural. In this context of extremes, Perón died in 1974, and his wife Isabel took power. The conflict deepened, as the right fought back against the Montoneros, and strikes crippled the country. The military overthrew her in 1976.

The military government that emerged from the coup was extraordinarily violent. It intensified what became known as the "Dirty War" against perceived ideological enemies. One of the more chilling accounts of that internal war is *The Flight*, a book consisting of an interview with a naval officer who worked at the infamous military intelligence unit at the Navy School of Mechanics. Prisoners were drugged and put on airplanes:

> In their unconscious state, the prisoners were stripped, and when the commander of the airplane gave the order, which happened according to where the plane was, the hatch was opened and they were thrown out naked, one by one.

That's the story. A gruesome story, but true, and no one can deny it. I can't get rid of the image of the naked bodies lined up in the plane's aisles, like something in a movie about Nazis.[7]

The military regime referred to the period as a "Process of National Reorganization," or "**Proceso**," led by General Jorge Rafael Videla. That reorganization would destroy the urban guerrillas, eliminate leftists, attempt to bring back traditional Catholic cultural values and generally seek to restore the idealized vision of Argentina of a different era. Particularly because of ties the Montoneros had with provincial governors and other political actors, the military associated virtually anyone with leftist subversion. Estimates of deaths during this "process" range upward of 30,000. As in other countries, the violence politicized many women, whose husbands and sons had disappeared. In 1977, the "**Mothers of the Plaza de Mayo**" held their first silent protest (see Box 12.1).

These mothers were not the only protestors. There were other family-based groups, but also civil libertarians and religious movements.[8] Some of them had existed prior to the dictatorship and shifted their activities in opposition to it. One example is the Argentine League for the Rights of Man and Permanent Assembly for Human Rights, which was founded in 1937, but during the Proceso began systematically collecting information on almost 6,000 of the disappeared. These local and national-level groups then linked up with international actors in the United States and Europe, which raised their profile and also made it more difficult—though definitely not impossible—for the military government to target those groups. There was, therefore, a very important international influence for what otherwise was a domestic issue. As political scientist Alison Brysk has argued, "Argentine human rights protest combined with other national movements to shape a new international climate of issue awareness and legitimacy—especially in the United States."[9]

The dictatorship itself also had far-reaching (and much more damaging) international implications. Argentina became a member of the Chile-led Operation Condor, which abducted and/or killed political opponents when they had fled their country of origin. The junta also actively supported the Contra rebels in Nicaragua and was involved in Central America as early as 1977, concerned that President Jimmy Carter was becoming too "soft" on Communism. Argentine military intelligence helped to organize the first Contra battalion to fight the Sandinista government.

The military government's attack on labor (which included military occupation of key factories in addition to repression), along with a cut in tariffs, hit industry hard and increased unemployment. At the same time, the government was concerned about unemployment becoming too high, which could push workers into the opposition, so it took on a large amount of debt. External debt grew from $6.4 million in 1969 to $64.7 million in 1989. Following the same logic, no major state industries were privatized. The government was also unable to reduce inflation, which consistently ran over 100 percent, and in 1980 a series of bank failings prompted capital flight. Meanwhile, an overvalued peso hurt export industries. Internal schisms within the armed forces were an

BOX 12.1

The Mothers of the Plaza de Mayo

International: The Plaza de Mayo is the main plaza in Buenos Aires, where the presidential building (the "Casa Rosada") and other key political institutions are located and has been a central geographical point for politics throughout Argentine history. In 1977, a newly formed group of local women (only fourteen to begin with) began a silent and peaceful protest in the plaza in front of the Casa Rosada against the dictatorship's repression.

They became a formal organization in 1980 and by 1982, the Madres claimed to have 2,500 members.[10] They forged ties with domestic and international human rights nongovernmental organizations and helped to bring together the opposition after the disastrous Falklands-Malvinas war with Great Britain. The movement was remarkable for its ability to oppose the military government in a way that would have been virtually impossible in any other form. Their marches punctured the military's carefully crafted image of saviors, an image that was all too often accepted abroad, such as in the United States.

National: Their goal was to find out what had happened to their children, who had disappeared. They were initially ignored, but they kept coming back, thus posing a dilemma for the military junta. In an era of fear and brutality, this act represented a major

act of defiance. Eventually they wore white handkerchiefs and carried signs with photos of their children, with the phrase "Where Are They?" They were explicitly nonviolent and their marches were largely silent. Their role as women and mothers allowed them to move more freely and to avoid being tagged as "subversive" to the same degree as men. For these reasons, they consciously avoided allowing men to march with them.

Local: Over time, the movement splintered as disagreement spread about what types of local issues should be pursued. After the dictatorship ended, democratic governments gradually began seeking answers to their questions, and the common enemy of the military regime no longer existed. The organization took on a more ideological message, focusing on social justice and socialism more generally, which prompted some women to leave. In 2006 they held their last march for the disappeared but continued to march on behalf of other issues they considered important.

Discussion Questions

- In what ways can the unity of a locally organized group be affected by political change at the national level?
- Why are international connections so important for human rights activists who live in a dictatorship?

---

obstacle to coherent economic policy making, as free market advocates clashed with traditional state capitalists.

Facing severe problems at home, in 1982 the government followed the time-honored strategy of stirring nationalist sentiment by going to war. The

Islas Malvinas (or Falkland Islands, depending on who you're asking) were taken by Great Britain in 1833 and have been claimed by Argentina ever since. The military leadership assumed that the United States would not respond (because it was an anti-Communist ally) and that Great Britain would not pursue war. They turned out to be wrong on both counts, and Argentina was routed in the ensuing war in just two months. The islands continue to be a bone of contention, as even today successive Argentine governments demand their return. Back in 1982, the military was therefore in a position where it showed itself unable either to run an economy or to win war. Soon thereafter, President (and retired General) Reynaldo Bignone called for elections to be held in 1983.

This was a transition by imposition, as the armed forces left power very unpopular, in disarray, and in a position of considerable weakness. This meant that, unlike in Chile for example, the new civilian government immediately sought not only to investigate but also to prosecute human rights abuses. UCR candidate **Raúl Alfonsín** won 52 percent in the 1983 presidential election, which marked the first time a Peronist candidate (Ítalo Lúder, a former senator who once had been acting president in 1975 while Isabel Perón took sick leave) had lost a free election. The military budget was cut, salaries reduced, positions eliminated, and new laws passed that shifted power from military commanders to the Ministry of Defense. Meanwhile, the military believed that Alfonsín's social democratic leanings were overly leftist, which created yet another undercurrent of tension. The prestige of the armed forces was badly damaged. At the same time, the collapse of the military regime left a very bad taste in the mouths of many military officers and therefore it took years to stabilize civil-military relations and establish any sense of trust between elected officials and the military leadership.

The Postauthoritarian Era

Raúl Alfonsín was not in an enviable position. The public clamored for justice for the massive abuses of human rights. Alfonsín had made a campaign promise to bring officers to trial, which of course was anathema to the armed forces. Four military rebellions occurred between 1987 and 1990, though they never had broad enough support to seriously threaten Argentine democracy. Nonetheless, they prompted the legislature to pass a "Full Stop Law" (*ley de punto final*) in 1986 that ended prosecutions. It also included a "Law of Due Obedience" that protected junior officers from prosecution if they were just following orders, which was intended to pacify the armed forces sufficiently to end the rebellions. These laws would not be rescinded until 2003. In 1988 the legislature also passed a new Defense Law that expressly prohibited the participation of the armed forces in internal security. This was a particularly important reform, because it formally denied the military any legal right to intervene in domestic politics. The share of military spending went from 3.8 percent in 1985 to 1.7 percent in 1995. The long era of military influence was over.

The Dilemma of Balancing Political and Economic Demands

For the economy, Alfonsín tried to balance the need for market stabilization with recognition of political resistance to its effects. His first presidential address emphasized, for example, that the state must be beholden neither to international finance nor to local oligarchies, while also avoiding taking control of national businesses. He faced serious economic problems. Inflation rose, while there were rapid changes—both up and down—in the exchange rate, wages, and the interest rate that discouraged investment and hampered economic growth. By 1985 inflation had risen to 1,800 percent.

In response, in 1985 Alfonsín passed the Austral Plan, the centerpiece of which was the replacement of the old peso with a new currency, the austral. It also imposed austerity, with wage and price controls along with budget cuts to tame the inflation tiger. By 1988, the minimum wage was lower than it was in 1980. Not surprisingly, his policies were politically unpopular, which raised the profile of the Peronist Party as it criticized Alfonsín for failing to consider the consequences for workers. Indeed, the plan soon proved ineffective because wage freezes combined with inflation to seriously cut into living standards. Although Alfonsín did manage to pass legislation like the Austral Plan, Peronists blocked many initiatives and slowed others down, thus making his job even more difficult.

Argentine federalism and presidentialism had a negative impact as well. The president, who has considerable power, still has to constantly fight regional elites to forge national policy. Those regional leaders are far more concerned with their own constituencies than with coherent policy making at the national level. In a survey of seventy-five countries, Argentina ranked last in terms of tax collection, social security contributions, and payment of minimum wages.[11] As a result, there are constant battles over resources. Elected officials at the state and local levels have the authority to write their own laws governing revenue sharing, so their relationship with the national government is practically impenetrable. At any given time, therefore, the Argentine president cannot necessarily count on his or her decisions to carry much weight. In particular, governors can effectively drag their feet or dictate how national laws will be interpreted.

Market Reforms Under Carlos Menem

Carlos Menem was elected in 1989 at yet another turbulent moment. Menem was a Peronist who had curried the favor of Perón himself, had served in a number of different party positions since his youth, and had been imprisoned after the coup. He seemed to offer a breath of fresh air in difficult times. Alfonsín actually resigned six months before his presidency ended because of massive looting and a major loss of legitimacy. Foreign debt was about $63 billion, inflation was almost 5,000 percent, and gross domestic product (GDP) was negative. Not surprisingly, this led to major social unrest. In that turbulent context, Menem won the presidency while his party won a majority in the senate (28 of 46 seats) and almost a majority in the lower house (124 of 254). He therefore had a solid mandate to embark on reforms to halt hyperinflation and encourage economic growth.

Much of the election outcome's uncertainty hinged on the fact that Menem ran on a traditional populist Peronist platform. Given the wave of Peronist-led strikes that had hit the country during the 1980s, there was broad concern that a Menem victory would entail a new cycle of state spending and inflation. Despite his campaign promises, however, Menem immediately signaled that he planned to enact market-oriented reforms that would be markedly anti-Peronist. He surrounded himself with business leaders and economists, and abandoned the rhetoric that had brought him to the presidency. That also meant rejecting most of what Peronism originally signified and what Menem had promised, which was an activist state.

Economic problems were deeply entrenched. Hyperinflation was stubborn, going upward of 3,000 to 5,000 percent in the late 1980s and in the very beginning of the 1990s. Real wages fell during the same period. Menem's economic policies were the opposite of traditional Peronism, because they weakened labor and reduced the role of the state in the economy. Between 1990 and 1993, over 100,000 public sector workers were fired or retired. President Menem named Domingo Cavallo as Minister of the Economy in early 1991, and he created the "Convertibility Plan," which pegged the peso to the dollar. The Central Bank was required to keep in reserve (in dollars or gold) the entire amount of money supply in the country, and it could print money only if reserves grew higher than the existing money supply.

Menem had already been privatizing hundreds of state-owned industries, including the national telephone company and national airline, which brought the necessary capital to the Central Bank to cover any demand for dollars. The main idea was that fiscal stability would encourage Argentines to keep their pesos and thereby eliminate any desire for a run on dollars. The initial results were very positive, particularly because inflation dropped very quickly. Consumers then felt more confident and GDP began to grow again. Menem, though, was not universally popular. Unemployment remained stubbornly in double digits, for example, and there were large strikes in 1996. The mid-1990s saw the rise of a new political party, the Front for a Crisis in Solidarity (FREPASO). It brought together a host of small leftist parties, the unifying theme of which was the corruption of the Menem administration. FREPASO joined forces with the UCR to form an anti-Peronist electoral bloc. Their new Alliance for Jobs, Justice, and Education won a plurality in the 1997 midterm elections. As a result, Menem found many of his initiatives blocked by the legislature.

Economic recovery, however, gave Menem an important political boost. He successfully pushed for constitutional reform that allowed him to run for reelection in 1995 (later he unsuccessfully tried to gain a third term). He won the election with 45 percent of the vote over the FREPASO candidate's 29 percent. The UCR stumbled along at only 17 percent and was never able to recover the support it had once enjoyed.

As political scientist Steven Levitsky has argued, the fluid nature of the Peronist party structure allowed it not just to survive but even to thrive in a time of rapid economic change.[12] The party is mass-based and populist, and those origins meant it never developed a strong bureaucratic hierarchy. The relationship between the party and unions, which formed the core of Peronist support, were never formalized, so could change over time and adapt to changing conditions in the country. The result is that party leaders like Menem could change the party's direction without destroying it. And, as we shall see, in the future new leaders would swing the party back toward its traditional roots.

There was also a rise of opposition organization at the local level. Given the economic turmoil, unions and political parties alike suffered from a legitimacy crisis. Protests broke out in towns during 1993 and 1994, and so were called *puebladas* (town revolts). They were directed largely at local officials and focused on receiving back wages while also protecting existing jobs that were threatened by structural adjustment policies. Though usually brief, their intensity led to the fall of several provincial governments.[13] When the national money supply dried up in 2001, local groups also sprang up to provide a formal framework for bartering. Over three million people participated in such barter groups in 2001 and 2002.

Fernando de la Rúa of the FREPASO/UCR alliance won the 1999 presidential election with 48 percent of the vote over the Peronist Eduardo Duhalde (at 38 percent). At that time, both the Argentine politics and the country's economy appeared to be more stable than they had been in years. Meanwhile, the Convertibility Plan had fostered steady economic growth. A dollar peg provides a large dose of predictability, because the U.S. dollar does not fluctuate wildly. On the other hand, it takes considerable power from the government, in some cases leaving it unable to respond effectively to crisis. For Argentina, the crisis came in 1999 when Brazil devalued its currency. The Menem administration had been borrowing to repay past debt, so the appearance of economic stability was only that. Brazil was (and is) a major trading partner, so the devaluation suddenly made Argentine goods much more expensive for Brazilian consumers. The economy slid into recession, and debt ballooned.

The Return of Economic Crisis

The credit crunch is what eventually brought the economy crashing down. For a time, the International Monetary Fund (IMF) continued lending, in part because it had been touting Argentina for years as an example of success. At the end of 2000, for example, the IMF issued an aid package, which the government touted as proof that the international community had confidence in the direction of the economy. Domingo Cavallo returned and tried to find way to swap the debt, which would postpone payment but increase the interest rate, thus of course inflating the debt. But when it became clear in 2001 that convertibility was doomed, the IMF announced it would not provide the $1.24 billion loan that Argentina needed.

The end of 2001 and the beginning of 2002 were a time of economic collapse and political upheaval in Argentina. The recession had made it even more difficult for the government to pay the country's debts, and reserves were dwindling. To avoid capital flight, President de la Rúa limited bank account cash withdrawals, leaving people unable to access their money and prompting riots. The flow of capital between banks slowed to a trickle, and therefore loans for any purpose quickly became very difficult to obtain. Inflation actually became negative, indicating that demand was extremely low and people simply did not have money. Legislative elections in 2001 demonstrated the broad discontent with politics, as participation dropped and the number of spoiled votes rose. The major unrest that followed all these developments forced the president's resignation in December 2001.

There were major local implications. In 2002, neighborhood assemblies also appeared, particularly in lower-income areas of Buenos Aires. They included members of the middle class who had been hit hard and whose job status was either unemployed or unstable. These unique assemblies informally took on the characteristics of local government, with committees focusing on different topics (such as services and health). Like the town revolts, they did not affiliate with any political party, but instead worked to find solutions to local problems. One of their dilemmas, however, was that their perception of the political was not uniform. That meant the members often disagreed about whether to work within existing political channels, or to take more drastic steps such as occupying buildings. Regardless, the movements did create a sense of empowerment for people who otherwise felt alienated from politics. Organizing local food distribution was a prominent example, as the sense of state absence fostered cooperation and interaction that had not existed before. The assemblies eventually dissolved, but many of their members became part of new organizations.

Federalism in Argentina also contributed to the economic crisis. The political system grants considerable authority to state governments in a complex relationship known as "coparticipation." So, for example, national taxes get redistributed to state governments. It also allows for state governments to become heavily indebted and run budget deficits, which in turn has periodically prompted national bailouts of insolvent states. As the financial crisis deepened and the national government was unable to fill state coffers, the provinces used their authority to find other solutions. Short of cash, some provinces began to print their own money, which was not convertible elsewhere. Capital flight ensued, as Argentines who held dollars began to get them out of the country.

After de la Rúa's resignation, a period of confusion set in, which only inflamed the crisis. A period of what has been called *parliamentarization* of Argentine presidentialism set in, as presidents left office in bewildering rotation when confidence in their governments sank. FREPASO even dissolved completely. The vice president had already resigned, so the presidency went to the president of the senate, Ramón Puerto, who did not want the job and resigned after two days. The position then went to the president of the Chamber of Deputies, Eduardo Camaño, who also lasted only two days. At that point, the legislature voted for Governor Adolfo Rodríguez Saá, who was in office for a very unpopular week. The legislature then turned to Eduardo Duhalde, a Peronist senator, in early 2002. He remained in office for a year and a half.

Duhalde's most important move was to end the dollar peg in January 2002. The immediate result was devaluation and inflation as prices shot up. Unemployment went over 20 percent and the poverty rate increased to 45 percent. Duhalde announced that Argentina would default on its debt, arguing that the state needed to address the needs of its citizens rather than follow neoliberal dictates. But no such assistance was forthcoming, and millions of Argentines scrambled one way or another to find ways to make ends meet. After police killed two protestors in 2002, Duhalde called for new elections to be held the following year as a way to promote stability.

The crisis had important national political repercussions. In particular, the party system sustained a major shock as popular confidence in parties' ability to govern evaporated. The UCR continued its decline. Yet it is also important to keep in mind what did *not* occur, namely, military intervention. Rut Diamint, an expert on Argentine civil-military relations, writes that "the armed forces avoided participation in the process of negotiation that arose with the shift in government, did not voice an institutional position, were not present in the private meetings between candidates, and expressed no political preferences regarding the alternatives that were discussed among Peronist leaders."[14] There still remains a gulf between civilian and military leaders, as the former have not articulated a clear defense policy over the years, and there is still distrust. The fact that Argentine democracy remained in place, however, was an historic achievement. A 2009 poll by *Latinobarómetro* showed that 67 percent of Argentines would not accept a military government under any circumstances. That does mean that almost a third would possibly accept one, but given the country's history of coups it is a relatively low percentage. Meanwhile, 70 percent disagreed that the military should remove a president who was violating the constitution.

The Era of the Kirchners

Peronism got quite a black eye because of the economic crisis but still persevered, in large part due to its continued strong regional links, which served to maintain a solid base of support. A little-known governor of Santa Cruz province, **Néstor Kirchner,** ran on the Peronist ticket in the presidential election of 2003 (another a reminder about how governors are natural presidential candidates in federal systems). A very political tarnished Carlos Menem also ran, and in the first round Menem received 24 percent of the vote to Kirchner's 22 percent. Realizing he had no chance of gaining the majority necessary to win the second round, Menem chose to drop out, and Kirchner became president. He campaigned and then governed on the strategy of focusing on Argentina's domestic economic problems rather than the pressing concerns of foreign creditors. In his inaugural speech, he made no bones about the fact that the state would once again become a major player in the economy: "You must understand that the state will play a leading role; the state's presence or absence constitutes a political attitude." The traditional notion of Peronism thus reemerged.

ANALYZING DOCUMENTS

When Néstor Kirchner took office in 2003, Argentines were looking for solutions to the political and economic turmoil that had plagued the country since 2001. Kirchner rejected the model that had brought on the crisis, and promised a new strategy that would bring the state back into the economy and reduce inequality.

Néstor Kirchner's Inaugural Speech (2003)

The Argentine people have shown a strong preference for the future and change; the level of participation in the elections showed that by thinking differently and respecting diversity, the vast and total majority of Argentines want the same things even if we think differently.

It is not necessary to do a detailed review of our problems in detail to know that our past is full of failure, pain, confrontation, and energies wasted on unproductive struggles, to the point of creating serious confrontations between leaders and the people they represent; to the point of seriously creating confrontations between Argentines.

...

During the nineties, the demands made included obtaining economic gains, especially in terms of controlling inflation. The measure of that success was the profits for the strongest economic groups, the absence of extended stock market growth, and the magnitude of speculative investments. The consolidation of poverty and the condemnation of millions of Argentines to social exclusion, national fragmentation and the enormous and unending foreign debt did not matter.

Thus, in a practice that should not be repeated, it was very difficult to distinguish pragmatic solutions from surgery without anesthesia. An effort was made to reduce politics solely to obtaining electoral results...

At the center our plan is rebuilding national capitalism, which will generate alternatives that will allow us to restore upward social mobility. It is not a matter of closing yourself off to the world, it is not a matter of reactionary nationalism, but rather of intelligence, observation and commitment to the nation. It is enough to see how the most developed nations protect their workers, industries and producers. It involves, therefore, the creation of an Argentina with social progress, where children can aspire to live better than their parents had, based on their effort, capabilities, and work.

That is why it is necessary to promote active policies that will spur the country's development and economic growth, the generation of new jobs, and a better and fairer distribution of income. You must understand that the state will play a principal role; the state's presence or absence constitutes a political attitude.

Of course, it is not a matter of once again of creating pendulum, ranging from omnipresent and overwhelming private activity to a deserter and absent state, continually swinging from one extreme to the other, in what would seem to be an authentic national obsession that prevents us from finding a fair, sensible and necessary balance.

...

We are not inventing anything new. In the 1930s, the United States overcame the worst economic and financial crisis of the century in this manner.

...

I come to propose a dream. I want a united Argentina. I want a normal Argentina. I want us to be a serious country but also I want a more just country. I hope that that by taking this path a new and glorious nation, will rise up. Ours.

Discussion Questions
- What type of focus does Kirchner suggest a national government should have?
- Does Kirchner seem hostile to international actors?

Source: El Historiador: http://www.elhistoriador.com.ar/documentos/misceláneas/discurso_de_nestor_kirchner_25_de_mayo_de_2003.php

---

Ironically, Kirchner's position was strikingly similar to that of Menem in 1989. Faced with soaring inflation and economic uncertainty, he stepped in as a savior to succeed discredited leaders, but he did so in a very different manner. He worked with the IMF to restructure the country's debt and reduce total payments, and managed to do so from a position of strength. President Kirchner took a hard economic line, announcing in 2005 that he would offer only 35 percent of the value of the country's $82 billion in debt. He also indicated that Argentina was done with the IMF, a move that would have seemed unthinkable not long before. Although international financial institutions wield tremendous power, large developing countries still have some leverage. Economic "contagion" can take hold when the economies of large developing countries crash, thus leaving dangerous doubts in the minds of international investors about other developing economies, and so the IMF among other institutions gave Argentina more leeway than it might have in the past, and accepted terms much more favorable to Argentina. Kirchner was widely lauded for these actions and had Congress pass a law limiting changes in repayment terms beyond that level. By 2010, in fact, Argentina had a lower debt to GDP ratio than the United States.

Much of the ensuing economic growth, however, was linked directly to government spending, particularly in public works. As foreign investment had fallen, Kirchner looked to export taxes, particularly beef, for revenue. In addition, the Venezuelan government bought Argentine bonds, though stopped once the global recession hit. When severely cold weather swept into the country in 2007, the precarious nature of the economy was evident, as President Kirchner was forced to halt gas exports and shortages prompted protests.

Politically, he worked quickly to neutralize opposition. He persuaded Congress to impeach two Supreme Court justices, and the others eventually were pressured to retire. Following long Peronist tradition, Kirchner established a clientelist network with loyalists in important policy positions. He reached out to labor, including the "piquetero" movement, which had sprung up around Buenos Aires in the 1990s in response to economic crisis. The word comes from the English *picket* and refers to a mobilization strategy of blocking roads. That involved approving wage increases and refraining from using police force to disrupt protests. These movements developed in a manner that mirrored national politics, so that collective action was also often accompanied by personalism and clientelism. The piqueteros became politically influential, and remained so even when the economy improved. In part because of their support, in 2005 Kirchner's wife, **Cristina Fernández de Kirchner**, won the senate seat for Buenos Aires.

Kirchner, not unlike Perón, has always been difficult to pin down ideologically. Because of his tendency toward increasing the state's role in the economy, along with his public disagreements with both the IMF and the United States, he has often been labeled as "leftist." His nationalization of the postal service, water utilities, railroads, and other businesses clearly articulated a prominent role for the government. But in general he has followed a state capitalist model that is more in line with traditional Peronism, which was never conventionally "leftist." His antagonism toward international financial institutions is similarly more nationalist than leftist. International influences have also changed greatly since 2001. The response to the crash demonstrated the strong presence of such institutions, but their leverage was short-lived. The size of the Argentine economy, and more specifically the implications of a default, provided Kirchner with a bargaining power with those institutions that few observers anticipated.

More so than his predecessors, he also took on the military amnesty laws, which had been a fixture of Argentine politics. For years, human rights organizations had faced what one scholar called *the Scilingo Effect*, referring to the confession mentioned earlier in the chapter.[15] Scilingo's confession prompted others to confess as well, but there was no consensus about how to respond. A major dilemma was that the existence of amnesty laws meant that even if the truth about the disappeared became known—no guarantee—there could be no prosecution. Just months into Kirchner's presidency, he sent a bill to Congress to overturn the amnesty, which overwhelmingly approved it. The Supreme Court upheld the constitutionality of the law and in 2007 went further by ruling that past pardons were themselves unconstitutional. These decisions set the stage for hundreds of officers to be tried (with dozens already sentenced), including members of the ruling juntas. General Videla himself was already in prison for charges of child abduction since the military government had taken the young children of the disappeared and given them to promilitary families to be raised as their own. Carlos Menem had originally pardoned him in 1990 after he had started serving a life sentence for murder. The amnesty repeal opened the door for a new murder trial.

Kirchner's reforms have not only been aimed at the military. Women's rights have expanded. Already, in 1991 Argentina established congressional quotas for women, whereby they had to constitute 30 percent of candidates. Although compliance with the law has been uneven, the number of women winning elections rapidly increased, and therefore women's issues gained greater visibility. That in turn has meant that the parties have incorporated such issues to a greater degree than in the past. Because provincial politicians establish congressional lists, the quota law has had the effect of increasing women's influence both at the local level at the time of selection and then at the national level after election.

In 2010, the government implemented a program that trained judges on gender equality and women's rights, spearheaded by Carmen Argibay, the first woman to serve on the Supreme Court. The second female justice, Elena Highton, set up the Supreme Court Women's Office, which among other tasks organizes workshops on gender issues. Abortion is illegal and has been traditionally been off the legislative table, but more members of Congress have been arguing it should come up for a vote. Argentina also became the first country in Latin America to legalize "neutral" marriages, meaning that homosexual couples could marry. That set it apart from most of the Western Hemisphere.

Kirchner reformed the Supreme Court in 2003, which had historically been considered ineffective, illegitimate, and even detrimental to democracy despite its formal importance in the constitution. Carlos Menem increased the number of judges from five to nine, thus obtaining a majority that deferred to him and allowing even greater expansion of presidential prerogatives. The effect was that a large number of judges had some type of personal tie to Menem, which left them open to pressure. In 1992, a survey showed that 93 percent of Buenos Aires attorneys believed the judiciary was either "not independent" or "marginally independent."[16] Kirchner's reforms actually reduced presidential influence over the selection of nominees to the court, established criteria for their professional credentials, increased the transparency of the nomination process, and provided mechanisms for the public to weigh in on the choices.[17] Creating a positive popular image of the court was important for Kirchner because decisions in his favor would enjoy greater legitimacy. Five of Menem's judges resigned under public pressure or were impeached, thus providing Kirchner the opportunity to utilize the new process. He left two vacancies, however, and was criticized for packing the court just as Menem had. A compromise came in the form of reducing the number of justices to seven.

Research has shown that the court does offer at least some measure of horizontal accountability: "The probability of a justice's voting against the government depends on the political alignment of the justice, but the appointment power is bounded and does not by itself lead to complete political control of the Court."[18] The court has actually gone against the wishes of the president in a number of important cases. Nonetheless, public opinion of the court remains quite low, though that can also reflect a generalized lack of confidence in any branch of government. Such sentiments do not change quickly.

Although debates about presidential reelection have raged elsewhere in the region, President Kirchner, who remained very popular, chose not even to run for a second term, for which he would have been eligible. Instead, he served a single four-year term and his wife, Cristina Fernández de Kirchner, became a candidate in his place. In 2007 she won with a large plurality, with 45 percent versus only 22 percent for the second place candidate, Elisa Carrió of the UCR. That percentage difference was great enough to avoid a runoff. Cristina

Fernández had considerable political experience, having served in both the provincial and national legislatures since 1989. She was a senator for Buenos Aires at the time of her presidential election. Néstor Kirchner's decision not to run again was the source of much speculation. It seemed intended to establish the precedent of handing power to a spouse, who then would perhaps hand power back in the case of a winning election in the future, thus establishing a type of dynasty not embodied by a single individual. No matter the reason, the couple proved themselves to be a potent political force.

She largely kept the same cabinet and advisers as her husband and did not display a drastic difference in governing. She faced the immediate problem of a credit shortage, not only abroad but at home as well. As the credibility of the banking system was still damaged, few depositors wanted to keep their money in for more than 180 days.[19] Meanwhile, because income taxes were so widely ignored or avoided entirely through the informal economy, one of the few ways the government had of raising revenue was to tax exports. President Fernández did so aggressively, which later created political problems for her.

In 2009, Néstor Kirchner won a seat in the legislature for the Buenos Aires district. There is some irony in that move, because as this discussion has shown the legislature plays a small role in Argentine politics, whereas the president is very powerful. On average, members of Congress don't stay longer than one term, and little attention gets paid to executive-legislative horizontal accountability. Local party lists are made by provincial leaders, which sharply curtails an individual's ability to act independently. As in Brazil, provincial leaders are very important. If you cross the local party boss, then you may find your name off the next list. There is more incentive to keep those bosses happy than to become a nationally known expert on policy issues. This dynamic also means that no political actor has an incentive to create a transparent and well-functioning bureaucracy. From Kirchner's perspective, going into the legislature kept him in an elected position (in addition to being the president's spouse) with plenty of limelight.

Accountability and the Kirchners

President Fernández faced a sometimes hostile opposition. This was best exemplified by a 2008 bill raising agricultural export taxes, which farmers vehemently opposed and publicly protested. The economy suffered as farmers went on strike and supporters joined them in the streets of Buenos Aires. Interestingly enough, her own vice president (Julio Cobos) used his tiebreaking vote against her wishes. He had already caused controversy by running with Fernández in the first place because he was a member of the UCR, and he was therefore forced to resign his party membership. In 2008 Fernández nationalized (or rather renationalized, as it had been in government hands in the past) the national airline, which was heavily in debt. That move had legislative support, but more controversial was the decision to nationalize the private pension system, a total of about $30 billion. Critics argued that she did so to pay off the country's debt rather than the stated aim of protecting citizens' social security during the global economic crisis. Supporters asserted that the funds were losing so much money that the state had no choice but to take them over.

In general, over time both Kirchner and Fernández became more vocal as they felt under fire. They blamed foreign companies and an intransigent opposition for policy failures and denied charges that they were understating inflation. This in turn led to many rallies and counterrallies in Buenos Aires and elsewhere. At the same time, though, it is noteworthy that the ultimate negotiations still had to go through the legislature, and the democratic process continued to function despite the discord, even if imperfectly. No one looked to the armed forces.

The 2009 midterm election saw the Kirchner's Front for Victory coalition lose its majority, which put the executive and legislative branches on a collision course. Néstor Kirchner resigned as president of the Peronist party in recognition of the failure to maintain a majority. Tensions remained evident even within the executive branch. In 2009 President Fernández sought to fire the president of the Central Bank for refusing to free up requested reserves to repay national debt. He argued that because Congress was not in session, he did not have authority to disburse the money. President Fernández was eventually forced to back down by federal courts. The media, which of course also contributes to horizontal accountability, has had a similarly rocky relationship. The major Argentine newspaper *Clarín*, which is part of the larger media company "Clarín Group," has fought repeatedly with the Kirchners, who have tried to force the group to divest itself of its many different component parts.

President Fernández initially struggled to garner the same level of popularity that her husband enjoyed during his presidency. She continued to fight her own vice president, as Julio Cobos cast the tiebreaking vote to increase the floor on social security spending, which President Fernández then vetoed, claiming the state did not have adequate resources to fund the increase (thus also muddying any argument about bring "leftist"). At the same time, though, her political opponents were hardly unified, with the UCR competing with the center-right Republican Proposal (PRO), created in 2005. By 2011, her approval ratings were improving after dipping under 30 percent in 2008, and she won the 2011 presidential election handily, with 54 percent. Her closest competitor won only 17 percent. Yet by 2013 her approval dropped again because of inflation and sluggish growth.

Néstor Kirchner's sudden death of a heart attack in late 2010 raised new questions about President Fernández's ability to successfully bridge the executive-legislative divide and advance her political agenda. It also resolved the question of succession, as Kirchner would have been eligible to run for president again in 2011, and it was widely believed he would do so. As Kirchner cast a very long shadow over Argentine politics, his death immediately created a Peronist power vacuum, particularly because he exerted strong control over the party itself. But as the party structure allows for movement within it, Kirchner and Fernández had risen from obscure positions to the highest level of power, and others within the party may well do the same. No matter who eventually takes that role, it is also true that opposition to Peronism remains divided. As is the case in numerous other Latin American countries, there is no united front against the government, and so Peronism remains strong.

Contemporary Argentina and International Influence

The Kirchner and Fernández administrations inserted Argentina more into regional affairs. The seemingly indifferent attitude of the U.S. government, where support was channeled almost entirely through the IMF during the 2001 crisis, soured U.S.-Argentine relations. Those relations had been positive in the years when it had seemed the economic model was a success, but not so much when the Menem model was discarded. Since Néstor Kirchner's election, the relationship has been prickly though not overtly hostile. Overall, the Kirchners have been focused much more on strengthening regional ties in South America than repairing U.S.-Argentine relations.

In addition to confronting the IMF, after 2003 Argentina has taken a more active role in regional organization. Argentina was a founding member of MERCOSUR (the South American Common Market) and remains one of four member countries, along with Brazil, Paraguay, and Uruguay, with other countries joining as associate members. The organization has facilitated greater movement of both goods and people for Argentina. Before he died, in 2010 Néstor Kirchner became the first General Secretary of the Union of South American Nations (UNASUR). This organization, modeled on the European Union, is part of a broad effort to encourage political and economic cooperation—and eventually formal union—in the region.

Argentina also continues involvement in high-profile international disputes. The long-standing conflict with Great Britain over the Falklands/Malvinas gets the most attention, but it has also fought Uruguay through legal channels (including the International Court of Justice in the United Nations) to stop a pulp mill on the Uruguay River between the two countries. The Argentine government argues that it is polluting the river and that a treaty requires approval for projects on that river. Uruguay rejects both claims. After the International Court of Justice ruled in Uruguay's favor, the Fernández administration agreed to a binational commission to jointly measure pollution.

Conclusion and Comparative Perspective

In 2011 IMF announced that it no longer trusted the Argentine government's reporting of inflation. Particularly because of its prickly history with the IMF, the government of Cristina Fernández responded by announcing it would pursue criminal charges against anyone who published claims that inflation was higher. International influences thus clashed with national politics. Inflation reverberates to all levels, and consequently any lack of faith in its reporting cannot be taken lightly. The stakes were high in a country with a recent experience with economic collapse, and for a government that had been painstakingly restoring economic growth. If the reports were true, then inflation was second highest in the region to Venezuela.

Argentina is an exceptional case in many ways, though it shares similarities with Latin American counterparts. After the glory days of the late nineteenth century, its economy has never lived up to its promise and democracy has been wobbly. Its political institutions—executive, legislative, and judicial—have so often been at bitter odds, and in general stability has been hard to come by. As in Brazil, the extreme nature of Argentine federalism serves to amplify problems, as the president and legislators coexist in a sometimes uneasy web of relationships that make compromise difficult and therefore exacerbate already-existing tensions with local interests. Interestingly, though, Peronists were both blamed for the economic crisis (under Menem) and then lauded for solving it (under Kirchner). Long having shed its reliance on the person on Juan Perón, the party is now a flexible clientelist creature, able to adapt to virtually any circumstance.

The austerity policies of the 1990s had a similar outline as other Latin American countries, such as Mexico. Spending and subsidies were cut, nationalized industries were sold off, and inflation was attacked. Argentina took it a step further with the dollar peg, but like other South American countries—Bolivia, for example—the results were initially held up by national and international leaders alike as a model and later derided when they led to economic implosion and serious social unrest.

As in Chile, Argentina suffered military resistance after the transition from authoritarian rule. Contentious politics have been a constant in Argentina, yet despite the economic crash of the 2001–2002, the country has remained democratic since 1983 and the military has stayed in its barracks for many years. In a country historically beset by nondemocratic changes of government, this is no small achievement. Executive-legislative disputes may be bitter, but they stay within the political rules of the game. A 2009 poll showed that 21 percent of Argentines believed a coup was possible, while 75 percent agreed that democracy might have problems but was preferable to any other form of government. This suggests that democracy is strong, but that a solid proportion of Argentines do not always feel it fulfills their needs. Kirchner's inaugural speech acknowledged the precarious situation for many at the local level.

The ties that the Kirchner and Fernández governments had with countries like Venezuela provide an interesting point of comparison. The term *leftist* is tossed around quite often, but Argentina demonstrates that it can be used simplistically. On the one hand, their governments did pursue greater state intervention and even nationalization, as President Hugo Chávez did. On the other hand, they also worked to assure investors that the economy was stable, and the tough negotiations with the IMF involved continued repayment of debt. Ideology in this case is not easy to pigeonhole.

TABLE 12.1 Argentine Economic Indicators, 1991–2011

Year	GDP Growth	Inflation	Unemployment	Poverty Rate	Human Development Index
1991	10.0	84.0	6.5	—	0.882
1992	8.9	17.6	7.0	—	0.853
1993	5.8	7.4	9.6	—	0.885
1994	8.3	3.9	11.5	12.3	0.884
1995	−3.1	1.6	17.5	—	0.829
1996	4.4	0.1	17.2	—	—
1997	8.4	−0.1	14.9	—	0.827
1998	3.9	0.7	12.9	—	0.837
1999	−3.4	−1.8	14.3	16.3	—
2000	−0.8	−0.7	15.1	—	—
2001	−4.4	−1.5	17.4	—	0.856
2002	−10.9	41.0	19.7	45.4	0.853
2003	8.8	3.7	17.3	—	—
2004	9.0	6.1	13.6	29.4	—
2005	9.2	12.3	11.6	26.0	0.869
2006	8.5	9.8	10.2	21.0	—
2007	8.7	8.5	8.5	—	0.866
2008	6.8	7.9	8.0	—	—
2009	0.9	7.7	8.7	11.3	—
2010	8.4	11.1	7.8	—	0.805
2011	8.9	9.8	7.3	—	0.810

Sources: *Unemployment: GDP and Inflation: Preliminary Overview of the Economies of Latin America and the Caribbean,* 1994–2012.
Poverty rate: Social Panorama of Latin America. Economic Commission for Latin America, 1990–2012.
Human development index: United Nations, *Human Development Report,* 1990–2013.

Key Terms

- Radical Civic Union Party (UCR)
- Juan Domingo Perón
- Justicialist (Peronist) Party
- Proceso
- Mothers of the Plaza de Mayo
- Raúl Alfonsín
- Carlos Menem
- Néstor Kirchner
- Cristina Fernández de Kirchner

Critical Thinking Questions

- What are the key reasons the Argentine economy did not keep up with the developed world after the turn of the twentieth century?
- In what ways was President Menem's dollar peg an effective strategy to stabilize the economy? Why did it ultimately backfire?
- To what degree have the Kirchners followed the traditional political and economic model of Peronism?
- Analyze the key reasons why the Argentine military has remained out of politics since 1983 despite serious political and economic turmoil.
- How does federalism in Argentina differ from other Latin American examples? In what ways does it affect political stability?

Further Sources

Books

Blustein, Paul. *And the Money Kept Rolling In (and Out): Wall Street, the IMF, and the Bankrupting of Argentina* (New York: Public Affairs, 2005). This is a very readable account of the 2001–2002 economic crisis, with an emphasis on the influence of global finance and international institutions. The author is a reporter for the *Washington Post.*

Epstein, Edward and David Pion-Berlin (eds.). *Broken Promises? The Argentine Crisis and Argentine Democracy* (Lanham, MD: Lexington Books, 2006). A wide-ranging book on the economic crisis, by primarily Argentine scholars. It examines social movement, the military, the police, policy makers, and many other relevant political actors to provide a holistic view of that crisis.

Levitsky, Steven. *Transforming Labor-based Parties in Latin America: Argentine Peronism in Comparative Perspective* (New York: Cambridge University Press, 2002). The central question for this book is how Peronists managed to persevere and even thrive despite the economic shift toward neoliberalism. It focuses on the structure of the party itself, which was very flexible and therefore able to adapt in a way that political parties elsewhere could not.

Lewis, Paul. *The Agony of Argentine Capitalism: From Menem to the Kirchners* (Santa Barbara: Praeger, 2009). This is a well-written, highly detailed, and accessible analysis of the economic reforms begun during Carlos Menem's presidency, and what their long-term impact has been on Argentina.

Spiller, Pablo T. and Mariano Tommasi. *The Institutional Foundations of Public Policy in Argentina* (New York: Cambridge University Press, 2007). Viewing politics as the cooperation (or lack thereof) between political institutions, this book examines major institutions in Argentina to understand what incentives drive coordination and political change.

Web Sites

Argentina and the IMF (http://www.imf.org/external/country/arg/index.htm). From the Web site of the International Monetary Fund, there is a lengthy collection of documents dealing with its relationship with Argentina. It goes from 1991 until the present.

Buenos Aires Herald (http://www.buenosairesherald.com/). This is a long-standing English-language newspaper based in Buenos Aires. It includes local, national, and international news.

Central Bank of Argentina (http://www.bcra.gov.ar/index_i.htm). The bank has an English version of its Web site, with an extensive number of links to financial reports, economic statistics, press releases, and other information.

Merco Press (http://en.mercopress.com/). This news site focuses on the South Atlantic, with heavy coverage of Argentina. It even includes a permanent section on the Falklands/Malvinas, with updates about that conflict.

The National Security Archive: Argentina (http://www.gwu.edu/%7Ensarchiv/NSAEBB/NSAEBB73/index.htm). The National Security Archive has declassified many U.S. documents relating to the Argentine dictatorship and Dirty War. They focus in particular on the repression in Argentina and what the role of the U.S. government was in human rights abuses.

Endnotes

1. Barrionuevo, Alexei. "Inflation, an Old Scourge, Plagues Argentina Again." *The New York Times*, February 5, 2011.
2. Levitsky, Steven and María Victoria Murillo. "Building Castles in the Sand? The Politics of Institutional Weakness in Argentina." In Steven Levitsky and María Victoria Murillo (eds.), *Argentine Democracy: The Politics of Institutional Weakness* (University Park, PA: The Pennsylvania State University Press, 2005), 21.
3. Quoted in Romero, Luis Alberto. *A History of Argentina in the Twentieth Century*. (University Park: The Pennsylvania State University Press, 2002), 61.
4. Munro, Dana Garnder. *The Latin American Republics: A History*, 2nd edition. (New York: Appleton-Century Crofts, Inc, 1950), 193.
5. Katz, Jorge and Bernardo Kosacoff. "Import-Substituting Industrialization in Argentina, 1940–1980: Its Achievements and Shortcoming." In Enrique Cárdenas, José Antonio Campo, and Rosemary Thorp (eds.), *An Economic History of Twentieth Century Latin America*, Vol. 3 (New York: Palgrave, 2000), 282–313.
6. O'Donnell, Guillermo A. *Modernization and Bureaucratic-Authoritarianism: Studies in South American Politics* (Berkeley: Institute of International Studies, 1973), 75.
7. Quoted in Verbitsky, Horacio. *The Flight: Confessions of an Argentine Dirty Warrior* (New York: The New Press, 1996), 49.
8. Navarro, Marysa. "The Personal is Political: Las Madres de Plaza de Mayo." In Susan Eckstein (ed.), *Power and Popular Protest: Latin American Social Movements* (Berkeley: University of California Press, 1989), 251.
9. Brysk, Alison. *The Politics of Human Rights in Argentina: Protest, Change, and Democratization* (Stanford: Stanford University Press, 1994).
10. Brysk 1994, 170.
11. Spiller, Pablo T. and Mariano Tommasi. "Political Institutions, Policymaking Processes, and Policy Outcomes in Argentina." In Eduardo Stein and Mariano Tommasi (eds.), *Policymaking in Latin America: How Politics Shapes Policies* (Washington, DC: Inter-American Development Bank, 2008), 73.
12. Levitsky, Steven. *Transforming Labor-Based Parties in Latin America: Argentine Peronism in Comparative Perspective* (New York: Cambridge University Press, 2002).
13. Villalón, Roberta. "Neoliberalism, Corruption, and Legacies of Contention: Argentina's Social Movements, 1993-2006." In Richard Stahler-Sholk, Harry E. Vanden, and Glend David Kuecker (eds.), *Latin American Social Movements in the Twenty-First Century* (Lanham, MD: Rowman and Littlefield, 2008), 253–269.

14. Diamint, Rut. "Crisis, Democracy, and the Military in Argentina." In Edward Epstein and David Pion-Berlin (eds.), *Broken Promises? The Argentine Crisis and Argentine Democracy* (Lanham: Lexington Books, 2006), 163.
15. Feitlowitz, Marguerite. *A Lexicon of Terror: Argentina and the Legacies of Torture* (New York: Oxford University Press, 1998), Chapter 6.
16. Chavez, Rebecca Bill. *The Rule of Law in Nascent Democracies: Judicial Politics in Argentina* (Stanford: Stanford University Press, 2004), 52.
17. Ruibal, Alba M. "Self-Restraint in Search of Legitimacy: The Reform of the Argentine Supreme Court." *Latin American Politics & Society* 51, 3 (Fall 2009): 59–86.
18. Spiller, Pablo T. and Mariano Tommasi. *The Institutional Foundations of Public Policy in Argentina* (New York: Cambridge University Press, 2007), 125.
19. Lewis Paul H. *The Agony of Argentine Capitalism: From Menem to the Kirchners* (New York: Praeger, 2009), 168.

CHAPTER 13

Chile

LEARNING OBJECTIVES

- Identify how the three levels of analysis interact in Chile.

- Use theoretical propositions to understand political and economic development in Chile.

- Explain how and why political and economic development in Chile differs from other Latin American countries.

TIMELINE

1818	Independence from Spain
1891	Civil war
1924–1932	Civil-military rule
1970	Election of Salvador Allende
1973	Allende overthrown and military government installed
1978	Political amnesty decreed
1989	Democratic elections
1998–2000	Augusto Pinochet under arrest in Great Britain
2005	Constitutional reforms passed
2006	Michelle Bachelet elected; Augusto Pinochet dies
2010	Sebastián Piñera elected

In 2010, billionaire center-right politician Sebastián Piñera was inaugurated president of Chile. He was exultant, with his characteristic broad smile, as he had wanted the presidency for years and it marked the end of twenty years in power for the opposition coalition, the Concertación. His inauguration was literally rocky, since aftershocks of the recent massive 8.8 earthquake shook

311

visiting heads of state. It was an important moment in Chilean political history, because a candidate of the right had not been elected for more than forty years. At a national level, Chileans had decided it was time for a change.

In many ways, Chile is a country of extremes, though politically in recent years it has found moderation. From a symbolic point of view, geography offers a poignant picture. A very slim country wedged between Argentina to the east, Peru to the north, Bolivia to the northeast, and the Pacific Ocean to the west, Chile includes the bitterly cold South Pole and the driest place on earth in the north (the Atacama Desert). In political terms, Chile has periodically enjoyed some of the most stable periods of democracy in Latin America (including the present) while also experiencing one of the most infamous dictatorships (1973–1990) of the twentieth century. Economically, Chilean policy makers have experimented with socialism but also with a style of capitalism that

CHILE
Population: 17.1 million
Size: 292,000 square miles
Capital: Santiago
Currency: peso

Map of Chile

surpassed any other country in the Western Hemisphere and generated positive macroeconomic outcomes but also high levels of economic inequality. Given its economic success in recent years, although it relies heavily on commodities—particularly copper—it does not fit well with dependency theory and defies easy generalization.

Historical Roots of Political and Economic Development

The seeds of stability, albeit of an avowedly elitist kind, were sown in the years following independence from Spain in 1818. For over a decade afterward, the country suffered intense and bloody internal warfare. Under the influence of the conservative Diego Portales (an individual of critical political importance despite never having been president), a new constitution was ratified in 1833, which would launch Chile on a path of political constancy enjoyed by very few other Latin American countries. With the perceived threat of indigenous peoples (the Mapuche) in the south, political elites came together at the national level more quickly than elsewhere. As in many other countries, throughout the eighteenth century the split between Liberals and Conservatives was a hallmark of politics, but from 1831 until the civil war of 1891 Chilean presidents alternated power much more peacefully than elsewhere.

International factors are also central to understanding Chilean political and economic development. As noted in Chapter 2, border disputes with Bolivia and Peru led to the War of the Pacific (1879–1883), which had important and far-reaching consequences. The result was an economic boom for Chile, and humiliation for Bolivia and Peru. The issue of ocean access remains a highly relevant issue in Bolivia today, while current disputes over fishing rights based on land boundaries remain a bone of contention between Chile and Peru.

National Divisions in Chile

Chilean politicians were keenly aware of the potential wealth in the barren north, which further raised the stakes for policy decisions: What should the state's role be in extracting and taxing? What should the role of foreign investment be? The Liberal-Conservative split in Chile eventually led to armed confrontation that also changed the nature of executive and legislative power. President José Manuel Balmaceda, associated with the Liberal Party, became embroiled in bitter struggle with a more conservative legislature, which denied funding for his projects and refused approval of his ministerial choices. When in 1891 he attempted to enact a budget without congressional approval, the conflict expanded to civil war, with the opposition led by the navy and parts of the army (and even joined by discontented nitrate workers). When it was clear that his side would lose, Balmaceda committed suicide.

The long-term result was that Congress took extensive control over politics. Rhetorically, this meant saving the country from the tyrannical whims of the president, but in practice it entailed constant changes of cabinet and little leadership. This era is generally labeled the "Parliamentary Period" but that is a bit misleading. In a true parliamentary system, the executive has the authority to dissolve the legislature, but in the Chilean case the president held no sway over Congress. This state of affairs was especially problematic because the early years of the twentieth century were marked by economic uncertainty, urbanization, and labor unrest (based in part on the booms and busts of the nitrate industry). Further, as late as 1920 only 5 percent of the population voted, and the political system was dominated by landowners and political machines.[1] The average Chilean had no say, and autonomous local political organization was suppressed.

World War I wrought more change from international actors. Historically, Great Britain and Germany had invested heavily in Chile, but they were being replaced by investors from the United States. Global demand for copper was also growing. After the war, however, copper prices dropped and the country went into a depression. Given urbanization and labor activism, this is also the period when in 1912 the Socialist Workers Party, which would later become the Communist Party, was formed. This is an example of local leaders with common political goals coming together to form a national-level party. Into this situation blazed Arturo Alessandri, who won the presidency in 1920 on a platform of reform. Like his predecessors, he faced a Congress that routinely blocked his decisions. In 1924, the army created a junta, made demands for political change, and ultimately prompted Alessandri to resign and leave the country for Italy.

Military Rule in Chile

Military intervention of this type was rare in Chile, particularly when compared to the rest of the region. The armed forces considered themselves the ultimate saviors of the nation (the "Patria") but for the most part remained out of politics. After the War of the Pacific, flush with victory and funding, the Chilean army began receiving extensive training and arms from Prussia, a close relationship that would last until Germany's defeat in World War II (not surprisingly, it also meant that many Nazis fled to Chile).

This period of military activism was marked by national conspiracy and intrigue. A second coup in 1925 brought Alessandri back to Chile. He named a commission to write a new constitution, which was ratified a few months later. The 1925 constitution, which remained in effect until it was suspended after the 1973 coup, shifted political power back toward the executive. The presidential term limit was expanded to six years, and Congress' authority to fire cabinet ministers was revoked. Furthermore, the president had the ability to enact budgets if Congress balked, which ended decades of precedent. It also officially separated church and state, which served to dissolve that long-standing difference between Liberals and Conservatives.

A new constitution, however, did nothing to alleviate the political crisis in the country. Colonel Carlos Ibáñez del Campo, who had played an important role in the 1924 coup and was a rival of Alessandri's, was minister of war and pressured Alessandri to resign, which he did once again not long after the constitution went into effect. Although he would not run for the presidency until 1927 (when he won with 98 percent of the vote), Ibáñez remained the most powerful political figure in Chile. Under his presidency, the country became increasingly authoritarian, with suppression of labor, attacks on opposition politicians, and extensive use of decree power.

Part of his support rested on economic growth, which was slowly petering out, and of course would then be hit by the global crash of 1929. The price of nitrates, which had been a consistent source of revenue, began falling when European companies engineered synthetic substitutes. International influence came in other ways as well. Before Ibáñez became president, the government had contracted the services of Princeton Professor Edwin Kemmerer, foreshadowing the high level of U.S. involvement in the Chilean economy forty years later. Kemmerer, known as the "Money Doctor," advised many governments, mostly in Latin America. His advice for Chile, as for other countries, was to adhere to the Gold Standard, create an independent Central Bank, and maintain balanced budgets. These measures encouraged foreign investment, but the combination of falling nitrate and copper prices (which had been a major source of revenue since the nineteenth century) and debt, followed later by the crash of the U.S. stock market, brought on depression and renewed political strife.

As Ibáñez was weakened by adverse economic conditions, the opposition—including many military officers—became more vocal, and violence in 1931 finally prompted the president to resign (he later received an amnesty and in 1952 once again was elected president). The next seventeen months were tumultuous, with coups, countercoups, rapid changes of government, and even a self-proclaimed "Socialist Republic" under the flamboyant leadership of Colonel Marmaduque Grove, which lasted only 100 days. A presidential election in 1932 brought Alessandri back to the presidency and ushered in forty-one years of uninterrupted democratic rule in Chile.

CHILEAN POLITICAL INSTITUTIONS

Last constitution: 1980, amended in 2005

Unitary system with fifteen regions

Executive: Presidential, four-year term; runoff of top two candidates if no majority is reached; one nonconsecutive reelection is allowed

Legislative: Bicameral; lower house is the Chamber of Deputies (120 members) and the upper house is the Senate (38 members)

Judicial: Supreme Court with no influence over legislation; Adversarial judicial system

Contemporary Politics in Chile

In the post-1932 era, several political and economic developments emerged. First, political parties split along three main ideological lines—left, center, and right— with clear social class differences that eventually led to serious conflict. The Socialist (created in 1933 in the wake of the short-lived Socialist Republic) and Communist parties represented the core of the left, and with effective local organizing made important gains by appealing to voters who felt disconnected from national politics. The old Conservative Party splintered, with several different parties occupying the center. The middle was occupied by the Radical Party until perceptions of corruption splintered it in the 1950s. In its place would eventually coalesce the Christian Democratic Party, founded in 1957. The right (particularly the United Conservative Party) would fuse with like-minded Liberals, though they would not form a unified party—the National Party—until 1966. This confusing stew of parties was summed up nicely in a 1932 newspaper article:

> The Socialists of today are the Radicals of yesterday and the Liberals of the day before yesterday. The vanguard has changed in name, but the nature is the same. As much can be said of those stigmatized today as oligarchs; they are the same ones that yesterday were Conservatives and the day before yesterday Ultramontanes. Between them both is the centre, which today is Radical and yesterday was Liberal. The names change: humanity does not.[2]

No matter the name of a given party, in this tripartite environment the center became the anchor, which in part accounts for why Chile did not experience dictatorship. Chileans and outside observers alike believed that democracy would endure forever. As the author of a widely read guide to Latin American politics wrote glowingly in 1941, "Chile is as democratically minded and governed as any state in the Americas."[3]

Another important political reality was that the military leadership was chastened by the debacles of the late 1920s and early 1930s, and consciously stayed out of politics. Historically, civilians had shown very little interest in defense issues, and therefore a tacit modus operandi came about, whereby the military was left to develop its own doctrines and perceptions of security threats, and in return it would not meddle in political affairs. In fact, the armed forces became proud of their noninterventionist stance. The advent of the Cold War, however, represented a serious problem for this arrangement. For as the Chilean left gained an important foothold in democratic politics at both the local and national levels, the military was left to its own devices, which opened the door to international influence, particularly the United States. Its developing military doctrine displayed antidemocratic features, combining anti-Communism with geopolitical theory, which portrayed the country as a living organism and the military as the surgeon, ready to cut out cancerous Communist tumors.

Economically, international copper prices began to improve in the 1930s and would rise even more after the onset of World War II. Alessandri increased tariffs and subsidies, and Chile embarked on a project of import substitution industrialization (ISI). To facilitate the state's relationship with business, in

1939 the government created the Corporación de Fomento de la Producción (CORFO), a state-run economic development agency that is still in place.

Labor unions in Chile increased their political influence during this period, which reflected the growing connection of political parties to the local level, down to factories. It would also entail growing class conflict. In 1936, the Workers' Confederation of Chile (CTCH) became the largest union in the country, but until the 1950s there was no united labor organization. In 1953 the United Center of Chilean Workers (CUT) brought the major unions together and lasted until the 1973 coup. Throughout the mid-twentieth century, local influences were extremely important. Although Alessandri sought to control labor, overtime unions and activists became more independent of the state. This would eventually represent a threat to elite interests. Nonetheless, rural unionization remained illegal.

In the post-1932 period, Chilean democracy grew in fits and starts. On the one hand, it expanded when women were granted the right to vote in 1949 (illiterates were denied the right until 1970). On the other hand, the 1948 Law for the Permanent Defense of Democracy outlawed the Communist Party and set up banishment areas for those the government considered subversive. It provided legal cover to ensure more labor compliance and would not be repealed for a decade.

Theory and Politics of Chilean Development and Democratic Breakdown: Local, National, and International Influences

From a modernization perspective, Chile in the 1960s should have been a clear case of successful development. Chileans had imbibed capitalism, albeit with a strong role for the state, democracy had persevered for several decades, and even by Western-defined values, was "modern." We should have expected democracy to continue, but the 1973 coup crushed it. For an explanation we are better served by Guillermo O'Donnell's concept of bureaucratic-authoritarianism, as the decline of the ISI model sparked popular sector discontent.

Given Chile's democratic institutions, labor found expression in well-organized political parties on the left. The Chilean state was an active player in the economy to varying degrees over time. In the 1950s and early 1960s, for example, Carlos Ibáñez and Jorge Alessandri (son of former president Arturo Alessandri) were periodically forced to reduce spending as a means of combating inflation.

In the 1960s, international influences in Chile reached all new highs, particularly from the United States. The copper industry was dominated by U.S. companies such as Anaconda and Kennecott, which combined controlled the four largest mines in the country. From the perspective of dependency theory, this was a classic case of exporting a valuable raw material—largely in the hands of foreign interests to boot—and then importing finished goods. Dependency theory would predict that the core would do whatever possible to maintain the arrangement, and indeed the copper companies were dismayed by labor agitation and began complaining to the U.S. government of Marxist infiltration.

Further, the Central Intelligence Agency funneled approximately $12 million to the campaign of Eduardo Frei Montalva, a Christian Democrat who won the presidency in 1964. The United States and the Chilean right were particularly concerned about **Salvador Allende**, a Socialist Senator and physician who first ran for president in 1952 and whose radical message of reform was ideologically alarming.

A declassified memo from President Lyndon Johnson's National Security Council put it succinctly in 1964: "If Allende wins and stays in power, we are in trouble."[4] On the left, the Cold War also resonated. Under Moscow's direction, the Chilean Communist Party did not become radical, and instead focused on a more moderate strategy that included discussing reforms with the Christian Democrats. The Socialist Party—Allende's party—moved much more sharply to the left by the mid-1960s, showing solidarity with Fidel Castro's Cuba. In response, the right, much of which had supported Frei in 1964 as a bulwark against the Socialists, coalesced into the National Party.

President Frei's strategy was to seek a middle road between political extremes under the slogan "Revolution in Liberty." He enacted land reform, which included expropriation, as a way of alleviating the high concentration of land in very few hands. In practice this meant taking land from owners, repaying them with government bonds, and then redistributing it. He also promoted a variety of policies aimed at the poor, such as education and housing, and even a partial nationalization of copper, because the left was not the only group that resented its domination by foreign interests. However, the right generally opposed his policies, while the left viewed them as not going far enough, reflecting the class difference that became increasingly stark and irreconcilable.

Nonetheless, many people from poor neighborhoods who had always felt excluded were energized and believed that real change was possible. Actors at the local level, therefore, were more active than ever before in Chilean history. The stage was set for the presidential election of 1970, for which the left joined in the Unidad Popular (Popular Unity) coalition, which promised a "Peaceful Road to Socialism." The coalition put Salvador Allende forward as its candidate, and he pledged to enact the more radical reforms desired by the left. The right, the fringes of which were increasingly violent, considered him dangerous.

After Allende's election, the intense international pressures to oust him played an important role in his downfall. Nonetheless, a closer look reveals the many national factors that contributed to the fall of Allende's government and his death. He won only a plurality, which meant by law the decision had to be made by Congress. He won 36.2 percent of the total vote, while former president and candidate of the right Jorge Alessandri garnered 34.9 percent and Christian Democrat Radomiro Tomic trailed with 27.8 percent. Despite the fact that the far right and the administration of Richard Nixon wanted otherwise, and the former even tried to kidnap the Commander in Chief of the Army René Schneider and blame it on the left (he was killed in the process), congressional leaders chose Allende after he agreed to constitutional guarantees intended to cement his commitment to democratic rule.

Allende's economic program included full nationalization of the copper industry (passed unanimously because even the right viewed it in nationalist rather than ideological terms), further rural expropriation and redistribution, wage increases, and eventually nationalization of a wide range of smaller businesses. Before long, the Christian Democrats moved into open opposition and extremist groups on the right formed to foment violence and disrupt the administration's policy initiatives, labeling them as communist. The crisis spread to the local level, down to the streets, most famously with women banging pots to protest food shortages and inflation, along with strikes by truck owners concerned that their small businesses might be nationalized.

The U.S. government made it known to the opposition that it wanted Allende removed from power, and did what it could to strangle the economy, such as blocking Chile's access to international credit. The Cold War context transformed local and national labor protests into a global struggle, because the U.S. government saw them as directed by Cuba for the benefit of the Soviet Union. As a memo by National Security Advisor Henry Kissinger put it, under Allende Chile would "become part of the Soviet/Socialist world, not only philosophically but in terms of power dynamics; and it might constitute a support base and entry point for expansion of Soviet and Cuban presence and activity in the region."[5] How much the United States participated in the coup itself is a matter of long-standing dispute, but there is no doubt that the Nixon Administration signaled in every way possible to conservative elements in the Chilean military that a coup would be viewed in very positive terms.

Perhaps the most critical miscalculation was that of the Christian Democrats, who believed that—based on forty years of an apolitical military—the armed forces would overthrow the government and then immediately work with civilians to call new elections within a short time and reconstruct Chile's tattered democracy. They could not have been more wrong. Contrary to widespread expectations, the military immediately displayed both its brutal tactics and its refusal to set a timetable for restoration of democratic institutions. On September 11, 1973, the armed forces bombed the presidential palace (known as La Moneda, or "the Mint," because that was its function in the colonial era), suspended the 1925 constitution, and began rounding up—and sometimes summarily executing—thousands of political prisoners, many of them in the National Stadium in the middle of Santiago. Allende died in the attack by suicide (he was later exhumed, and in 2012 a court confirmed that he took his own life). Before his death, he made a dramatic radio speech, condemning the coup conspirators and asking his supporters to keep up hope.

We should also consider the role of national political institutions in the breakdown of democracy in Chile. Salvador Allende was elected by a plurality, and even after favorable congressional elections in March 1973, when the Unidad Popular added six seats in the Chamber of Deputies and two in the Senate, like many other Chilean presidents he never had majority support. In a presidential system, however, he did not need to negotiate or compromise to enact policies, and instead sought to circumvent Congress, using executive powers like decrees, to further the Unidad Popular's program. This was exacerbated by the fact that the Unidad Popular itself was deeply split internally. Political scientist Arturo Valenzuela has argued that a parliamentary system would have been better equipped to handle a polarized multiparty system by creating incentives for coalition building.[6] Of course, whether or not that would have resolved the crisis peacefully is impossible to say. But as it stood, Allende did not have a simple majority to pass legislation and the opposition did not have the necessary two-third majority to impeach him. The armed forces therefore cut the Gordian knot.

Years of Dictatorship: 1973–1990

The repression was far worse than almost anyone believed possible, given Chile's relatively stable history and the fact that the military intervened far less than in most Latin American countries. However, many within the armed forces had been developing deeply held anti-Communist and antireformist beliefs. After the coup, those that dissented were imprisoned or killed. One of Allende's closest military allies, General Carlos Prats González, fled to Argentina and was murdered there. Air Force General Alberto Bachelet, father of future president Michelle Bachelet, was detained, tortured, and then died in prison. In the first months of the dictatorship, tens of thousands of people were arrested.

The military's self-proclaimed role was messianic, intended to cleanse the nation and deliver it from ideological evil. As mentioned in Chapter 2, Latin American militaries have often displayed such views, and the Chilean case was a perfect example of the "politics of antipolitics." Political parties were immediately banned by decree, and any act or movement that included reference to class struggle or somehow threatened the notion of family was also made illegal.

Transformation of National Political Institutions

The military government's project, then, was to remake Chilean political institutions. The army commander in chief, **Augusto Pinochet**, quickly assumed control and named a constitutional commission, which met from 1973 to 1978, and its work would culminate in the 1980 charter, which remains in place—albeit with major revisions—today. It included a prominent role for the armed forces, which would "watch over" the political system and had broad political prerogatives. Presidents could not fire commanders in chief, the military could force a meeting of the National Security Council, retired commanders in chief could become designated senators, and the language in the constitution was left intentionally vague as to allow the military leadership the right to intervene if it believed civilians were destroying the constitutional order, as the military was deemed obedient to the nation, but automatically to a particular government in power.

All political institutions were revamped. For example, legislative elections now utilize a **"binomial electoral system."** Each congressional district elects two representatives, but to win both seats a party must get over two-thirds of the total district vote. Given the difficulty of achieving that feat, the second largest party (or coalition of parties) has a better chance of representation. As part of the 1980 constitution, the military government's intent was to protect parties on the right, which were not as popular as the center and left. Under the military government, Chile became a unitary system, so power is concentrated in the central government (although some decentralization has been taking place more recently) and not in the fifteen regions of the country.

A New Economic Direction

The economic policy of the military government made it stand out even more in comparative perspective. Other dictatorships around Latin America tended to keep the inherited state capitalist model, and initially Pinochet did the same. Continued problems with inflation (over 300 percent in 1975) and sluggish growth led him to turn toward a group of Chileans who were eventually dubbed the "**Chicago Boys.**" These were about 100 economics students who attended the University of Chicago from 1957 to 1970, originating with an exchange with Chile's Catholic University. One of the most outspoken, Sergio de Castro, became minister of the economy in 1975 and economic strategy quickly became more radically market-oriented.

Under their direction, the government embarked on a series of measures that made Chile one of the most capitalist countries in the world, through privatization of state enterprises (but not all of the copper industry, which was still viewed in nationalist as well as economic terms, just as in Mexico with oil), deregulation, cuts in state spending, elimination of price controls, reduction of tariffs and encouragement of foreign investment and trade. Even *El Mercurio*, the conservative newspaper that supported the Pinochet regime, noted later that during the first four years of reforms, the economy was controlled "by a small and select team that seldom explains its reasons and...does not communicate its decisions in advance."[7] The dictatorship, meanwhile, ensured that labor was kept under strict control.

Neoliberal reforms reached into every aspect of life and the regime celebrated them as Chile's entrance into modernity. One of the most prominent was the pension system, as after intense (and largely closed door) debate the government phased out most of its participation and instead channeled compulsory social security funds into private accounts, administered by Pension Fund Managing Corporations (AFPs), which profit from management fees. The new system was launched in 1981, and although it was often heralded as a hallmark of capitalism's success, and was even studied as a possible model for the United States, by the twenty-first century it had become increasingly unpopular because of high fees and the uncertainty of the market. Critics also point to the system's neglect of large sectors of the population: "in order to get a decent pension or a decent health package one needs more than just a positive attitude toward modernity, one needs to be a young male, to have a stable job, and a high income."[8]

Privatization was also introduced into the educational system, with incentives to create private schools, as well as measures intended to encourage enrolling in private health plans, and for private businesses to build housing. It was, as the government intended, almost the precise opposite of Allende's economic policies. The essential drawback of these plans, as with the overhaul of social security, was that they benefited males, the young, relatively well-off, and the economically active.

Politically, the dictatorship outlawed parties, denied the right to strike, crushed labor unions, and targeted anyone associated with the left, especially the Socialist and Communist Parties. To facilitate political control, soon after the coup the government created the Directorate of National Intelligence (DINA), which would be housed in the army and run by Colonel (later General) Manuel Contreras. The DINA coordinated state repression, both nationally but also with an aggressive international presence. Within Chile, it spied on its own citizens, made arrests without warrants, then interrogated, tortured, and sometimes killed its victims at locations scattered around Santiago and other parts of the country. At the international level, Contreras founded "Operation Condor," an agreement with fellow South American dictatorships to share intelligence and even make abductions on behalf of other military intelligence services. The international reach of DINA also went to Washington, DC, where in 1976 one of its operatives (a U.S. citizen) set off a car bomb that killed former Defense Minister Orlando Letelier and a U.S. citizen colleague of his, Ronni Moffitt. That terrorist attack initiated a slow erosion of U.S. support for the Pinochet government.

By the late 1970s, Pinochet made several moves that consolidated his own position and set a political framework for the future. In 1977 he announced the "Chacarillas Plan," a vision of a military-controlled government that would gradually (with no specific timetable) provide more space for civilians, but with a strong oversight role for the armed forces. This launched Pinochet's notion of a "protected" democracy that would be reined in by the watchful eyes of the military leadership. That same year, he called for a referendum condemning President Jimmy Carter, who had criticized the regime's human rights record. In 1978, he ousted fellow junta member Air Force General Gustavo Leigh, who was outspoken in opposition to Pinochet's seemingly indefinite role as president, and even of the military's indefinite running of the government. That year the junta also decreed an amnesty, so that any alleged political crimes committed between 1973 and 1978 could not be prosecuted. Finally, in 1980 the new constitution was approved in yet another national vote, with 67 percent voting in favor and 30 percent against (which itself demonstrated the small but growing opposition to the government). Taken together, all these measures consolidated Pinochet's personal position and also that of an authoritarian political structure, "protected" from the whims of democratic elections.

What Pinochet could not foresee were the national consequences of international economic crisis. The rapid rise of oil prices in 1979 combined with an overvalued Chilean peso caused a balance of payment problem with a sharp drop of exports. In 1982, inflation hit 20.7 percent (and remained over 20 percent until 1986) and gross domestic product dropped 14 percent from 1981. Meanwhile, in the same span of a year the unemployment rate rose from 16 to 26 percent, and it continued to go up. The government responded with a devaluation (as Sergio de Castro was pushed out in favor of Hernán Büchi, who in 1989 became a losing presidential candidate), an increase of selected tariffs and state takeover of failing banks. For many Chileans, resentment about economic deprivation fed into local political protest, and the country saw the first major rallies and strikes of the dictatorship, led by labor. Soon thereafter, the still illegal political parties took a more active role. Women were also critical to the effort.

Protest Against the Military Government: Local and National Factors

Women were at the forefront of the political struggle against the dictatorship. The theme of motherhood was central, as an initial rationale for protesting was that the dictatorship, which claimed to be protecting families, was in fact destroying many. The deaths and disappearances of family members was the initial impetus for many women, and also provided justification for political action. Motherhood also provided some measure of protection, since the government was less likely to attack women openly, though of course such protected status had limits. These movements epitomized local action, as they often originated at the neighborhood—the most local—level. Their organizational efforts then provided them with national influence (and international attention), which facilitated a cohesive and organized stand against the dictatorship. This was a slow process, as women were not even sure how to define themselves. Were they feminists, or just activists? As one woman who became politically active in the early 1980s put it, "Ours was, therefore, a very gradual definition as a feminist collective, privately at first and only then publicly."[9] One important example of connecting the local to the international is the *arpillera* (see Box 13.1), colorful sewn pictures that depicted suffering and repression, which became a symbol of resistance to the military regime.

This helps to explain *why* women were protesting but does not explain much about whether the efforts were successful. Susan Franceschet has argued that the weakness of Chilean political parties during the dictatorship provides the answer.[10] In the 1970s and 1980s, Chilean social movements were stronger than opposition political parties, which were prime targets for repression. The strength of the women's movement, which was aided by international attention, and the presence of many different nongovernmental organizations compelled parties to take women's issues—of all kinds, not simply that related to the dictatorship—into account as a way to attract support. Thus, even after the end of the dictatorship, women continued to work within parties to effect change.

The recognition of the role women's groups played in defeating the dictatorship was reflected in the creation in 1991 of the cabinet-level National Women's Service (known by its Spanish acronym SERNAM). Its mission is to promote policies and programs aimed at equal rights and opportunities for men and women and to eliminate gender discrimination. Its first minister, Soledad Alvear, eventually became a presidential contender for the Concertación. There is debate about whether SERNAM has lived up to its promise, in particular because the transition from authoritarian rule also splintered the movement, because no consensus emerged regarding political priorities. Plus, although women did become prominent in politics, their platforms did not place women's issues at the forefront. Nonetheless, SERNAM remains an important legacy of women's protests during the dictatorship and, in fact, some key issues have

BOX 13.1

Arpilleras in Chile: The Power of Local Protest

International: An *arpillera* (in English literally *burlap*) is a brightly colored sewn picture to be hung on a wall, which becomes three dimensional as fabric and cloth are applied to it. They were created by poor Chilean women after the coup, as a way to supplement the family income, but then more and more to articulate the horrors of the regime through art. They started originally in church basements around Santiago, but especially through the church and by smuggling them out of the country, their resistance art became known outside Chile, and they received money for material from abroad as well as media attention. This raised the profile of protests against the human rights abuses committed by the government.

National: The women initially found refuge in the Vicariate of Solidarity, sponsored by the Catholic Church, which provided a safe space for the work. They were able to sew messages and scenes—such as depictions of abductions or torture—that otherwise could not be expressed out loud for fear of government reprisal. The art form subsequently spread and eventually came to the attention of the Pinochet government, which even attempted to confiscate them.

Local: This was protest starting at the most local level, with personal motivations of justice and household income. The women sewing the arpilleras represent an excellent example of how even the most local actions can reverberate nationally and internationally.

Discussion Questions
- Why would art produced at the local level have national and even international effects?
- Can you think of reasons why such local initiatives get started in the first place?

been addressed, such as making divorce legal in 2004 against the wishes of the influential Catholic Church.

At the national level, the economic crisis of the early 1980s helped to forge new ties between the previously antagonistic opposition parties. In spite of arrests, protests were common until 1986, when an assassination attempt on Pinochet led to a renewed wave of repression. Nonetheless, Pinochet remained confident of his popularity, banking on the long-standing argument that he and the armed forces had saved the country from a Communist takeover. Transitory articles of the 1980 constitution required him to hold a plebiscite to determine whether he would remain in office until 1997 or if there should be general democratic elections instead. The announcement of the plebiscite for 1988 was the spark the opposition needed to unite.

That year the Christian Democrats came together with sixteen other parties to form the "Concertación de Partidos por el No" (Coalition of Parties for the

No). They were given some latitude to advertise their side (such as signs with the word *No* prominent) but still were harassed and the state-controlled media pushed the government's "Yes" campaign. The energy of the "No" campaign could not be denied, though, as exemplified by the Socialist opposition leader and future president Ricardo Lagos going on a television show and pointing his finger at the camera while lecturing Pinochet on his abuse of power.

Believing he would win, Pinochet allowed the vote to be reasonably free and fair, but the "No" won 55 to 44 percent. Despite concerns that Pinochet might not accept the results, the Commander in Chief of the Air Force quickly acknowledged the opposition's victory and Pinochet felt compelled to accept the outcome. This set in motion a pacted transition, which entailed a period of fifteen months during which fifty-four constitutional reforms were negotiated. As with all such transitions, the military remained protected, but the opposition did receive concessions. For example, the size of the senate increased from 26 to 38 as way to dilute the power of the designated senators, and language about banning "totalitarian" ideas was removed. Elections were then held in 1989. After Pinochet's defeat, the opposition coalition would be changed to "Coalition of Parties for Democracy" and would thereafter be dubbed simply the **Concertación**.

Its candidate was Patricio Aylwin, the Christian Democrat who had initially supported the coup but had since publicly apologized for doing so. He won the election handily, with a majority of 55 percent, compared to the right's candidate, Hernán Büchi, with 29 percent, and independent Francisco Javier Errázuriz at 15 percent. The parties of the Concertación also won 72 of 120 seats in the lower house (the Chamber of Deputies) and 22 of the 38 elected senate seats. On March 11, 1990 Aylwin was sworn in and Chilean democracy began again.

Redemocratization in Chile was almost entirely a local and national process. Certainly, there was a measure of international pressure, as most countries in the region had shed their authoritarian governments and by the late 1980s the United States was no longer supportive of the Pinochet government. The combination of mass protests, increasing disillusion by Chilean business (which considered the regime's poor image as an obstacle to foreign investment), and the new cohesion of the opposition ultimately was most responsible for the results.

The Return of Democracy: 1990 and Beyond

Even the word *democracy* requires some attention. From a procedural point of view, where competitive, free and fair elections decided by a universal electorate determine which representatives will enter political office—a polyarchy—Chile was democratic. Much beyond that, however, was less clear at the time. The pro-military elements of the 1980 constitution have already been mentioned. Oddly enough, the former dictator remained Army Commander in Chief, which he would hold until 1998, and he could not be removed. The military's budget could not be cut under 1989 levels, adjusted for inflation. Finally, the Pinochet government amended a 1954 law guaranteeing the military a share of earnings of the state copper company CODELCO to include 10 percent of all copper earnings. The new civilian government was therefore saddled with a politically influential military.

Further, many Chileans were suffering after years of economic reforms made without any popular participation. The so-called Chilean miracle had a darker side. Inequality was rife: In 1990, the Gini coefficient in Chile was 55.9, among the highest in Latin America, and it would continue to rise (56.1 in 1996 and 57.1 in 2000).[11] In 1990 the poverty rate was also 33.3 percent. There was no doubt that macroeconomic stability had been achieved, as overall indicators like inflation and economic growth remained positive. Clearly, though, the benefits of the model were not being felt by a large portion of the Chilean population.

The neoliberal model itself, however, was not immediately challenged. Moderated by repression and years in exile, even many (though certainly not all) members of the Socialist Party, the backbone of the Unidad Popular, believed the stability of the model meant it should continue. Perhaps best exemplified by Ricardo Lagos, they espoused a Social Democratic strategy of embracing the market while seeking to soften its worst effects. As he campaigned in 1999 he wrote, "Chile's development requires that we integrate more and better in the global economy. To do this, we need to increase our competitiveness in a stable and socially just manner."[12] In practice, this meant increasing the state's role to a degree within the framework of generally limited state involvement in the economy and an explicit policy of forging free trade agreements with countries around the world (including the United States), which also decreases the state's scope of influence.

Globalization in Chile thus entails a policy of increased insertion into global markets, encouraging and facilitating foreign investment, and marketing Chilean products (such as wine and fish) abroad. Nonetheless, a significant proportion of the copper industry remains in state hands, and copper revenue is a critical source of export revenue.

Therefore, during the 1990s the governments of Patricio Aylwin and Eduardo Frei Montalva (son of the former president, who was in office from 1994 to 2000) steered a course based on consensus at the national political level. The economic model would remain largely unchanged, little effort would be made to reduce military influence, and the parties of the Concertación would endeavor to set aside their differences as much as possible. All remembered the cleavages that had set the events of 1973 in motion. For those who did not feel part of this consensus, however, the refusal to challenge the inherited economic model chafed, which gradually contributed to a decline of support for the Concertación and numerous local protests. Nonetheless, this strategy certainly yielded a number of positive results. The governments of the Concertación successfully decreased unemployment, curbed inflation, and also brought down the percentage of Chileans living in poverty.

Despite the democratic advances made in Chile, serious social problems also remain. The **Mapuche**, Chile's largest indigenous group—there are approximately 800,000, or about 5 percent of the total population—have had a complicated relationship with the government. A 1972 law was passed to redistribute land to Mapuche communities but was barely implemented because of the military coup (and the military government gave the land back to the original owners). The Concertación addressed indigenous rights in its 1989 platform and passed a new indigenous law in 1993, which established a state development agency. The National Corporation for Indigenous Development (CONADI) set aside funds for development projects and prohibited the sale of some indigenous lands to nonindigenous groups, though it did allow for land transfer.

This became an issue in 2003, when the state energy company Endesa pushed to dam the Bio-Bio River at an area inhabited by the Mapuche for a major electricity project, arguing that a 1982 law trumped the Indigenous Law by allowing the state to expropriate private property for energy purposes. Presidents Frei and Lagos both agreed, and in 2003 the Mapuche families finally gave up their protests and agreed to receive compensation and land in return for leaving. However, the Mapuche also hold an annual march in Santiago to draw attention to Mapuche rights. For them, the problem is one of nationality, where their very identity is being challenged. One Mapuche organization summed it up as a problem of sovereignty: "This is the root of the problem, the other elements...poverty, marginality, lack of land, etc....are the effects and not the cause of the conflict."[13]

Legacies of Dictatorship: Human Rights

Another lingering challenge was to address the various legacies of the dictatorship. In the area of human rights, soon after his inauguration President Aylwin created the National Commission for Truth and Reconciliation, which became known as the Rettig Commission for its chair, Raúl Rettig, a respected politician and diplomat. The commission's task was to provide information on politically motivated deaths during the dictatorship. It released a report in 1991, providing details of deaths and disappearances, counting 2,279 individuals killed for political reasons (as more facts became known, that number would rise to 3,197). As a concession to the restive military, the names of perpetrators were not included, though all evidence regarding crimes was given to the courts.

Given the 1978 amnesty, however, there was little chance that many crimes could ever be prosecuted. Despite some high-profile exceptions, such as the prosecution and imprisonment for former intelligence chief Manuel Contreras, the vast majority of human rights abuses went untouched. In fact, military resistance to investigation led to two high-profile shows of force. The 1990 *ejercicio de enlace* (readiness exercise) and the 1993 *Boinazo* (a phrase referring to the *berets*, or *boinas*" that the soldiers wore) were both rooted in resistance to civilian investigations of allegations of military corruption, and constituted public displays intended to force the government to back off. Pinochet's threats were taken seriously, though by the late 1990s it seemed inconceivable that a military rebellion could occur.

The brake on human rights cases gradually eased, and activists received an unexpected international benefit in Europe. In 1996 a Spanish judge, Baltasar Garzón, had begun investigating the murder of Spanish citizens in Chile and included charges of genocide and terrorism. He called for Pinochet's arrest, arguing that domestic amnesties did not apply to international law. This call went ignored until Pinochet traveled to Great Britain for back surgery. Citing international agreements, Garzón had the British police arrest Pinochet in his hospital bed. For the next fifteen months, he would remain under house arrest while the

British government (through a special committee in the House of Lords) debated whether he should be extradited to Spain or allowed to return to Chile.

This political hot potato was resolved by claiming he was medically unfit to stand trial, and therefore could return home. This same rationale would be used several more times as Chilean courts deliberated his fate in the face of numerous different cases against him. He died in 2006 without ever being convicted. The aura of impunity embodied by Pinochet, however, was forever dispelled, and the courts became more active in pursuing human rights cases. Thus, the international influence was an important element in sparking greater national judicial activism. Particularly important was a new national legal interpretation of human rights abuses, which stipulated that a "disappearance" did not prove death, but instead could be considered an ongoing kidnapping. This in turn allowed judges to move forward with cases that otherwise would be halted by the amnesty. The irony, however, was that if death was ever proved, then the investigation would cease and the perpetrator would go free.

The Rettig Commission's report was an important—albeit limited—step toward establishing the facts and confirming the truth about political violence during the dictatorship, but it did not address the even more sensitive topic of torture. No comprehensive effort had ever been made to determine how many Chileans had been tortured but not killed, and it was not something people wanted to discuss much, but the victims' scars had never healed. President Lagos finally brought the issue to the fore in 2003 by creating the National Commission on Political Imprisonment and Torture, led by Bishop Sergio Valech. The 2004 Valech Report ultimately determined that 28,456 people had been tortured, and it also provided the shocking details of different types of torture techniques.

■■■■■■■■ ANALYZING DOCUMENTS ■■■■■■■■

Torture is a difficult subject for societies to discuss. In Chile there was no national consensus about how to address torture until over a decade after the dictatorship had ended. The Valech Report considers how the nation was divided in terms of that response.

Valech Report, Informe de la Comisión Nacional Sobre Prisión Política y Tortura (Chapter One) (2004)

Consciously or unconsciously, a conspiracy of silence about torture was slowly extended over the country. With the passing of time many believed that even though poor treatment had been common against prisoners of the military government, torture per se had not been massive. However, those who had been tortured—most of the time, also in silence—guarded their memory, the marks, and the consequences of cruel, inhumane and degrading treatment, according to the Universal Declaration of Human Rights, which literally had changed or destroyed their lives.

Others believed it was just and necessary to search for truth and justice in the cases of the detained-disappeared or of executed prisoners, victims of summary or incomplete judgment, or in the so-called emblematic cases of violations of human rights, but that it was wasn't possible to find justice in the case of victims of political imprisonment and torture. How would it be possible to prove a torture irrefutably thirty years later? What sense would there be in addressing these issues when the events seemed so distant?

...

Today, months after listening to intimate accounts, whispers, related with pain and even weeping, and seeing the physical and psychological scars, in addition to family and social wounds—some without any possible reparation to restore what has been lost— of so many Chileans who were imprisoned and tortured, we are left with no doubt that this part of the truth obliged us to complete, in the best way possible, the reparation and justice that country owes these brothers, to advance on the always difficult and necessary path of reencounter and reconciliation among Chileans.

More than thirty thousand people have come before us; we have seen and heard them. More than thirty thousand people have dared to bring themselves to our offices or to respond to our calls in the regions. And more than thirty thousand times we have listened to the stupor, the fear, the impotence that still comes from violation of dignity by agents of the State, from whom we expect—or ought to expect—respect for people, protection of the weak and a scrupulous adherence to the law. In this way we've realized, in the first person, that the corruption of power is the worst of all corruptions, because it undermines the essential foundations of credibility that all citizens await from State institutions.

But why the silence of the victims? One can understand that of the victimizers, who in their turn are also victims of their own actions. But why the silence of the victims?

After giving it much thought, we realized that it is a silence based not only on fear, despite so much fear! Also there is an aspect of elemental dignity. It's once thing to present oneself to the family after having been detained. Protestations of innocence are not a burden and there is even some pride for having suffered an injustice or a suffering for a cause one deems noble. It is also human to want to show oneself as dignified and not humiliated. But to lift the veil of torture, humiliation, and of physical and psychological violation, is very difficult to do, even with one's own spouse. And this same understandable silence was deepening the damage of the suffering not shared, of the destroyed confidences, of that which we prefer to put on the shelf of nightmares and to erase the archives of history.

...

We don't wish to prolong this presentation. The pages of the report will explain precisely what we seek to summarize. In the name of all the members of this Commission, of all that have worked with this Commission, or all that assisted generously to fulfill this task— to whom we thank from the heart—we hope that with this shared task will be another contribution to *never again*, which everyone yearns for, and to the firm handshake with which Chile desires to resolve in brotherhood so much pending debt among brothers in the same nation.

Discussion Questions
- In what ways can the local level be affected by torture sponsored by the national level?
- In what ways was the Chilean nation divided with regard to its response to torture?

Source: http://www.gobiernodechile.cl/comision_valech/ (translation by the author)

The Politics of National Consensus

As mentioned, the Concertación was founded on the ideal of consensus and the need to work together as harmoniously as possible. For the Christian Democrats, this meant accepting a presidential primary system in 1999, which was won by Ricardo Lagos, a member of the center-left Party for Democracy (PPD) created in 1988 as an offshoot of the Socialist Party, which could follow similar principles without the historical ideological baggage of the label. In the general election, he failed to win an absolute majority and barely gained a plurality (47.96 to 47.51 percent), but won in the runoff against Joaquín Lavín, a member of the right's Independent Democratic Union (UDI) party and mayor of a wealthy area of Santiago. The coalition had survived the change of presidential party leadership, but the vote totals indicated that its popularity had dropped considerably.

Lagos' six years were marked by solid economic growth, and the president was committed to a number of economic, political, and judicial reforms that modified the economic model to a greater degree. He introduced reforms that increased health coverage, for example. After years of being stymied by the right in Congress, Lagos finally managed to put a package of important constitutional reforms up for a successful vote in 2005. They removed the designated senators, changed the composition of the National Security Council to remove the military's prerogatives, and gave the president the right to fire commanders in chief. With the judicial system, Lagos also worked to change the system from inquisitorial to adversarial, which provided more opportunity for the accused to defend themselves.

Further, the reforms reduced the presidential term from six years to four. Since Bachelet's election, the presidential and lower house elections are concurrent (occurring at the same time). This facilitates greater coalition building between presidential and legislative candidates of the same party, who see mutual benefit in assisting each other and defining key issues they will jointly address.

In the 2005 Concertación primaries, Christian Democrat Soledad Alvear (who had been the first minister of SERNAM) conceded to Socialist Michelle Bachelet. As mentioned, Bachelet's father was arrested after the coup and died in prison. His daughter lived in exile until 1979. President Lagos named her minister of health (where she was associated with Plan AUGE, which expanded health care coverage) and later as the first female minister of defense in Latin America, as she had received a Master's Degree from the Chilean Army War College.

Like Lagos before her, Bachelet won a plurality (45.96 percent) but not a majority against a divided right (with both Joaquín Lavín and Sebastián Piñera running) and then won a very slim majority (53.49 to 46.50 percent) in the 2006 runoff. She also benefited from the continuing investigation into embezzlement by Augusto Pinochet and his family, who were accused of funneling over $20 million into U.S. banks (particularly the Riggs Bank). This was a thorny issue for the right, which had remained close to Pinochet and his legacy, which was now clouding.

President Bachelet's approval rating was high (63 percent) one month into her term, and her message of reform resonated. However, she immediately faced a host of problems. She had campaigned on a platform of change and had thirty-six specific measures she wanted to introduce, such as elderly health care reform, pension reform, and a change in the binomial electoral system. She had, however, also emphasized her commitment to maintaining fiscal responsibility and a balanced budget, so there were immediately limitations to the scope of reforms that required greater government spending.

During 2006, she faced a major strike by secondary students, who demanded lower fees and a restructuring of the educational system, and quickly thereafter a strike by copper miners for higher wages. These represented local-level efforts to compel the government to make policy adjustments. As a result she shuffled her cabinet mere months after taking office, and although her response was criticized as slow and inconsistent, she reached accords with both students and miners. Then in early 2007, the capital's new transportation system "Transantiago," which had been conceived during the Lagos administration, went into effect and broke down immediately, leaving people stranded and unable to get to work. Later that year, the country's largest union, the United Center of Workers (CUT) launched a strike for increased wages, which included members of Bachelet's own party. A core element in these strikes was the idea that although copper prices were high, the government was maintaining a surplus instead of investing in social programs. The consensus about the benefits of the neoliberal model made it difficult for Bachelet to please her constituencies on the left.

In late 2007, the Christian Democrats expelled one of their own members from the party for refusing to pass a funding bill for Transantiago, which demonstrated the continued fraying of the coalition. In January 2008, Bachelet shook up her cabinet once again, saying she was starting fresh for the second half of her term. By then, her approval ratings had fallen dramatically, hovering around 40 percent. Interestingly, Bachelet became more popular as the global economic crisis exploded in late 2008. Her government had refused to use copper revenue to drastically increase social spending, choosing instead to save it while prices remained high. That proved prescient, because when prices dropped she was able to introduce a $4 billion stimulus package and provide small payments to the most poor.

Bachelet also continued the pattern of hesitancy toward regional economic and political alliances. She declined to join the Bank of the South, designed by Venezuelan President Hugo Chávez as a counterweight to U.S.-dominated financial institutions. Like her predecessors, she has forged ties with Asian countries, including a free trade agreement with China.

In 2009, Sebastián Piñera ran again as part of a united coalition of the right against former president Frei for the Concertación. Discontent with the latter manifested in an independent candidate, Marco Enríquez-Ominami, who left the Socialist Party. With no candidate gaining a majority, Piñera defeated Frei in a 2010 second round, 52 to 48 percent. It marked a major political shift in Chile, as the right won the presidency for the first time in the postauthoritarian era. That it occurred so smoothly was testament to the strength of Chilean democracy. Nonetheless, he faced significant opposition because he struggled to address issues like education and environmental protection, so that by 2011 his own approval had dropped precipitously in the face of large national student strikes. The change of government did not mean that discontent disappeared.

After working at the United Nations, in 2013 Michelle Bachelet returned to Chile to much fanfare, and she announced her candidacy for the presidency. Neither coalition has a monopoly on the office anymore. The Piñera administration successfully pushed new laws that made voting voluntary and registration automatic. This will bring more voters who previously felt disenfranchised into the political mix. There is a high number of voters, especially the young, who don't feel attached to either coalition so their support is up for grabs.

Conclusion and Comparative Perspective

Sebastián Piñera's election marked an important moment in Chilean political history, as it demonstrated a clear democratic maturing. After decades, the right returned to power smoothly and democratically. This did not mean there was no controversy or disagreement, but rather that Chilean polyarchy was getting stronger. Yet at the same time, the two coalitions have seen their support dwindle. Even after the close election of 1999, predicting the Concertación's imminent demise has almost become a popular political sport. From an institutional perspective, however, there is still a strong incentive to maintain the coalition, because the individual parties would fare much more poorly in both presidential and legislative elections. The same logic holds for the right.

In general, economic growth has been solid but not spectacular, despite several years of relatively high copper prices. Like other countries that have undergone market reforms, inequality is stubbornly high and underdevelopment is still a major challenge. At the same time, Chile weathered the global recession quite well, and poverty has been consistently decreasing, which has also occurred in Brazil. As local political actors are becoming more politically active, both coalitions must balance the increasing local and national demands with the economic model, which include a small role for the state and a very open economy. The decentralization of a unitary state echoes Colombia.

Chile's pacted transition from authoritarian rule was similar to those that occurred in Brazil and Uruguay, where the armed forces retained considerable political influence, though only in Chile was there a former dictator who continued to be a problem for democratically elected civilian governments. That meant greater military autonomy for a long period than elsewhere. Yet with regard to presidentialism, we see the opposite trend. Unlike Bolivia, Colombia, Ecuador, Venezuela, and Nicaragua, Chile not only maintained prohibition on immediate reelection, but it actually reduced the length of the presidential term.

Economically, like so many other countries Chile is heavily dependent on a primary product, in its case copper. The country's economic fortunes at any

TABLE 13.1 Economic Indicators in Chile, 1991–2011

Year	GDP Growth	Inflation	Unemployment	Poverty Rate	Human Development Index
1991	7.3	18.7	8.2	—	0.880
1992	10.9	12.7	6.7	—	0.848
1993	6.6	12.2	6.5	—	0.882
1994	5.1	8.9	7.8	23.2	0.891
1995	9.0	8.2	7.4	—	0.893
1996	6.9	6.6	6.4	19.7	—
1997	6.8	6.0	6.1	—	0.844
1998	3.2	4.7	6.4	17.8	0.826
1999	−0.8	2.3	9.8	—	0.825
2000	4.5	4.5	9.7	20.2	—
2001	3.4	2.6	9.9	—	0.831
2002	2.2	2.8	9.8	—	0.839
2003	3.9	1.1	9.5	18.7	—
2004	6.0	2.4	10.0	—	0.859
2005	5.7	3.7	9.2	—	0.867
2006	4.0	2.6	7.7	13.7	0.874
2007	4.6	7.4	7.0	—	0.878
2008	3.7	8.9	7.7	—	—
2009	−1.5	−1.4	9.7	11.5	—
2010	5.3	2.5	8.3	—	0.813
2011	6.0	3.0	7.1	—	0.817

Sources: Unemployment: GDP and Inflation: *Preliminary Overview of the Economies of Latin America and the Caribbean*, 1994–2012.
Poverty rate: *Social Panorama of Latin America*. Economic Commission for Latin America, 1990–2012.
Human development index: United Nations, *Human Development Report*, 1990–2013.

given time are therefore deeply affected by its price. However, Chile has gone much farther than any other Latin American country in diversifying its international trade partners and reaching out to Asia. With an influx of foreign investment and a very stable economy, it has enjoyed considerable macroeconomic success. Nonetheless, the increase of protests by workers and students demonstrates the depth of local popular concern about the national effects of economic policy. This has not been as severe as in Bolivia or Ecuador, but still serves as a reminder about how positive national economic indicators can mask important local problems.

Key Terms

- Salvador Allende
- Augusto Pinochet
- Binomial electoral system
- Chicago Boys
- Concertación
- Mapuche

Critical Thinking Questions

- In what ways has the nature of women's local political participation been different under the dictatorship versus the postauthoritarian era?
- Analyze the conditions that made it easier for civilian governments in Chile to reduce military prerogatives. Can these conditions be replicated elsewhere in Latin America?
- How have domestic versus international factors been more important when understanding political change in Chile?
- What are the main positive outcomes of the Chilean economic model? In what ways has it created problems?
- Discuss the role that presidential government has played in Chilean political crises. To what degree would a parliamentary government likely have changed political outcomes?

Further Sources

Books

Franceschet, Susan. *Women and Politics in Chile* (Boulder: Lynne Rienner, 2005). This is an analysis of women's marginalization from politics in Chile, using the lens of citizenship as a means of explaining why, despite the high-profile entrance of several women to high political office, women's movements and efforts to promote women's interests have remained weak.

Haughney, Diane. *Neoliberal Economic, Democratic Transition, and Mapuche Demands for Rights in Chile* (Gainesville: University Press of Florida, 2006). A well-written discussion of the obstacles indigenous Chileans face as they seek to protect their indigenous roots. She argues that the state's emphasis on neoliberal economics blocks any acceptance of indigenous demands.

Oppenheim, Lois Hecht. *Politics in Chile: Socialism, Authoritarianism, and Market Democracy*, 3rd edition (Boulder: Westview, 2007). The book is an accessible overview of Chilean politics, focusing on the post-1970 period. It has very useful notes and bibliography.

Stern, Steve J. *Remembering Pinochet's Chile: On the Eve of London 1998* (Durham: Duke University Press, 2004). This is the first part of a trilogy analyzing the complexities of memory in Chile. It includes examples and interviews of how people from all different walks of life—and different ideologies—remember the dictatorship and how they related to it.

Weeks, Gregory. *The Military and Politics in Postauthoritarian Chile* (Tuscaloosa: University of Alabama Press, 2003). This is an analysis focusing primarily on the post-1990 period, examining how the relationship between the civilian government and the armed forces unfolded in both formal and less formal means.

Web Sites

The Chilean Government (http://www.chileangovernment.cl/). The government maintains a Web site for the English-reading audience, focusing on its international connections. This includes a discussion of political institutions, free trade agreements, and details about each region of the country.

Report of the Chilean National Commission on Truth and Reconciliation (http://www.usip.org/publications/truth-commission-chile-90). This is the full text (including copies of the decree, notes, and a guide to the English edition) of the Rettig Commission's report in English, posted by the U.S. Institute of Peace.

Villa Grimaldi (http://www.villagrimaldi.cl/). The Villa Grimaldi Park for Peace is the site of the infamous detainment and torture center in Santiago, where President Bachelet was also taken. The Web site has an English version as well, and it provides history, testimonies, names of the missing, and even names of the torturers who were there.

National Security Archive: Chile Documentation Project (http://www.gwu.edu/~nsarchiv/latin_america/chile.htm). The National Security Archive is a nongovernmental research institute that works to declassify previously secret documents of the U.S. government. It includes many documents (in PDF format) about the relationship with the Pinochet government.

The Santiago Times (http://www.santiagotimes.cl). This is an English-language newspaper about Chilean current events available online (including RSS feeds). It covers a wide range of topics from across Chile.

Endnotes

1. Loveman, Brian. *Chile: The Legacy of Hispanic Capitalism* (New York: Oxford University Press, 2001), 164–5.
2. Quoted in Drake, Paul. "Chile, 1930–1958." In Leslie Bethell (ed.), *The Cambridge History of Latin America* (Cambridge: Cambridge University Press, 1991), 279.
3. Gunther, John. *Inside Latin America* (New York: Harper and Brothers, 1941), 259.
4. Papers Relating to the Foreign Relations of the United States 1964–1968, volume XXXI, *South and Central America; Mexico* (Washington: United States Government Printing Office, 2004), 553.
5. Haslam, Jonathan. *The Nixon Administration and the Death of Allende's Chile* (London: Verso, 2005), 56.
6. Valenzuela, Arturo. "Party Politics and the Crisis of Presidentialism in Chile: A Proposal for a Parliamentary Form of Government." In Juan J. Linz and Arturo Valenzuela, *The Failure of Presidential Democracy: The Case of Latin America*, volume 2 (Baltimore: The Johns Hopkins University Press, 1994), 91–150.
7. Quoted in Valdés, Juan Gabriel. *Pinochet's Economists* (New York: Cambridge University Press, 1995), 21.
8. Borzutzky, Silvia. *Vital Connections: Politics, Social Security, and Inequality in Chile* (Notre Dame, IN: University of Notre Dame Press, 2002), 240.
9. Quoted in Schild, Verónica. "Recasting 'Popular Movements': Gender and Political Learning in Neighborhood Organizations in Chile." In Richard Stahler-Sholk, Harry

E. Vanden, and Glen David Kuecker (eds.). *Latin American Social Movements in the Twenty-First Century: Resistance, Power, and Democracy* (Lanham, MD: Rowman and Littlefield Publishers, Inc., 2008), 225.

10. Franceschet, Susan. "Explaining Social Movement Outcomes: Collective Action Frames and Strategic Choices in First- and Second-Wave Feminism in Chile." *Comparative Political Studies* 37, 5 (June 2004): 499–530.

11. Perry, Guillermo and Michael Walton. *Inequality in Latin America and the Caribbean: Breaking with History?* (Washington, DC: World Bank, 2004).

12. Lagos, Ricardo. *Mi idea de país* (Santiago: Prosa, 1999), 95.

13. Quoted in Haughney, Diane. *Neoliberal Economics, Democratic Transition, and Mapuche Demands for Rights in Chile* (Gainesville: University Press of Florida, 2006), 199.

GLOSSARY

Abertura Period of political opening in Brazil from 1979 to 1985.

Alfonsín, Raúl President of Argentina (1983–1989).

Allende, Salvador President of Chile (1970–1973); overthrown by a coup.

American Revolutionary Popular Alliance (APRA) Peruvian reformist political party created in 1924 that became a target for political elites.

Batista, Fulgencio Dictator of Cuba from 1952 to 1959; overthrown by revolution led by Fidel Castro.

Binomial electoral system Chilean electoral system that requires over two-third vote to get both seats in a district.

Brazilian Landless Workers' Movement Influential grassroots movement in Brazil founded in 1980.

CAFTA-DR Free trade agreement between the United States, Central American countries, and the Dominican Republic.

Capitalism An economic system characterized by market supply and demand with minimal state intervention.

Caracazo 1989 riots in Caracas that left at least 300 dead.

Cardoso, Fernando Henrique President of Brazil (1995–2003).

Castro, Fidel Led the revolution that overthrew Fulgencio Batista; leader of Cuba from 1959 until 2006.

Castro, Raúl Brother of Fidel Castro; head of the Cuban armed forces and president of Cuba beginning in 2006.

Caudillo A military figure who develops a large following and establishes some variant of authoritarian rule at the regional level.

Centralist A political system with a strong central authority.

Chávez, Hugo Venezuelan president (1999–2013).

Chicago Boys Group of Chilean economists educated at the University of Chicago who advised the military government.

Civil society Groups organizing at the local level to push for change of some sort.

Commodity A primary product that is mined or cultivated.

Communism An ideology characterized by total government control over politics and the economy.

Concertación Chilean center-left coalition founded in 1988.

confederal A political system where regional governments are more powerful than the central government.

Confederation of Indigenous Nationalities of Ecuador (CONAIE) Politically influential ethnic movement in Ecuador.

Conservative Those committed to maintaining many of the political and social characteristics of the Spanish (or Portuguese) regimes.

Corporatism A set of formal institutions that facilitate clientelist rel.

Correa, Rafael Populist president of Ecuador (2006–present).

Coup d'état The sudden overthrow of a government.

Creoles Native-born and lighter skinned colonial elites.

Democratic socialism A political system in which citizens have the opportunity to vote and there is considerable debate in legislatures about what types of socialist policies to pursue.

Dependency theory A theory focused on how less-developed countries are dominated economically by the developed world, exporting primary products and importing finished goods.

Devalue To make one's own national currency worth less than others. This spurs exports.

Dollarization The conversion of a currency to the U.S. dollar.

Dutch disease The dilemma whereby a country rich in natural resources will see its currency appreciate to the detriment of other domestic industries.

Ejido A traditional system of communal land in Mexico.

Embargo   Laws intended to block trade between one country and another.

Estado Novo   Corporatist era in Brazil led by President Getulio Vargas from 1937 to 1945.

Exchange rate   The value of one country's currency versus another.

Farabundo Martí National Liberation Front (FMLN)   Guerrilla organization in El Salvador that later became a political party.

Federal   A political system where a central government and regional governments share authority.

Fernández de Kirchner, Cristina   President of Argentina (2007–present).

Fuero   Special privileges and immunity, especially for the military and clergy.

Fujimori, Alberto   Populist president of Peru (1990–2000) who resigned in disgrace and was later convicted of human rights abuses.

Gini coefficient   A statistical measure of income inequality.

Gross domestic product (GNP)   The value of all goods and services produced within a country in one year.

Guerrilla   A combatant who uses hit-and-run tactics and knowledge of local terrain to confront a conventional army.

Guevara, Che   Argentine revolutionary who became a leader of the Cuban revolution.

Hacienda   A large plantation.

Horizontal accountability   The ability of the executive, legislative, and judicial branches to hold each other politically accountable.

Human development index (HDI)   A measure derived from life expectancy at birth, average years of schooling, and average income.

Hyperinflation   Inflation that is at least 50 percent a month.

Ideology   A set of ideas that are aimed at a specific political goal.

Informal economy   Refers to people who perform work and earn money that is not sanctioned or recorded by the government.

Institutional Revolutionary Party (PRI)   The postrevolutionary Mexican political party that dominated Mexican politics until the 2000 presidential election.

International Monetary Fund (IMF)   An international institution that makes loans and became a clearinghouse for loans.

Justicialist (Peronist) Party   Argentine political party founded in 1946 and originally centered on Juan Perón (see also Juan Perón).

Kirchner, Néstor   President of Argentina (2003–2007).

La Violencia   A decade (1948–1958) of severe political violence in Colombia, resulting in over 100,000 dead.

Liberal democracy   A broad definition of democracy that goes beyond holding elections and includes a wider array of rights.

Liberals   Those committed to an emphasis on the separation of church and state, on international trade, and in general a challenge to the traditional order.

Lula   President of Brazil (2003–2011).

Mapuche   Largest indigenous group in Chile.

Menem, Carlos   President of Argentina (1989–1999).

Mestizos   People of mixed race between Iberian conquerors and natives.

Modernization theory   A theory claiming that underdeveloped countries can advance by copying the model of already developed countries.

Morales, Evo   Former coca grower union leader who in 2005 became the first Bolivian president of indigenous descent.

Mothers of the Plaza de Mayo   Influential Argentine protest organization founded in 1977.

Nation   Deeply shared common characteristics that create a sense of identification for a large group of people.

Nongovernmental organization (NGO)   An organization with political goals that is independent of any government.

Noriega, Manuel   Dictator of Panama from 1981 to 1989. Overthrown by a U.S. invasion.

North American Free Trade Agreement (NAFTA)   An agreement between Canada, Mexico, and the United States to reduce trade barriers, which went into effect in 1994.

Organization of American States (OAS)   A regional organization based on the principles of the United Nations.

Ortega, Daniel   Former Sandinista guerrilla leader and later president of Nicaragua.

Pact of Punto Fijo   1958 power-sharing pact in Venezuela between the major political parties.

Paramilitaries   Armed organizations that operate apart from the military.

Peasant   People in rural areas engaged in agriculture.

Peninsulares   Spanish- and Portuguese-born colonial elites.

Perón, Juan Domingo   Populist leader and periodic president in Argentina. His movement still bears his name (see also Justicialist Party).

PDVSA   The state oil company of Venezuela (Petroleum of Venezuela), which is central to generating government revenue.

Pinochet, Augusto   President and dictator of Chile (1973–1990).

Plan Colombia   Antidrug initiative launched by the United States and Colombia in 2000.

Platt Amendment   Passed in 1901; inserted into the Cuban constitution to guarantee the right of the United States to intervene.

Polyarchy   Concept developed by Robert Dahl that focuses on competitive elections as a core aspect of democracy (see also procedural democracy).

Populism   A style of governing characterized by personalism and a high level of connection between the executive and the population.

Procedural democracy   A narrow definition characterized by competitive elections and universal suffrage (see also polyarchy).

Proceso   Period of Argentine military dictatorship from 1976 to 1983.

Radical Civic Union Party (UCR)   Moderate political party in Argentina that is the oldest in the country.

Remittances   Money sent from migrant workers back to their country of origin.

Revolution   Radical armed overthrows of the entire political system.

Revolutionary Armed Forces of Colombia (FARC)   Guerrilla organization founded in 1964 and still active.

Revolutionary Nationalist Movement (MNR)   Bolivian reformist and corporatist political party created in 1941.

Rousseff, Dilma   President of Brazil (2001–present).

Sánchez de Lozada, Gonzalo   Twice president of Bolivia (1993–1997; 2002–2003), forced to resign in 2003 and went into exile.

Sánchez, Yoani   Cuban opposition blogger.

Sandinista National Liberation Front (FSLN)   Guerrilla organization in Nicaragua that overthrew Anastasio Somoza Debayle in 1979 and later became a political party.

Santos, Juan Manuel   Former defense minister who was elected president of Colombia in 2010.

Self-coup   An illegal dissolution of other state institutions by the president, leaving power entirely in his or her hands.

Shining Path   Very violent guerrilla force created in Peru in 1980.

Socialism   An ideology that focuses on government ownership over means of production to achieve economic equality.

Somoza Debayle, Anastasio   Dictator of Nicaragua from 1967 to 1979; overthrown by the Sandinistas.

Special Period in Peacetime   Era of economic deprivation in Cuba from 1991 to the mid-1990s.

State   The concrete institutions that allow a government to function domestically and as part of an international system.

Technocrats   Individuals in bureaucracies who have technical expertise on specific issues. In theory they are apolitical.

Undocumented immigrants   Latin American migrants living in the United States without legal status.

United Socialist Party of Venezuela (PSUV)   The broad political coalition party created by President Hugo Chávez.

Uribe, Alvaro   President of Colombia (2002–2010).

Vertical accountability   The degree to which national authorities are held accountable to voters.

War of the Pacific   War between Bolivia, Chile, and Peru from 1879 to 1884.

Workers' Party or PT   Influential Brazilian political party founded in 1980.

World Bank   An international institution whose purpose is to fund and coordinate development projects.

Zelaya, José Manuel   Honduran president who was overthrown in 2009.

BIBLIOGRAPHY

Abreu, Marcelo de P., Afonso S. Bevilaqua, and Demosthenes M. Pinho. "Import Substitution and Growth in Brazil, 1890s-1970s." In Enrique Cárdenas, José Antonio Campo, and Rosemary Thorp (eds.). *An Economic History of Twentieth Century Latin America*, Volume 3 (New York: Palgrave, 2000): 154–175.

Allende, Isabel. *The House of the Spirits* (New York: Bantam, 1993).

Alvarez, Bernardo. "How Chávez Has Helped the Poor." *Foreign Affairs* 87, 4 (2008): 158–160.

Alvarez, Sonia E. "The (trans)formation of Feminism(s) and Gender Politics in Democratizing Brazil." In Jane S. Jaquette (ed.). *The Women's Movement in Latin America: Participation and Democracy*, 2nd Edition (Boulder: Westview Press, 1994): 13–63.

Anderson, Leslie E. "The Authoritarian Executive? Horizontal and Vertical Accountability in Nicaragua." *Latin American Politics & Society* 48, 2 (2006): 141–169.

Archer, Ronald and Matthew Soberg Shugart. "The Unrealized Potential of Presidential Dominance in Colombia." In Scott Mainwaring and Matthew Soberg Shugart (eds.). *Presidentialism and Democracy in Latin America* (New York: Cambridge University Press, 1997): 110–159.

Arias, Enrique Desmond. *Drugs and Democracy in Rio de Janeiro* (Chapel Hill: University of North Carolina Press, 2006).

Avellaneda, Claudia N. "Mayoral Quality and Local Public Finance." *Public Administration Review* 69, 3 (2009): 469–486.

Avilés, William. "Despite Insurgency: Reducing Military Prerogatives in Colombia and Peru." *Latin American Politics and Society* 51, 1 (2009): 57–85.

Avritzer, Leonardo. *Participatory Institutions in Democratic Brazil* (Baltimore: The Johns Hopkins University Press, 2009).

Baer, Werner. *The Brazilian Economy: Growth and Development* (Boulder: Lynne Rienner Publishers, 2008).

Barrionuevo, Alexei. "Inflation, an Old Scourge, Plagues Argentina Again." *The New York Times*, February 5, 2011.

BBC News, "Ecuador Defaults on Foreign Debt," December 13, 2008.

Beer, Carolina C. "Electoral Competition and Fiscal Decentralization in Mexico." In Alfred P. Montero and David J. Samuels (eds.). *Decentralization and Democracy in Latin America* (Notre Dame, IN: University of Notre Dame Press, 2004): 180–200.

Bemis, Samuel Flagg. *The Latin American Policy of the United States: An Historical Interpretation* (New York: Harcourt, Brace and Company, 1943).

Bermann, Karl. *Under the Big Stick: Nicaragua and the United States since 1848* (Boston: South End Press, 1986).

Betancourt, Rómulo. *Venezuela: Oil and Politics* (Boston: Houghton Mifflin, 1979).

Bolívar, Simón. *El Libertador, Writings of Simón Bolívar* (New York: Oxford University Press, 2003).

Booth, John A., Christina J. Wade, and Thomas W. Walker. *Understanding Central America* (Boulder: Westview Press, 2010).

Borzutzky, Silvia. *Vital Connections: Politics, Social Security, and Inequality in Chile* (Notre Dame, IN: University of Notre Dame Press, 2002).

Bourne, Richard. *Lula of Brazil: The Story So Far* (Berkeley: University of California Press, 2008).

Bowman, Kirk F. *Militarization, Democracy, and Development: The Perils of Praetorianism in Latin America* (University Park, PA: The Pennsylvania State University Press, 2002).

Brysk, Alison. *From Tribal Village to Global Village: Indian Rights and International Relations in Latin America* (Stanford: Stanford University Press, 2000).

Brysk, Alison. *The Politics of Human Rights in Argentina: Protest, Change, and Democratization* (Stanford: Stanford University Press, 1994).

Bushnell, David and Neill Macaulay, *The Emergence of Latin America in the Nineteenth Century*, 2nd Edition (Oxford: Oxford University Press, 1994).

Buxton, Julia. "Venezuela's Contemporary Political Crisis in Historical Context."

Bulletin of Latin American Research 24, 3 (2005): 328–347.

Crandall, Russell. *Driven By Drugs: U.S. Policy Toward Colombia,* 2nd edition (Boulder: Lynne Rienner Publishers, 2008).

Cardoso, Fernando Henrique. *The Accidental President of Brazil* (New York: PublicAffairs, 2006).

Cardoso, Fernando Henrique and Enzo Faletto. *Dependency and Development in Latin America* (Berkeley: University of California Press, 1979).

Carey, John. "Strong Candidates for a Limited Office: Presidentialism and Political Parties in Costa Rica." In Scott Mainwaring and Matthew Soberg Shugart (eds.). *Presidentialism and Democracy in Latin America* (New York: Cambridge University Press, 1997): 199–224.

Carranza Valdés, Julio, Juan Valdés Paz, and Raúl J. Rosales. "Institutional Development and Social Policy in Cuba: The 'Special Period.'" *Journal of International Affairs* 58, 1 (2004): 175–188.

Castañeda, Jorge G. "Latin America's Left Turn." *Foreign Affairs* 85, 3 (2006): 28–43.

Castellanos Moya, Horacio. *Senselessness* (New York: New Directions, 2008).

Centeno, Miguel Angel. *Blood and Debt: War and the Nation-State in Latin America* (University Park: The Pennsylvania State University Press, 2002).

Centeno, Miguel Angel and Fernando López-Alves. "Introduction." In Miguel Angel Centeno and Fernando López-Alves (eds.). *The Other Mirror: Grand Theory through the Lens of Latin America* (Princeton: Princeton University Press, 2001): 3–23.

Centeno, Miguel Angel and Alejandro Portes. "The Informal Economy in the Shadow of the State." In Patricia Fernández-Kelly and Jon Shefner (eds.). *Out of the Shadows: Political Action and the Informal Economy in Latin America* (University Park: The Pennsylvania State University Press, 2006): 23–48.

Cepeda Ulloa, Fernando. "Colombia: The Governability Crisis." In Jorge I. Domínguez and Michael Shifter (eds.). *Constructing Democratic Governance in Latin America,* 2nd Edition (Baltimore: The Johns Hopkins University Press, 2003): 193–219.

Chasteen, John Charles. *Born in Blood and Fire: A Concise History of Latin America* (New York: W.W. Norton and Company, 2001).

Chavez, Rebecca Bill. *The Rule of Law in Nascent Democracies: Judicial Politics in Argentina* (Stanford: Stanford University Press, 2004).

Cheibub, José Antonio. *Presidentialism, Parliamentarism, and Democracy* (New York: Cambridge University Press, 2007).

Chinchilla, Norma Stoltz. "Feminism, Revolution, and Democratic Transitions in Nicaragua." In Jane S. Jaquette (ed.). *The Women's Movement in Latin America: Participation and Democracy* (Boulder: Westview Press, 1994): 177–197.

Collier, David and Steven Levitsky. "Democracy with Adjectives: Conceptual Innovation in Comparative Research." *World Politics* 49, 3 (1997): 430–451.

Collier, Ruth Berins and David Collier. *Shaping the Political Arena* (Princeton: Princeton University Press, 1991).

Conaghan, Catherine M. "Ecuador: Correa's Plebiscitary Presidency." In Larry Diamond, Marc F. Plattner, and Diego Abente Brun (eds.). *Latin America's Struggle for Democracy* (Baltimore: The Johns Hopkins University Press, 2008): 199–213.

Conrad, Joseph. *Lord Jim & Nostromo* (New York: The Modern Library, 1999 [1904]).

Coppedge, Michael. "Venezuela: Popular Sovereignty versus Liberal Democracy." In Jorge I. Domínguez and Michael Shifter (eds.). *Constructing Democratic Governance in Latin America* (Baltimore: The Johns Hopkins University Press, 2003): 165–192.

Coppedge, Michael. "Venezuela: Democratic despite Presidentialism." In Juan J. Linz and Arturo Valenzuela (eds.). *The Failure of Presidential Democracy: The Case of Latin America,* Volume 2 (Baltimore: The John Hopkins University Press, 1994): 322–347.

Coppedge, Michael. *Strong Parties and Lame Ducks: Presidential Partyarchy and Factionalism in Venezuela* (Stanford: Stanford University Press, 1994).

Corrales, Javier. "Presidents, Ruling Parties, and Party Rules: A Theory on the Politics of Economic Reform in Latin America." *Comparative Politics* 32, 2 (2000): 127–149.

Craske, Nikki. *Women and Politics in Latin America* (New Brunswick, NJ: Rutgers University Press, 1999).

Dahl, Robert A. *Polyarchy: Participation and Opposition* (New Haven: Yale University Press, 1971).

Degregoria, Carlos Iván. "The Origins and Logic of Shining Path: Two Views." In David Scott Palmer (ed.). *Shining Path of Peru* (New York: St. Martin's Press, 1992): 33–44.

De Jesus, María Carolina. *Child of the Dark* (New York: Signet Books, 1962).

De la Cruz, Rafael. "Decentralization: Understanding a Changing Nation." In Jennifer L. McCoy and David J. Myers (eds.). *The Unraveling of Representative Democracy in Venezuela* (Baltimore: The Johns Hopkins University Press, 2004): 181–201.

De la Fuente, Alejandro and Laurence Glasco. "Are Blacks 'getting out of Control'? Racial Attitudes, Revolution, and Political Transition in Cuba." In Miguel Angel Centeno and Mauricio Font (eds.). *Toward a New Cuba? Legacies of a Revolution* (Boulder: Lynne Rienner Publishers, 1997): 39–52.

Denissen, Marieke. "Reintegrating Ex-Combatants into Civilian Life: The Case of the Paramilitaries in Colombia." *Peace and Change* 35, 2 (2010): 328–352.

DePalma, Anthony. *The Man Who Invented Fidel: Castro, Cuba, and Herbert L. Matthews of the New York Times* (New York: Public Affairs, 2006).

Diamint, Rut. "Crisis, Democracy, and the Military in Argentina." In Edward Epstein and David Pion-Berlin (eds.). *Broken Promises? The Argentine Crisis and Argentine Democracy* (Lanham: Lexington Books, 2006): 163–179.

Dixon, Kwame. "Transnational Black Social Movements in Latin America: Afro-Colombians and the Struggle for Human Rights." In Richard Stahler-Sholk, Harry E. Vanden, and Glen David Kuecker (eds.). *Latin American Social Movements in the Twenty-First Century: Resistance, Power, and Democracy* (Lanham: Rowman and Littlefield Publishers, Inc., 2008): 181–195.

Dodson, Michael and Donald W. Jackson. "Horizontal Accountability and the Rule of Law in Central America." In Scott Mainwaring and Christopher Welna (eds.). *Democratic Accountability in Latin America* (New York: Oxford University Press, 2003): 228–265.

Donna Lee, Van Cott. *Radical Democracy in the Andes* (New York: Cambridge University Press, 2009).

Drake, Paul. "Chile, 1930-1958." In Leslie Bethell (ed.). *The Cambridge History of Latin America* (Cambridge: Cambridge University Press, 1991): 267–310.

Drake, Paul W. *Between Tyranny and Anarchy: A History of Democracy in Latin America: 1800-2006* (Stanford: Stanford University Press, 2009).

Dunkerley, James. *The Pacification of Central America* (New York: Verso, 1994).

Eaton, Kent. "Subnational Economic Nationalism? The Contradictory Effects of Decentralization in Peru." *Third World Quarterly* 31, 7 (October 2010): 1205–1222.

Eckstein, Susan. "Power and Popular Protest in Latin America." In Susan Eckstein (ed.). *Power and Popular Protest: Latin American Social Movements* (Berkeley: University of California Press, 1989): 1–60.

Eduardo A. Gamarra. "Hybrid Presidential and Democratization: The Case of Bolivia." In Scott Mainwaring and Matthew S. Shugart (eds.), *Presidentialism and Democracy in Latin America* (New York: Carmbridge University Press, 1997).

Eisenhower, Milton S. *The Wine Is Bitter: The United States and Latin America* (New York: Doubleday and Company, Inc., 1963).

Eisenstadt, Todd A. "Mexico's Postelectoral Concertacesiones: The Rise and Demise of a Substitutive Informal Institution." In Gretchen Helmke and Steven Levitsky (eds.). *Informal Institution and Democracy: Lessons from Latin America* (Baltimore: The Johns Hopkins University Press, 2006): 227–248.

Eisenstadt, Todd A. "Agrarian Tenure Institution Conflict Frames, and Communitarian Identities: The Case of Indigenous Southern Mexico." *Comparative Political Studies* 42, 1 (2009): 82–113.

Ellner, Steve. *Rethinking Venezuelan Politics: Class, Conflict, and the Chávez Phenomenon* (Boulder: Lynne Rienner Publishers, 2008).

Erikson, Daniel. *The Cuba Wars: Fidel Castro, the United States, and the next Revolution* (New York: Bloomsbury Press, 2009).

Feitlowitz, Marguerite. *A Lexicon of Terror: Argentina and the Legacies of Torture* (New York: Oxford University Press, 1998).

Fernandes, Sujatha. "Barrio Women and Popular Politics in Chávez's Venezuela," *Latin American Politics & Society* 49, 3 (2007): 97–127.

Franceschet, Susan. "Explaining Social Movement Outcomes: Collective Action Frames and Strategic Choices in First- and Second-Wave Feminism in Chile." *Comparative Political Studies* 37, 5 (2004): 499–530.

Franko, Patrice. *The Puzzle of Latin American Economic Development*, 3rd Edition (Lanham: Rowman and Littlefield Publishers, Inc., 2007).

Friedman, Elisabeth J. *Unfinished Transitions: Women and the Gendered Development of Democracy in Venezuela, 1936-1996* (University Park: The Pennsylvania State University Press, 2000).

Fuentes, Carlos. *The Campaign* (New York: HarperPerennial, 1990).

Fukuyama, Francis (ed). *Falling Behind: Explaining the Development Gap Between Latin America and the United States* (Oxford: Oxford University Press, 2008).

Gallegos, Rómulo. *Doña Bárbara (Translated by Robert Malloy)* (New York: Peter Smith, 1948).

Garner, Paul. *Porfirio Díaz* (New York: Longman, 2001).

Gonzalez-Perez, Margaret. *Women and Terrorism: Female Activity in Domestic and International Terror Groups* (New York: Routledge, 2008).

Guevara, Aleida. *Chávez, Venezuela and the New Latin America: An Interview with Hugo Chávez* (Melbourne: Ocean Press, 2005).

Guevara, Che. *Guerrilla Warfare, with an Introduction and Case Studies by Brian Loveman and Thomas M. Davies, Jr.* (Lincoln: University of Nebraska Press, 1985).

Gunder Frank, Andre. *Capitalism and Underdevelopment in Latin America: Historical Studies of Chile and Brazil* (New York: Monthly Review Press, 1967).

Gunther, John. *Inside Latin America* (New York: Harper and Brothers, 1941).

Haber, Stephen, Herbert S. Klein, Noel Maurer, and Kevin J. Middlebrook. *Mexico Since 1980* (New York: Cambridge University Press, 2008).

Harrison, Lawrence. "Promoting Progressive Cultural Change," In Lawrence E. Harrison and Samuel P. Huntington (eds.). *Culture Matters: How Values Shape Human Progress* (New York: Basic Books, 2000): 296–307.

Hartlyn, Jonathan. "Colombia: The Politics of Violence and Accommodation." In Larry Diamond, Juan J. Linz, and Seymour Martin Lipset (eds.). *Democracy in Developing Countries: Volume 4, Latin America* (Boulder: Lynne Rienner Publishers, 1989): 291–334.

Haslam, Jonathan. *The Nixon Administration and the Death of Allende's Chile* (London: Verso, 2005).

Haughney, Diane. *Neoliberal Economics, Democratic Transition, and Mapuche Demands for Rights in Chile* (Gainesville: University Press of Florida, 2006).

Hawkins, Kirk. "Is Chávez Populist? Measuring Populist Discourse in Comparative Perspective" *Comparative Political Studies* 42, 8 (2009): 1040–1067.

Hellinger, Daniel C. *Venezuela: Tarnished Democracy* (Boulder: Westview Press, 1991).

Holden, Robert H. *Armies without Nations: Public Violence and State Formation in Central America, 1821-1960* (New York: Oxford University Press, 2004).

Hornbeck, J. F. *NAFTA at Ten: Lessons from Recent Studies.* CRS Report for Congress RS21737, February 21, 2004.

Houtzager, Peter P. and Adrian Gurza Lavalle. "Civil Society's Claims to Political Representation in Brazil." *Studies in Comparative International Development* 45, 1 (2010): 1–29.

Hristov, Jasmin. *Blood & Capital: The Paramilitarization of Colombia* (Athens: Ohio University Press, 2009).

Htun, Mala and Timothy J. Power. "Gender, Parties, and Support for Equal Rights in the Brazilian Congress." *Latin American Politics & Society* 48, 4 (2006): 83–104.

Inkeles, Alex and David H. Smith. *Becoming Modern: Individual Change in Six Developing Countries* (Cambridge: Harvard University Press, 1974).

International Herald Tribune. "Peru Removes Army Chief, Says Spat with Chile Over." December 6, 2008.

Jameson, Kenneth P. "Dollarization in Latin America: Wave of the Future or Flight to the Past?" *Journal of Economic Issues* 37, 3 (2003): 643–663.

Jennissen, Therese and Colleen Lundy. "Women in Cuba and the Move to a Private Market Economy." *Women's Studies International Forum* 24, 2 (2001): 181–198.

Jones, Bart. *Hugo! The Hugo Chávez Story from Mud Hut to Perpetual Revolution* (Hanover, NH: Steerforth Press, 2007).

Karl, Terry Lynn. "Dilemmas of Democratization in Latin America." *Comparative Politics* 23, 1 (1990): 1–21.

Katz, Jorge and Bernardo Kosacoff. "Import-Substituting Industrialization in Argentina, 1940-1980: Its Achievements and Shortcoming." In Enrique Cárdenas, José Antonio Campo, and Rosemary Thorp (eds.). *An Economic History of Twentieth Century Latin America*, Volume 3 (New York: Palgrave, 2000): 282–313.

Klepak, Hal. "Cuba's Revolutionary Armed Forces: Last Bulwark of the State? Last Bulwark of the Revolution? In Philip Brenner, Marguerite Rose Jiménez, John M. Kirk, and William M. Leo Grande (eds.). *Reinventing the Revolution: A Contemporary Cuba Reader* (Lanham, MD: Rowman and Littlefield Publishers, Inc., 2008): 63–73.

Kline, Harvey F. *State Building and Conflict Resolution in Colombia: 1986-1994* (Tuscaloosa: The University of Alabama Press, 1999).

Kline, Harvey F. *Chronicle of a Failure Foretold: The Peace Process of Colombian President Andrés Pastrana* (Tuscaloosa: University of Alabama Press, 2007).

Krauze, Enrique. "Looking at Them: A Mexican Perspective on the Gap with the United States." In Francis Fukuyama (ed.). *Falling Behind: Explaining the Development Gap Between Latin America and the United States* (Oxford: Oxford University Press, 2008): 48–71.

Lagos, Ricardo. *Mi Idea De País* (Santiago: Prosa, 1999).

Latell, Brian. *After Fidel: Raul Castro and the Future of Cuba's Revolution* (New York: Palgrave Macmillan, 2005).

Levitsky, Steven. *Transforming Labor-Based Parties in Latin America: Argentine Peronism in Comparative Perspective* (New York: Cambridge University Press, 2002).

Levitsky, Steven and María Victoria Murillo. "Building Castles in the Sand? The Politics of Institutional Weakness in Argentina." In Steven Levitsky and María Victoria Murillo (eds.). *Argentine Democracy: The Politics of Institutional Weakness* (University Park: The Pennsylvania State University Press, 2005): 25–44.

Lewis Paul H. *The Agony of Argentine Capitalism: From Menem to the Kirchners* (New York: Praeger, 2009).

Linz, Juan J. "Presidential or Parliamentary Democracy: Does It Make a Difference?" In Juan J. Linz and Arturo Valenzuela (eds.). *The Failure of Presidential Democracy: The Case of Latin America*, Volume 2 (Baltimore: The Johns Hopkins University Press, 1994): 3–87.

Lipset, Seymour Martin. "Values, Education, and Entrepreneurship." In Seymour Martin Lipset and Aldo Solari (eds.). *Elites in Latin America* (New York: Oxford University Press, 1967): 3–60.

López-Alves, Fernando. *State Formation and Democracy in Latin America, 1810-1900* (Durham: Duke University Press, 2000).

Loveman, Brian. *For La Patria: Politics and the Armed Forces in Latin America* (Wilmington, DE: Scholarly Resources, 1999).

Loveman, Brian. *Chile: The Legacy of Hispanic Capitalism* (New York: Oxford University Press, 2001).

Loveman, Brian. *The Constitution of Tyranny: Regimes of Exception in Spanish America* (Pittsburgh: University of Pittsburgh Press, 2003).

Loveman, Brian and Thomas M. Davies, Jr. (eds.). *The Politics of Antipolitics: The Military in Latin America* (Wilmington, DE: SR Books, 1997).

Lucero, José Antonio and María Elena García. "In the Shadows of Success: Indigenous Politics in Peru and Ecuador." In A. Kim Clark and Marc Becker (eds.). *Highland Indians and the State in Modern Ecuador* (Pittsburgh: University of Pittsburgh Press, 2007): 234–247.

Lunda, Francisco Vidal and Herbert S. Klein. *Brazil Since 1980*. (New York: Cambridge University Press, 2006).

Lynch, John. *Caudillos in Spanish America, 1800-1850* (Oxford: Clarendon Press, 1992).

Mahoney, James. *The Legacies of Liberalism: Path Dependence and Political Regimes in Central America* (Baltimore: The Johns Hopkins University Press, 2001).

Mainwaring, Scott. "The Crisis of Representation in the Andes." In Larry Diamond, Marc F. Plattner, and Diego Abente Brun (eds.). *Latin America's Struggle for Democracy* (Baltimore: The Johns Hopkins University Press, 2008): 18–32.

Mainwaring, Scott, Ana María Bejarano, and Eduardo Pizarro Leongómez. *The Crisis of Democratic Representation in the Andes* (Stanford: Stanford University Press, 2006).

Mainwaring, Scott and Matthew Soberg Shugart. "Conclusion: Presidentialism and the Party System." In Scott Mainwaring and Matthew Soberg Shugart (eds.). *Presidentialism and Democracy in Latin America* (New York: Cambridge University Press, 1997): 394–437.

Martz, John D. and David J. Myers. *Venezuela: The Democratic Experience* (New York: Praeger Publishers, 1977).

McCann, Bryan. *The Throes of Democracy: Brazil Since 1989* (London: Zed Books, 2008).

McClintock, Cynthia. "Peru: Precarious Regimes, Authoritarian and Democratic." In Larry Diamond, Juan J. Linz, and Seymour Martin Lipset (eds.). *Democracy in Developing Countries: Latin America* (Boulder: Lynne Rienner Publishers, 1989): 335–385.

McCoy, Jennifer L. "From Representative to Participatory Democracy? Regime Transformation in Venezuela." In Jennifer L. McCoy and David J. Myers (eds.). *The Unraveling of Representative Democracy in Venezuela* (Baltimore: The Johns Hopkins University Press, 2004): 263–295.

Melo, Marcus André. "Unexpected Successes, Unanticipated Failures: Social Policy from Cardoso to Lula." In Peter R. Kingstone and Timothy J. Power (eds.). *Democratic Brazil Revisited* (Pittsburgh: University of Pittsburgh Press, 2008): 161–184.

Menchú, Rigoberta. *I, Rigoberta Menchú: An Indian Woman in Guatemala* (New York: Verso, 1984).

Mendoza, Plinio Apuleyo, Carlos Alberto Montaner, and Alvaro Vargas Llosa. *Guide to the Perfect Latin American Idiot* (Lanham: Madison Books, 2000).

Merton, Robert. *Social Theory and Social Structure, 1968 Enlarged Edition* (New York: The Free Press, 1968).

Miguel, Luis F. "Political Representation and Gender in Brazil: Quotas for Women and Their Impact." *Bulletin of Latin American Research* 27, 2 (2008): 197–214.

Miller, Francesca. "The Suffrage Movement in Latin America." In Gertrude M. Yeager (ed.). *Confronting Change, Challenging Tradition: Women in Latin American History* (Wilmington, DE: SR Books, 1997): 157–176.

Montaner, Carlos Alberto. "Culture and the Behavior of Elites in Latin America." In Lawrence E. Harrison and Samuel P. Huntington (eds.). *Culture Matters: How Values Shape Human Progress* (New York: Basic Books, 2000): 56–64.

Montero, Alfred P. *Brazilian Politics* (Cambridge, MA: Polity, 2005).

Mujal-León, Eusebio. "Tensions in the Regime." *Journal of Democracy* 20, 1 (2009): 20–35.

Munck, Gerardo L. *Measuring Democracy: A Bridge Between Scholarship and Politics* (Baltimore: The Johns Hopkins University Press, 2009).

Munro, Dana Garnder. *The Latin American Republics: A History*, 2nd Edition (New York: Appleton-Century Crofts, Inc., 1950).

Navarro, Marysa. "The Personal Is Political: Las Madres De Plaza De Mayo." In Susan Eckstein (ed.). *Power and Popular Protest: Latin American Social Movements* (Berkeley: University of California Press, 1989): 241–258.

O'Donnell, Guillermo A. *Modernization and Bureaucratic-Authoritarianism: Studies in South American Politics* (Berkeley: Institute of International Studies, 1973).

O'Donnell, Guillermo. "Human Development, Human Rights, and Democracy." In Guillermo O'Donnell, Jorge Vargas Cullell, and Osvaldo M. Iazzetta (eds.). *The Quality of Democracy: Theory and Applications* (Notre Dame, IN: University of Notre Dame Press, 2004): 9–92.

O'Neill, Kathleen. "Decentralization in Bolivia: Electoral Incentives and Outcomes." In Alfred P. Montero and David J. Samuels (eds.). *Decentralization and Democracy in Latin America* (Notre Dame: University of Notre Dame Press, 2004): 35–66.

O'Neil, Shannon. "The Real War in Mexico." *Foreign Affairs* 88, 4 (2009): 63–77.

Orias Arredondo, Ramiro. "Peru: The Trauma of Post Democratic Consolidation." In Russell Crandall, Guadalupe Paz, and Riordan Roett (eds.). *The Andes in Focus: Security, Democracy & Economic Reform* (Boulder: Lynne Rienner Publishers, 2005): 67–89.

Palacios, Marco. *Between Legitimacy and Violence: A History of Colombia, 1875-2002* (Durham: Duke University Press, 2006).

Papers Relating to the Foreign Relations of the United States 1964–1968, Volume XXXI, South and Central America; Mexico (Washington: United States Government Printing Office, 2004).

Pastor, Manuel and Carol Wise. "The Fox Administration and the Politics of Economic Transition." In Russell Crandall, Guadalupe Paz, and Riordan Roett (eds.). *Mexico's Democracy at Work: Political and Economic Dynamics* (Boulder: Lynne Rienner Publishers, 2005): 89–118.

Penfold-Becerra, Michael. "Electoral Dynamics and Decentralization in Venezuela." In Alfred P. Montero and David J. Samuels (eds.). *Decentralization and Democracy in Latin America* (Notre Dame: University of Notre Dame Press, 2004): 155–179.

Pereira, Anthony W. "Public Security, Private Interests, and Police Reform in Brazil." In Peter R. Kingstone and Timothy J. Power (eds.). *Democratic Brazil Revisited* (Pittsburgh: University of Pittsburgh Press, 2008): 185–208.

Pérez, Jr., Louis A. *Cuba: Between Reform and Revolution* (New York: Oxford University Press, 1995).

Perry, Guillermo and Michael Walton. *Inequality in Latin America and the Caribbean: Breaking with History?* (Washington, DC: World Bank, 2004).

Przeworski, Adam, Michael E. Alvarez, José Antonio Cheibub, and Fernando Limingi. "What Makes Democracies Endure? In Larry Diamond and Marc F. Plattner (eds.). *The Global Divergence of Democracies* (Baltimore: The Johns Hopkins University Press, 2001): 167–184.

Ramos Escandón, Carmen. "Women's Movements, Feminism, and Mexican Politics." In Jane S. Jaquette (ed.). *The Women's Movement in Latin America: Participation and Democracy* (Boulder: Westview Press, 1994): 199–221.

Richmond, Douglas W. *Carlos Pellegrini and the Crisis of the Argentine Elites, 1880-1916* (New York: Praeger, 1989).

Robertson, William Spence. *History of the Latin-American Nations* (New York: D. Appleton and Company, 1922).

Rodriguez, Francisco. "An Empty Revolution." *Foreign Affairs* 87, 2 (2008): 49–62.

Rodríguez, Francisco and Adam J. Gomolin. "Anarchy, State, and Dystopia: Venezuelan Economic Institutions before the Advent of Oil." *Bulletin of Latin American Research* 28, 1 (2009): 102–121.

Romero, Luis Alberto. *A History of Argentina in the Twentieth Century* (University Park: The Pennsylvania State University Press, 2002).

Romero, Simon. "Bolivia Reaches for a Slice of the Coast That Got Away." *The New York Times*, September 24, 2006.

Roett, Riordan. *Brazil: Politics in a Patrimonial Society*, 3rd edition (New York: Praeger, 1984).

Rostow, W.W. *The Stages of Economic Growth: A Non-Communist Manifesto* (New York: Cambridge University Press, 1961).

Rueschemeyer, Dietrich, Evelyne Huber Stephens, and John D. Stephens. *Capitalist Development and Democracy* (Chicago: University of Chicago Press, 1992).

Ruibal, Alba M. "Self-Restraint in Search of Legitimacy: The Reform of the Argentine Supreme Court." *Latin American Politics & Society* 51, 3 (2009): 59–86.

Saint-Germain, Michelle A. and Cynthia Chavez Metoyer. *Women Legislators in Central America: Politics, Democracy, and Policy* (Austin: The University of Texas Press, 2008).

Santiso, Javier. *Latin America's Political Economy of the Possible* (Cambridge: The MIT Press, 2006).

Sawyer, Mark Q. *Racial Politics in Post-Revolutionary Cuba* (New York: Cambridge University Press, 2005).

Scheina, Robert L. *Latin America's Wars: The Age of the Caudillo, 1791-1899* (Washington, DC: Brassey's, Inc., 2003).

Schild, Verónica. "Recasting 'Popular Movements': Gender and Political Learning in Neighborhood Organizations in Chile." In Richard Stahler-Sholk, Harry E. Vanden, and Glen David Kuecker (eds.). *Latin American Social Movements in the*

Twenty-First Century: Resistance, Power, and Democracy (Lanham, MD: Rowman and Littlefield Publishers, Inc., 2008): 217–232.

Schoultz, Lars. *Beneath the United States: A History of U.S. Policy Toward Latin America* (Cambridge: Harvard University Press, 2008).

Seligson, Mitchell A. "The Rise of Populism and the Left." In Larry Diamond, Marc F. Plattner, and Diego Abente Brun (eds.). *Latin America's Struggle for Democracy* (Baltimore: The Johns Hopkins University Press, 2008): 77–91.

Shepherd, William R. *Latin America* (New York: Henry Holt and Company, 1914).

Shugart, Matthew Soberg and Scott Mainwaring. "Presidentialism and Democracy in Latin America: Rethinking the Terms of the Debate." In Scott Mainwaring and Matthew Soberg Shugart (eds.). *Presidentialism and Democracy in Latin America* (New York: Cambridge University Press, 1997): 12–54.

Silva, Eduardo. *Challenging Neoliberalism in Latin America* (New York: Cambridge University Press, 2009).

Smith, Peter H. "The Changing Agenda for Social Science Research on Latin America." In Peter H. Smith (ed.). *Latin America in Comparative Perspective: New Approaches to Methods and Analysis* (Boulder: Westview Press, 1995): 1–29.

Smith, Peter H. *Latin America: Political Change in Comparative Perspective* (New York: Oxford University Press, 2005).

Somoza, Anastasio. *Nicaragua Betrayed: As Told to Jack Cox by as told by former President Somoza* (Boston: Western Islands Publishers, 1980).

Spiller, Pablo T. and Mariano Tommasi. *The Institutional Foundations of Public Policy in Argentina* (New York: Cambridge University Press, 2007).

Spiller, Pablo T. and Mariano Tommasi. "Political Institutions, Policymaking Processes, and Policy Outcomes in Argentina." In Eduardo Stein and Mariano Tommasi (eds.). *Policymaking in Latin America: How Politics Shapes Policies* (Washington, DC: Inter-American Development Bank, 2008): 69–110.

Stefanoni, Pablo and Hervé Do Alto. "The Emergence of Indigenous Nationalism in Bolivia." In Francois Polet (ed.). *The State of Resistance: Popular Struggles in the Global South* (London: Zed Books, 2007): 29–34.

Stepan, Alfred. *The Military in Politics: Changing Patterns in Brazil* (Princeton: Princeton University Press, 1971).

Sweig, Julia E. and Michael M. McCarthy. "Colombia: Staving off Partial Collapse." In Russell Crandall, Guadalupe Paz, and Riordan Roett (eds.). *The Andes in Focus: Security, Democracy & Economic Reform* (Boulder: Lynne Rienner Publishers, 2005): 11–43.

Taibo, II, Paco Ignacio. *An Easy Thing* (New York: Penguin Books, 1990).

Tanaka, Martín. "From Crisis to Collapse of the Party Systems and Dilemmas of Democratic Representation: Peru and Venezuela." In Scott Mainwaring, Ana María Bejarano, and Eduardo Pizarro Leongómez (eds.). *The Crisis of Democratic Representation in the Andes* (Stanford: Stanford University, 2006): 47–77.

Tate, Winifred. *Counting the Dead: The Culture and Politics of Human Rights Activism in Colombia* (Berkeley: University of California Press, 2007).

Taylor, Matthew M. *Judging Policy: Courts and Policy Reform in Democratic Brazil* (Stanford: Stanford University Press, 2008).

Taylor, Steven L. *Voting amid Violence: Electoral Democracy in Colombia* (Boston: Northeastern University Press, 2009).

Uriarte, Miren. "Rediscovering Lo Local: The Potential and the Limits of Local Development in Havana." In Alexander I. Gray and Antoni Kapcia (eds.). *The Changing Dynamic of Cuban Civil Society* (Gainesville: University Press of Florida, 2008): 90–115.

Valdés, Juan Gabriel. *Pinochet's Economists* (New York: Cambridge University Press, 1995).

Valenzuela, Arturo. "Party Politics and the Crisis of Presidentialism in Chile: A Proposal for a Parliamentary Form of Government." In Juan J. Linz and Arturo Valenzuela (eds.). *The Failure of Presidential Democracy: The Case of Latin America*, Volume 2 (Baltimore: The Johns Hopkins University Press, 1994): 91–150.

Vélez, Fredy Rivera and Franklin Ramírez Gallegos. "Ecuador: Democracy and Economy in Crisis." In Russell Crandall,

Guadalupe Paz, and Riordan Roett (eds.). *The Andes in Focus: Security, Democracy and Economic Reform* (Boulder: Lynne Rienner Publishers, 2005): 121–149.

Verbitsky, Horacio. *The Flight: Confessions of an Argentine Dirty Warrior* (New York: The New Press, 1996).

Villalón, Roberta. "Neoliberalism, Corruption, and Legacies of Contention: Argentina's Social Movements, 1993-2006." In Richard Stahler-Sholk, Harry E. Vanden, and Glend David Kuecker (eds.). *Latin American Social Movements in the Twenty-First Century* (Lanham, MD: Rowman and Littlefield, 2008): 253–269.

Walker, Thomas W. and Christine J. Wade. *Nicaragua: Living in the Shadow of the Eagle, Fifth Edition* (Boulder: Westview Press, 2011).

Waltz, Kenneth. *Man, the State and War: A Theoretical Analysis* (New York: Columbia University Press, 1959).

Weeks, Gregory. *U.S. And Latin American Relations* (New York: Pearson Longman, 2008).

Welna, Christopher and Gustavo Gallón (eds.). *Peace, Democracy, and Human Rights in Colombia* (Notre Dame, IN: University of Notre Dame Press, 2007).

Weyland, Kurt. "Clarifying a Contested Concept: Populism in the Study of Latin American Politics," *Comparative Politics* 34, 1 (2001): 1–22.

Wiarda, Howard J. *The Soul of Latin America* (New Haven: Yale University Press, 2003).

Wolf, Sonja. "Subverting Democracy: Elite Rule and the Limits to Political Participation in Post-War El Salvador." *Journal of Latin American Studies* 41 (2009): 429–465.

Woodward, Jr., Ralph Lee. *Central America: A Nation Divided*, 3rd Edition (New York: Oxford University Press, 1999).

Wuhs, Steven T. *Savage Democracy: Institutional Change and Party Development in Mexico* (University Park: The Pennsylvania State University Press, 2008).

Yashar, Deborah. *Contesting Citizenship in Latin America* (New York: Cambridge University Press, 2005).

INDEX